REGNUM STUDIES IN MISSION

Shaping Christianity in Greater China
Indigenous Christians in Focus

Series Preface

Regnum Studies in Mission are born from the lived experience of Christians and Christian communities in mission, especially but not solely in the fast growing churches among the poor of the world. These churches have more to tell than stories of growth. They are making significant impacts on their cultures in the cause of Christ. They are producing 'cultural products' which express the reality of Christian faith, hope and love in their societies.

Regnum Studies in Mission are the fruit often of rigorous research to the highest international standards and always of authentic Christian engagement in the transformation of people and societies. And these are for the world. The formation of Christian theology, missiology and practice in the twenty-first century will depend to a great extent on the active participation of growing churches contributing biblical and culturally appropriate expressions of Christian practice to inform World Christianity.

REGNUM STUDIES IN MISSION

Shaping Christianity in Greater China

Indigenous Christians in Focus

Edited by Paul Woods

First published 2017 by Regnum Books International

Regnum is an imprint of the Oxford Centre for Mission Studies
St. Philip and St. James Church
Woodstock Road
Oxford OX2 6HR, UK
www.ocms.ac.uk/regnum

09 08 07 06 05 04 03 7 6 5 4 3 2 1

British Library Cataloguing in Publication Data
A catalogue record for this book is available from the British Library

ISBN: 978-1-506477-26-8

Typeset by Words by Design

This book was made possible by financial support from OMF UK.

Distributed by Fortress Press in the US and Canada

Contents

Introduction

Paul Woods

This book is an integrated collection of essays emerging from a conference entitled 'The Shaping of Christianity in China: A Fresh Look at the Contributions of Indigenous Christians', held at the Oxford Centre for Mission studies in May 2015. The event was held to mark the 150th anniversary of the China Inland Mission, now known as OMF International.

It has been common to view the mission enterprise itself and the writing of its history as the preserve of Western people, traditionally seen as the bearers of the gospel from the West to the Rest, the civilisations beyond Christendom. However, as the world has become more multilateral and as the demographic centre of the church moves south and east, theologians, historians, and missiologists have begun to take a less Eurocentric view. With this in mind, as possible themes for a 150th anniversary CIM/OMF conference were considered, it seemed appropriate that the event should focus on the activities and contributions of Chinese Christians within an endeavour traditionally characterised as Western driven.

The conference and its call for papers generated a significant response among mission scholars, historians and, theologians, and it was extremely difficult to choose papers for the event and subsequently for this volume. What is presented here can only represent a very small part of the history of the shaping of Christianity in China. The historical incidents and personalities described here can only manifest a tiny scratching of the huge surface of a remarkable enterprise which is still on going. It is unfortunate that the conference included only a relatively small amount of discussion of Roman Catholic believers and was totally silent about the Eastern Orthodox Church. It would also have been wonderful to have received contributions about minority peoples in Greater China. With the exception of one piece on Watchmen Nee, the great heroes of twentieth-century Chinese Christianity were not mentioned; Liang Fa, John Sung, Wong Ming Dao, and other great leaders have been discussed thoroughly, critically, and with much appreciation elsewhere. I was delighted to receive and work with the paper concerning what I call 'a lost strand' in the great tapestry of Chinese Christianity: a brief study of poems by Catholic literati in Fujian.

Each essay reflects its author's individual interest and position. There was considerable freedom to write and present under the overall broad theme, the result of which is a somewhat eclectic collection, yet one which fits together remarkably well to provide the 'fresh look' which was of such importance to the conference organisers. In moving from conference to book, considerable effort was expended to craft a coherent whole arranged historically. In addition, a slight change was made to the title. 'Shaping Christianity in Greater China: Indigenous Christians in Focus' is less of a mouthful than the conference title, and the use of 'Greater China' acknowledges the different histories and societies of the Mainland, Taiwan, and Hong Kong, while hopefully avoiding political issues. The original 'fresh look' of the conference has become 'in focus', which I believe is an acceptable change.

The variety of material here suggests that 'shaping' and 'Christianity' should perhaps both be plural – a huge diversity of processes and results is summarised in these pages. As well as its geographical scope of the China Mainland, Taiwan, and Hong Kong, the *liang'an sandi* (兩岸三地, lit. *two banks, three places*), the material covers a span of time from the end of the Ming Dynasty until the Sichuan earthquake of 2008. Also, a range of Christian denominations and traditions is explored in the work: Anglicans, Presbyterians, Roman Catholics, Charismatics, and various kinds of independents rub shoulders within its pages. This is, of course, how it should be.

A recurring theme is what we might call 'history from below'; in many cases scholars were only able to access indigenous Chinese Christians in records and biographies which principally concerned Western missionaries. It is to be hoped that in yet to be written histories of our time and its Christian endeavour, future authors will not have to work so hard to draw in indigenous actors from the edge of the stage and that the diversity which was always there will be obvious to all. Another important motif is *histoire croisée*, the studies in this book resulting from and representing the intersection of researcher and researched, culture and politics, different denominations, complex local circumstances, West and East, and God and his servants.

With apologies to David Bosch and his remarkable 'Transforming Mission', we can use dual interpretations of the words 'Shaping Christianity' to approach this current volume. While most of the articles can be considered as depicting Chinese believers' shaping of Christianity in their world, in some cases we can discern how the gospel influenced Greater China as Chinese Christian people took their message beyond the doors of the church and sought to shape and improve the lives of their compatriots. Either way, it should be said that this volume does not seek to present or explore a Chinese contextual theology – nothing so grand. Consistent with a focus on the contributions of a broad swathe of Chinese Christians, both ordinary people (so-called) as well as full-time Christian ministers, the articles presented here concern practical ministry and day-to-day transformation of Chinese Christians within their society.

Before looking briefly at the chapters in the book, a comment about the contributors, brief descriptions of whom can be found at the end of the volume. In keeping with the focus on indigenous Christians and history from below, and without in any way compromising the quality of the volume, it was decided to bring together a group of established academics and emerging postgraduate students, a mixture of Chinese and Western authors, representing various parts of the Chinese world as well as Europe and North America. The corporate hybridity of the authors is in some small way an echo of the hybridity in the Chinese church over its remarkable history. With this in mind it was decided to retain as much of the authors' personal character as an edited volume can allow. British and American spellings reflect authors' preferences in a collection edited in the UK by an Englishman; readers will find both simplified and traditional Chinese characters. In keeping with the historical portraits in the work, many traditional romanisations of Chinese names were retained in order to facilitate further research in original English language sources while as far as possible modern *hanyu pinyin* was added for clarity. Chinese personal names – of authors and historical figures – are usually presented in traditional surname-given name format.

The book is divided into five parts. The first three chapters can be thought of as foundational or introductory. *David Killingray* sets the scene as a sympathetic outsider; a historian whose area of expertise is Africa gives a historical overview of Christian mission, and then turns to indigenisation and the contributions of locals to their churches around the world. Following this, *Lian Xi* provides a critical but fair assessment of Western missionaries and their role in the making of what he calls 'vernacular Christianity'. From the other side of the Taiwan Strait, *Kuo Ya-pei* focuses on a Presbyterian Christian, Li Chunsheng, and his dissatisfaction with the efforts of Western missionaries as well as his own struggles to live as a Confucian Christian or perhaps a Christian Confucian.

The second main part of the book is entitled 'Writing the Faith' and contains four papers dedicated to various aspects of literature ministry by Chinese believers. The written word has long been treated with great respect in China, and as in may other parts of the world, the church has benefited hugely from literature as a means of edification and influence. *Liu Yanyan* gives us a brief glimpse of poems written to honour Roman Catholic missionaries by Confucian literati in Fujian. It is a tantalising look at Christianity viewed through the eyes of elite gentlemen scholars from southeast China and expressed through the idiom of classical Chinese poetry. Returning again to Taiwan, *Stephen Donoho*'s exploration of the Presbyterian Church's *Church News* gives a fascinating insight into how Taiwanese Christians discussed everyday issues and theological responses to them – theology from below, if you like. Donoho's use of a local system for the romanisation of the language used on the island may prove challenging for those familiar with the Mainland's *hanyu pinyin*, but its Taiwanese feel is a reminder that the volume concerns Christianity in *Greater China* (中華大地) and not only the Mainland. Back on the Mainland, *Zhou Yun*'s discussion of Li Guanfang looks at the life and work of a female educator and patriot whose Christian and Chinese identities were inseparable. Li's contribution resonates with the dual readings of 'shaping Christianity', as her efforts were directed at bringing change to her country. The final article under the 'writing' title is by *Monica Romano*, who looks in depth at the work of Chinese Bible translators, Catholic and Protestant. Their attempts to render the Bible into Chinese had to negotiate theology, tradition, culture, translation theory, and sometimes political sensitivities, and were foundational in shaping the faith in China.

The third large part of book is called 'Building the Faith', as the articles within it describe the work of Chinese believers in consolidating and advancing the work of the gospel. A local clergy is important for the church to make progress and *Peter Cunich* describes in sympathetic detail the policies and activities of the Kwangsi-Hunan mission of the CMS which from the inception of its work sought to identify and train local men for the Anglican priesthood. In an age when we are almost expected to criticise western missionaries uniformly for their highhandedness and paternalism, Cunich brings us a more rounded picture of the reality in one area of China. The medical doctor Kao Gin-cheng is the subject of a biographical study by *Lauren Pfister* and *Liu Jihua*. Dr Kao was a Christian leader in Gansu in the Republican period who served local people selflessly and openly as a believer in Christ. He established a Christian community and cooperated with the famous CIM Cable and French 'trio'. The themes of community and medical care continue in *Christina Wong*'s piece on three Presbyterian institutions in Guangzhou in the early part of the twentieth century. Female missionaries from the United States trained and employed young Chinese women who became part of a strong Presbyterian church with an influence deep into the broader community. The contribution of the church to society is also explored in the last paper in this section. *Bai Limin* introduces us to the life and work of Wang Hengtong, a Christian educator who made significant contributions to the mainstream Chinese education system. Both Wong and Bai show how open-minded western Christians were able and willing to empower Chinese colleagues and pass the baton on to them. Indeed, Bai talks of a blurring of boundaries between missionaries and local believers in the endeavour to deliver high quality education to Chinese people.

'Living the Faith' is the title of the fourth part of the book. *Paul Woods*' article on the indigenous believers' attitudes and activities during the Boxer Rebellion also looks at blurred boundaries and the questions of otherness and identity within Chinese Christianity at the time. *Stephen Williams* contributes the only theological paper of the collection, in which he looks at Watchman Nee and some of his discipleship teaching, which emerged later in his classic, *The Normal Christian Life*. An exploration of a particular application of discipleship comes in *Charles Weber*'s account of the anti-opium struggle of the late nineteenth and early twentieth centuries. Weber looks at the influence of the church in China and Britain at the time and profiles three leading Chinese Christian figures in the anti-opium movement.

The final part of the book, 'Commending the Faith', relates to more modern movements in the church, which seek to make the gospel relevant to society. *Niki Alsford* discusses Shoki Coe and the various aspects of his ministry. Coe was passionate that the church should address issues of modern life and is known as the father of the term 'contextualisation'. Identity and otherness were constantly negotiated in Coe's life and Alsford narrates this skilfully. The creative tension between local and global also lies at the heart of *Kwok Wai Luen*'s study of three contemporary leaders in Hong Kong's church. Kwok reveals the multiple hybridity of these leaders, theologically, culturally, and with regard to their interpretation of the gospel, as they have shaped Christianity in the Special Administrative Region. For the last chapter of the book we return to the Mainland, with Easten Law's account of an NGO in southwest China and how it has been influencing society there in the aftermath of the 2008 Sichuan earthquake.

This volume is, if you like, yet *another* book on the Chinese church, and I am mindful of Qoheleth's ancient warning that 'of making many books there is no end, and much study wearies the body' (Ecc 12:12). However, I believe this collection is a worthwhile addition to the many tomes about China's church because of its theme and subject matter, the unity and diversity within its pages, its historical scope, and the eclectic group of authors.

The editor would like to express his thanks to those authors, for their patient and cooperative spirit, to the Oxford Centre for Mission Studies, who hosted the conference in 2015, and to OMF, whose anniversary celebrations prompted the event. Special thanks to David Killingray and Peter Rowan (National Director of OMF in the UK) for their vision and drive in making both conference and book realities!

The character on the front cover is 'fu', which means 'blessing' and forms part of the Chinese word for 'gospel'. It was written by Mr Ma Guangzhao, a retired Beijing calligrapher who is the uncle of the editor's wife. In using it the editor expresses his respect and admiration for Mr Ma and his work.

Paul Woods
Oxford
February 2017

Part One

Locating the Faith

The Role of Indigenous Christians in the Global Church

David Killingray

The spread of the Christian Gospel and the growth of the church across the world over two thousand years have largely been due to the work of countless unnamed Christians who gossiped the good news in their own language and among peoples of their own culture. They are in the records of God, rarely noted in the register of man. The command to spread the gospel was implicit in Jesus' incarnation and explicit in his 'Great Commission' in Matthew 28:19, given not just to a handful of apostles, but to all believers throughout the ages. Even before that we read how the Gerasene man, healed of his mental impairment, was sent by Jesus to tell his own people in the non-Jewish towns of the Decapolis of God's grace and mercy (Mark 5:1-20). And that was the pattern for converts in the New Testament gospels and epistles. At Pentecost people heard in their own language the message of salvation and the church grew in number. When the early church in Jerusalem was persecuted and the Christians 'scattered', they 'preached the word wherever they went' (Acts 8:8). Church leader Philip was instrumental in the conversion and baptism of the proselyte 'Ethiopian' official on his long journey home from Jerusalem to Meroe astride the middle valley of the Nile (Acts 8:26-39). The Apostle Paul wrote of his approach to 'win as many as possible' to Christ: 'To the Jews I became like a Jew, to win the Jews. To those under the law I became like one under the law.' (1 Cor 9:20). At the end of several epistles are listed names of people from across the Roman imperial world actively preaching the Christian message, often to their own people. It may have been that Paul, the archetypal missionary, 'planted' churches then 'watered' by Apollos, 'but God made it grow' (1 Cor 3:6).

This chapter is not specifically on China. Indeed, I am not a specialist on that vast country with its millions of people. What I set out to do here is to provide a brief global perspective on the processes of indigenisation of the church over the past 250 years whereby, as a result of missionary endeavour from the global 'North', a large part of the world was made aware of the Christian gospel. In this broad comparative approach it is possible to ask pertinent questions about the diffusion of the Christian message, whether policies differed from one region or denomination to another, and whether there were areas of the world marked by missionary exceptionalism. Did the ecclesiastical structures of the originating foreign denomination inhibit or help to promote transfer of control to indigenous leaders? For example, why did the Anglican Church in West Africa retreat from promoting African clergy in its hierarchy in the late nineteenth century? Given its great size and the many missions at work in China, did Christian work there have a different pattern from elsewhere, and if so why and how? To what extent did European perceptions of the target culture determine strategies and policies towards indigenous peoples? And did multiplicity and complexity of languages, and difficulty in understanding culture, or the date when foreign missionary work began, influence the shaping of policies on the roles of indigenous Christians in the church? Two intrinsic questions are what is meant by 'Christianity' and also what is meant by 'conversion'?[1]

Historiography

The vast literature on missionary work in the nineteenth and early twentieth centuries produced by the bureaucratised mission agencies, primarily acclaimed the work of white (occasionally black) missionaries from Europe and North America. Mission reports, magazines, and memoirs overwhelmingly promoted the image of European activity at home and in foreign parts of the world. However, indigenous workers did not go altogether unnoticed: they appear in the literature as occasional profiles, often identified by a single name and, from the 1890s onwards, occasionally with an accompanying photograph.[2] They are 'faithful' assistants, credited with translation work, registered as responsible for evangelism and the planting and running of churches. Even if not given great prominence, indigenous workers do appear in missionary magazines and journals, partly to encourage home readers to acknowledge the value and fruit of the 'civilising' and Christianising mission.[3] As with all less-visible groups of people, at one time thought to be of little significance to history, or indeed 'people without history' – women, children, non-Europeans – their presence can be gleaned from the condescending pages of the past by modern eyes acute to their presence, role and significance in mission work. On rare occasions a biography written by a European applauds the work of a prominent indigenous

1 See J.D.Y Peel, 'The Christianization of African society: some possible models', in Edward Fasholé-Luke, Richard Gray, Adrian Hastings & Godwin Tasie, eds, *Christianity in Independent Africa* (London: Rex Collings, 1978), 443-454. Some recent books worthy of attention are Norman Etherington, ed, *Missions and empire: Oxford history of the British Empire* (Oxford: Oxford University Press, 2005); Peggy Brock, Norman Etherington, Gareth Griffiths & Jacqueline Van Gent, *Indigenous evangelicals and questions of authority in the British Empire 1750-1940* (Leiden: Brill, 2015); Tolly Bradford, *Prophetic identities: Indigenous missionaries on British colonial frontiers, 1850-75* (Vancouver: University of British Columbia Press, 2013); and Edward E. Andrews, *Native apostles: Black and Indian missionaries in the British Atlantic world* (Cambridge, MA: Harvard University Press, 2013).

2 E.g. H.M. Bentley, *W. Holman Bentley: The life and labours of a Congo pioneer* (London: The Religious Tract Society, 1907), opp. 160, 277 and 343 for three photographs of Don Zwau M.D. Nlemvo (1865-1938), Holman's 'assistant translator'.

3 E.g. in the pages of the *Regions Beyond*, the home journal of the Regions Beyond Mission, whose issues for the years 1878-1887 I have recently read through.

convert, such as Bishop Samuel Ajayi Crowther or Pastor Hsi (Shengmo),[4] or an individual missionary draws specific attention to the role of an indigenous agent.[5] Another way of looking at the barely visible indigenous Christian workers is through missionary statistics, the data recorded at mission conferences held either on the field or the often much larger meetings in the metropole. For example, the statistics compiled for the World Missionary Conference in Edinburgh, 1910, show that there were 19,280 Protestant 'foreign missionaries' on the mission field, aided by 98,388 'native workers'.[6] The role of indigenous Christians was increasingly recognised in the mission churches of the late 1940s-60s, the decades of decolonisation and the emergence of new independent states in Asia and Africa. This was accompanied by a new historiographical awareness by a small but growing number of scholars, both in the 'northern' world as well as in the new states, who were intent on researching and writing history which gave a primary place to Asians and Africans. In Europe and North America religious history by then was increasingly becoming a specialist interest among historians; indeed, it would not be unreasonable to suggest that materialistically minded historians often ignored or disdained religious belief. In Asia and Africa, where different shapes and expressions of indigenous and new forms of religious belief were so significant and widespread, historians could not ignore their role or the conflicting claims made by older belief systems such as Buddhism, Hinduism, and Islam. In Africa, for example, it was difficult to engage with the historical cultural landscape without immediately being aware of the power and influence of religious belief in inter-communal relationships. Many anthropologists had studied religious beliefs, and historians (particularly of Africa) often relied on such work as one starting point for their own research. If at times in the years of nationalism (late 1950s-early 1970s), religion was interpreted as too closely involved in primary or secondary resistance to colonial rule, it did provide an agenda for later researchers to deconstruct and to present a more sophisticated indigenous history.

The traditional mission-orientated history of global Christianity is provided by Latourette's monumental seven volume work written in the 1930s-40s.[7] For Africa the specific work is by Groves, written and published in the 1940s-50s.[8]

---

4 Jesse Page, *Samuel Crowther: The slave boy who became Bishop of the Niger* (London: S.W. Partridge & Co, 1888); Mary Geraldine Taylor, *Pastor Hsi of North China: One of China's Christians* (London: Morgan & Scott, 1900); both books went into several editions.

5 A.W. Lee, *Charles Johnson of Zululand* (London: Society for the Propagation of the Gospel, 1930), ch.VIII, 'Native agents'; Lee comments on the need for the 'native agency' (102-103) and also draws attention to the work of the Rev. Titus Mtemba who planted and nurtured churches among the Hlubi peoples (110-111).

6 World Missionary Conference, *A statistical atlas of Christian missions* (Edinburgh: World Missionary Conference, 1910), 63. In 1924-25 the Church Missionary Society world-wide recorded 1,233 foreign missionaries aided by 15,183 'paid native helpers', quoted by Roland Allen, *The spontaneous expansion of the Church and the causes which hinder it* (1927; 2nd edn London: World Dominion Press, 1949), 11.

7 K.S. Latourette, *A history of the expansion of Christianity*, 7 vols (New York: Harper, 1937-44).

8 C.P. Groves, *The planting of Christianity in Africa. vols.1-4* (London: Lutterworth Press, 1948-58). The first volume begins in 1840.

It is not unfair to say that these volumes deal primarily with 'foreign' missionary activity and that indigenous Christians, when occasionally mentioned, play only an incidental role in the work of mission. The handful of scholars who began to work in the 1950s-60s on the roles played by African Christians in the growth and development of the church needed skills somewhat different from those deployed in the comfortable settings of university libraries at Yale and Birmingham. In praising Latourette's work, Andrew Walls comments: 'Since his time, much fundamental research has been conducted on the primary sources, oral and written, and new perspectives have been taken up in which Africans, Asians, and Latin Americans figure as the principal agents of Christian expansion'.[9] In this new endeavour what was required was knowledge of one or more African languages, a deep awareness of the African cultural context, and a willingness to seek out and read local church records along with official documents with eyes alert to the role of indigenous Christians, allied to solid field work which also engaged with oral evidence. A major and pioneering piece of research was Shepperson and Price's study of John Chilembwe, Nyasaland church leader who led a forlorn rising against the British in 1915.[10] Research on major West African church leaders began in the 1950s pioneered by scholars such as J.F.A. Ajayi and E.A. Ayendele, whose London doctoral theses soon became books.[11] Such studies rested on archival and secondary sources located in Europe and Africa.

In East Africa indigenous orientated studies were given a stimulus by the work of John V. Taylor, whose study of the Buganda church, subtitled 'an attempt at understanding', was based on his research as a missionary priest through the 1950s.[12] A further study, also published in the SCM 'World Mission Studies' series, by Welbourn of Makerere University College, looked at African independent churches in Uganda and Kenya.[13] The creation of the University College in Dar es Salaam, and the arrival of Terry Ranger as professor of history in 1963, provided a further centre for a growing number of scholars who took seriously indigenous belief systems and the role of African Christians in the historic and contemporary churches.[14] The white authorities in

9 Andrew Walls, 'A History of the expansion of Christianity reconsidered: Assessing Christian progress and decline', in Walls, ed, *The cross-cultural process in Christian history* (Maryknoll, NY: Orbis Books, 2002), 8.

10 George Shepperson & Thomas Price, *Independent African: John Chilembwe and the Nyasaland rising of 1915* (Edinburgh: Edinburgh University Press, 1958).

11 J.F.A. Ajayi, *Christian missions in Nigeria 1841-1891: The making of a new elite* (London, Longmans, 1965); E.A. Ayendele, *The missionary impact on modern Nigeria 1842-1914: A political and social analysis* (London: Longmans, 1966); also *Holy Johnson: Pioneer of African nationalism 1836-1917* (London: Frank Cass, 1970).

12 John V. Taylor, *The growth of the church in Buganda* (London: CMS Press, World Mission studies series, 1958).

13 F.B. Welbourn, *East Africa rebels: A study of some independent churches* (London: CMS Press, World Mission Studies series, 1961).

14 See T.O. Ranger & Isaria Kimambo, eds, *The Historical Study of African Reli*gions (London, Heinemann, 1972); T.O. Ranger & John Weller, eds, *Themes in the Christian history of Central Africa* (London: Heinemann, 1975). When Ranger moved to the University of California Los Angeles he helped to establish a regular newsletter, *African Religious Research* (November 1971 to

South Africa had viewed with concern the activities of 'Ethiopian' or independent African churches since the Bambatha 'rising' of 1906. By 1945 the South African government had recognised more than 800 independent African-led churches to which Sundkler's classic study on Bantu Prophets added another 123.[15] Similar patterns of independency were developing elsewhere in the Christian world at the same time, including in Europe, and were being recorded by historians, to which I will turn later.

The Early Church

In the introduction to his book on the conversion of the 'Old World', Richard Fletcher comments that 'by the year 1000 Christian communities had been planted from Greenland to China'.[16] This was a considerable achievement, beginning in the urban centres of the Roman Empire, which became officially Christian in the early fourth century, and spreading beyond the imperial frontiers. As Fletcher says: 'There was a variety of ways in which such communities might come into existence, by means of trading settlements, diplomatic contacts, veterans returning from service in the Roman army in the course of which they had been converted, cross-frontier marriage, the settlement of prisoners carried away from the homelands by barbarians, and so on'.[17] The great North African scholar Augustine of Hippo in his influential book *City of God* discounted the idea of Christianity as exclusive to the Roman hegemon and argued that a universal gospel was for the whole world. Would that we knew more about the way knowledge of Christianity was spread and took root in the very early medieval world. Certainly by the eighth to tenth centuries the church in Europe had become a mission church sustained by sympathetic secular rulers, monastic orders given to prayer, piety and charity, devout bishops and a system of parishes, many with faithful priests, all of which brought ordinary people into contact with the church. Great names of church leaders stand out: Augustine who preached in Kent, Alcuin in York, Bishop Boniface; but the Cornish landscape is littered with the names of minor saints. Some of those are obscure men and women, similar to 'the venerable man Boso [who] has sweated much among the Slav people to convert them to God'.[18] Some rulers, such as Charlemagne, had a more violent purpose, converting the Saxons by the sword. On various frontiers both the Latin Church and the eastern Byzantium Greek Church confronted Islam and Paganism.

April 1975), which later received a 'measure of existence' in the newly established *Journal of Religion in Africa*.

15 B.G.M. Sundkler, *Bantu prophets in South Africa* (London: Lutterworth Press, 1948). Twenty years later a researcher identified many more independent churches in sub-Saharan Africa, David B. Barrett, *Schism and renewal in Africa: An analysis of six thousand contemporary religious movements* (Nairobi: Oxford University Press, 1968).

16 Richard Fletcher, *The conversion of Europe* (London: HarperCollins, 1997), 1.

17 Fletcher, *Conversion*, 25.

18 Henry Mayr-Harting, 'The West: The age of conversion (700-1050)', in John McManners, ed, *The Oxford illustrated history of Christianity* (Oxford: Oxford University Press, 1990), 99.

Missionary Activity During the 'Age of European Reconnaissance'

European modern missionary endeavour came in two bursts of activity, a smaller one accompanying the 'age of reconnaissance' in the sixteenth and seventeenth centuries, and a much larger and more sustained movement from the 1790s onwards. The first overseas area of European intrusion in the sixteenth century was in the 'New World' of the Americas by the Spanish from Mexico south to Paraguay and the Portuguese in Brazil. The large Aztec, Maya and Inca polities of Mexico and Peru collapsed in the face of Spanish military might aided by local indigenous enemies, and the vacuum was filled by the Spanish state and the priests of Roman Catholic religious orders. Despite the weight of Spanish religious enculturation and the severities of the Inquisition, much of the new popular Catholicism was a syncretic blend of indigenous beliefs and practices and Christian ideas.[19] Similarly in Brazil, heavily dependent on sugar produced by imported African slaves, the new Catholic faith co-existed and mingled with religious beliefs from various parts of West Africa. In their global commercial and religious expansion Iberian travellers and clergy encountered the old indigenous Thomist church in southern India and the churches that had existed in China since the millennium; they also experienced strong resistance and hostility from the Monophysite church in the highlands of Ethiopia. The Spanish planted Roman Catholic Church in Japan endured great persecution. In the Spanish-ruled Philippines the indigenous clergy often proved resistant both to colonial rule and foreign clerical domination until the Spanish-American war of 1898, then transferring their support to nationalist efforts resisting the presence of the United States. In Africa Portuguese Catholics found fertile soil in the Kingdom of Kongo when the King – the *mani Kongo* – in 1491 voluntarily converted and established a Church under Kongolese control which over the next three centuries produced its own indigenous priests, prophets and martyrs.[20] It was a pronouncedly syncretic church, but tolerated by the Catholic authorities who, unlike the Spanish in the Americas, had not come as colonial conquerors but as visitors. In Canada during the seventeenth and eighteenth centuries French Catholic priests helped spread knowledge of Christianity within the Great Lakes region and further west; the native Americans and métis, or mixed race communities, viewed later British and Protestant control as inimical to their interests.

---

19 See John Lynch, *New worlds: A religious history of Latin America* (New Haven: Yale University Press, 2012), ch.1, 'Religion and empire'. Also C.R. Boxer, 'The problem of the native clergy in the Portuguese and Spanish Empires from the sixteenth to the eighteenth centuries', in Geoffrey John Cuming, ed, *The mission of the Church and the propagation of the faith: Studies in Church history 6* (Cambridge: Ecclesiastical History Society, 1970), 88-105.

20 John Thornton, 'The development of an African Catholic Church in the Kingdom of Kongo, 1491-1750', *Journal of African History*, 25 (1984), 147-67. Also Thornton, *The Kongolese Saint Anthony: Dona Beatriz Kimpa Vita and the Antonian movement, 1684-1706* (Cambridge: Cambridge University Press, 1998). Richard Gray, *Black Christians and white missionaries* (New Haven, CT: Yale University Press, 1990). On this, and much more see Adrian Hastings, *The Church in Africa 1450-1950* (Oxford: Clarendon Press, 1994), ch.3.

The Modern Missionary Movement since 1790

The modern missionary age was marked by the foundation of missionary agencies in Europe and the Americas intent on evangelising Asia, Africa, and the Pacific. India was William Carey's objective for the Baptist Missionary Society in 1792, southern Africa was the field first chosen by the London Missionary Society (LMS) in 1795, while the Church Missionary Society (CMS), founded in 1799 and exercised by the campaign to abolish the transatlantic slave trade by Britain, looked first to West Africa. The American Board of Commissioners for Foreign Mission (ABCFM), founded in 1810, sent its first missionaries to British India and Native American communities. Christianity took root in non-European regions in a variety of ways. In the West African colony of Freetown the first churches were established by black Christian immigrants from Britain and America; in Hawaii the queen regent Ka'ahumanu welcomed the first Congregational missionaries led by Hiram Bingham and effectively made Christianity the state religion;[21] in Madagascar the initial foothold of the LMS was gained through King Radama's ambition to promote schools and literacy in Antananarivo.[22] Invariably foreign mission activity resulted in the employment of local Christian converts as interpreters, catechists, translators, and evangelists. It was obvious that indigenous converts could and should be primary agents; they were on the spot, spoke the language, understood the culture, and also were cheaper to employ than white missionaries who often suffered higher mortality rates or were invalided home. In India these ideas were made explicit by the Danish Tranquebar Mission in Tamil Nadu in the early eighteenth-century and nearly one-hundred years later by William Carey at Serampore.[23] An earlier approach adopted by the Italian Jesuit priest Robert de Nobili in India advocated total personal identification in language, dress and mode of living with those he sought to reach.

By the mid-nineteenth century administrative heads of missions in Europe and the United States, and many missionaries in the field, saw the wisdom and necessity of what was increasingly referred to as 'native agency'. Henry Venn of the CMS and Rufus Anderson of the ABCFM both argued that native churches should be 'self-reliant, self-supporting and self-governing'.[24] Similar ideas were taken up by Bishops Tozer and Steere of the Universities Mission to Central Africa, by Roman Catholic missions, and promoted by the German

---

21 Susanna Moore, *Paradise of the Pacific: Approaching Hawaii* (New York: Farrer, Straus and Giroux, 2015).

22 Gwyn Campbell, *David Griffiths and the missionary 'History of Madagascar'* (Leiden: Brill, 2012); see Campbell's introductory section.

23 See the essays by Nickhiles Guha & E. Johnson Rathinasamay in Roger E. Hedlund, ed, *Christianity is Indian: The emergence of an indigenous community* (Delhi: Mylapore Institute for Indigenous Studies, 2000; 2nd rev edn, 2004), 77-85 and 199-211.

24 Venn's 'African Native Agency Commission' (1845) sought 'the social and religious improvement of Africa by means of her own sons', an idea endorsed by the conference on missions at Liverpool in 1860. See Peter C. Williams, *The ideal of the self-governing church: A study in Victorian missionary strategy* (Leiden: Brill, 1990). Also K.J. T. Farrimond, 'The policy of the Church Missionary Society concerning the development of self-governing indigenous churches, 1900-1942', PhD thesis, University of Leeds, 2004.

missionaries Christian Keysser in in New Guinea and Christian Guttmann in German East Africa. The result in West, East and Central Africa was a steady stream of locally-trained ordained indigenous pastors. This also occurred in southern Africa, although in societies with dominant white minorities and sharply divided by race, African clergy were restricted to ministering to Africans. At the World Missionary Conference in Edinburgh, 1910, it was widely recognised that the mission church 'has, in many places, reached, and in others is fast reaching, maturity; and is now fitted and willing, perhaps in a few cases too eager, to take upon itself its full burden of responsibility and service'.[25] The idea of 'native agency' was slightly more palatable in non-colonial territories of the world. Roland Allen, drawing on his experience in China, wrote in 1927,

> that if our object was to establish in that country a Church which might spread over the six provinces which then formed the diocese of North China, that object could only be attained if the first Christians who were converted by our labours, understood clearly that they could by themselves, without any further assistance from us, not only convert their neighbours, but establish churches.[26]

Such a policy had been pursued vigorously by the Anglican church in West Africa until the 1870s, and Africans, including 'recaptives' liberated from slave ships in Freetown, were trained and ordained as pastors and catechists, but laymen working as traders, seamen, artisans, and colonial officials, planted and spread the Gospel across a large part of the region.[27] Samuel Ajayi Crowther, rescued as a child from a slave ship, was consecrated as the first Anglican African bishop in 1864, his diocese an ill-defined area of Equatorial Africa, Venn urging European missionaries in the region to 'voluntarily place themselves under his jurisdiction'. By contrast the CMS in India had no indigenous clergy in 1854; the BMS with 56 churches in 1867 had a single Indian pastor; however, seven years later the LMS in Travancore had ordained eleven ministers and 210 'native preachers'.[28]

The tide turned against indigenous preferment in the CMS church in West Africa after 1860 with the growth of pseudo-scientific ideas of race which demeaned the idea of African ability and advancement and thus of an autonomously led church in Africa. Late in the next decade European colonial imperialism began its steady advance in Africa and elsewhere. Colonial rulers anxious to avoid communal unrest in Islamic regions of Africa and areas of Hindu predominance in India excluded most European missions although could

---

25 Report of Commission II, p.3, quoted by Brian Stanley, *The World Missionary Conference: Edinburgh 1910* (Grand Rapids, MI: Eerdmans, 2009), 133.

26 Roland Allen, *The spontaneous expansion of the Church*, 1.

27 See Ajayi, *Christian missions*, Ayendele, *Missionary impact*, and Jehu Hanciles, *Euthanasia of a mission: African church autonomy in a colonial context* (Westport, CT: Praeger, 2002). See also the Church Missionary Society's *Register of missionaries and native clergy from 1804 to 1904* (London: Church Missionary Society, n.d., c.1905).

28 Brian Stanley, 'Christian missions, anti-slavery and the claims of humanity c.1813-1873', in Gilley & Stanley, eds, *The Cambridge history of Christianity. vol.8. World Christianities c.1815-c.1914* (Cambridge: Cambridge University Press, 2006), 457.

not bar the way to individual itinerant Christians who carried the Gospel with them. In French colonies republican administrators were generally anti-clerical and sought to restrict Christian mission activity. In British colonies, by the 1880s, in both the Anglican church and the colonial State, formally educated Africans began to be by-passed or overlooked for office as the growing rancour of racial discrimination closed many doors of opportunity once open to them. In such circumstances it is not surprising that some African Christians – and also Christians in other parts of the Imperial dominated world – reacted by breaking away from mission control to assert the independency of their own churches. Such movements happened across Africa although secession should not necessarily be seen as an assertion of anti-colonialism, as a good number of scholars in the past have suggested. In some cases it may well have been so, but often the break was with intent to reform, links with parent or overseas denominations maintained.[29] The Niger Delta Pastorate did not cease being Anglican (and nor did its Bishop 'Holy' Johnson), and Mojola Agbebi's Native Baptist Church continued to function as a Baptist body although its members dressed in African clothes and conducted services in Yoruba. In southern Africa independency was often referred to as Ethiopianism, viewed with increased suspicion by the white authorities as a result of the Bambatha 'rebellion' of 1906.[30] Europeans saw their lack of control over African independent churches as likely to lead to syncretism, a reversion to 'traditional' African beliefs and cultural practices such as polygyny, acceptance of slavery, and clitorosectomy. Indeed, the latter was a major issue in the Gikuyu church in Kenya in the 1920s-30s and led to the creation of break-away independent churches.

The impact of the First World War in Africa led to new opportunities for Africans to take a primary role in mission churches. It also spawned large independent churches, led by revivalist prophets who tried to make sense of the great catastrophe of not only the war itself but also the influenza pandemic of 1918-19 which hit the continent with such ferocity. Some of these revivalists, for example William Wadé Harris in West Africa, stressed confession of sins, adherence to the Bible, the need for prayer, and a closer communion with God, and were favourably viewed by the Methodists. In some instances European missionaries were actively involved in revivals such as that in East Africa in the 1930s, which drew on Keswick ideas of holiness and emphasised public confession and ecstatic expressions of the work of the Holy Spirit.[31] The growth

29 For a study of these Zionist churches see Robert J. Houle, *Making Africa Christian: Africans reimagining their faith in colonial South Africa* (Bethlehem, PA: Lehigh University Press, 2011); for West Africa see Adam Mohr, 'Out of Zion into Philadelphia and West Africa: Faith Tabernacle congregations, 1897-1925', *Pneuma*, 32, 1 (2010), 56-79; 'Faith Tabernacle Congregation and early Pentecostalism in colonial West Africa, 1910s-1941', *Journal of Religion in Africa*, 43 (2013), 196-221, and 'Zionism and Aladura's shared genealogy in John Alexander Dowie', *Religion*, 45 (2015), 239-251.

30 Hastings, *Church in Africa*, 478-499.

31 Derek R. Peterson, *Ethnic patriotism and the East African Revival: A history of dissent, c.1935-1972* (Cambridge: Cambridge University Press, 2012); Kevin Ward & Emma Wild-Wood, eds, *The East African revival: History and legacies* (Farnham: Ashgate, 2012).

of African Pentecostalism which dates back to the early years of the twentieth century owed much to influence from Europe and North America.[32]

Andrew Walls splendidly captures how Christianity came to engage with African communities:

> I recall a survey of how the numerous congregations within one densely populated area of Nigeria had come into being. Time after time the seminal figure was a new court clerk who was a Christian, or a worker on the new railway, or a tailor, carrying his sewing machine on his head, or some other trader. Some such stranger, or a group of strangers, had arrived and had started family prayers, stopped work on Sunday, and sang hymns instead, and some local people got interested. Or perhaps the initial impetus came from people from that village who had gone elsewhere – to school, to work, to trade, in more than one case to jail – and on return home sought the things they had found in their travels. The survey yielded no instance of a congregation founded by a missionary, and hardly one founded by any official agent of the church at all. In most cases the role of the mission had been to respond – sometimes, through straitened resources, belatedly and minimally – to an initiative within the community.[33]

And Adrian Hastings' words on the growth of the church in Africa could equally be applied to other parts of the non-European world:

> The Christian advance was a black advance or it was nothing. It was one in which ever so many more people were involved but very few of whom we can even name. It used and depended upon the missionaries to some extent and it was used by them to a very considerable extent, but in general the black advance was far more low-key and often entirely unplanned and haphazard.[34]

As in Africa, so globally, the major challenge for European missions was reliance upon an indigenous clergy and church leaders. Rely they certainly had to; the numerical strength of a growing church indicated that. This was an enduring subject of debate, particularly in colonial territories subject to Western imperial dominance, less pronounced in the non-colonial world where missions had more of a suppliant role. But allied to this were other questions: how valid was indigenous conversion and could local people be effective evangelists in upholding the purity of faith; could and would autonomous churches adhere to orthodox faith in the face of local culture; and significantly would foreign missionaries be willing to accept and respect the autonomy of local Christian pastors which challenged their authority? Allied to this was the question of what did indigenous autonomy actually imply. Clearly the attaining of the 'three selves' of ecclesial independence could take several stages rather than occurring simultaneously. It did not mean leaving a denomination, but what was essential was achieving the degree of indigenous ecclesiastical authority

32 See Adam Mohr, 'Out of Zion', 56-79; 'Faith Tabernacle Congregation', 196-221, and 'Zionism and Aladura's shared genealogy', 239-251.

33 Andrew Walls, 'The evangelical revival, the missionary movement, and Africa', in M.A. Noll, D.W. Bebbington, & G.A. Rawlyk, eds, *Evangelicalism: Comparative studies of popular Protestantism in North America, the British Isles, and beyond, 1700-1990* (New York: Oxford University Press, 1994), 316; also in Walls, *The missionary movement in Christian History: Studies in the transmission of faith* (Maryknoll, NY: Orbis Books, 1996), 87.

34 Hastings, *Church in Africa*, 437-438.

that Bishop 'Holy' Johnson, perhaps naively, envisaged when in 1901 he promoted 'the Niger Bishopric Endowment Fund for the establishment of an "Independent African Bishopric" in the Niger Delta'.[35]

In regions of British India 'native agents' had been pre-eminent in evangelical expansion. This was so in south India and Assam where in the nineteenth and twentieth centuries the work of spreading the Christian message was primarily undertaken by Indian preachers and teachers, often winning converts from the outcastes and very poor. For example, V.S. Azariah (1874-1945), the first Indian bishop of the Anglican church, 'was the chief inspirational force behind mass movements that brought roughly 200,000 outcaste Mala and Madigas, tribals and low-caste non-Brahmins into his fledgling church during his lifetime'.[36] As Frykenberg states 'missionaries were neither the primary vehicles of the Christian message nor the primary agents of conversion with the cultural matrix or "mother tongue" of each people, [but] they were the primary vehicles of modern learning, science and medicine'.[37] And the latter encouraged a desire among Indians to govern their own church affairs free of foreign domination. That spirit of independency was well-established and is perhaps well captured in the ideas and words of the Sikh-Hindu Christian convert Sadhu Sundar Singh, who never accepted European modes of thought: 'Indians need the Water of Life, but not the European cup'.[38]

A further evidence of independency was the willingness of an autonomous church to become a mission church. The West African Anglican church was indeed such as it spread out with its African clerics, catechists, and evangelists from Freetown to regions such as the lower Niger and beyond, which often constituted cross-cultural mission as African Christians entered territories characterised by languages and cultures markedly different from their own.[39] The same process occurred in India as indigenously-run churches adopted mission societies 'native to the soil', sending missionaries to neighbouring ethnic groups and to people of their own ethnic origin but overseas, for example John Rangiah's Baptist mission to the Telegu-speaking settlers in South Africa.[40] In the Pacific Ocean region, indigenous converts played a vital role as missionary evangelists by travelling to different islands to preach, teach and plant churches, for example Polynesians to the New Hebrides and to the Solomon Islands.[41] Among those faithfully engaged in this pioneer missionary

---

35 Ayendele, *Holy Johnson*, 328-335.

36 Susan Billington Harper, 'Azariah', 'Vedanayagam Samuel', in Gerald H. Anderson, ed, *Biographical dictionary of Christian missions* (Grand Rapids, MI, Eerdmans, 1998), 35-36, and further Harper, *In the shadow of the Mahatma: Bishop V.S. Azariah and the travails of Christianity in British India* (Grand Rapids, MI: Eerdmans, 2000).

37 Robert Eric Frykenberg, 'Christian and religious traditions in the Indian Empire', in Gilley & Stanley, *Cambridge history of Christianity. vol.8*, 487-488.

38 Ibid., 489.

39 There are numerous examples, e.g. T. Jack Thompson, *Touching the heart: Xhosa missionaries to Malawi, 1876-1888* (Pretoria: University of South Africa, 2000).

40 See Stanley, *World Missionary Conference*, 100.

41 Darrell Whiteman, *Melanesians and missionaries: An ethnological study of social and religious change in the Southwest Pacific* (Pasadena, CA: William Carey Library, 1983), chs.3 & 4. See also

endeavour was Ta'unga (1868-98), a Cook Islander, one of more than 20 Polynesian missionaries who went to New Caledonia before any Europeans missionaries arrived there.[42] A more formal later development of this in 1925 was the formation of the Anglican Melanesian Brotherhood which continues its work of indigenous evangelism today, including a recent history of 'martyrs' killed in service in 1999-2000.[43]

In the life of the church and in evangelistic effort the significant and often specific role of women should not be overlooked. Frequently women constituted the largest number of members of a church or congregation. Christianity came with new ideas of human equality and gender roles, and strictures against practices that disadvantaged women. For many women the Gospel brought not only a message of a new and different spiritual experience, but also of a potential new domestic order and relationships with new social freedoms, such as access to formal education and earned money. In societies where women were customarily marginalised or demeaned, they could now find distinctive places where they alone as Christians could function. Not all female converts were poor. India's remarkable Pandita Ramabai was a high caste Hindu-Christian, intellectually gifted and independent-minded, whose spiritual pilgrimage took her from Hinduism to Anglo-Catholicism and then via Holiness ideas to evangelicalism, with a striking ministry of care for orphans and widows, and translation work.[44] In West Africa elite women often played a major role in prophetic churches; for example the Aladura Cherubim and Seraphim society was founded jointly by Moses Orimolade and Christiana Abiodun Akinsowon in the mid-1920s.[45] South African Bible women's prayer groups helped promote faith among women, some of whom were not literate, but also gave them a platform for them to protest at restrictions placed on black people by the white authorities.[46]

Raeburn Lange, *Island ministers: Indigenous leadership in nineteenth-century Pacific Islands Christianity* (Canterbury, NZ: Macmillan Brown Centre for Pacific Studies, 2005).

42 Charles W. Foreman, 'Ta'unga', in Anderson, *Biographical dictionary of Christian missions*, 657. Also R.G. & Marjorie Crocombe, eds, *The works of Ta'unga: Records of a Polynesian traveller in the South Seas, 1833-1898* (Canberra: Australian National University Press, 1968).

43 Whiteman, *Melanesians and missionaries*, 194-198 and 469-470.

44 Robert Eric Fryckenberg, *Christianity in India* (Oxford: Oxford University Press, 2008), 380-411, devotes most of his chapter on 'Trophies of Grace' to Ramabai.

45 Elizabeth Isichei, *A history of Christianity in Africa* (London: SPCK, 1995), 291-292. See also Philomena Njeri Mwaura, 'Gender and power in African Christianity: African Instituted churches and Pentecostal churches', in Ogbu U. Kalu, ed, *African Christianity: An African story* (Trenton, NJ: Africa World Press, 2007), ch.16; Isabel A. Phiri, D.B. Govinden & S. Naders, eds, *Her stories: Hidden histories of women of faith in Africa* (Pietermaritzburg: Cluster Publications, 2002); and Rosalind I.J. Hackett, 'Women as leaders and participants in the Spiritual churches', in Hackett, ed, *New religious movements in Nigeria* (Lewiston, NY: Edwin Mellen Press, 1987), 191-208.

46 See the essays by Deborah Gaitskell, 'Power in prayer and service: Women's Christian organizations', in Richard Elphick & Rodney Davenport, eds, *Christianity in South Africa: A political, social & cultural history* (Cape Town: David Philip, 1997), ch.15; 'Praying and preaching: The distinctive spirituality of African women's church organisations', in Henry Bredekamp & Robert Ross, eds, *Missions and Christianity in South African history* (Witwatersrand: Witwatersrand University Press, 1995), 211-232; and 'Devout domesticity? A

I hesitate as a non-specialist to say anything on the role of indigenous church activity in China, the subject of this book, but perhaps a few thoughts are in order. Missionaries in China in the first half of the nineteenth-century acknowledged the vastness of the country and the degree of the challenge. John Van Nest Talmage in 1848 recognised that the country could only be evangelised via a Chinese agency and based on the idea of a self-propagating, self-governing and self-supporting Chinese church. His thinking was in line with that of Venn and Anderson, and he helped to bring this about in south Fujian (Banlam) in the 1850s, through a joint venture by the Dutch Reformed Church of America and English Presbyterian missionaries in cooperation with Chinese congregations. Thus was established 'ecclesial devolution', what David Cheung has called 'the first Protestant church' in China.[47] In Shandong the American Presbyterian missionary John Livingston Nevius, with his annual programme of Bible teaching for Chinese pastors, promoted the idea of independent churches. In his sixties he advised the nascent Korean church where his ideas helped shape its self-standing growth and development.[48]

In Fuzhou, south-east China, Christian independency was helped by denominational structure; the 'Methodist conference system was unique among the Fuzhou missions in the symbolic equality and the degree of real power that it allowed to the Chinese preacher', argues Dunch. By 1881 the American Board had ordained only two Chinese clergy, and the CMS seven, while the Methodists had admitted 53 men to probationary or full membership in their annual conference. As Dunch continues: 'It is...clear that the Methodist missionaries simply accorded more than the other missionaries did, and this trust was institutionalized in their Chinese structures'.[49] James Hudson Taylor's China Inland Mission (CIM), founded in 1865, faith-based, under-girded by prayer, nondenominational, primarily employed lay-people including many Chinese, and direction was handled by a council in Shanghai rather than from overseas. The term 'Inland' in its title indicated the purpose of penetrating to every province of China. Taylor's aim was that each missionary, man and woman, should identify closely with Chinese culture. The purpose of CIM evangelism, stated Taylor, was not to denationalise but to Christianise the Chinese people. 'We wish to see Chinese Christians raised up – men and women truly Christian, but withal Chinese in every right sense of the word. We wish to see churches of such believers presided over by pastors and officers of their own countrymen, worshipping God in the land of their fathers, in their

---

century of African women's Christianity in South Africa', in Cherryl Walker, ed, *Women and gender in Southern Africa to 1945* (Cape Town: David Philip, 1990), 251-272.

47 David Cheung, *Christianity in modern China: The making of the first Protestant church* (Leiden: Brill, 2004).

48 Everett N. Hunt, Jr., 'John Livingston Nevius, 1829–1893: Pioneer of three-self principles in Asia', in Gerald H. Anderson, et al., eds, *Mission legacies: Biographical studies of leaders of the modern missionary movement* (Maryknoll, NY: Orbis, American Society of Missiology series, No. 19, 1994); and Hunt, 'The legacy of John Livingston Nevius', *International Bulletin of Missionary Research* 15, 3 (July 1991), 120, 122–4.

49 Ryan Dunch, *Fuzhou Protestants and the making of modern China 1857-1927* (New Haven, CT: Yale University Press, 2001), 24.

own tongue, and in edifices of a thoroughly native style of architecture. ... Let us in everything not sinful become like the Chinese, that by all means we may "save some".'[50] And yet Taylor, the founder and Director General of the CIM, struggled to exercise autocratic control of the Mission, and its workers, which over time assumed many of the marks of a separate denomination.[51] Lian Xi's measured assessment is that by 1900, the year of the Boxer uprising, 'it was clear that no significant independent Christian communities had endured in China', and he quotes D.E. Hoste, Taylor's successor who had concluded that 'the system hitherto in general use...practically postpones indefinitely the independence and self-government in the native churches'.[52]

Despite these instances of indigenisation, the vast majority of Chinese churches throughout the nineteenth-century and well into the second decade of the twentieth-century remained subject to foreign control and direction. At the great nation-wide Protestant missionary conferences in 1877 and 1890 there were no known Chinese delegates, and for the 1907 conference fewer than ten of 1,100 delegates. By 1900 there were nearly 500 ordained episcopal priests but a Chinese bishop was not appointed until 1926; in 1905 there were 3,440 foreign Protestant missionaries in China, some 300 ordained Chinese pastors assisted by well over 10,000 Chinese staff. There were, of course, Chinese church leaders and evangelists who steadfastly worked independently of foreign mission control, for example Pastor Hsi Shengmo of Shanxi, who established opium refuges and cooperated with CIM missionaries but retained autonomy of action.

The promotion of indigenous-led independent churches rested in part on the ideas and attitudes of foreign missionaries but was also vitally determined by the local political environment. Chinese Christians' demands for independency were encouraged by the upsurge of anti-foreign feeling in the country in 1900, the revolution of 1911, and the Fourth of May Movement in 1919 in reaction to the terms of the Treaty of Versailles, and later with the successes of the Nationalist Guomindang government after 1927. Much more far-reaching for the Chinese church was the victory of the Communist Party in 1949 followed by the subsequent expulsion of foreign missionaries. Although it meant persecution for Chinese Christians it also gave them space to breathe and think

---

50 Howard & Geraldine Taylor, *Hudson Taylor and the China Inland Mission. vol.2. The growth of a work of God* (London: Morgan & Scott, 4th edn, 1920), 90-91. See Daniel H. Bays, *A new history of Christianity in China* (Chichester: Wiley-Blackwell, 2012), 68-69.

51 See Alvyn Austin, *China's millions: The China Inland Mission and late Qing society, 1832-1905* (Grand Rapids, MI: Eerdmans, 2008), 104-105, on Taylor's *Principles and practices of the CIM* (1867) and the letter he wrote on retiring as Director General in 1904. Austin's study is one of the few scholarly studies of the CIM not written by an 'insider'. The reference to a 'separate denomination' is from Bob Whyte, *Unfinished encounter: China and Christianity* (London: Collins, 1980), 119-123.

52 Lian Xi, *Redeemed by fire: The rise of popular Christianity in modern China* (New Haven, CT: Yale University Press, 2010), 31. Referring to D.E. Hoste, 'Possible changes and developments in the native churches arising out of the present crisis', *Chinese Recorder* (October 1900), 509-510.

in a church context that was solely Chinese.[53] The turmoil of more than twelve years of war followed by Communist rule in China disrupted mission activities and broke-up churches, driving Chinese Christians into new looser and more informal ecclesial bodies. In 1955 a foreign Christian wrote that 'Sects have multiplied since the Communist conquest, largely at the expense of the established denominations. Some observers estimate that a majority of Chinese Christians are no longer in any organized church, but in small worshipping groups without any organizational connection at all.'[54]

A similar process happened in Japan which, following the First World War, became more nationalistic as the regime responded to social, political, economic and military challenges, some occasioned by the policies of the Western powers, others due to the rise of Japanese militarism and its aggression in China. Protestant mission agencies, both large and small, were reluctant to devolve control of the church to Japanese leaders. The matter was resolved by the growth of a hostile, and particularly anti-British, Japanese nationalism and the passing of the Religious Bodies Act in 1940 which effectively placed all Christian churches, schools and universities, under the control of an authoritarian government.[55]

The Post-Colonial Years since c.1960

In the second half of the twentieth-century when religious belief and practice in the West was arguably in decline and social institutions increasingly secularised, the opposite was happening in the 'southern' portion of the world. The centre of gravity of Christianity now shifted towards Africa, Asia and Latin America. By 2000 there were more Anglicans in Nigeria than in the whole of Europe and North America. In China, in the face of State hostility, the number of Christians had increased in number, outstripping the membership of the Communist Party. Most of this Christian expansion was due to indigenous evangelism, and the resulting new denominations, churches and house fellowships were decidedly independent and owed little to foreign mission activity. As Andrew Walls has recently written: 'What is certain is that Christianity is now a predominantly non-Western religion, the profession principally of African and Asian and Latin American people, and that it is currently moving progressively in that direction'.[56]

---

53 William R. Schenk, 'The origins and evolution of the Three-Selfs in relation to China', *International Bulletin of Missionary Research* (January 1990), 28-35.

54 Dr Charles West, *Christian News Letter*, July 1955, quoted by Welbourn, *East African Rebels*, 3.

55 A. Hamish Ion, *The cross and the rising sun. vol.2. The British Protestant missionary movement in Japan, Korea, and Taiwan, 1865-1945* (Waterloo, ON: Wilfred Laurier University Press, 1990), ch.8. And for the history of a small British evangelical faith mission see Esther Maxton, 'A band of evangelists, native and "foreign": the story of Japanese initiatives in indigenizing the Japan Evangelistic Band 1903-1940', forthcoming PhD thesis, Middlesex University, 2017.

56 Andrew F. Walls, 'Afterword: Christian mission in a five-hundred year context', in Walls & Cathy Ross, eds, *Mission in the 21st Century: Exploring the five marks of global mission* (London: Darton, Longman and Todd, 2008), 199.

One major movement has been the growth of Pentecostalism, a truly twentieth-century phenomenon which saw astonishing expansion worldwide after 1960. Pentecostal churches with their emphasis on the power and the gifts of the Holy Spirit, faith healing, speaking in tongues, and charismatic worship may have links with overseas 'parent' denominations, but most are autonomous in one way or another. They often fulfil the 'three selves' of Venn and Anderson, but they can be very weak in the fourth self, that of self-theologising. Pentecostalism first attracted serious scholarly attention by its growth in Latin America after 1960,[57] one reason for which, according to Edward L. Cleary, was that local pastors set up independent churches and then 'learned on the job, proving themselves by probity of life and success in extending the movement through drawing in members'.[58] By the year 2000 African Christians numbered *c*.350 million, Pentecostalists over 120 million, some 20 percent of all Christians in the continent, and members of African Initiated Churches (other than Pentecostalists) 34 million, that is one in ten of all African Christians. African Independent/Initiated Churches (AIC), of all sizes and shapes, some led by 'prophets' and often very syncretic in their theology, could be found all over sub-Saharan Africa and throughout the world where Africans had migrated. David Maxwell, writing of the expansion of Protestant Christianity in Africa since the 1980s, says that most was of 'the low-level face-to-face kind. The range of localities expanded to include the townships and the middle-class black suburb, alongside the village. And enhanced communications and social mobility swelled the ranks of the proselytisers from labour migrants, catechists and evangelists to include nurses, teachers and civil servants on placement, returning students, often accompanied by their Christian Union and Scripture Union brethren, and urban churches on "crusade" determined to establish rural branches.'[59]

Conclusion

Scholarly work on indigenisation is well in hand and new dimensions of that work are still required to produce a history of the spread of the Gospel which gives due credit and recognition to mission agencies but particularly to the numerous local Christians who have gossiped the 'word' wherever they found

57 David Martin, *Tongues of fire: The explosion of Protestantism in Latin America* (Oxford: Blackwell, 1990); Martin, *Pentecostalism: The world their parish* (Oxford: Blackwell, 2002). See also Michael Bergunder, *The South Indian Pentecostal movement in the twentieth century* (Grand Rapids, MI: Eerdmans, 2008).

58 Edward L. Cleary, 'The transformation of Latin American Christianity c.1950-2000', in Hugh McLeod, ed, *The Cambridge history of Christianity. vol.9. World Christianities c.1914-2000* (Cambridge: Cambridge University Press, 2006), 381.

59 David Maxwell, 'Post-colonial Christianity in Africa', in McLeod, ed, *Cambridge history of Christianity. vol.9*, 408-409; also Allan Anderson, 'The Pentecostal and Charismatic movements', in ibid., pp. 89-106; and Anderson & Edmond Tang, 'Independency in Africa and Asia', in ibid., 107-128. In addition: Allan H. Anderson, *African transformation: African initiated Christianity in the twentieth century* (Trenton, NJ: Africa World Press, 2001), and Ogbu Kalu, *African Pentecostalism: An introduction* (Oxford: Oxford University Press, 2008).

themselves. Ogbu U. Kalu in his preface to one of his recent books described his task as seeking 'to build up a group of African church historians who will tell the story as an African story by intentionally privileging the patterns of African agency without neglecting the roles of various missionary bodies'.[60] And that is what is required for the new direction of church history written by other Africans, Asians, Pacific islanders, and Latin Americans. Churches in those now dominant Christian areas of the contemporary world, once dependent upon European agencies, are now 'sending' churches; thus, Korean missionaries are to be found in all corners of the globe, and Brazilian Protestants minister in Portuguese-speaking Africa. Additionally the process of 'reverse' migration which began in the 1950s as peoples from the Caribbean, Asia and Africa moved to Europe and North America, has been followed by 'reverse mission' so that today there are African-led churches (including some mega-churches) filled with black and white faces across the northern hemisphere from Kiev to Chicago.

Indigenous Christians have had to work out how to navigate their way of faith in new state structures and political orders sometimes hostile to Christianity or certain forms of Christian action. This has ranged widely from indigenous churches that opposed all secular authority (Alice Lenshina's Lumpa Church in Zambia, mid-1950s to mid-1970s) to Chinese Christians who asserted their right to meet on their own terms and not those imposed by a communist regime which had declared all religious belief and practice as counter-revolutionary. Remarkably, the church in China emerged from the dark decade following the Cultural Revolution (what Bays has called 'a black hole' in China's Christian history) to thrive rapidly in the climate of a changing regime that embraced economic reform and tolerated Christian practice as long as it did not challenge the authority of the State.[61] Chinese Christians had to work out their own course, either independence from the State or accommodation with it through the revived Three-Self Patriotic Movement. Elsewhere in the world independency has spawned new theologies that pronounced 'Liberation', 'Asian', and 'Black' identities, a 'rethinking' of what it meant to be Christian in a specific part of the world or personal situation, giving rise to hybrid forms that often challenge orthodox Christian praxis.

And yet while all this attracted the attention of scholars, there was the everyday business of Christian evangelisation at grassroots level. In conclusion, perhaps one brief story will suffice to illustrate this. An African mother brought her hydrocephalic spina bifida child to a hospital. While there the mother became a Christian believer. Her husband later said: 'When my wife came from [the hospital], she was different. She brought a Bible home and started preaching to neighbours and everybody. I accepted Jesus through her and now

60 Obgu U. Kalu, ed, *African Christianity: An African story* (Trenton, NJ: Africa World Press, 2007), xi.

61 Bays, *New history of Christianity in China*, 187-190.

things are different for all of us. Our child is better and is in school. Thank you for the Bible you gave to her, we read it all the time.'[62]

62 Personal communication, July 2016.

Missionaries in the Making of Vernacular Christianity in China

Lian Xi

In scholarly excavations of the history of Christianity in modern China, the field of the indigenous church has yielded some of the most valuable finds in recent decades. The other chapters in this volume attest to the richness of both the historical artifacts of Chinese Christianity – unearthed from a century and a half of Chinese-language sources – and historical insights that can be gained from them. Since the 1980s, scholarly attention has increasingly shifted from a Eurocentric focus to one that features indigenous leaders and church members as the prime historical agents in the making of Chinese Christianity. Meanwhile, a new silence at times appears to have befallen mission studies. One major recent reappraisal of Chinese Christianity concludes that, "looking broadly across the stage of History, it just did not much matter what the foreign missionaries did" during the late-Qing and Republican periods. The "real achievement, the construction of a vibrant and firmly grounded Christian community, has been that of the Chinese Christians themselves."[1] There is an aura of irrelevance about the missionaries.

Did the missionaries matter in the making of Chinese Christianity? (A curious question, perhaps, if we consider their extraordinary role in the making of modern China.[2]) Should we vacate the field of mission history as we extend our probe into homegrown Christianity? Or should we dig our way deeper into both the history of the indigenous church and that of Western missions? Are we in fact able to separate the two or is there a continuum that we disregard at the risk of a diminished understanding? Pearl Buck's question posed in 1927 – which eventually hurled her into a storm of theological controversies – can be raised again in our time with a different twist: "Is there a place for the foreign missionary?"[3]

---

1 Daniel H. Bays, 'Reflections on Protestantism and modern China', *The Chinese Historical Review*, 20, 1 (May 2013), 14.

2 Both Jonathan D. Spence and Yu Yingshi recently reaffirmed the crucial role that mission Christianity played in introducing modernity to late-Qing and Republican China. See '余英时、史景迁谈1898-1989世纪交替中的中国知识分子', *Guanchazhe*, August 6, 2013, http://www.guancha.cn/YuYingShi/2013_08_06_163875.shtml (accessed 17 February, 2016).

3 Pearl S. Buck, 'Is there a place for the foreign missionary?', *The Chinese Recorder*, 58 (February 1927), 100-107. Buck's vehement criticism of missions eventually led to her forced resignation as a Presbyterian missionary. See Lian Xi, *The conversion of missionaries: Liberalism in American Protestant missions in China, 1907-1932* (University Park, PA: Pennsylvania State University Press, 1997), ch.3.

The answers to these questions have as much to do with the nature of the missionaries' work and their actual accomplishments as with our perceptions, both popular and academic, of Western missions. In modern times, such perceptions have been shaped by historical circumstances, intellectual preoccupations, and political needs. In China during the 1920s, late-Qing xenophobic antagonism to Western missions – sometimes echoed in caustic quips from Western critics such as Mark Twain[4] – gave way to Communist-instigated denunciations of foreign missions as "cultural invasion."[5] For its part, the missionary enterprise, protected by Western gunboats, yielded from time to time to the temptation of religious chauvinism, which expressed itself in such unfortunate claims as "The Christian Occupation of China," the title of the massive survey of Protestant work in China published in 1922. Preoccupied with their own institutional advances in the evangelization of the Middle Kingdom, the missions largely overlooked homegrown expressions of Chinese Christianity. As Daniel Bays observes, the 1936 *Handbook of the Christian Movement in China under Protestant Auspices* produced by the National Christian Council included "vast statistics" on mission societies and denominational churches "but did not even mention the names of the True Jesus Church, the Assembly Hall, the Jesus Family, or the China Christian Independent Church Federation, all of which were well established by that time."[6] The indigenous churches were invisible.

The full-scale Japanese invasion of China beginning in 1937 brought horrendous suffering to the people, but also catapulted Western missionaries into the new role as allies and defenders of the Chinese – heroic figures who delivered the helpless from the terror of the Japanese military. Minnie Vautrin, American educational missionary at Ginling College, turned the campus into a sanctuary for thousands of local women and girls during the Rape of Nanking.[7] In 1940, as the Japanese army advanced into Yangcheng, Shanxi, an English China Inland Mission (CIM) probationer-turned-independent missionary named Gladys Aylward led 100 orphans on an exodus for more than two hundred miles over the mountains to safety in West China. Her story was later featured in a post-war BBC radio series, called *The Undefeated*, about war heroes

4 See Mark Twain, 'To the person sitting in darkness', *North American Review*, February 1, 1901.
5 Yang Weihua 杨卫华, 'Zhongguo fan zongjiao lilun de chengxing: 1920 niandai fei zongjiao huayu fenxi' 中国反宗教理论的成型: 1920年代非宗教话语分析, *Aomen Ligong Xuebao 澳门理工学报*, 3 (2013), http://jds.cass.cn/Item/24493.aspx (accessed 10 June, 2015). See also Tao Feiya 陶飞亚, '"Wenhua qinlue" yuanliukao' "文化侵略"源流考, *Wen shi zhe文史哲*, 5 (2003).
6 Daniel H. Bays, 'The growth of independent Christianity', in Bays, ed, *Christianity in China: From the eighteenth century to the present* (Stanford, CA: Stanford University Press, 1996), 309-10.
7 See Suping Lu, ed, *Terror in Minnie Vautrin's Nanjing: Diaries and correspondence, 1937-38* (Champaign, IL: University of Illinois Press, 2008); Hua-ling Hu, *American goddess at the Rape of Nanking: The courage of Minnie Vautrin* (Carbondale, IL: Southern Illinois University Press, 2000).

returning home, and also found its way into the 1958 Hollywood film *The Inn of Sixth Happiness* featuring Ingrid Bergman.[8]

The Communist victory in 1949 and the end of the missionary era brought strident official castigations of modern Western missions. Mao himself observed sarcastically in 1949 that the so-called American efforts to deepen friendships between the US and China had included the "spiritual aggression" of American missions forced upon the Chinese after the Opium War.[9] In Chinese Communist Party (CCP) propaganda throughout the Mao era, "Western missions" and "cultural invasion" were synonymous. The first serious academic study of Christian missions, produced by Gu Changsheng and published 1981, was initially instructed by the authorities to bear the title "the history of the imperialists' use of religion in their aggression against China." It was the author's patient insistence and intricate negotiations through personal connections that enabled the monograph finally to appear under the more neutral title *Missionaries and Modern China*.[10]

In the West, questions about the missionary connection with imperialism have also featured in scholarly assessments of modern Christian missions. In Kenneth Scott Latourette's seminal work *A History of Christian Missions in China* published in 1929, he conceded that the story of the missionary movement in China was "inextricably bound up with the whole history of the Western invasion of China."[11] However, he also suggested that Christian missions represented an effort to bring the best of the spiritual resources of the West "to counteract the evils attendant upon their commerce, industry, and use of force."[12]

Latourette wrote as an insider, one who was "thoroughly committed to the enterprise of Christian missions."[13] The publication of his work coincided with the emergence in the West of missiology as a theological discipline in the 1920s and 1930s, one that was primarily concerned with the methodology and effects of Christian missions and utilized sources in Western languages.[14] As a whole, and in the United States in particular, academic studies of the China missions by secular scholars did not arise until the 1960s. To John King Fairbank, it was "intellectual abdication" for American historians to neglect

8 'Gladys Alward, missionary to China', Biographical Sketches of Memorable Christians of the Past, http://justus.anglican.org/resources/bio/73.html (accessed 10 June, 2015); Huijuan Li, 'From "The small woman" to a religious-secular saint', unpublished graduate seminar paper, 2014.

9 Mao Zedong, '"Youyi", haishi qinlue' '友谊', 还是侵略 ['Friendship', or aggression], August 30, 1949, in *Mao Zedong Xuanji 毛泽东选集 [Collected works of Mao Zedong]*, 4 vols. (Beijing: Renmin chubanshe, 1991), 4, 1505-6.

10 Chen Xulu, 'Foreword', in Gu Changsheng, *Chuanjiaoshi yu jindai Zhongguo 传教士与近代中国 [Missionaries and Modern China]* (Shanghai: Shanghai renmin chubanshe, 1981), 2; Gu Changsheng, various conversations with the author, 1993-2012.

11 Kenneth Scott Latourette, *A history of Christian missions in China* (New York: MacMillan, 1929), 4.

12 Ibid., 202.

13 Ibid., vii.

14 Nicolas Standaert, 'New trends in the historiography of Christianity in China', *The Catholic Historical Review*, 83, 4 (October 1997), 574.

Chinese history in general and the Christian missions in particular, and to reduce "the missionary in foreign parts" to "the invisible man of American history."[15]

Academic works produced since the 1970s by North American and European scholars have brought the China missionaries out of historical oblivion. We have come to see them as playing a vital role in the introduction of Western modernity. They helped transform education, medicine, publishing, the urban landscape, and village life; their work generated upward social mobility and changed the Chinese view of themselves and of the outside world. It is perhaps not surprising that the first wave of studies focused on the missionaries. One thinks of Ellsworth Carlson's *The Foochow Missionaries* (1973); Edward Gulick's *Peter Parker and the Opening of China* (1974); Irwin Hyatt's 1976 monograph on Shandong missionaries T. P. Crawford, Lottie Moon, and Calvin Mateer; Adrian Bennett's study of Young J. Allen (1983); Jane Hunter's *Gospel of Gentility* (1989), among others.[16] Until at least the 1980s, available sources on Chinese Christianity were primarily in Western languages, in the form of missionary publications, correspondence, and reports. Western modes of thinking about the history of the Chinese church also dominated early studies of Chinese Christianity. As D. E. Mungello points out, "China was viewed as a mission field cultivated by Western missionaries [and] the story of Christianity's development in China was merely another chapter in a long series of mission histories."[17] That is particularly the case with books on denominational mission work.[18] In these accounts, the missionaries were the prime makers of Chinese Christianity.

---

15 J John King Fairbank, 'Assignment for the '70s', *The American Historical Review*, 74, 3 (February 1969), 863, 868. Among notable, early monographs are Paul A. Cohen, *China and Christianity: The missionary movement and the growth of Chinese antiforeignism, 1860-1870* (Cambridge, MA: Harvard University Press, 1963); Liu Kwang-ching, ed, *American missionaries in China: Papers from Harvard seminars* (Cambridge, MA: Harvard University Press, 1966). Joseph R. Levenson's *Confucian China and its modern fate: A trilogy* (Berkeley, CA: University of California Press, 1958-65), completed before his untimely death in 1969, includes a section in its first volume that discusses the missionaries' failure to bring about a 'Christian-Confucian syncretism'.

16 See Irwin Hyatt, *Our ordered lives confess: Three nineteenth-century American missionaries in East Shantung* (Cambridge, MA: Harvard University Press, 1976); Adrian A. Bennett, *Missionary journalist in China: Young J. Allen and his magazines, 1860-1883* (Athens, GA: University of Georgia Press, 1983); Jane Hunter, *The Gospel of gentility: American women missionaries in turn-of-the-century China* (New Haven, CT: Yale University Press, 1989). Kathleen Lodwick's *Crusaders against opium: Protestant missionaries in China, 1874-1917* (Lexington, KY: The University Press of Kentucky, 1996) belongs to the same category.

17 D. E. Mungello, 'Reinterpreting the history of Christianity in China', *The Historical Journal*, 55, 2 (2012), 535.

18 See, for example, Walter Nind Lacy, *A hundred years of China Methodism* (Abingdon: Cokesbury Press, 1948); A. J. Broomhall, *Hudson Taylor and China's open century, 7 vols.* (Sevenoaks: Hodder & Stoughton and OMF, 1981-1989); G. Thompson Brown, *Earthen vessels and transcendent power: American Presbyterians in China, 1837-1952* (Maryknoll, NY: Orbis, 1997).

Beginning in the 1980s, what Nicolas Standaert calls a "major paradigm shift" occurred in the field.[19] A China-centered approach to the study of Chinese Christianity began to emerge, with increased use of Chinese-language sources and a new focus on the Chinese response to Christianity, as seen in Jacques Gernet's *Chine et christianisme* (1982). There is a new sensitivity to the Chinese as historical agents – opponents of missions in some cases, but also reformers, rebels, revolutionaries, modernizers, church leaders, visionaries, and individuals otherwise discovering a new faith and frame of meaning as well as new resources for their life's struggles. New studies done in mainland China as well as in other areas of the Chinese-speaking world have also yielded fresh findings. Together, these works have reshaped our understanding of China's encounter with Christianity and of the emergence of a spirited Chinese Christianity beyond the design of Western missions.[20] Notable studies in this vein include fine works by D. E. Mungello, R. G. Tiedemann, Robert Entenmann, Alan Richard Sweeten, Tao Feiya, and those who contributed to Daniel Bays' edited volume *Christianity in China* (1996). More recently, the deeply researched and provocative monographs by Eugenio Menegon and Henrietta Harrison shine the spotlight on Catholic communities in coastal Fu'an and the Fen River valley of central Shanxi, respectively.[21]

However, the new approach has often left us with a historical drama in which the players on the center stage are Chinese and the missionaries fade into the indistinct background or assume adversarial roles. The risk we now face is a new kind of invisibility of the missionaries, as if the likes of Robert Morrison, Hudson Taylor, Griffith John, W. A. P. Martin, Lottie Moon, Timothy Richard, Samuel Pollard, and hundreds of other pioneers could just be left in the footnotes. Ryan Dunch's *Fuzhou Protestants and the Making of a Modern China, 1857-1927* (2001) stands in striking contrast to Carlson's book concerning Christianity in the same treaty port city. Jessie Lutz's edited volume *Pioneering Chinese Christian Women* (2010) is populated with a whole different set of historical figures from Jane Hunter's *Gospel of Gentility*. In my own recent work *Redeemed by Fire* (2010), which explores the rise of popular Christianity in modern China, Jonathan Goforth, the great Canadian missionary, and Marie Monsen, a charismatic Norwegian, are foils to the

19 Standaert, *New trends in the historiography of Christianity in China*, 573.

20 Much of what may be called 'China-centred' scholarship on Chinese Christianity produced since the 1980s has focused on the Catholic church in the Ming-Qing period. See Mungello, *Reinterpreting the history of Christianity in China*, 540-44.

21 See R. G. Tiedemann, 'Christianity and Chinese "heterodox sects": Mass conversion and syncretism in Shandong Province in the early eighteenth century', *Monumenta Serica*, 44 (1996), 339-382; D. E. Mungello, *The forgotten Christians of Hangzhou* (Honolulu: University of Hawaii Press, 1994); D. E. Mungello, *The Spirit and the flesh in Shandong, 1650-1785* (Lanham, MD: Rowman & Littlefield, 2001); Robert Entenmann, 'Catholics and society in eighteenth-century Sichuan' and 'Christian virgins in eighteenth-century Sichuan', in D. Bays, ed, *Christianity in China: From the eighteenth century to the present* (Stanford, CA: Stanford University Press, 1996); Eugenio Menegon, *Ancestors, virgins, and friars: Christianity as a local religion in late imperial China* (Cambridge, MA: Harvard University Asia Center, 2009); Henrietta Harrison, *The missionary's curse and other tales from a Chinese Catholic village* (Berkeley, CA: University of California Press, 2013).

indigenous Shandong revivalists of the 1930s. Daniel Bays' *A New History of Christianity in China* (2012) builds on his earlier works on indigenous Chinese Christianity to remedy what he calls the "lamentable non-recognition" of Chinese Christians, for instance the "anonymity of the Chinese scholars who toiled, some for decades, with the missionary translators to create the Union version of the Bible." And he highlights the work of a long list of neglected, frustrated, or untapped Chinese talents – from Jesuit priest-turned educator Ma Xiangbo, St. John's Yan Yongjing to evangelist and theologian Chen Chonggui.[22] In this story, the missionary appears without his halo, and much less frequently than in earlier mission studies.

The redirecting of the spotlight to indigenous Chinese Christians should not deter us, however, from recognizing the basic historical chain of events in the rise of Chinese Christianity. Western missionaries, as carriers of the Gospel and initiators of China's encounter with Christianity, must be granted their critical role in the making of that movement. This is not to deny the historical agency of Chinese Christians, or to suggest that missionaries provided the blueprint and laid down the exact denominational or theological foundation upon which local Christians subsequently built the Chinese church (although many missionaries did attempt that). Instead, we can picture the missionaries as kindling a bushfire. As we shall see later, for those who were engulfed by the new faith, conversion was not a "religious defeat...the most humiliating" of "all forms of cultural defeat," as Arthur Schlesinger, Jr. claims.[23] What missionaries did was to set in motion a religious and social movement, which turned out to be a "spontaneous expansion" rather than "directed propagation" (to borrow Erik Zürcher's characterization of the rise of Buddhism in early China).[24] Christianity became a homegrown, vernacular faith that was able to respond to local needs and give voice to communal aspirations. As such it was able to defy both the Chinese authorities and – if necessary – foreign missionaries who stood in the way of that bushfire.

In that development, the relationship between the missionaries and Chinese Christians conformed to no single, uniform pattern but was often characterized by a complex interplay of personalities and circumstances. It is true, as Jessie Lutz points out, that for the first hundred years of the Protestant movement in China, missionaries in most cases "remained the authoritative tutors in doctrine and they assumed most administrative responsibilities."[25] It is also true, on the other hand, that in the Taiping movement that drew more than a million "God

22 Daniel H. Bays, *A new history of Christianity in China* (Chichester: Wiley-Blackwell, 2012), 73, 81, 97-98.

23 Arthur Schlesinger, Jr., 'The missionary enterprise and imperialism', in John King Fairbank, ed, *The missionary enterprise in China and America* (Cambridge, MA: Harvard University Press, 1974), 366. Schlesinger does later allow that 'Christianity...was not just a faith imposed by external force. On occasion it answered questions or filled needs in native societies' (p. 371).

24 Erik Zürcher, *Bouddhisme, Christianisme et societe chinoise* (Paris: Julliard, 1990), 24, as quoted in Mungello, *Reinterpreting the history of Christianity in China*, 539.

25 Jessie G. Lutz & R. Ray Lutz, 'The invisible China missionaries: The Basel Mission's Chinese evangelists, 1847-1866', *Journal of the International Association for Mission Studies*, 12 (October 1995), 214.

Worshipers" in the early 1850s (in contrast to the combined communicant membership of mission churches of about 350 in 1853),[26] Hong Xiuquan, "God's Chinese son," claimed a form of revealed Christianity superior to what the Western brethren were preaching; Hong also freely annotated and edited the Bible to make his rebellion fit into God's cosmic scheme.[27] In Alvyn Austin's *China's Millions* (2009), we meet Xi Shengmo, the Overcomer of Demons, "an austere, charismatic figure, immaculately dressed in a white gown with a scarlet ribbon across his chest that read 'Jesus came into the world to save sinners.'" According to Austin, Xi "manipulated the missionaries adeptly, playing them off against each other and against other contenders to his leadership."[28] We also learn that such was the Overcomer of Demon's influence on the English missionaries in Shanxi that the latter started to cast out demons and came to "learn the secret language of demonology, a phenomenon rarely seen in Britain in three hundred years."[29]

In the revival movements in Shandong during the 1930s, we also see the line between missionaries and the Chinese momentarily disappear when both were drawn into Pentecostal ecstasies. An American missionary attending an all-night native revival meeting felt "a strong electric current" going through his body; he also testified to the Spirit coming to him at midnight in the presence of his rapturous congregation to shake him "as I would shake a rag" and drew from deep inside him "a great burst of joyous laughter," which his Baptist upbringing had never given him and which likely released his flock from the former bondage of excessive deference.[30]

It appears that in the intricate, varied, and constantly evolving relations between missionaries and indigenous Christianity, the issue of the missionaries' dominance, or power, vis-à-vis local Christians and Chinese authorities, is crucial. Did the missionaries become part of the oppressive or intrusive structure of power that dominated local lives, or were they allies in local resistance to that power? Did the missionaries – and the Gospel they introduced – empower believers, strengthen their collective identity, and bring cohesion to their community or did they do the opposite? Did the missionaries operate under terms set by themselves or by the local people? Andrew Walls has suggested that "the fundamental missionary experience is to live on terms set by others" and to be "the very converse of the cultural imperialism with which it is often quite justifiably charged."[31] In most of Africa, the humbler missionary strategy was the norm until the 1880s.[32] The corruption of that

26 Lian Xi, *Redeemed by fire: The rise of popular Christianity in modern China* (New Haven, CT: Yale University Press, 2010), 24.
27 See Jonathan D. Spence, *God's Chinese son: The Taiping Heavenly Kingdom of Hong Xiuquan* (New York: W. W. Norton, 1996).
28 Alvyn Austin, *China's millions: The China Inland Mission and the late Qing society, 1832-1905* (Grand Rapids, MI: William B. Eerdmans, 2007), 258.
29 Austin, *China's millions*, xxvi.
30 Lian Xi, *Redeemed by fire*, 100.
31 Andrew F. Walls, *The cross-cultural process in Christian history: Studies in the transmission and appropriation of faith* (Maryknoll, NY: Orbis, 2002), 41-42.
32 Walls, *Cross-cultural process in Christian history*, 97.

experience happened afterwards. In China, the assertion of Western power after the Opium War compromised the missionary movement early on, leaving us in many cases with the ills, the intrusiveness, and the ineffectiveness of an alien Christianity that plagued the missions until indigenous Christian movements erupted outside denominational churches or weakened foreign control within them.

That, however, is not the entire story. In spite of the structural flaws of the Western missionary enterprise and the racial as well as cultural prejudices of many individuals, Western missionaries also entered into robust and fruitful relationships with the local people and responded to their deepest needs. They did it through shared prayers, friendships, the translation of hymns and the Bible, the uplift of women, the fight against opium, as well as extensive literacy, educational, medical, and relief work, and through the creation of communities of faith and love. Despite the violent disruptions caused by the Communist revolution, especially during the Cultural Revolution years, there is a degree of continuity, in diminished denominational – or non-denominational or even sectarian – forms, between the missionary and the post-missionary eras.

The contemporary explosive growth of Protestant Christianity, with distinct roots in the indigenous, independent movements of the Republican period,[33] also retain intricate, though often indirect, ties to missionary Christianity. In a search for historical explanations for the emergence of Wenzhou as "China's Jerusalem" – with Christians accounting for some fourteen percent of the current local population of 7.6 million[34], the highest percentage in all of China outside the minority areas – both anthropologist Cao Nanlai and independent Wenzhou researcher Shen Jia have suggested the importance of its missionary past.[35] Alvyn Austin is at least partially right when he claims that "the enduring indigenous Protestant church in Wenzhou dates from [the 1860s]," when one-legged CIM missionary George Stott started his work there.[36] Stott was followed by Methodist missionary William E. Soothill, who completed a romanized translation of the Bible into the Wenzhou dialect,[37] thereby enabling biblical and a degree of general literacy in a matter of weeks instead of years,

33 See Lian Xi, *Redeemed by fire*, ch.9.

34 Shen Jia 沈迦, 'Jie Su Huilian de jiubei, daoxia yige shiji de geku' 借苏慧廉的酒杯，倒下一个世纪的歌哭, *Aikanwang 爱看网*, June 23, 2014, https://www.ai-kan.net/?p=107711 (accessed 10 June, 2015).

35 Nanlai Cao, *Constructing China's Jerusalem: Christians, power, and place in contemporary Wenzhou* (Stanford, CA: Stanford University Press, 2010), 15-16. See also Shen Jia 沈迦, *Xunzhao Suhuilian 寻找苏慧廉* [Searching for William E. Soothill] (Beijing: Xinxing chubanshe 新星出版社, 2013). Wenzhou Christianity's more direct historical ties are with independent Christianity of the Republican period, particularly the Little Flock that arose at the expense of both Methodist and CIM mission churches during the early 1930s. See Ni Tuosheng (Watchman Nee), 'Wangshi de shushuo 往事的述說 [The narration of things past]', 1932, in *Ni Tuosheng zhushu quanji 倪柝聲著述全集* [Complete works of Watchman Nee], 33 vols. (Hong Kong: Manna Publisher, 1995), 33: 21.

36 Austin, *China's millions*, 235.

37 William Edward Soothill, *A mission in China* (Edinburgh and London: Oliphant, Anderson & Ferrier, 1907), 206.

which traditional mastery of essential Chinese characters would require. (Soothill also ran an opium refuge, built a fine hospital, gathered a large Methodist flock, became one of the great Western Sinologists of modern times, and, upon his return to Britain, was named Professor of Chinese at Oxford in 1920.) All that was inseparable from what eventually became a naturalized Christianity in the area, whose vigorous expansion in our time has alarmed the provincial Party leadership of Zhejiang into desperate but useless attempts to "turn down the temperature" of Christianity in the province – through targeted demolition of churches and forced removal of more than 1,200 church crosses between 2014 and 2015.[38]

Nowhere is the continuity between missionary and post-missionary eras – and the collective role of missionaries in partnership with local people in fostering vernacular Christianity – more evident than in Yunnan province in southwestern China. There, writer Liao Yiwu discovered "a pattern" in the dissemination of the Gospel, which he reported in *God is red*:

> locals had inherited their Christian faith from their parents and grandparents who had benefited from the teachings of a certain foreign missionary. Was the missionary English, French, German, American, Australian, or New Zealander? They didn't know. To them, it was not important. Through the efforts of that foreign missionary, who had found a fertile ground in which to plant the seeds of faith, Christianity had taken root earlier than it had in other parts of China. Three or four generations later, Christianity was part of the heritage of each individual family and an integral part of local history. It was a path filled with strife and blood.[39]

Liao Yiwu's investigation focuses on the Miao tribal people in east-central Yunnan. A parallel history is found in the Upper Salween River, or Nujiang, valley along Yunnan's western border with Myanmar. The inhabitants of that wet, wild, and almost perpendicular country are the Lisu, a hunting and gathering tribe whose ancestors had trekked southwest over the harsh terrain of the Sino-Tibetan borderlands near the Himalayas.[40] Here in the misty gorge of the Salween the Lisu clung to a precarious existence of slash and burn migratory agriculture on narrow plots of red-soil fields wrestled from rocks and pristine forests. For hundreds of years they had had to contend with extreme poverty; domination and exploitation by the Han Chinese and the tribal headmen they appointed; torrential monsoon rains that sent loosened rocks tumbling down canyon sides, smashing hamlets and fields, earthquakes, malaria, typhoid, and other sicknesses that terrified them and sent them,

38 Zhao Sile 赵思乐, 'Shizijia zhi zhan: weishenme Wenzhou shengchan jiaotang 'dingzihu'?' 十字架之战: 为什么温州盛产教堂"钉子户"？*Duan* 端, September 2, 2015, https://theinitium.com/article/20150901-mainland-wenzhou-church-protest (accessed 22 December, 2015).

39 Liao Yiwu, *God is red: The secret story of how Christianity survived and flourished in Communist China*, trans. Wenguang Huang (New York: HarperOne, 2011), xviii-xix.

40 T'ien Ju-K'ang, *Peaks of faith: Protestant mission in revolutionary China* (Leiden: Brill, 1993), 6.

helpless, to the wizard, who would order livestock to be killed off one by one and offered as sacrifice to the spirits, reducing families to dire want.[41]

In 1909, James O. Fraser (1886-1938) of the China Inland Mission arrived in western Yunnan as one of the missionary pioneers in the region. The first five years were enervatingly slow, but during that time he made steady gains in his study of the Lisu language, which had no written script. He jotted down phrases and, with the help of a young Burmese Karen evangelist, developed a romanized system based on the Latin alphabet to represent Lisu sounds. It would become known as the "Fraser script," which was used to translate the Bible, starting with Mark's gospel.[42]

Among minority peoples of Yunnan province, the longing for the "return" of their written language ran deep, and painful tales abounded about its loss in the dim past. The Lisu recalled a primordial moment when the Mother-God gave words to the forefather of the Lisu, who found a piece of deerskin and wrote them down. Then he laid the deerskin out in the sun to dry. A careless lad, he got distracted before the ink had dried and went off to play. Then a wild dog came and ate up his piece of deerskin. And that is why the Lisu had no books.[43] The storied loss of language left a deep hole in the Lisu consciousness – an acute sense of deprivation. Yet the Lisu legends handed down from one generation to the next also foretold the coming of a fair-skinned Lisu king. "And when that man comes from the far country, he will bring books in the Lisu language."[44]

For the Lisu tribesmen from the mountains, Fraser was the prophesied king, and the books had arrived. According to fellow CIM missionary Isobel Kuhn, Fraser's "white-man appearance so monopolized interest that no one remembers his message."[45] In any event, Fraser's work had turned a corner; the illiterate could be taught to read the "speaking paper" in a matter of weeks. Copies of the books were snatched up eagerly. Fraser reported that people were "tumbling over themselves in their earnestness."[46] He then made a farsighted decision: he would rely on Lisu evangelists, rather than Western missionaries, to spread the Gospel.[47] Despite their extreme poverty, the new tribal churches were made self-supporting, and unpaid preachers undertook evangelistic journeys into the mountains.[48]

41 Isobel Kuhn, *Nests above the abyss* (Toronto: OMF International, 1947), 3-6.
42 Eileen Fraser Crossman, *Mountain rain: A biography of James O. Fraser, pioneer missionary to China* (Wheaton, IL: Harold Shaw Publishers, 1982), 69, 74, 139; Jin Jie 金杰, 'Jidujiao chuanbo dui Lisu zu yuyan wenzi jiqi shiyong de yingxiang yanjiu 基督教传播对傈僳族语言文字使用的影响研究 [On Christian evangelization's influences on the Lisu language]' (Ph.D. thesis, Yunnan University, 2013), 38; Shi Fuxiang 史富相, 'Fu Nengren, Badong he Yang Sihui fufu' 傅能仁、巴东和杨思慧夫妇, *Nujiang fangzhi 怒江方志* [Nujiang chronicles], 1997, 1.
43 Leila R. Cooke, *Fish Four and the Lisu New Testament* (London: China Inland Mission, 1947), 11-12.
44 Cooke, *Fish Four and the Lisu New Testament*, 12.
45 Kuhn, *Nests above the abyss*, 18.
46 Crossman, *Mountain rain*, 162; Cooke, *Fish Four and the Lisu New Testament*, 23-24.
47 Crossman, *Mountain rain*, 161.
48 Ibid., 174.

As Lisu Christianity spread northward along the Upper Salween valley, indigenous evangelists were joined by foreign reinforcements – CIM, Church of Christ, and Assemblies of God missionaries. The latter held rainy season Bible classes to train Lisu *mapa* (evangelists) and *mizipa* (deacons) to carry the Gospel into villages and to start new congregations.[49] The communal solidarity that Lisu Christian villagers developed offered a degree of mutual protection against oppressive, hereditary tribal headmen and rapacious Han Chinese officials. Occasional intervention in legal disputes by missionaries also strengthened the hands of local Christians in the defense of church property or in resisting the headmen's order to grow opium poppies.[50] Meanwhile, the missionaries dispensed medicine for bacterial infections and common ailments such as malaria and dysentery.[51] To supplement the local staple diet of Indian corn, they also introduced grape vines, fig trees, oranges, and other fruit trees, at times from cuttings sent from Florida and California.[52] During the Republican period, the frontier administrative offices in the valley maintained only a broken system of Chinese schools, often taught by opium sots; local Christians countered with their own schools to teach the Lisu language, which drastically improved literacy rates.[53]

In 1937, CIM missionaries Allyn and Leila Cooke, working with local church leaders, completed the Lisu translation of the entire New Testament in the Fraser script.[54] (The Lisu Old Testament, translated by two Lisu pastors living in Burma, would arrive thirty years later.[55]) As Yunnan anthropologist Jin Jie points out, the emergence of the Lisu Bible helped bridge regional differences in the Lisu language, leading to what Australian linguist David Bradley calls "increased dialect homogeneity."[56] That in turn has helped strengthen the collective Lisu identity. In *Imagined Communities*, Benedict Anderson argues that "print languages laid the bases for national consciousness." It is for that reason that "the Thai government actively

49 Yi Liya 伊里亚口述, 董国华翻译, 洪俊记录整理, 'Jidujiao zai Gongshan de Chuanbo 基督教在贡山的传播, *Nujiang wenshi ziliao xuanji 怒江文史资料选辑* [Selected literary and historical materials of Nujiang]', 2 (1984); Gertrude Morse, *The dogs may bark, but the caravan moves on* (Joplin, MO: North Burma Christian Mission, 1998), 343.

50 See Russell Morse, 'Meiguo Dianzang Jidujiaohui Moershi zhi Fugong shezhijuzhang de xin 美国滇藏基督教会莫尔仕致福贡设治局长的信 [Russell Morse of the American-run Yunnan-Tibet Christian Church to the head of the Preparatory Administrative Bureau of Fugong]', July 17 (June 9 of the Lunar Calendar), 1945 民国三十四年 阴六月九日, in Han Junxue 韩军学, ed, '*Zhongguo Dian-Gui-Qian sanshenqu Jidu zongjiao shiliao huibian 中国滇桂黔三省区基督宗教史料汇编* [A Collection of Historical Materials on Christianity in Yunnan, Guangxi, and Guizhou]' (unpublished manuscript); Shi Fuxiang, *Fu Nengren, Badong he Yang Sihui fufu*, 45-56.

51 Gertrude Morse, *Dogs may bark*, 340-41.

52 Ibid., 192; Eugene Morse, *Exodus to a hidden valley* (New York: Reader's Digest Press, 1974), 7; Shi Fuxiang, *Fu Nengren, Badong he Yang Sihui fufu*, 45-56.

53 Cooke, *Fish Four and the Lisu New Testament*, 59-60; Li Daosheng 李道生, 'Fugong Jidujiao qingkuang diaocha 福贡基督教情况调查 [Unpublished Fugong County government report, 1985]'.

54 Cooke, *Fish Four and the Lisu New Testament*, 12; Jin Jie, *Jidujiao chuanbo*, 35.

55 Jin Jie, *Jidujiao chuanbo*, 36.

56 Ibid., 92-93.

discourages attempts by foreign missionaries to provide its hill-tribe minorities with their own transcription-systems and to develop publications in their own languages."[57] Had Anderson looked a little further north, he would have seen a similar drama playing out in the Upper Salween Valley, in which Protestant missionaries were the midwife of both an indigenous Lisu Christianity and a renewed Lisu consciousness.[58]

Throughout the 1930s and 1940s, church membership soared. In the early 1950s, a report by the new government of the People's Republic noted that Lisu Christians were economically better off and had greater influence in local affairs than non-Christians because of their abstinence from opium and drinking.[59] Needless to say, their better education and hygiene as well as access to Western medicine also made a difference.

The outbreak of the Korean War in 1950 led to a nationwide, state-orchestrated patriotic campaign that featured denunciations of American imperialism. Lisu Christians proved unresponsive, as did many other tribal Christians. They had never participated in Chinese nationalism. Their response to the government's anti-American exhortations includes the following:

> American missionaries created written characters for us, enabling our adults and children to learn to read and write. They told us about the benefits of believing in Jesus and abolishing superstition. They educated us to work hard and to live thriftily. They drew no distinction between Americans and our tribe – all believers are members of a single family. What is wrong with that?[60]

In the Nujiang valley, as official hostility and violence against Christians intensified through the 1950s, one Lisu publicly declared, "Christianity has already penetrated into our flesh and blood and it will not be easy to tear it away from us."[61] In 1958 came a massive police operation in the region against alleged "counterrevolutionaries" who were plotting to establish a "Lisu kingdom." Christians bore the brunt of the witch-hunt; churches were razed or closed. More than 10,000 were arrested; thousands perished. Tens of thousands fled across the border to Burma. Those Christians that remained were driven underground.[62] In one village, the faithful reportedly recovered from the rubble a post that had supported the church before it was torn down, and carved passages from the Lisu New Testament on it.[63] In Lanping county, a former lay evangelist hid his Lisu Bible in a cave, where he read it two or three times a week when he took the buffalos out to graze. When the Party relaxed its

---

57 Benedict Anderson, *Imagined communities: Reflections on the origins and spread of nationalism* (1983, rev edn London: Verso, 1991), 44-45.

58 Jin Jie, *Jidujiao chuanbo*, 155. That has happened even as the growth of the local church also hastened the decline of traditional Lisu singing and dancing (which the missionaries banned) and weakened its oral literature, particularly traditional verse employed in Lisu divination and witchcraft.

59 Undated CCP directive (early 1950s) as quoted in T'ien Ju-K'ang, *Peaks of faith*, 69.

60 T'ien Ju-K'ang, *Peaks of faith*, 71.

61 T'ien Ju-K'ang, *Peaks of faith*, 73.

62 Nujiang government official (name omitted), interview with the author, Liuku, December 8, 2014. See also Lian Xi, 'China's gospel valley', *The Christian Century*, September 30, 2015.

63 Bobby Morse, interviews with the author, Lijiang, December 9, 2014.

religious policies in 1979, he took the lead in reviving church worship in his village.[64] The missionaries were long gone, but the Lisu Bible they left behind endured.

In this way, Christianity survived the radical Mao years and has flourished in the post-Mao era. The Fraser script, the language of the Lisu Bible, has also outlasted an official Lisu romanization system introduced in the 1950s with the help of Soviet linguists.[65] Today, Christians account for an estimated 30 percent of the overall Lisu population.[66] In Fugong County, the heart of the so-called "Gospel valley" of Nujiang prefecture, some 350 churches have been built.[67] Christians make up about seventy percent of Fugong's roughly 90,000 residents, whose exceptionally low crime rate makes the county an oasis in this heroin-infested province bordering the infamous "Golden Triangle."

In retrospect, it was a convergence of historical developments and local circumstances that helped make possible the successful transmission of Protestantism and its transformation into a vibrant homegrown faith: The completion of the British colonization of Burma in 1886 opened a back door into the otherwise inaccessible southwestern interior of China. The absence of strong tribal or local political power, or well-developed religious and cultural institutions, left the Upper Salween valley open to outside influences. The Christian faith, once transplanted, went through extensive naturalization under local leadership. The Lisu Bible brought the divine message to a people bereft of the written word and helped foster and sustain a rejuvenated Lisu ethnic consciousness on the margins of Han Chinese, Burmese, and Tibetan civilizations. Christianity also offered the benefits of literacy, education, and Western medicine, as well as the advantage of a Protestant ethic and lifestyle over the wasteful, even ruinous, traditional practice of ritual sacrifice, excessive drinking, and the modern curse of opium addiction,[68] There was local Lisu agency in every aspect of the church's work.

However, we must not leave out the missionaries. Without them bringing the Gospel to the mountainous edge of the Middle Kingdom, there would have been no Lisu Christianity. The innovation of the Fraser script made possible the Lisu sacred book, in the same way that the innovation of the "Pollard script" (named after Samuel Pollard) paved the way for the Miao-language Bible and

---

64 Zhu Falin 朱发林, interview with the author, Liuku, December 8, 2014; Zhu Fade 朱发德, ed, *Dianxi Jidujiao shi 滇西基督教史* (Kunming: Yunnan minzu yinshuachang 云南民族印刷厂, 2008), 426-27.

65 Jin Jie, *Jidujiao chuanbo*, 44.

66 Paul Hattaway, *Operation China: Introducing all the peoples of China* (Pasadena, CA: Piquant, 2000), 302.

67 Yang Yi 扬伊, 'Fugong xian de fanzuilü wei ling?' 福贡县的犯罪率为零?, *Zhongguo minzu zongjiao wang 中国民族宗教网*, August 22, 2014 http://www.mzb.com.cn/html/report/140829475-1.htm (accessed 10 June, 2015).

68 See also Qin Heping 秦和平, 'Dianxi bufen shaoshu minzu diqu Jidujiao lishi wenti chutan 滇西部分少数民族地区基督教历史问题初探 [A preliminary inquiry into the history of Christianity among some minority peoples of Western Yunnan]', *Shijie zongjiao yanjiu 世界宗教研究*, 3, 1987.

Miao Christianity. For the Lisu and countless other groups of people in China, it was a vernacular Christianity that has found life – a faith that speaks the language of pains and hopes of the local people instead of the venerated doctrines of Western denominations. Yet it would be historical amnesia to forget how that language came into being.

As the rest of this volume demonstrates, we have entered into a new phase in our exploration of the rise of Christianity in modern China. In the latest historical reenactments of the drama of two centuries of Chinese Christianity, the stage has come alive with the appearance – long overdue – of indigenous characters. But shall the missionaries who once dominated the stage remain? If we wish to maintain an unimpaired historical memory, the answer to Pearl Buck's question must be in the affirmative.

The Dawn of Indigenous Consciousness – A "Chinese" Convert's Criticism of the Western Missionary

Kuo Ya-pei

Li Chunsheng (李春生) was born in 1838 to a poor family in Xiamen. His father was a boatman, who could not afford to give Li any formal education. Li went to literary school at 6 but had to drop out after a brief stay. He converted to Christianity in 1851 at age 14. Li never talked about his conversion directly, except some insinuation that it was a decision imposed by his father. The church connection, however, opened new doors for him. Li learned English subsequently and gained the opportunity of apprenticeship in foreign companies. He worked for Elles & Co in Xiamen in the mid-1850s, and started his own trading firm in 1861. The Taiping uprising soon destroyed the trading network that he built. In 1864, through Jamieson Elles' liaison, Li met John Dodd, a Scottish merchant, and agreed to help the latter with his business adventure in Taiwan. Li subsequently moved to Taipei and worked as the general manager at Dodd. & Co. In the coming decades, Li established himself as one of the most prominent businessmen in north Taiwan, accumulating an enviable amount of wealth and assets and winning government titles and social influence. In 1895, when the Japanese took over Taiwan, Li was one of the first Taipei residents who welcomed and collaborated with the colonial regime. In 1896, he was awarded with the Order of the Rising Sun (6th class, Silver Rays) by the Japanese emperor, for his facilitating role in the relatively peaceful process of power transition in the city. On the invitation of Taiwan's General-Governor Kabayama Sukenori (樺山資紀), Li visited Japan in the same year. After the trip, he retired from the daily operation of his business and "devoted himself to the expounding and propagating of Christian doctrines." He was elected as an elder of the Presbyterian church in Dadaocheng (大稻埕) in 1901, and died in 1924.[1]

Li Chunsheng authored twelve works in his lifetime, nine of which are extant, including one collected volume of essays (1894), one travelogue (1896), two books that address religious conflicts in China (1903, 1906), three philosophical tracts (1907, 1908, 1911), and one commentary on the Bible

1 The most complete narrative of Li's life story; see 中西牛郎, 泰東哲學家小傳 [Simple biography of the Eastern philosopher Li Chunsheng], in *李春生著作集* [Collection of works by Li Chunsheng] (台北：南天書局, 2004), *附冊* [supplementary volume], 13-204.

(1914).[2] The subjects that his works touch on are wide, ranging from international relations, to politics and policy, and to philosophy and religion in China, Japan and Taiwan. The earliest piece was published in 1873 and the latest in 1914. They are important sources for studying the turmoil of late-imperial China, the colonial expansion of Japan and cultural and intellectual development in Taiwan, providing first-hand records on the life and thinking of a non-elite man away from the power centers of the nation-states. They are also unique because of the Christian perspective shooting through his writings of different periods and on different subjects, even when religion was not the topic immediately at hand. For expanding our understanding of East Asia's church history beyond mission-centered narratives, they are invaluable for offering a rare glimpse into how the first generation of East Asia's indigenous Christians viewed their place in the larger community of believers. Most historical material on the early formation of Christian communities in China comes from church archives, which by nature place the missionaries at the center of the storyboard. The collection of Li Chunsheng's major works is an exception to this general nature of the sources on Christian missions. It contains the original voice of a Chinese Christian without expurgation, and thus a chance to examine the early formation of the indigenous consciousness in an individual convert.

In the mid-nineteenth century, the new paradigm that highlighted the imperatives of fostering a self-supporting, self-governing, and self-propagating church started to shape the direction and style of Christian missions across the globe. In China, although the Western missionaries had been using help from the indigenous since the beginnings of the church history, only after the mid nineteenth century had the indigenization of church leadership become a heated topic of debate.[3] Many started to experiment with new structures of church organization and to put more emphasis on the role of the local participants, with the most famous case being Hudson Taylor's China Inland Mission founded in 1865. How did the discourse and concept of indigenization, brought to the mission fields by the missionaries, impact the local believers' understanding of the church and their role in it?

Li Chunsheng's case revealed that in as early as the 1870s, the convert in China had started to consciously grope for a perspective on the church affairs that was distinct from that of the missionary. Taken as a whole, Li Chunsheng's understanding of Christianity was no doubt deeply shaped by catechisms and other materials composed by the missionary. In spite of this indebtedness, Li held misgivings over the way in which the foreign missionary carried out the mission in China. The cultural incompetence of the missionary, according to Li, caused blunders in translation as well as strategic mistakes, and constituted the primary reason for Christianity's low social status and small following in

2 For a brief history of these texts' recent reprint, see '編者序' (compilers' preface), in *著作集*, v-vii.

3 For the debate among missionaries in China, see General Conference of the Protestant Missionaries of China, ed, *Records of the General Conference of the Protestant Missionaries of China held at Shanghai, May 10–24, 1877* (Shanghai, 1878).

China. Through his notes of the missionary's blunders and mistakes, Li demonstrated a heightened awareness of the difference in cultural knowledge between the convert and the missionary. Rather than feeding into an anti-foreignism, however, this awareness came with a sense of personal responsibility and a conscious effort to prepare himself for a more active role in church leadership. In spite of his harsh criticism of the missionary, Li never showed any intention of leaving the congregation established by the foreigners. Throughout his life, he continued to display a stout activism in the synodic polity of the Presbyterian church in Taiwan.

Li's Understanding of Christianity

Given the transnational nature of his life experience, Li Chunsheng should probably not be readily treated as a typical Chinese Christian. Born in the mainland, Li spent most of his adult life in Taiwan, half of which was under Japanese rule. Modern scholars have thus pointed out that Li's life seems to have typified Talcott Parsons' notion of "the marginal man."[4] This marginality derived not only from Fujian and Taiwan's peripheral locations on the map of China, but also from Li's identity as an outsider to elite culture. Li climbed the social ladder and became a man of wealth and importance in his community through his acumen and skills in foreign trade. This career path fundamentally differed from that of the majority of educated Chinese. Whatever knowledge he had of the Confucian classics and classical Chinese, he gained it through self-study and could claim no expertise in it. As such, he was never part of the cultural and ideological system integral to the functionality of the Chinese empire. This distance from China's elite culture explains Li's ease with his own transnational identity. Since the 1870s, Li had been admirer of Japan. He had frequently invoked modern Japan as the contrasting role model for China's attempt at reforms.[5] After the Japanese takeover of Taiwan, Li enthusiastically supported the new regime, and was proud to join the Japanese "brotherhood."[6]

Nevertheless, Li remained a "Chinese" Christian in several accounts. Li came to age in mainland China, and received his formal and informal education there. This means that Chinese was his primary language of communicating. Even after he moved to Taiwan, he relied on Chinese publications for information about both the Christian and non-Christian affairs. In spite of his relative ease with the colonial regime on post-1895 Taiwan, Li never attempted

4 古偉瀛, '從棄地遺民到日籍華人: 試論李春生的日本經驗' [From a forsaken subject of the abandoned land to a Japanese Chinese: Tentatively on Li Shunsheng's Japanese experience], in 李明輝, ed, *李春生的思想與時代* [The thought and times of Li Chunsheng] (台北: 正中書局, 1995), 204-5.

5 Cf. 黃俊傑 & 古偉瀛, '新恩與舊義之間: 李春生國家認同之分析 [Between newly bestowed favor and old committed loyalty: An analysis of Li Chunsheng's national identity]', in *時代與思想*, 216-56.

6 Li ended his travelogue of 1896 with a reference to the notion of brother [between himself and his Japanese friends. See 李春生, 東遊六十四日隨筆 (Random notes during sixty-four-day trip to Japan), in *著作集*, vol.4, 227.

to learn Japanese. In this sense, he spent his whole life in the sinophone orbit of norms and values, whose boundaries expanded way beyond the Chinese polity. Li composed all his short and long works in Classical Chinese, eagerly demonstrating his proficiency in the language earmarked for the Chinese elite. The frequent references to and citations from the Classics furthermore indicated a learned familiarity with the literary practice in China.[7] Even after the ceding of Taiwan to Japan, China, especially the progress of the Christian mission in China, continued to be the most central concern in his writings. Out the eleven titles dated after 1895, eight were printed in Fuzhou, China, and all of them tried to appeal to the Chinese reader on the mainland. In this sense, Li never stopped speaking as a Chinese Christian.

This identity was already quite clearly articulated in the early stage of his career as a writer. Li Chunsheng's first datable essay occurred in 1873. In this year, he submitted an opinion piece titled "Religious Affiliation Has a Direct Bearing on the Soul" (*Linghun xi yu jiaomen* 靈魂繫於教門) to *The Church News* (Jiaohui xinbao 教會新報), the trans-denominational weekly run by the American Methodist missionary Young John Allen. In the subsequent four years, he contributed fourteen more pieces to *The Global Magazine* (*Wanguo gongbao* 萬國公報), the sequel to *The Church News*. These essays, together with others composed probably in the 1880s and early 1890s, were strung together to form a section in his *The New Collection of the Main Deck* (*Zhujin xin ji* 主津新集), published in Taipei in 1894. Altogether, they attested to Li Chunsheng's attentive consumption of the missionary's discourse on Christianity as well as his strong interest in engaging with debates in the larger Christian community beyond his own church.

In this group of essays, one finds the author, a young Christian in his late thirties and early forties, trying to formulate his own apologetics for the Christian faith. His formulation, in many ways, was not original; it carried characteristics of the narrative strategy that many Protestant missionaries associated with *The Church News* and *the Global Magazine* had relied on. Central to this strategy was to graft Christianity onto some cultural elements native to the Chinese elite, and thus tone down its foreignness in their eyes. W. A. P Martin, for example, in his *Evidences of Christianity* (*Tiandao suyuan* 天道溯源) (1954), famously followed Matteo Ricci's precedent in the sixteenth century and argued that Christianity was the lost religion of the Chinese people in antiquity.[8] Martin claimed that the majority of Christian doctrines reinforce the teachings of Confucianism. The only divergence between them lay in the Christian monotheist faith in God which, according to Martin, had given Christianity its unique strength in carrying out its moral tenets, and made it the most effective means for achieving the Confucian ideal of "transformation

7 李明輝, '轉化抑或對話? –李春生所理解的中國經典 [Transformation or dialogue? – the Chinese classics understood by Li Chunsheng]', in 李明輝, ed, *近代東亞變局中的李春生* [Li Chunsheng in the transformation of early modern East Asia] (台北: 台大出版中心, 2010), 25-65.

8 W. A. P Martin (丁韙良), *天道溯源* [Evidences for Christianity] (台北: 文泉出版社, 1967), 5a.

through teaching" (教化). This attempt to utilize the cultural capital of Confucianism and to boost the esteem of Christianity was accompanied by an all-out denigration of other religions. Buddhism and Daoism, with their practice of idolatry, were blamed for representing the most sinister elements of Chinese culture.[9]

Although there is no indication that Li Chunsheng had read *Evidences of Christianity*, the framework of his apologetics resembled that of the most influential Christian catechism of the nineteenth century.[10] The affinity between Christianity and Confucianism was the cornerstone of Li's representation. He readily equated the Christian Lord to the High Lord mentioned in the Confucian Classics, and contended that Christianity had its cultural roots in China.[11] Conversion in this light constituted a return to the orthodox belief of antiquity. Li's attitude towards other religions also mirrored closely the position of the Protestant missionary in mid-nineteenth century. The Christian conception of idolatry formed the backbone of Li's dismissal of Buddhism and other forms of cultic worship in China. The Christian God was the only true god of "veracity, vitality and dignity" (真實活潑無妄);[12] others were only man-made and fake icons.[13] The promotion of the worship of the former, as such, stood for the best remedy to rampant idolatry in Chinese society, fostered by heterodox teachings of Buddhism and Daoism.[14] Last but not least, Li's apologetics unabashedly represented Christianity as a civilizing force that the states should utilize. He specifically linked Christianity with the West's wealth and power (*fuqiang* 富強) in the modern era, and repeatedly referred to the Christian Bible as containing the guiding principle of "decline and prosperity, demise and survival [in this world]."[15]

Despite adherence to this established pattern of narrative, Li made significant departures from the missionary's typical representation of Christianity. Li's depiction of his own religion explicitly placed more emphasis on the supernatural dimension. He not only equated Christianity with the Confucian notion of Heavenly Way (*tiandao* 天道), but also gave the Christian God a strong anthropomorphic spin. To him, although Confucius refused to address mythical subjects, the sage evidently had his faith in Heaven as a

---

9 Ibid., 65a-69a.

10 W. A. P Martin's *Evidences of Christianity* was one of the most widely circulated texts in the second half of the nineteenth century. It went through thirty to forty editions before 1912, and was used across denominations as a material for the missionary's language training. The discursive pattern in the catechism was influential for the general representation of Christianity in China.

11 李春生, '物各有主' [Things all have their respective masters], 主津新集 [The new collection of the main deck], in *著作集*, Vol.2, 82-83.

12 李春生, '靈魂繫於教門' [Religious affiliation has a direct bearing on the soul], *主津*, 69.

13 李春生, '稽道追元' [To examine the Way and trace its origin], *主津*, 88.

14 李春生, '致惑有由' [Confusion has its cause], *主津*, 90-94.

15 李春生, '書道相契' [The relationship between books and the Way], *主津*, 71; '釋癡道人之辯' [Explanation of the idiotic Daoist's polemics], *主津*, 78; '應籌相安論' [On the plan for a peaceful relationship between Christians and non-Christians], *主津*, 79.

deity.[16] This belief, according to Li, for thousands of years, was kept from all of the sage's followers, making them vulnerable to the temptation of idol worship.[17] Li therefore never shunned away from the fact that central to the Christian religion was its cultic worship. Li was aware that such worship had been distained by the high-minded gentlemen (*junzi* 君子).[18] Yet, Li viewed it as simply an integral part of human existence. Buddhism and Daoism both attempted to address this religious need and thus offered something that Confucianism failed to offer. Their popularity in China proved the indigenous longing for a sort of communion with the supernatural, a longing that only Christianity could answer. As such, Li openly placed Christianity, together with Buddhism and Daoism, in the category of the Way of Spirits (*shendao* 神道). Among different ways of spirits, the Christianity was the most righteous (*zheng* 正), because the monotheistic god, being the only true god, had the ultimate power to determine the destiny of humans. In the global reality of the nineteenth century, Li found the strongest evidence for the trueness of his God. The Christian West's hegemony around the globe, to him, testified to the work and power of their god. The Western nations' wealth and power, Li believed, was bestowed upon them for their faithful allegiance to the Christian religion.[19] Although the causal relationship between the Christian faith and the West's civilizational potency had been a recurrent topic in the missionary tracts,[20] in Li's hands, it turned explicitly and utterly transactional.

Differences with the Missionary

Li was not unconscious of his differences with the missionary. In a series of essays that tried to answer the question of why Christianity has spread so slowly in China, Li Chunsheng directly criticized the way in which the mission had been carried out. Central to his criticism was the missionary's language skills. In Li's view, at the early stage of the mission, much of the Christian vocabulary was rendered into Chinese too rashly, without appreciation of the precise connotations of the chosen translations in Chinese language. In addition, due to the lack of coordination among different denominations, many terms ended up having multiple Chinese renderings.[21] These blunders in language deployment set the mission off on the wrong foot. Chinese who were curious about Christianity were confused and turned away by the unintelligible terminology. Those who were dubious, similarly, could not access its content and grew more hostile.[22] The inadequate linguistic representation had subjected

16 李, *癡道人*, 77.

17 李, *致惑*, 90-94.

18 李, *靈魂*, 67.

19 李, *稽道*, 89; 李春生, 拂塵中義 [To wipe the dust and elaborate on the meaning], *主津*, 113.

20 Cf. Kuo Ya-pei, '"Christian Civilization" and the Confucian Church: The origin of secularist politics in modern China', *Past & Present*, 218 (February 2013), 242-47.

21 李春生, 天道滯行 [The delay in the spread of the Heavenly Way], *主津*, 72.

22 李, *拂塵*, 110.

Christianity to "suspicion and controversy," leading to its reputation as a heresy. It had cost tens of thousands of Chinese their opportunity of repentance and redemption before death.[23]

The language in which Christianity had been represented to the non-Christians had to be revised. Li suggested that all chapels, in his opinion, should declare themselves as "the sacred palace of the High God who created the world" (*zhuzai zaohua shangdi sheng dian* 主宰造化上帝聖殿); all lecture halls should announce themselves as representing "the entry door to the Heavenly Way" (*tiandao yimen* 天道儀門).[24] Li argued that all of these changes would render the Christian idioms into "dignified and respectable" (*weiyan suzheng* 威嚴肅整) Chinese, "fittingly and smoothly" (*qie qia* 切洽) conveying their intended meanings.[25] Similarly, Li regarded the rendering of Christianity into a "teaching" (*jiao* 教) was regrettable. The term, according to him, had become a rather hackneyed label that gave no positive meaning. "There were so many schools of teaching in the world, and they almost all did harm to people. The name had become worthless and conjured nothing but derision."[26] In contrast, "Heavenly Way," his preferred rendering, had extensive references in the classics, and gave an exceptionally lofty impression.

The dispute over translation inevitably touched on the question of mission strategy as a whole. Here, Li's position constituted no radical departure from that of the missionary. The proposal of appropriating "the Heavenly Way" into Christian usage, for example, constituted no a novelty at the time. W. A. P Martin's catechism, for one, not only featured 天道 (the heavenly way) in his title, but also systematically deployed it as the appellation of the supreme being in the text. Even Li's justification for such rending – it clarified once and for all that Christianity offered what "all of Confucius's best disciples aspired to but failed to procure"[27] – trod on the known path of utilizing Confucianism as a stepping stone for building Christianity's image. Instead of a calling for a revision of the existent translational scheme, Li's plan urged a more rigorous and systematic implementation.

Underneath Li's support of the formulated strategy, there were also irreconcilable differences, one of which was Li's willingness to expound on the anthropomorphic nature of both the Confucian heaven and the Christian god. Looking back to the first moment of Christianity's legalization in China, Li wished for a different introduction in the treaties that in 1858 brought the proscription to an end. Rather than "encouraging good deeds" (*quan ren weishan* 勸人為善), he would have preferred phrases such as "the righteous

23 李春生, *續論天道滯行* [Continuing on the delay in the spread of the Heavenly Way (I)], *主津*, 80-82.

24 李春生, *天道*, 73. Li later added two more possible ways of presenting the lecture hall: 'the beginning of the Heavenly Way' 天道入門 and 'the lecture room of the Heavenly Way' 天道講室. See 李, *續論* [Continuing on the delay of the Heavenly Way], 主津, 81.

25 李, *天道*, 73; *續論* (I), 81.

26 李, *續論* (I), 81.

27 Ibid.

tenets that propagate the Heavenly Way, and guide people back to their roots" (*boyang tiandao, dao ren baoben fanshi zhengli* 播揚天道，導人報本反始正理).[28] Placing the notion of the Heavenly Way in the center of Christianity's Chinese identity, Li's proposed revision conveyed a stronger sense of Christianity's religious character. *Baoben fanshi* (returning to one's roots), as a classical reference, had been a set phrase that explained the purpose of Heaven worship since the ancient times. In a later essay of 1893, Li gave further elaboration on his opposition against the missionary's representation. Christianity, to him, was more than a set of teachings that "encourage good deeds." The jealous god of Christianity was capable of using human violence to express his displeasure and to dispense punishment for misdeeds. Colonialism in its most aggressive form of territorial infringement and racial subjugation was for Li such an example. The West's belligerence, to him, was unintelligible until one considered it as being perpetuated by God to signal his wrath over the non-Western nations' heathenism.[29] Similarly, when commenting on the British involvement in the opium trade, Li also broached on a person hypothesis that the black calamity in China could be the retribution from God for its rejection of Christianity.[30] Li's Christian god was by no means a peace-loving being. Based on such understanding, Li had to question whether the missionary had misrepresented the Western faith and given out a false image of the supreme being.

Li's criticism of the missionaries grew harsher and more personal after the 1870s. In a longer essay composed in 1882 and published in *Pictorial Newspaper* (*huatu xinbao* 畫圖新報), a magazine published by the American Presbyterian Church in Shanghai, Li revisited the issue of language, and sought to "expose where the missionaries had fallen short."[31] In his view, the missionaries' negligence of language training was not simply a technical issue; it was a sign of the church leadership's stubbornness (*guzhi* 固執) and indolence (*yinxun* 因循).[32] The Westerners had from the very beginning ignored the risk of miscommunication. Their strategy that concentrated on "tameness and patience, together with the material interests and secular power" (*Ren ren bing yong, li hai jian shi* 仁忍並用，利害兼施), achieved nothing but giving them the reputation of "holding the Bible in one hand and poison in another." From Li's viewpoint, the mistake was gross. Mingling commerce with preaching, they tampered with the divide between the Way (*dao* 道) and the secular (*su* 俗). Some of them even took up pivotal positions in the government (*ju ming weizhi* 居命位置) and grew negligent of their self-discipline (*shu fang jiandian* 疏防檢點). These involvements with non-religious matters compromised their judgment, and led them away from

28 Ibid.
29 李春生, 比權（下）[Power competition, II], *主津*, 152.
30 李春生, 天命臆說 [Speculative comment on the mandate of Heaven], *主津*, 29.
31 李, *拂塵*, 111.
32 Ibid.

concentrating on the situation at hand. The missionaries mistook China for Judea, and wrongly believed that the Confucians in China, just like the Pharisees in Judea, had prepared the ground for the spread of their faith. This underestimation of the communicative challenge explained to Li why translation had received such a low priority in comparison to other things.[33]

In another essay dating from the early 1890s, Li stated his position more bluntly: the Westerners should be held responsible for the tardiness of the China mission.[34] In this essay, he repeated an allegation that he had broached before: "the human means have not been exhausted" (*renshi wei jin* 人事未盡). Although God was the final arbiter of how the mission would turn out, this should have been no excuse for the lack of human effort. The missionaries had brought Christianity to China but had not done their best to propagate it.[35] He singled out the Society for the Diffusion of Christian and General Knowledge among the Chinese (*Guangxuehui* 廣學會), the trans-denominational organization founded by the Scottish Presbyterian missionary Alexander Williamson in 1887, as a case in point. Missionaries associated with this organization placed a premium on bringing wealth and power to China and mistakenly believed conversion would mechanically ensue. Their approach was dishonest and ineffective. It delayed the dissemination of the gospels and wasted the opportunity to save the souls of the Chinese people. This kind of divergence of focus from the objective of the mission, a sign of methodological inconsistency, meant that the work of propagation was done merely half-heartedly. It had done nothing but sheer harm to China. Ultimately, Li predicted, the delay of missionary work in China would bring larger catastrophe to the world. Exactly because the mission had been a transnational enterprise, when God sent disasters and calamities as the token of his anger, they would be directed not only at the Chinese, but also at the foreigners for their parts in the failure.[36]

The disaffection towards to the missionary enterprise grew deeper after Li's first publication. In his 1903 book-length analysis of the conflict between Christians and non-Christians in China, he accused the foreigners of "losing their resolution and honesty as soon as they arrived in China", and lacking determination in propagating their faith.[37] In his 1914 elaboration on the Bible, he once again argued that the unique strength of Christian teachings rested in the correctness of its divination and prophecy, yet the missionaries "kept them a secret tucked away from the people."[38]

33 Ibid.

34 李春生, *教事問訊* [Inquiries about religious affairs], *主津*, 125.

35 Ibid., 126, see also 李, *拂塵*, 109;

36 李, *教事*, 127-28.

37 李春生, 民教冤獄解 [The unjust charge between Christians and non-Christians], in *著作集*, vol.3, 35.

38 李春生, 聖經闡要講義 [Lecture material for expounding the Bible], in *著作集*, vol.3, 171.

The Self-Standing Church

Li's growing awareness of the fundamental differences between his own outlook and that of the missionaries coincided with a rudimentary discussion of the indigenous church. Li's earliest reference in this regard occurred in an essay published in 1875. In this essay, Li Chunsheng tried to respond to a comment made on the pages of *the Global Magazine*. According to this certain Retired Scholar of Clear Brook (*Qingxi jushi* 清溪居士),[39] despite Christianity's resemblance to what the Heavenly Way was supposed to be like, its Western origin had made it hard to be accepted in the East, thus its small following. To Li, this proposition fundamentally violated his faith in Christianity as universally applicable. Christianity was a religion of the whole world, and not merely of a certain race or region. Its tardiness in coming to China offered no counterevidence against this principle of universalism. After all, God's decision could not be gauged and comprehended by the human mind. Who could predict what God had planned for China's future? Li further explained that religion, as the core of morality, should have nothing to do with cultural customs (*su* 俗). In spite of Christianity's reputation as the Western religion, Li asserted, it was the full embodiment of the Heavenly Way, and thus had universal applicability. Christians across the globe were joined by their faith, but they did not need to alter or abandon their cultural identities. Rather, the Christian institution had proved to be capable of accommodating particular customs in different places. "The Heavenly Way remains one, while the congregations [of different locations] took different forms [according their customs.]" The cultural differences found expression through the institution.[40]

Li's portrait of the church being an internally diverse community naturally begged the question about its formation in China. After the praise of the church's accommodation of cultural variations, Li asked, "Are we Chinese Christians uniquely denied of the joyful choice of building our own church?" He then answered his own question with an analysis of the makeup of the Christians in China. The indigenous church could not be built without activism from its constituency. "At the present, most of those who have repented and joined the faith come from the middle to lower classes. They are either seriously impoverished or ailing. Only a few of them know how to read and write, and are dedicated to explaining the Scripture and propagating the Heavenly Way. Still they are far apart from each other and could make no difference by working alone." Li concluded his piece with a plea to his interlocutor. If he, a non-believer, had recognized that Christianity was the teaching of the Heavenly Way, why not step forward and join the cause? With this plea, Li made his case. The apathy of the educated Chinese, who, even upon recognizing Christianity's worth, would still refuse to lend a hand, in the

39 居士 was commonly adopted by lay Buddhists as a self-appellation.

40 李春生,「釋疑」書後 [Response to 'Explanation of Doubts'], *主津*, 75.

final analysis, constituted the largest impediment to not only the mission, but also the indigenization of the Christian church.[41]

Li never came back to the question of the church indigenization until the early 1890s. In a hypothetical conversation between himself and a foreign missionary, Li confessed through the mouth of the latter that most of his ideas for mission, based on his knowledge of the native culture and language, were meant to be implemented under the "self-standing church" (*zili jiaohui* 自立教會). Yet, judging from the overwhelming hostility towards Christianity in China, Li was afraid that the indigenous church would take generations to realize.[42] Under these circumstances, the communication of his ideas of mission, going against the grain of the day, would naturally become a criticism of the current framework created by the missionary. Yet insofar as it represented the genuine voice of the Christian church's indigenous constituency, Li, hoped, the criticism might expediently point to a solution for the mission's deadlock in China.[43] Without dwelling on the issue, Li's comments lucidly illustrated his belief in the trajectory for an indigenous church. His intellectual strife for an indigenous perspective on Christianity, based on more informed knowledge of the local culture, was premised on an anticipation of a changed ecclesiastical leadership. It was the manifestation of his dedication to the dream of indigenization.

Conclusion

In this paper, I focused on Li Chunsheng's writings before 1895 and demonstrated that as early as the 1870s, the search for a culturally amicable model of church operation had started. This search emanated from the awareness of the Western missionaries' foreignness to the cultural norms, and the concomitant sense of responsibility in revising their methods. In this early stage of groping, the idea of a self-standing church had been entertained. There is no doubt that Li learned this notion or its specific rendering in Chinese from the missionary. Yet, how Li turned this imported notion and a remote hope into an inspirational guideline for action in the here and now was completely original.

The indigenous consciousness that emerged during the two decades before 1895, rather than alienating him from the missionary-led congregation, motivated him to deepen his involvement in it. He was elected to be an elder in Dadaocheng, Taipei, in 1902. Two years later, he witnessed and participated in the founding of the first self-governing organ, the classis, of the Presbyterian Church of North Taiwan.[44] As such, Li readily stepped into the leadership role

41 Ibid., 75-76.

42 李, 教事, 126.

43 Ibid.

44 There were only thirteen elders at the first meeting of the classis. See 郭和烈, '自甲午戰爭至北部中會成立' [From the First Sino-Japanese War to the founding of the classis of the church of the

in the rise of the indigenous Presbyterian church. In 1905, with the formation of the advisory board, the Missionary Council, all of the foreign missionaries were removed from the daily operation of the church.

The process that Li Chusheng witnessed and participated, that is, the Presbyterian church's transition in Taiwan into a self-governing body under indigenous leadership, from a conventional vantage point of the mission history, demonstrated how the theology of mission conceived in the West in the mid-nineteenth century shaped Christianity's form of existence globally. Yet, from the viewpoint of the convert, indigenization was often a precarious and tension-ridden process; it entailed simultaneously an acceptance of the missionary's vision and a rejection of his tutelage. Herein lies the double meaning of Li's intellectual strife. After all, his antagonist comments on the missionary enterprise, whilst expressing defiance against the foreign leadership, also announced his willing collaboration in a project that was foreign in origin and brought to his world by the Western missionary.

North], in 鄭連明, ed, *台灣基督長老教會百年史* [A centennial history of the Presbyterian Church of Formosa, 1865-1965] (S.I.: 台灣基督長老教會, 1965), 101.

Part Two

Writing the Faith

Chinese Literati and their Christian Poems in the Seventeenth Century

Liu Yanyan

Since their arrival in China during the latter part of the Ming dynasty, the Jesuits and their form of Christianity have appeared in Chinese poetry. The official Li Rihua (李日華, 1565-1635), the well-known philosopher Li Zhi (李贄, 1527-1602),[1] and the novelist Tang Xianzu (湯顯祖, 1550-1616) all wrote poems about the Jesuits; their poems were published in the works of the respective authors and not in a collective work. These poems were composed mainly by non-Christian literati, either as a gift to the missionaries or to show positive attitudes toward them.

Another group of poems came from converts such as Xu Guangqi (徐光啟, 1562-1633), one of the "three pillars of Chinese Christianity",[2] and Wu Li (吳歷, 1632-1718), the accomplished painter, poet, Jesuit priest, and the first person to use the term *Tianxue shi* (天學詩 Poetry of the teaching of Heaven) to refer to Catholicism. He "succeeded in crafting a sizable body of Chinese Christian poetry, aesthetically and theologically successful."[3] As a matter of fact the Fujian literati collection appeared earlier than Wu Li's poetry and its topics include Christian doctrines, eulogies to missionaries concerning their difficult journey to China, and their work as missionaries, authors, and translators of western writings. The group of poets included officials, literati from lower circles, converts, and common people. It is delightful that the collection *Minzhong zhugong zengshi* (閩中諸公贈詩 Poems offered by Fujian Literati) has been preserved in the Bibliothèque Nationale de France, although unfortunately it has not yet been thoroughly studied.[4]

---

1 O. Franke, *Li Tschi und Matteo Ricci: Abhandlungen der Preußischen Akademie der Wissenschaften, Jahrgang 1938, Nr.5* (Berlin: Verlag der Akademie der Wissenschaften, 1939), 23-24.

2 Fang Hao 方豪, *Zhongguo tianzhujiao renwu zhuan* 中国天主教人物传. *vol.1* (Beijing: Zhonghua shuju, 1988).

3 Jonathan Chaves, 'Wu Li (1632-1718) and the first Chinese Christian poetry', *Journal of the American Oriental Society*, 122, 3 (2002), 507. Xu Guangqi left eight poems, covering subjects such as the Ten Commandments, the Eight Beatitudes, the Fourteen Works of Mercy, and the Seven Cardinal Virtues Overcoming the Deadly Sins. They may be described as a journeyman's work, intended for a didactic purpose.

4 Although this collection has gone largely unnoticed, scholars Fang Hao 方豪 (Yingyin minzhong zhugong zengshi chaoben xu 影印閩中諸公贈詩抄本序 in *Fang Hao liushi zidinggao 方豪六十自定稿 vol.1* (Taipei: Xuesheng shuju, 1969), 2267-2273, and Mingmo qingchu lühua xiren yu shidafu zhi jinjie 明末清初旅華西人與士大夫之晉接 in *Fang Hao liushi ziding gao* 方豪六十自

About the Collection

The poems are an important primary source about the 25-year mission work of Italian Jesuit Giulio Aleni (1582-1649) in Fujian. They can be considered a product of Aleni's successful mission work and were dedicated to missionaries in the years 1624 to 1641 and collected by a church in Jinjiang (晋江) between 1639 and 1641. Aleni had already won fame among the literati in his first ten years (1625-1635), converted more than ten thousand people, published many Christian texts, and built eight main prefectural and 15 district churches.[5] His success caused him to be nominated "Vice-Provincial of the Society of Jesus in South China" while his scholarship earned him the accolade "the Confucius from the West (*Xilai Kongzi* 西來孔子) from Fujian's literati."[6]

According to the cover of the original manuscript, the poems were all to be published in one grand collection called *Xichao chongzheng ji* (熙朝崇正集, Collection for Revering Orthodoxy in our August Dynasty) and arranged not according to the age and official rank of the poets, but by temporal order as a present. The handwritten manuscript includes 29 pages. The table of contents is not consistent with the actual contents, in that it lists 70 poets, while 71 names appear in the collection. There are 84 poems in all; ten people wrote two poems each and a certain Lin Xun (林珣) produced four. The remaining authors wrote one poem each. In the collection we pick up numerous signs of the decline and fall of the Ming empire: government corruption was rampant and the eunuch clique manipulated irresponsible emperors and abused power to control affairs of state and persecute upright scholar officials. The people suffered heavy taxation and frequent disasters, resulting in serious peasant rebellions. The crisis of the Ming Empire and the influence of those opposed to Christianity in Fujian may explain why the work was not preserved in Mainland China.

About the Poets

Of the 71 poets, 23 came from Fuzhou prefecture, 22 from Quanzhou, 16 from Xinghua, 4 from Zhangzhou, two from Jianning, and one from Shaowu; there

---

定稿 Bd.1 (Taipei: Xuesheng shuju, 1969), 255-279) and Liang Zihan 梁子涵 (Ba Gu Baohu jiaoshou sheying de Xichao chongzheng ji 跋顧保鵠教授攝影的「熙朝崇正集」, *Dalu zazhi 大陸雜誌*, 21, 8 (1960), 17-21) were the first Chinese researchers to pay attention to it, and Lin Jinshui 林金水 ('Minzhong zhugong zengshi chutan 闽中诸公赠诗初探 [A preliminary survey of poems to Giulio Aleni by scholars in central Fujian]', in Chen Cunfu 陈村富, ed, *Zongjiao wenhua 宗教文化 (Religion and Culture), No.3* (Beijing: Dongfang chubanshe, 1998), 101-102) and Erik Zürcher ('Giulio Aleni's Chinese Biography', in Tiziana Lippiello & Roman Malek, eds, *'Scholar from the West': Giulio Aleni S.J. (1582-1649) and the dialogue between Christianity and China* (Nettetal: Steyler Verlag, 1997), 89) mention it. Only some of the poems have been interpreted and analyzed by Lin, 'Minzhong zhugong', and Dudink (*Christianity in late Ming China: Five studies* (Leiden: Rijksuniversiteit, 1995), 313) has translated Xie Maoming's poem into English.

5 Fei Laizhi 费赖之, *Zai hua yesuhuishi liezhuan ji shumu* 在华耶稣会士列传及书目. Trans, Feng Chengjun 冯承钧. *vol.1* (Beijing: Zhonghua shuju, 1995), 135.

6 *Yesuhui xilai zhuxiansheng xingshi* 耶穌會西來諸位先生姓氏, 311.

were three visiting Fujian from other provinces. Quanzhou, Xinghua, and Fuzhou prefectures were the key regions of Aleni's mission where the number of converts, churches, and Christian publications exceeded other regions. The 20 poets in this collection took official positions after obtaining the imperial *jinshi*-degree. Some were members of literati families and already highly regarded by people in their region. They had a positive attitude to the Jesuits and were interested in Western knowledge and used their influence to help the missionaries. Though they were sponsors, sympathizers and interested observers of the Christians and the missionaries, none stated publicly that they had converted to Christianity; indeed, there were few converts within the élite. Huang Mingqiao, the seventh poet in the collection and writer of *Tianxue Chuangai* (Overview of the Spread of Heavenly Teaching, 1639), was considered a convert[7] although we do not see any evidence.

The following table shows the name of the poets considered converts, their hometowns, educational background, and relevant works.

Name, Position in the Collection, Title	Origin (Prefecture)	Relevant Works
Lin Guangyuan 林光元 [20]	Puyang 莆陽 (Xinghua 興化)	*Dianjin shuo* 點金說 (On Alchemy); Reviser – *Kouduo richao* Vol 6
Dong Banglin 董邦廩 [22] Tribute student of 1630; College teacher in Chong'an district	Qiaoyang 樵陽 (Shaowu 邵武)	
Wang Yiqi 王一錡 [32] Tribute student	Futang 福唐 (Fuzhou 福州)	Appendix to 5th chapter of Aleni's *Zhifang waiji* 職方外紀 (Areas Outside the Concern of the Chinese Imperial Geographer)
Lin Shaozu 林紹祖 [38]	Puzhong 莆中 (Xinghua 興化)	
Pan Shikong 潘師孔 [44]	Taoyuan 桃源 (Quanzhou 泉州)	Reviser – *Shengmengge* 聖夢歌 (Song of the Holy Dream)
Xie Maoming 謝懋明 [45] State college student, Jinjiang district	Qingyuan 清源 (Quanzhou 泉州)	*Mike`er yiban bianyan* 彌克兒遺斑弁言 (Foreword to the Left Traces of Mike'er); Epilogue to *Kuangyi* 况義 (Aesop's Fables)
Su Fuying 蘇負英 [52]	Wenling 溫陵 (Quanzhou 泉州)	Reviser – *Shengmengge* (Song of the Holy Dream)

7 Note that Zurcher took Huang Mingqiao as a convert (*Giulio Aleni*, 126).

Lin Yi Jun 林一儁 [57]	Fuqing 福清 (Fuzhou 福州)	*Jiehuo* 解惑 (Clarifying Wrong Ideas); Foreword to *Shengmengge* (Song of the Holy Dream); Reviser – *Kouduo richao* Vol 4; Foreword to *Kouduo richao*

There is not much information about Lin Guangyuan (林光元),[8] but his conversion date can be roughly determined. Aleni visited Putian seven times, in 1631, 1632, 1633, 1637, 1638 and 1646.[9] Lin claimed to have studied longer with the missionaries than any other local supporters, and therefore we can assume that he was converted before 1632. Apart from Aleni he must have been in touch with the Polish Jesuit Andrzej Rudomina (*Lu Ande* 盧安德, 1594-1632), the Portuguese Jesuit Simão da Cunha (*Qu Ximan* 瞿西滿, 1589-1660) and Bento de Mattos (*Lin Bendu* 林本篤, 1600-1651). He would also have been familiar with Christian circles in Putian, who counted Ke Shifang (柯士芳) and Zhu Yuzhong (朱禹中, *aka* Dongji 東極), the editors of *Kouduo richao,* among their number[10] Lin's *Dianjin shuo* (點金說 On Alchemy) was written to refute a rumour that the missionaries were alchemists,[11] and in a poem in which he bore witness to the missionaries' lives he criticized those who believed it.

Lin Yijun obtained the *gongsheng* title during 1644-1661 and in 1668 worked as *xundao* (訓導 Assistant school instructor) first in the city of Fu'an and then in Quanzhou. He was one of the compilers of the first and fourth volumes of the *KDRC*. He also wrote a foreword to Aleni's *Shengmengge* (Songs of the Holy Dream) in 1637 and to Li Jiugong's *Wenxing Cuichao* (文行粹抄 Selected Copy on Ritual and Conduct) in 1678. When his son died from an unknown sickness Aleni comforted him with the story of Saint Job,[12] after which he wrote *Jiehuo* (解惑 Clarifying Wrong Ideas), a work unfortunately not preserved. He converted to Christianity in 1628 and is

8 Dudink ('Giulio Aleni and Li Jiubiao', in Tiziana Lippiello & Roman Malek, eds, *'Scholar from the West': Giulio Aleni S.J. (1582-1649) and the dialogue between Christianity and China* (Nettetal: Steyler Verlag, 1997), 193) stated that he was probably a relative of Lin Guangting, *zi* Zhongming (*juren* 1603), but did not prove it.

9 For his first journey to Putian see *KDRC*, *vol.2*, 152; *vol.3*, 176; *vol 4*, 245; *vol.7*. 458; *vol.8*, p. 528. For his last see *Siji Ai xiansheng xingji*, 931b.

10 The following persons appeared in *KDR* as reviser or editor: Lin Yijun 林一俊, Li Jiubiao 李九標, Li Jiugong 李九功, Zhang Geng 張賡, Yan Zanhua 嚴贊化, Chen Kekuan 陳克寬, Weng Heling 翁鶴齡, Lin Yunqing 林雲卿, Yan Weisheng 顏維聖, Lin Eryuan 林爾元,Yan Zhifu 顏之複, Luo Tianyu 羅天與, Chen Kesheng 陳克生, Yang Kui 楊葵, Chen Jingming 陳景明, Zhang Xun 張勳, Huang Weihan 黃惟翰, Zhu Yuzhong 朱禹中, Chen Jingyao 陳景耀, Ke Shifang 柯士芳, Li Sixuan 李嗣玄, Li Fengxiang 李鳳翔, Wu Huaigu 吳懷古, Feng Wenchang 馮文昌, Su Zhizan 蘇之瓚.

11 *Dian jinshuo*, 49-51.

12 *KDRC*, *vol.1*, 2a, and Zurcher, *Giulio Aleni*, 196-197.

mentioned frequently in *KDRC*, according to which he was interested in religious subjects and western knowledge, such as sacrifice, reward and punishment, the love of God, the Trinity, and geography. Another entry reports his refusal to marry a concubine.

Xie Maoming was from the literati class of Jinjiang. In the record of his conversion we read that while in his study he heard a voice from the air, saying: "Three and one is the way; do not separate them at all." He did not know the meaning, but in the first month of the same year Aleni visited Quanzhou and although they did not meet, on 17 November 1629 he smelled an extraordinary fragrance which he took as the symbol of an extraordinary man. Finally he met Aleni in the house of his cousin Zheng Dongli (鄭東里), eldest son of Zheng Hairu (鄭孩如) and relative of Zhang Geng (張賡, 1570-?), one of the "three Pillars of Fujian Christianity".[13] Xie was later baptized by Aleni.[14]

Su Fuying and Pan Shikong both came from Quanzhou prefecture and had written Christian works. Aleni had met Dong Banglin on his first journey into Shaowu prefecture and may have baptized him in Fuzhou.[15] Lin Shaozu 林紹祖 was mentioned in *KDRC* as consulting with Aleni on the subject of Buddhism. The Christian poets had many years of Confucian education and took part in the official exams but did not succeed in their efforts to become officials of the civil service. They contributed to mission, the publication of Christian works, and the establishing of churches and chapels. Their background enabled them to connect Confucian Humanism with Catholic concepts such as the "14 works of mercy",[16] which helped spread Christianity. More than 20 other poets could not be traced either in religious sources or local chronicles.

The collection indicates that the most fruitful field for Aleni's missionary activities was the lower echelon of the literati. However, there are only eight poets whose religious inclinations can be identified by their writings and other contemporary sources. Their names appear in the *Kouduo richao* (口鐸日抄 Diary of Oral Admonitions), a diary of Aleni's Fujian mission in the period 1630-1640 compiled by the converted Li brothers and other Chinese supporters. The foreword to *KDRC* states that all mentioned in it were converts.

13 Lin Jinshui 林金水 & Wu Huaimin 吴怀民, 'Ai Rulüe zai Quanzhou de jiaoyou yu chuanjiao huodong 艾儒略在泉州的交游与传教活动', *Haijiaoshi yanjiu 海交史研究*, 1 (1994), 66.

14 *Lixiu yijian, juan* 2, 24-25. Dudink (*Five studies*, 312-313) translated this into English.

15 For more on Su Fuying and Pan Shikong, see Fang (*Tianzhujiao renwu*, 268-270). The *KDRC* (*Vol.1*, 16b.) contains information on Aleni's first journey to the mountainous inland prefecture of Shaowu in 1631. In *Fujian tianzhujiao shi jiyao* 福建天主教史記要, Lin Quan 林泉 showed that Aleni stayed there for a month and became acquainted with the literati Mi Jiade 米嘉德, Dong Banglin 董邦廩, Deng Cai 鄧材 and Wu Weixin 吳維新. Mi Dejia became a pupil of Aleni, and also wrote a foreword for the *Xifang dawen* 西方答問.

16 *Tianru yitongkao*, 487-488.

The Poems

The rise of poetry societies and the development of printing in Fujian were the prerequisite for the poems offered to the missionaries. These poems were a sign of friendship from the literati who supported the missionaries during the Fujian persecution (1637-1639).[17] The contents of this collection can be divided into 6 groups: 1. Interaction between scholars and missionaries. 2. Dissemination of Christian doctrine. 3. Praise and worship of the journey and the works of Jesuits. 4. Criticism of immorality at that time. 5. The practice of mission. 6. Comparison of Christianity and Confucianism, and emphasis of the effects of Christianity and Jesuits in Ming Society. This collection communicated a positive response to Christianity.

The following two poems (translated by the author) were written by the converts Lin Guangyuan and Lin Yijun. Lin Guangyuan wrote a long poem in the ancient five syllable style.

大道早未聞，彳亍隨波靡.	Until hearing about the great way, my life was like[18] a wave.
誦法尼山徒，操戈滿前是.	They read the classics aloud like Confucius' disciples,[19] yet take up arms to attack each other.
作者有西賢，異地通心理。	There was an author, a western worthy; the foreign [works] connect to [our] heart and principle.[20]
發鑰開我扃，天衢平如砥。	[He] handed us the key to the door; the way to heaven is as smooth as a whetstone.
唐子還故都，望家驟驚喜。	[Like] the young Tang returning home, he was overwhelmed with joy[21] when he saw his family.
欽崇定一尊，紛紛敢妄儗。	Worship is due only to the eternal Lord [yet] many dare to doubt without reason.
聖學無二門，心傳只顧諟。	There are not two gates to the holy doctrine; the

17 Dudink, *Scholar from the West*, 34.

18 The literal meaning of *chichu* 彳亍 is 'walking slowly'. Here it means hesitation, indecision. *GDHYCD*, 200.

19 *Nishan* 尼山 is considered Confucius' birthplace. Cf. *ZWDCD, vol.3*, 764.

20 *Xinli* 心理 (lit: heart and principle) is a Neo-Confucian philosophical concept. While Cheng Yi and Zhu Xi advocated that nature is identical with principle (*xing ji li* 性即理), Lu Xiangshan held that heart is principle (*xin ji li* 心即理), a theory developed by Wang Yangming of the Ming dynasty. See Shimada Kenji (*Die Neo-Konfuzianische Philosophie: Die Schulrichtungen Chu Hsis und Wang Yang-Mings*, Übersetzt von Monika Übelhör (Hamburg: Gesellschaft für Natur- und Völkerkunde Ostasiens e.V., 1979), 115, 139. Also *ZWDCD*, vol.3, 5185.

21 *Tangzi* 唐子 (Young Tang) is from the chapter Xu Wugui 徐無鬼 of *Zhuangzi* 莊子. 莊子曰：「齊人蹢子於宋者，其命閽也不以完，其求鈃鍾也以束縛，其求唐子也而未始出域，有遺類矣夫！ Watson offers this translation: 'A man of Ch'i sold his own son into service in Sung, having dubbed him Gatekeeper and maimed him; but when he acquired any bells or chimes, he wrapped them up carefully to prevent breakage. Another man went looking for a lost son, but was unwilling to go any farther than the border in his search—there are men as mixed up as this, you know'. Burton Watson, *The complete works of Chuang Tzu* (New York & London: Columbia University Press, 1968), 268.

	mandate of heaven[22] is transmitted only by the heart.
墳索劫秦灰，異說始烽起。	The classics turned to ash in the fire of the Qin period, and various teachings began to spread.
語怪與談空，聽舌而食耳。	The talk about "extraordinary things"[23] and "emptiness"[24] was similar to hearing with the tongue and eating with the ear.
徒愛盡龍衫，百呈山鬼挾。	The followers [of the various teachings] liked to flock under the white dragon banner, [25] the epitome of a hundred mountain spirits.
爾建堂正師，衆義一時圮。	When the upright master built his hall, all other ideas were suddenly destroyed.
破彼疑関陳，疊我聖域址。	[He] refuted doubts about the Chen and Guan school, and nourished holy thought.
低徊繹詩書，乃愈有深旨。	[I] glanced down and read his works, and they penetrated deep into my mind.
隔世相鼓吹，出門合轍軌。	[The instructions] of different generations come together in harmony; all paths meet outside my door.
世福若綴疣，令人惜年齒。	Earthly happiness is like a trinket; therefore we should appreciate our lifetime.
顧影莽奔鞭，請事從茲始。[26]	Seeing our own shadow we run forward and look for the origin, where it all began.

Lin used quotations from Confucian classics to criticize the profit motive of the elite of his time as well as the chaos and disorder. The Confucian literati held public peace and state order as their ideal and intention and desired economic security and self-perfection for themselves. However, the reality was that the downfall of the Ming Dynasty was already obvious. Massive attacks from outside and numerous rebellions within, as well as constant competition between eunuchs and civil officials, showed the depth of the nationwide crisis in the late Ming period.

This poem expressed dissatisfaction with the immorality of some Confucians together with his glorification of Christianity, which he called *yizun* (一尊 the Eternal Lord). Christian doctrine was brought alongside the moral virtues of ancient China. The allusion to "young Tang" (*tangzi* 唐子), quoted from the

---

22 *Gushi* 顧諟: worship and serve the mandate of the Heaven. *HYDCD, vol.12*, 365.

23 *Yuguai* 語怪 comes from the chapter Shu'er 述而 of *Lunyu* 論語.

24 *Tankong* 談空 refers to discussion of mystery and emptiness in Buddhism. *ZWDCD, vol.8*, 1025.

25 *Shan* 衫 may be from *longshan* 龍衫, probably referring to *shan* 縿, a kind of material used to make flags in ancient China. It is mentioned in the chapter *Shitian* 釋天 of *Er'ya* 爾雅: '*Su sheng long yu shan* 素陞龍于縿 (a white dragon embroidered on a silk flag)' See *ZWDCD, vol.10*, 1168.

26 *DCFY, vol.11*, 26.

Zhuangzi, expressed the joy of the poet about seeing Christianity, just like the young man who had spent several years away from his homeland and was finally able to return. The poet also criticized people who spread rumours and attacked Christianity with terms such as *shangui* (山鬼), *tingshe* (聽舌) and *shi'er* (食耳). He witnessed the hardship of the missionaries' lives and their dedication to their faith and sought to convey the message that the missionaries did not seek wealth or fame but helped people to overcome the Seven Deadly Sins with the Seven Virtues.

He also mentioned worldly happiness, which was very popular not only in Buddhism, but also in the Christianity of the time. Topics such as "the meaning of life" and "good and evil" were discussed intensively in the first conversation between Aleni and Chinese scholars in Fuzhou. According to the Jesuits, true sages do not seek worldly happiness or wealth because these will undermine goodness and accelerate the spread of evil.[27] The approach to worldly happiness mentioned by Lin Guangyuan was an important Christian concept, but can also be connected with the disastrous political circumstances and material poverty of the common people at the time. According to him, worldly happiness is so short that people should appreciate life and search for the truth. In addition, he borrowed terms from Chinese history and the classics, such as *xinli* (心理) and *guanchen* (關陳) from Neo-Confucianism. *Xinli* is a central concept of Neo-Confucianism; Cheng Yi (程頤) and Zhu Xi (朱熹), regarded as founders of the School of Principle (*lixue* 理學), emphasized that "nature is identical with principle (*xing ji li* 性即理)", and Lu Jiuyuan (陸九淵, 1139-1193) represented the School of the Mind (*xinxue* 心學) with the thesis that "the heart is identical with principle (*xin ji li* 心即理)". Wang Shouren (王守仁, 1472-1529), known as Wang Yangming (王陽明), held to the interpretations of Lu Jiuyuan. *Guanchen* is an abbreviation of Zhang Zai (張載, 1020-1077) and Chen Xianzhang (陳獻章, 1428-1500). The former was one of the founders of Neo-Confucianism; because he came from the Guanzhong region (today's Shanxi) his teaching was known as Guanxue.[28] The latter came from the Guangdong province and was called *Baisha Xiansheng* (白沙先生 Mr. Baisha) because he settled in that district. He was a famous thinker and poet during the Ming Dynasty and the founder of the *Lingnan xuepai* (嶺南學派 Lingnan school).[29] Wang Shouren und Chen Xianzhang were considered significant figures of the Ming dynasty school of mind and their influence among the literati was a challenge to the orthodox philosophy of Zhu Xi.[30] The terms *fensuo* (墳索) and *qinhui* (秦灰) come from historiography. The first is an abbreviation of *sanfen basuo* (三墳八索), a chapter of the *Zhaogong shi'er nian* (昭公十二年) of the *Chunqiu Zuozhuan* (春秋左傳), which mentioned that a good historian should

27 *Sanshan lunxue ji*, 84.
28 Fung You-lan, *A history of Chinese philosophy*, *vol.2* (Princeton: Princeton University Press, 1953), 477-498.
29 Fung, *Chinese philosophy*, 594-596.
30 *Mingshi*, Bd. 24, *j*.282, 7222.

read following ancient texts: *sanfen* (三墳), *Wudian* (五典), *Basuo* (八索), and *Jiuqiu* (九丘). *Sanfen* were the legendary books of the Three Sovereigns and the *Wudian* belonged to the Five Emperors. There are two views about the *Basuo* and *Jiuqiu*; some believe that referred to the eight trigrams and a geographical chronicle, and others that they concerned the *Hetu luoshu* (河图洛书 Luo Shu Square).[31] The term *Qinhui* 秦灰 (Qin dynasty ashes) refers to the burning of texts in 212 BC, considered by Ming literati as causing the loss of ancient orthodox culture.[32] This poem shows resonances between the Jesuits and the school of mind. Both Neo-Confucian schools accepted that principle is the origin of the universe and the essence of morality, but their views of how human beings understand it are different. For the Jesuit, the idealism of the school of mind was a suitable philosophy to use in introducing the monotheistic God.

The second poem was by Lin Yijun and describes the doctrine and the virtue of missionaries, such as wisdom, aspiration and human warmth.

普天同大父，斯人皆吾與。	There is only one Great Father under heaven. He is with us.
真原久不明，魔役紛如許。	The true origin was for a long time unclear, [therefore] the servants of the devil were moving in droves.
宣尼悉憫秋，禹稷寧安處。	Confucius was the compassion for [the withered plants of] the autumn. Yu and Ji[33] would rather live in peace.
泰西有至人，梯航幾寒暑。	From the west came a man of virtue, who had travelled a difficult road for many years,
奉彼正教來，救茲陷溺侶。	and presented orthodox teaching to rescue his drowning companions.
苦勞既不辭，寧復知艱阻。	[He] spared no effort, even though [he] knew the difficulty and danger.
無量超性光，朗如幽室炬。	The infinite supernatural light is as bright as a torch in a dark room.
哀矜十四端，到處勤施予。	With 14 works of mercy, he constantly gave alms everywhere.
願拯衆靈魂，同入天堂所。	[He] wished to save all souls and go together to Paradise.
想彼一片心，是何惓惓緒。	[I] think of his heart, which is always sincere.
嗟我此方人，何為分爾汝。	Oh, why are the people of our country so different from you?

31 Cf. *Chunqiu zuozhuan zhengyi*, *j*.45, 2046.

32 Cf. *Zhifang waiji*, 4.

33 *Yuji* 禹稷 refers to Xia Yun 夏禹 and Hou Ji 后稷, legendary figures in ancient China. The former was famous for introducing flood control and as the founder of the Xia dynasty; the latter was considered a hero who introduced millet to the people and taught them cultivation skills.

屢以錐刀爭，戶庭生越楚。	They struggle for a small profit;[34] families bring forth conditions like Yue and Chu.[35]
幸聞仁者言，反欲加誹語。	Fortunately we hear the words of the wise, but others spread slanderous rumours.
總被異端迷，多因三仇沮。	They were always confused by heterodoxy, because of the three enemies.
撥雲一見日，痛悔應難禦。	Once the clouds are dispelled and the sun shines, they could not escape from deep remorse and pain.
曠觀斯世內，兄弟若相序。	If all in the world treated each other as their brother,
倘存遠邇情，便同小邾莒。	then there would be fraternity, and people would be as close as Zhu and Ju.[36]
矧吾教中儔，切勿微生齬。	Especially our companions in religion [definitely] do not fall out and disagree over trifles,
善功相勸勉，過失互箴矩。	[but] exhort each other to goodness, and encourage [each other] not to make mistakes.
期酬大主恩，立表為人佇。	[We] wish to repay the grace of God, and be a role model for others.
瀝血與披肝，和聲同律呂。[37]	[We] make every endeavour to achieve harmony.[38]

Many religious terms, such as *dafu* (大父), *shisiduan* (十四端), *tiantang* (天堂), *sanchou* (三仇), *mogui* (魔鬼), and *wuliang chaoxing guang* (無量超性光) are mentioned here. Chinese converts would be familiar with the terms *sanchou* (three enemies), referring to *roushen* (肉身 the flesh/the body), *shisu* (世俗 worldly customs), and *mogui* (魔鬼 the devil),[39] which appeared and were explained many times in *KDRC*. On 23 March 1631, the missionary Rudomina had shown converts 18 pictures concerning Christian concepts.[40] "The second picture showed a heart, about one half of which was caught in a net. Above it there were two angels. There also were three figures standing below the heart: one naked, one holding a sword and looking repulsive, and one richly adorned

34 The literal meaning of *zhuidao* 錐刀 is 'awl and knife'; here it means 'little profit'.

35 *Yuechu* 越楚 refers to ancient China's Yue and Chu states of the Spring and Autumn and Warring States periods (770-221 BC).

36 *Zhujü* 邾莒 refers to two small states in Shandong during the Spring and Autumn period, and allusions were made to them to exhort people to treat each other as brothers. The state of Yue was defeated by Chu in 334 BC. In 568 BC, the Jü and Zhu states launched a joint attack against the state of Zeng which was a dependency of Lu. See http://www.sdsqw.cn/history/preqin/200707/article_10835.html (accessed 30 March, 2015).

37 *DCFY*, *vol.11*, 33. Translated by the author.

38 *Lulu* 律呂 refers to a tool used to regulate the tone of a musical.

39 *KDRC*, vol.4, 6.

40 Eugenio Menegon, 'Jesuit emblematica in China', *Monumenta Serica: Journal of Oriental Studies*, 55 (2007), 396. This '18 pictures of the heart' [*Lun xintu yishiba* fu 論心圖一十八幅] is the famous series *Cor Jesu amanit sacrum* [The heart consecrated to the loving Jesus]. The original was engraved in Antwerp by Anton II Wierix (d.1604).

and of arrogant demeanor."[41] They respectively stand for the body, the devil, and the vulgar customs of the world, the missionaries' concrete way of suggesting that people never stop praying to the Lord for help.

Another interesting phrase in this poem, *aijin shisi duan* (哀矜十四端 14 works of mercy),[42] refers to the essential texts of the (Christian) Lord of Heaven, which Aleni arranged to fit the Chinese pattern of five classic texts. Aleni listed the following: (1) The Scripture of Faith (*Xinjing*, the Credo), (2) the Ten Commandments (*Shi jie*), (3) the Fourteen Works of Mercy (*Aijin shisi duan*), (4) the Seven Victories (*Qi ke*, the Seven Cardinal Virtues), and finally, to complete [the account of] the Lord's grace, (5) the Seven Sacraments (*Sagelemengduo zhi qi*). Some other parts of the catechism, like the Lord's Prayer and the Hail Mary, have been omitted.[43] This concept was thoroughly described by another Jesuit missionary Luo Yagu (羅雅穀 Giacomo Rho, 1592-1638) in his *Aijin xingquan* (哀矜行詮).[44] This approach also influenced the circle of converts, in the works of Xu Guangqi's *Shisi aijin ming* (十四哀矜銘), Yang Tingyun's *Daiyi xubian* (代疑續編 Sequel to the 'Treatise to Supplant Doubts') and *Tian shi mingbian* (天释明辨 Clear Discussion on [the Teaching of] Heaven and Buddhism), *Tianru tongyi kao* (天儒同异考 Similarities and *Differences between the Teaching* of the *Heaven* and the Confucianism) of Zhang Xingyao (张星曜).

In addition to writing, the converts established organizations to help the poor, the sick, orphans and widows, such as the *Tongshanhui* (同善会), considered a precursor of the modern charitable organisation.[45] The convert Wang Zheng (王徵) proposed the establishment of the *Renhui* (仁会 Ren Society) to practise Corporal and Spiritual Works of Mercy: "I was inspired by the *Aijin xingquan* written by the western scholar, Mr. Luo, to draw up this constitution of the Ren Society. I wish henceforth we could spare no effort, and draw together to let people get to the Promised Land, to restore the faulty of the world, to worship the grace of the Lord."[46] From this poem we see that the poet had already gained insight into Christian concepts and the task of mission. He was also devoted to propagating the faith.

The line *wuliang chaoxing guang, lang ru youshi ju* (無量超性光，朗如幽室炬) was similar to one of Aleni's statements, in which he explained that "the supernatural light shines brightly and can penetrate everywhere and makes all that is hidden visible; it transcends human nature and knows things beyond the

---

41 Zurcher, *Scholar from the West*, *vol.1*, 245-246.

42 Zurcher, *Scholar from the West*, *vol.2*, 730. *KDRC*, *vol.6*, 17a.

43 Zurcher, *Scholar from the West*, *vol.1*, 516-517.

44 Xu Zongze 徐宗澤, *Mingqing jian yesuhuishi yizhu tiyao* 明清間耶穌會士譯著提要 (Beijing: Zhonghua shuju, 1989), 70.

45 Han Siyi 韩思艺, 'Aijin yu zhoujiu: Mingmo qingchu yeru cishan sixiang he shijian de huitongyu zhuanhua 哀矜与赒救: 明末清初耶儒慈善思想和实践的会通与转化', *Jiannan xuebao 暨南学报 (哲学社会科学版) Jiannan Journal [of Philosophy & Social Sciences]*, *35*, *9*, 4.

46 Xu, *Mingqing*, 74.

reach of human beings. It is like the sun shining in space and illuminating all that is hidden. Without being inspired and illuminated by the Supreme Lord we cannot possess [that supernatural light], compared to which the light of our own nature is infinitely small."[47] He had already expounded on the distinction between the natural und supernatural in his work *Misa jiyi* (彌撒祭義 The Meaning of the Sacrifice of Mass):

> "Why are two candles placed on the altar? This refers to the two lights given by the Lord. One is the light of nature, which contains innate knowledge and ability; the other is the supernatural light which means blessing and protection [by the Lord]. It will make innate knowledge know what it could not know, make innate ability achieve what it could not achieve. 何以奉燭二座，蓋指天主賜人之光有兩種焉。 一為本性之光，良知良能是也. 一為超性之光, 即加庇默祐。令知良知所不能知，令行良能所不能行是也."[48]

Unlike other poems of the literati, these two were not limited to descriptions of the hardships endured by missionaries or their friendships with Chinese scholars. They cover many essential Christian concepts and express an understanding of doctrines, arguably the most fascinating part of the poetry. The converted poets' Confucian background meant that they were very well acquainted with classical literature and Chinese history, quoting from and alluding to both freely. They successfully used Christian terms in classical Chinese poetry; the Christian poems were doctrinally orthodox, even if some questioned their aesthetic value.

Conclusion

In contrast to the Christian poets, non-Christian poets focused on scientific works (especially mathematics and geography), and on the conduct of missionaries and their hardships during travel. In addition, they compared Christianity with Confucianism and admitted that there were similarities between them. The converts' poems convey mournful feelings about the immorality of the Confucians and the struggles between them, and we learn that the poets were not only followers of the missionaries and Christianity, but also totally devoted to advancing their faith and exhorting the people to abstain from evil. These poems may constitute the first use of Christian concepts in Chinese poetry.

The study of the converts' lives and thought is significant because of their contributions to the mission of Aleni. It is delightful that the poems have been preserved with along with the names and details of their writers. Because of this, many previously hidden converts can be traced and their stories recounted. This collection gives us a more general picture of mission in Fujian in the late

47 Cf. Erik Zurcher, *Kouduo richao: Li Jiubiao 's diary of oral admonitions: A late Ming Christian journal - Monumenta Serica Monograph Series LVI* (Nettetal: Steyler Verlag, 2007), 517-518 (*vol.1*) & 730 (*vol.2*). Also *KDRC, vol.6*, 17b.

48 Cf. *Misa jiyi*, 57.

Ming and the different circles with which the missionaries interacted socially. Sometimes, it is possible to deduce from the poems whether a poet was a convert or not.

The poems of Christian poets in this collection are special in reflecting directly the achievements and struggles of missionaries at that time. Many terms found in them, such as *tiantang*, *diyu*, *aijin shisiduan*, continued to be used as Christian concepts in the following centuries. The expression of Christian notions in poems and the connection with Confucian concepts no doubt helped in the propagation of Christianity. The historical significance of this collection and those indigenous Christians cannot be ignored.

Chinese Primary Sources

Dian jin shuo 點金說, in *FGGJ*, vol.7, 49–51.
Kouduo richao 口鐸日抄, in *YSH*, vol.7.
Lixiu yijian 勵修一鑒, in *FGGJ*, vol.7, 67-326.
Misa jiyi 彌撒祭義 (Shanghai: Tushanwan yinshuguan, 1931).
Mingshi 明史 (Beijing: Zhonghua shuju, 1974).
Sanshan lunxue ji 三山論學記, in *DCFY*, vol.3, 71-90.
Siji'ai xiansheng xingji 思及艾先生行蹟, in *XJH*, vol.2, 919-938.
Tianru yitong kao 天儒異同考, in *FGGJ*, vol.8, 429-558.
Tianxue chuangai 天學傳概, in *XJH*, vol.4, 1806-1814.
Xichao chongzhengji 熙朝崇正集, in *DCFY*, vol.11, 20-35.
Zhang Geng 张赓 & Han Lin 韩霖, 'Yesuhui xilai zhuxiansheng xingshi 耶穌會西來諸位先生姓氏', in Wu Xiangxiang 吴相湘, ed, *Tianzhujiao dongchuan wenxian sanbian 天主教東傳文獻三編* [Drittes Sammelwerk der Dokumente zur Verbreitung des Christentums nach dem Osten] – Zhongguo shixue congshu xubian 中國史學叢書續編; 21 (Taipei: Xuesheng shuju, 1972), 295-362.
Zhifang waiji jiaoshi 職方外紀校釋 (Beijing: Zhonghua shuju, 1996).

Collections of Texts and Dictionaries Consulted

Text	Abbreviated
Zhou Xiefan 周燮藩 & Wang Meixiu 王美秀, eds, *Dongchuan fuyin* 東傳福音 (Hefei: Huangshan shushe, 2005)	*DCFY*
Standaert, Nicolas 鐘鳴旦 & Adrian Dudink 杜鼎克, eds, *Faguo guojia tushuguan Ming-Qing Tianzhujiao wenxian* 法國國家圖書館明清天主教文獻 [Chinese Christian texts from the National Library of France] (Taipei: Ricci Institute, 2009)	*FGGJ*
Standaert, Nicolas 鐘鳴旦, Adrian Dudink 杜鼎克, Huang Yi-Nong 黃一農, Chu Ping-Yi 祝平一, Gu Baogu 顧保鵠, eds, *Xujiahui cangshulou Ming-Qing tianzhujiao wenxian* 徐家匯藏書樓明清天主教文獻 [Chinese Christian texts from the Zikawei Library] (Taipei: Ricci Institute, 1996)	*XJH*

Standaert, Nicolas 鐘鳴旦 & Adrian Dudink 杜鼎克, eds, *Yesuhui luoma dang'an guan Ming-Qing Tianzhujiao wenxian* 耶穌會羅馬檔案館明清天主教文獻 [Chinese Christian texts from the Rome Archives of the Society of Jesus] (Taipei: Ricci Institute, 2002) *YSH*

Zhongwen da cidian 中文大辭典 [Encyclopaedic dictionary of the Chinese language] (Taipei: Zhongguo wenhua daxue, 1985) *ZWDCD*

Hanyu da cidian 漢語大詞典 [Chinese dictionary] (Shanghai: Hanyu da cidian chubanshe, 2002) *HYDCD*

Gudai hanyu cidian 古代汉语词典 [Dictionary of Ancient Chinese] (Beijing: Shangwu yinshuguan, 2000) *GDHYCD*

Nineteenth-Century Churchgoers' Letters to the *Dailaam-Hwsviaa Kaohoexpoix*, an 'Amoy Dialect' Church Periodical

Stephen Donoho

Church Periodicals in the Zhefng Empire

The nineteenth and early twentieth centuries saw the establishment of thousands of churches in the Zhefng (*Qing* 清) Empire.[1] Scholars around the world are reflecting on the history of these churches in books and papers, drawing on archive material and letters from European and North American missionaries at the time. Though one can easily learn the missionaries' experiences and points of view, it is more difficult to gain the perspective of the Zhefng churchgoers who formed the greater part of these churches.

Some churches published periodicals for churchgoers written in one of the Zhefng Empire's languages, and because the missionaries were often involved in this, these periodicals went into missionary archives too. Although some of the content of these publications came from the missionaries, some material came from Zhefng churchgoers, and this provides a more complete picture of the churches at the time.

This article looks at one such periodical, the *Church News*, written in the 'Amoy Dialect' and put out by the Presbyterian Church of Daioaan (*Taiwan* 臺灣).[2] I will first summarise the background to the periodical's inception, the first ten years of its history, and the sort of content found in a standard issue. This will be followed by a short account of the parts contributed by the churchgoers, with some examples. In closing, I will take note of how we might use the *Church News* and other similar periodicals for writing the histories of churches in the Zhefng Empire.

1 I give the names of all persons, places, and organisations in the 'Amoy Dialect' using the Pofsit Daibuun writing system. For readers with no knowledge of this language, I provide the Modern Standard Mandarin forms in both the Gwoyeu Romatzyh and Characters systems, as well as any common historical name, the first time an item is mentioned, for example: Zhefng – Ching (清). The only name for which I have not done this is 'Amoy Dialect' (rightly, the 'Exmnng language'), which I always give in its historical form.

2 Daioaan – Tair'uan (臺灣); Taiwan.

Historical Background[3]

The Presbyterian Church of Daioaan began in 1865, when four representatives of the "Presbyterian Church in England" came to the island.[4] Some eighteen years before, the English Church had sent missionaries to the Zhefng Empire's mainland, and by the 1860s a small group of Presbyterian churches had been started in and around Exmnng (Xiamen).[5] Some of the churchgoers had friends and family on the nearby island of Daioaan, and it was from them that the English church got the idea of sending people there too. In 1860 some missionaries in Exmnng went to Daioaan on an exploratory trip; based on their report, the decision was made to put money toward initiating some church groups on the island.

The group that came to the island in 1865 compromised six persons. Three evangelists, Taan Cylo, Ngg Katix, and Ngo Bunsuo, and a medical doctor, James Maxwell, were to form the base of the new church. With them went Carstairs Douglas and Alexander Wylie, two experienced missionaries from the Exmnng church, who were to help with the first steps of the work. It was not easy; the "Opium Wars" had taken place between the Zhefng Empire and United Kingdom not long before, and some in Daioaan were not at all happy to see people from the country they had just been fighting now making their home on the island. In fact, when the mission group tried to start a small hospital in the island's capital, Daioaan-Hwsviaa (Tainan 臺南),[6] some local people were so angry that the local magistrate sent the mission group away for their own safety.

The group did not give up, moving the hospital to the safer city of Dvafkao (Takao 打狗), where Maxwell's medical knowledge and the evangelists' silver tongues soon brought them a small group of interested people.[7] Some of these decided to become part of the church, and in a few years small church groups

---

3 This overview of the Church's history is based on Edward Band, *Working his purpose out*: *The history of the English Presbyterian Mission, 1847-1947* (London: Presbyterian Church of England Publishing Office, 1948), ch.5-6; Lay Ingtzer [賴英澤], 'Nanbuh Jiawhuey Chwanjiaw Shyrchi [南部教會傳教時期], 1865-1875', in Jenq Lianming [鄭連明], ed, *Tair'uan Jidu Jaanglao Jiawhuey Baenian Shyy* [臺灣基督長老教會百年史] (Tairnan [臺南]: Tair'uan Jidu Jaanglao Jiawhuey Gongbawsheh [臺灣基督長老教會公報社], 1965), 6-30; Jason Johnston, *China and Formosa: The story of the mission of the Presbyterian Church of England* (London: Hazell, Watson, and Viney, 1897), chs.9, 16.

4 In 1876 the 'Presbyterian Church *in* England' was joined with the English Synod of the 'United Presbyterian Church' to form the 'Presbyterian Church *of* England'. This seems to have had no effect on the Church in Daioaan, which continued to take what money and missionaries the English Church could send. For the history of the English Churches' joining, see A.H. Drysdale, *History of the Presbyterians in England: Their rise, decline, and revival* (London: Publication Committee of the Presbyterian Church of England, 1889), 605-612.

5 Exmnng – Shiahmen (廈門); Amoy.

6 Daioaan-Hwsviaa – Tair'uan-Fuucherng (台灣府城). This city now goes by the name 'Dailaam' – Tairnan (台南); Tainan.

7 Dvafkao – Daagoou (打狗); 'Takow'. This city is now 'Koihioong' – Gaushyong (高雄); Kaohsiung.

were coming together all over the island's southwest. In fact, by 1867 the mission party were able to move their base of operations back to Daioaan-Hwsviaa, where the church is strong even today. As the church continued to develop, some members were given theological education and sent out as leaders of new groups. In time, schools and a theological college for future church leaders were started to help with this. The Presbyterian Church of England also sent more missionaries to the island, and they used their medical, theological, and educational knowledge to bring even more people into the Church. Within a decade of its foundation, the Presbyterian Church of Daioaan had over nine hundred members.

In 1881 James Maxwell, now back in Britain, sent a printing press to the church in Daioaan. At first, no one in the church had the necessary knowledge to make use of it, but one missionary, Thomas Barclay, had gained enough knowledge of printing while in the UK that on his return to Daioaan the church began to produce books and papers. A decision was made to put together a monthly periodical for all the Churches in southern Daioaan. The first issue of the *Dailaam Capital-City Church News* (*Dailaam-Hwsviaa Kaohoexpoix*) was sent out in 1885.[8] It was written in the "Amoy dialect," the island's most common language, in Latin script rather than the more common Chinese characters.[9] The publication seems to have met with churchgoers' approval; by 1895 the circulation was about 700 copies a month.[10]

The Presbyterian Church's *Church News*

Between 1885 and the end of 1895 the church put out 129 issues of the *Church News*. The content was mostly text, with a few woodblock and lithograph pictures. Each issue was between eight and twelve pages long and usually contained about eight parts. The first, "News" (*Siausid*), gave accounts of recent events, and the last, "Sabbath Bread" (*Zwjit-Sinlioong*), gave the next

---

8 *Dailaam-Hwsviaa Kaohoexpoix* – *Tair'uan-Fuucherng Jiawhueybaw* (台灣府城教會報); *Tair'uan Capital-City Church News*. When writing about the periodical in English, the missionaries always gave it the name '*Church News*'; I do the same here.

9 The chief language for writing in the Zhefng Empire was *Bungieen* (*Wenyan* 文言, Literary Chinese), always using Chinese Characters. Most churchgoers in Daioaan had little to no knowledge of *Bungieen* or the character script; their day-to-day language was Amoy. In the 1850s, missionaries from the UK and US developed a way of writing Amoy with the Latin alphabet, which they called 'common-language writing' (*Peq'oexji* – *Bairhuahtzyh* (白話字) abbreviated 'POJ.'). Church leaders soon found that this writing system was easy for the churchgoers to learn, and made ever greater use of it for Church purposes. For an overview of language in nineteenth-century Daioaan, see A. Heylen, *Japanese models, Chinese culture and the dilemma of Taiwanese language reform* (Wiesbaden: Harrassowitz Verlag, 2012), 16-21. For the history of POJ, see Henning Klöter, *Written Taiwanese* (Wiesbaden: Harrassowitz Verlag, 2005), ch.3.

10 At this time, the Church was made up of around 1,256 people. From the number of periodicals going out we cannot determine how many churchgoers were reading them. For the number of periodicals, see *Dailaam-Hwsviaa Kaohoexpoix* 141:90-91. For the number of churchgoers, see *Dailaam-Hwsviaa Kaohoexpoix* 131:15.

month's Bible readings. For the first eight years, these were the only parts found in every issue. In 1893, three more were added: "Sad and Glad Tidings" (*Song-Hy Su*), "Bible Questions and Answers" (*Kafngkiux Serngzheq ee Mng kap Irntab*), and "An Invitation to Prayer and Thanksgiving" (*Chviar Daixkef Habsym Ki'doir Siaxyn*). "Sad and Glad Tidings" was made up of short statements about weddings and funerals from the past month and into the near future. The second put ten Bible questions to the readers, half about the Old Testament and half about the New. Answers were also provided for the previous month's Bible questions. Finally, "An Invitation to Prayer and Thanksgiving" was a list of prayer requests and directions about thanksgiving to God.

The "News" and "Sabbath Bread" sections of the *Church News* together took up about two complete pages and the other regular parts of the periodical about one page between them. The remaining pages were taken up by articles on a variety of topics, the greater part of which concerned church matters, for example, discussions of the Bible or theology. However, the *Church News*' editors sometimes put in articles about matters well beyond the scope of their normal subjects, such as churches in the UK or the lives of animals in far away parts of the world. These papers were mostly written by missionaries, but some were submitted by Zhefng churchgoers, and it these which are of interest here. Through them, we can get a look at the churchgoers' experiences and views. They can also give us a different perspective on events about which our knowledge would otherwise come only from the missionaries. For this article, I have put these papers into two groups: (1) accounts of events in the near past, and (2) opinions on theological questions. Let us have look at examples of both.

Accounts of Recent Events

As noted above, the "News" part of every *Church News* was made up of short accounts of events in the recent past. Some issues had longer, more detailed accounts of such events, however, and these were often put into their own special part of the periodical, which normally gave the location in Daioaan where the event had taken place at the top. Sometimes there would be a single long piece of text, but other times there were pieces from different writers. Though the missionaries sent in many of these, quite a number came from local Christians. Here, I will look at three kinds of articles sent in by churchgoers: accounts of the home church groups, journeys, and uncommon events.

Accounts of the Home Church

During the period that we are looking at, the Presbyterian Church in Daioaan had very few ministers, who had to go from place to place caring for groups of churchgoers as needed. On a single journey, a minister might have to take care of baptisms, funerals, and weddings. In the meantime, the day-to-day work of organising the churchgoers, leading services, and bringing new people to the church was given to a group known as "evangelists" (*toandoi-siansvy*). Unlike the ministers, who at this time were all missionaries from the UK, the evangelists were chiefly from Daioaan. Most had been given some training in Bible and theology at the church's college, and had a good knowledge of POJ.

Some evangelists sent accounts of recent events at their church group into the *Church News*. From these, we can get an idea not only of what occurred at the church groups when the missionaries were not present – or at least as much as the editors would publish – but also the effect that these events had on the evangelists. Let us look at an account from "Brother Bengzw" the evangelist for a group of churchgoers in the Phveoo (Penghu, 澎湖), a small group of islands between Daioaan and the mainland.[11] (A quick note on the place-names in the account: "Mafkefng" is a city on the largest island in the Pveoo, and "Defngsvoaf" is an island to its north.)

> The brethren and I are well. Regarding their status, a few things are cheering; some love telling others what they know of the Gospel, and some have reformed their evil ways. Moreover, everyone is peaceful; no resentments trouble the group. Regarding our membership, it still has not grown. The Mafkefng brethren are as before; including men, women, young, and old, around twenty people gather each Sabbath. Saisu has around six or seven; on the Sabbath they usually gather at Qwnzeg's home for worship, but they sometimes come to Mafkefng. In alternate months, some of the Mafkefng brethren and I visit them for a week or two to check on their condition; this is more stable than our previous arrangement. Regarding the Defngsvoaf brethren, they often meet at Brother Harntwn's home. Including Harntwn's family, about ten people gather for worship each week. I often preach in the villages during the day, and in the city during the night. I have been somewhat successful; many people like to listen to me, but, alas, few believe. I entreat you to pray for us with all your might.[12]

The subjects of Bengzw's account are quite like those of other evangelists from this time. They normally talked about the churchgoers' lifestyles, and if these had got "better" or "worse" since their last letter. They often mentioned their hopes for the group, the evangelists recording what they had been doing to bring about the desired changes. Interestingly, this was much the same as the content of the missionaries' letters to the church leadership in the UK. I have

---

11 All the translations in this paper are my own. I have kept all proper names in Amoy, but have written them in Pofsit Daibuun, instead of the original POJ, which uses some unusual diacritics not supported in many typefaces, while Pofsit Daibuun employs the Latin alphabet alone. For an account of Pofsit Daibuun's advantages, see Juang Shenqshyung [莊勝雄], *Tzyshiunnhuah Puushyr Tairwen (PSDB): Tairyeu Jiawyuh yeu Fajaan* [資訊普實臺文：臺語教育與發展] (Tairjong [臺中]: Tair'uan Yeuwen Yanjeou Sheh [臺灣語文研究社], 2000), 3-14. When putting names into Pofsit Daibuun I used Chiou Yannling [邱艷菱] and Juang Shenqshyung [莊勝雄], *Puushyr Tair-Hwa Tsyrdean* [普實臺華詞典], 2nd edn (Tairjong [臺中]: Tair'uan Yeuwen Yanjeou Sheh [臺灣語文研究社], 2002).

12 *Dailaam-Hwsviaa Kaohoexpoix* 90:75. Mafkefng – Mhagong (媽宮); in Modern Standard Mandarin this city now goes by the name 'Maagong' (馬公). Saisu – Shiyeu (西嶼), Fisher Island. Defngsvoaf – Diingshan (頂山); this island is now 'Peqsoaf' – Bairsha (白沙).

not been able to find out if the missionaries were guiding the evangelists about what to say in their letters – it may have been that the evangelists' work was sufficiently similar to the missionaries' that the same subjects naturally came up in both sets of letters – but the similarity is interesting and deserves further attention.

Accounts of Journeys

As noted above, missionaries travelled from place to place, often over great distances. Accounts of these journeys sometimes featured in the *Church News*. Evangelists were responsible for the day-to-day lives of one or more groups of churchgoers and did not need to undertake as many journeys.[13] Nonetheless, from time to time an evangelist would have to travel, and accounts of their journeys are found in the *Church News*. Qor Denghofng was a teacher at the Church's college in Dailaam-Hwsviaa. He came originally from the Phveoo and sometimes went back there to see his family.[14] He sent an account of one of his journeys to the *Church News*. Though it is rather long, I have included the whole story, to give a sense of how these accounts were organised. (Another note on place-names: "Anpeeng," "Phoih'afqaf," and "Gu'dva'oafn" are cities in Daioaan; Saisu is an island in the Pveoo.)

> The college went on holiday, and on the thirteenth day of the sixth month, I boarded a boat at Anpeeng. Though the wind was light, the boat was nonetheless able to sail, and we entered Mafkefng harbour on the sixteenth. The Brethren had heard that I was coming, and were gathered to greet me. First, they asked for news of Daioaan; then, they described recent affairs in the Phveoo. They told me, "Few come to hear the Gospel, and, though we go out to spread the word, few show any interest." Everyone said the same thing, and I was dismayed along with them.
>
> Soon afterward, I took a boat to Defngsvoa, where I was welcomed by my family more warmly than on previous occasions; the reason was that I had been away rather longer this time. Whilst there, I had some opportunities to preach the word to my family. However, they showed no interest, which depressed me considerably.
>
> After I arrived at my home, the rain fell often, and the roads grew waterlogged. I dared not go out, and so was only able to preach the Word to a few friends in my own village. But, their hearts were hard, and they accepted it not. One person, one of my in-laws, said that they were willing to listen, but not to make a decision [i.e. a commitment to the Church].
>
> On the first day of the Seventh-month, I travelled to Saisu. When the brethren saw me, they rejoiced, and all were encouraged. On the second day, we gathered for worship; including the children, some six or seven people were present. I asked

13 The Church's 'booksellers' (*bexzheq-siansvy*), who went from place to place selling low-cost Bibles, tracts, hymnals, &c., may have gone on more and longer journeys than even the ministers. Accounts of these journeys were rare in the *Church News*; for one of the few examples, see *Dailaam-Hwsviaa Kaohoexpoix* 146:35.

14 Phveoo – Pernghwu (澎湖).

> them, "Do you usually gather on the Sabbath for worship?" They replied, "Yes, however, we merely gather to sing hymns, pray, and read the Bible; sadly, we have no one to expound the Gospel to us." I told them, "If you steadfastly believe in the Lord, then the Lord will send the Holy Spirit to quicken your hearts." To this, they said, "Yes, but when will an Evangelist be able to come live amongst us?" I responded, "If you earnestly pray to the Lord, then it will be so."
>
> I remained five days on Saisu, and daily walked the path of salvation with my friends and loved ones. However, they constantly said things like "We dare not evangelise, for we fear that an incident might result."
>
> On the twenty-seventh I saw that they were a bit better, so I gathered my things and went to Mafkefng. There, I boarded another boat, and by the twenty-ninth we were approaching Phoih'afqaf. On the first day of the eighth month we landed; in the afternoon, I went to Gu'dva'oafn, and by the third I had safely reached Hwsviaa.
>
> Based on what I saw of the churches in the Phveoo, I believe that they have not improved. The numbers in Mafkefng have not grown, and those in Defngsvoaf and Saisu are distinctly diminished; also, neither place has anywhere to build a chapel. My dearest wish is that our Lord will re-open the road, send an evangelist or teacher to them, and help them to find a place for a chapel.[15]

Qor's account of his journey is an unusually unhappy one, but it is representative of this type of writing. Evangelists' accounts of their journeys were made up of statements about where they had been, and what they had seen and heard. They recorded their experiences at the church groups along the way, usually in the order in which they happened. These stories are in some ways more detailed than the usual stories of the home church groups. Qor's account not only contains a record of his talks with various people, but also his feelings about these experiences, a kind of detail less common in accounts of home church groups. The narratives vary between writers, but generally speaking descriptions of travel contain the most detail.

Accounts of Uncommon Events

Although the vast majority of contributions by Zhefng churchgoers in the *Church News* were of the two kinds given above, some do not fit easily into either group, which I classify as "accounts of uncommon events." For example, on 23 March 1895, just before the end of the Zhefng-Japan War, the Imperial Japanese Navy took over the Phveoo. The sound of the guns was heard even in Dailaam-Hwsviaa, and it must have given great comfort to the church's leaders

15 *Dailaam-Hwsviaa Kaohoexpoix* 65:74. Anpeeng – Anpyng (安平). Phoh'afqaf – Pohtzaejiau (朴仔踥). Gu'dva'oafn – Nioudan'uan (牛擔灣). The names 'Kongtiantiatzoong' and 'Naixsugixzurn' are not Japanese, but Amoy; they were likely given to the officers by the churchgoers, who may have struggled to say their Japanese names. As Chinese characters can be used for writing both Amoy and Japanese, the churchgoers likely saw how the officers' Japanese names were written in characters, and then made new names for them from the Amoy sounds that these characters were also used to write.

when, a few weeks later, they received a letter from the church group in the Phveoo describing what had taken place. This letter, "written by Taxn Zernggoaan on behalf of all the Phveoo brethren," appeared in the next issue of the *Church News*.

> Doubtless you all know of the recent Japanese attack on the Phveoo islands; I need not go on about it here. Instead, I shall confine myself to Church matters, and to our relations with the Japanese believers.
>
> During the chaos here, the brethren were frightened, and remained at their homes. God protected them, and not one was hurt or killed. Truly we must be grateful for God's mercies. One matter, however, saddens us: Japanese soldiers occupied our chapel, and its door, windows, benches, tables, and everything else within, were all destroyed. However, afterward, a Japanese officer named Kongtiantiatzoong, who is also a believer, came and restored order. The chapel has since been cleaned out, and we meet every week for worship. A high-ranking Japanese officer named Naixsugixzurn, a Japanese doctor, and many soldiers all join us for worship. Unfortunately, our languages differ; so, in the morning, we hold worship, and the Japanese attend; in the afternoon, they hold worship with a Japanese pastor, and we attend. You may send an Evangelist here if you wish; everything is now peaceful. If an Evangelist does come, please have them bring *Peq'oexji* and *Qorngzwji* versions of the New Testament, hymnal, and all the Church's other books; many of the Japanese wish to buy them. Mr. Qor seems to know the situation; he lately came to Mafkefng to talk and worship with the Japanese.
>
> Brothers Kijiin, Zuylieen, and Uii are all well, and have also come to Mafkefng to worship. At present the chapel has only five benches. The chairs, table, shelves, clock, lamps, and book are almost completely gone. If an Evangelist is to come, I urge you to take the appropriate measures; otherwise, what is the point of one coming? […]
>
> Regarding the plague, Mafkefng is relatively quiet, but a few people have died in the countryside; we thank God that this instance of plague passed so quickly. All the brothers and sisters of Mafkefng have now returned. I also heard some good news from Mr. Qor: Daioaan is peaceful, and he plans to go immediately. When he arrives, he no doubt will tell you about our situation in more detail. In the meanwhile, we ask that you pray for our brothers and sisters here.[16]

Of course, Japanese interest in Daioaan was not limited to the Phveoo. The Treaty of Shimonoseki, which brought an end to the Zhefng-Japan War, also made Daioaan a part of the Japanese Empire. The Japanese soon took over the island, and for the next few years there was frequent fighting between the Japanese colonial government and local armed groups who refused to be ruled by them. During this time, the *Church News* was full of accounts of the fighting and other consequences of the change in government. Within a few years, the Japanese government was able to bring peace to the island, and the churchgoers' submissions to the *Church News* once again concerned mainly the home church group and people's travels.

---

16 *Dailaam-Hwsviaa Kaohoexpoix* 122:39-40. This was the same 'Mr. Qor' as in the earlier account, who had again gone to see his family. '*Qorngzwji*' was the local name for the character script.

Opinions on Theological Issues

The *Church News* often carried papers on theological subjects. Most issues contained a discussion of some part of the Bible, some had papers about the importance of recognising God's plan, and there were articles about the difference between "knowledge" and "wisdom."[17] Many of these were put together by the church's ministers, all missionaries at this time, but readers could also send in their views. In fact, the editors sometimes put theological questions to the readers in the hope that they would send in their thoughts. While accounts of recent events sent in by evangelists and other churchgoers were not normally connected with stories in previous issues, the theological papers come across more like a discussion. Not only were they all answers to the same theological question, but many also took note of answers to a given question found in earlier issues. Here, I will explore some papers that came in answer to a given theological question.

In *Church News* No.106, which came out in early 1894, the periodical's editors put the following theological question to their readers: "Seculars often accuse the Brethren of being unfilial toward their ancestors. Thus, some Brethren photograph their parents, and ostentatiously hang the portraits in the hall. Is this practice acceptable?"[18] It seems this was an interesting and important subject; the next four issues all contained churchgoers' opinions on this question. *Church News* No.107 presented two papers. One writer, Ngg Dekphiaw, had his doubts about the practice:

> If the purpose of taking the photograph is to give one's descendants the chance to see their ancestors' faces whenever they like, then I think that it is allowable. However, if the purpose of hanging the photograph is simply to silence the seculars, then I think that not hanging it is better. I fear that using photographs to silence the seculars will embroil one's children in trouble. Many people understand the Gospel but shallowly; by living near seculars, they are readily exposed to temptation. In some families, only a few are believers. If the believers pass away, then their offspring might look upon the pictures as they did their parents, and adore them wholeheartedly; this would be more harmful than venerating ancestral tablets.[19]

Note his position was that doing something in memory of the ancestors was not necessarily wrong. He even had a suggestion about how to do this in a way that would not make things harder for one's family in the future: "[I]f one still wants to photograph one's elders, and record their birth and death dates, then, rather than refraining, one should record these things in a book for future

17 For the paper on God's plan, see 'Dioh Qvoax Defngbin', *Dailaam-Hwsviaa Kaohoexpoix* 107:16. For that on 'wisdom' and 'knowledge', see 'Pian Zhongbeeng Diehui', *Dailaam-Hwsviaa Kaohoexpoix* 113:83.

18 *Dailaam-Hwsviaa Kaohoexpoix* 106:3.

19 *Dailaam-Hwsviaa Kaohoexpoix* 107:15-16.

generations. For, if one hangs the picture in the hall, then it might be venerated after their deaths."[20]

Right after this came a paper by Ngor Guxjiaa, whose view was somewhat different. Though he too was not in favour of for ancestor veneration, it was his opinion that keeping pictures of the ancestors could help the church to get the "seculars'" approval. He told a story in which he clarified how this might be done.

> I was walking down the road with an unbeliever and discussing the Gospel. He said to me, "Every point of the Gospel is sound, but it does not mention ancestor veneration." I told him, "Does veneration actually benefit the ancestors?...Indeed, what good is a bit of wood? You cannot use it to communicate with them, and it is a bother to maintain; the whole thing seems pointless. Thus, we followers of the true faith have decided not to keep up the tradition of venerating ancestors and creating ancestral tablets. When we true believers wish to honour our parents, we take a portrait of them, and record their birthdate and age, as well as their life's accomplishments, for example, being frugal, living ethically, ardently loving the Lord, behaving benevolently, and thinking broadly...We teach our children what our parents passed down to us, and learn from their examples." He listened, then replied, "That's amazing; your way far excels using mere tablets to remember one's ancestors!"[21]

Ngor's paper ended with a new question to his fellow churchgoers about ancestor veneration, which took the discussion in a new direction: "Almost no one practises tomb-sweeping any longer. However, I am not sure whether money-hanging is permitted; is it considered a heresy?[22]

In the next issue of the *Church News*, No. 108, there was a new answer to the original question. Ngg Onglieen also gave his support to the use of pictures, for reasons similar to Ngor's.

> I think that they are a good thing. When we evangelise, we know that some will slanderously observe our lack of ancestral tablets. However, we can always say to them, "What good is making a tablet from a plank of wood? It tells one's offspring nothing about what their ancestors were like in life. Thus, we use portraits, by which our offspring may learn how their ancestors were." Many acknowledge the truth of this.[23]

Ngg did not stop at giving his support to the putting up pictures of the ancestors. He also put some hard questions to those who were against it.

> Some argue against the portraits. They say that if we allow them, then our offspring, should they not be believers, might end up worshipping the portraits, and so not having them at all is best. I think that if one believes that, then it follows that one likewise cannot compile a genealogy, or let one's offspring know the day or month of their ancestors' births and deaths, else they will simply go out and buy an ancestral tablet. Indeed, I have seen people's homes burnt, and their

20 Ibid.

21 *Dailaam-Hwsviaa Kaohoexpoix* 107:15-16.

22 Ibid. 'Money-hanging' (*kuiezoar – guahjyy* 掛紙) is putting paper money at the top of one's doorframe as a gift to the ancestors.

23 *Dailaam-Hwsviaa Kaohoexpoix* 108:27-28.

> tablets and genealogies lost in the fire; they simply bought and inscribed new ones. We must concern ourselves with the present. If later generations want to serve our portraits, what is it to us? It is like the bronze snake that Moses cast; later generations worshipped that snake, but was this Moses' fault? Consider a bladesmith. He makes blades for people to use; if someone cuts his own throat with such a blade, has the bladesmith sinned? One simply cannot speak of the future. If we create portraits now, the seculars will admire our superior practices, and come to study us. Moreover, the filial can often gaze upon their predecessors. How is this a bad thing?[24]

However, not every act of respect for the ancestors gained Ngg Onglieen's support. Concerning "money-hanging" he said, "To me, this is clearly a heresy. According to the seculars who hang money, it helps their ancestors to build houses. *Hvai'aq*! If one hangs money today, and it rains tonight, then by tomorrow it will be gone. How, then, can it help to build a house? If one performs this nonsensical act, then one has surely committed heresy."[25]

In *Church News* No. 109, the discussion became more heated. A different Ngg Dekphiaw, who came from Dangkarng, had sent in a paper which said some sharp things about Ngg Onglieen's arguments.[26]

> I have once again read Brother Ngg's reasoning about portraits, and it smacks of sophistry…Putting portraits in a book does not matter, but if one hangs them in the hall, then the ignorant seculars might suspect that we believers worship them. Perhaps their claims will not affect our offspring, but how can we then get people to cast aside their ancestral tablets and idols? Nothing in this world is completely valueless, but people often do not know how to use the things of the world; how, then, can we scorn wooden tablets and clay idols, but value paper portraits? If we carry on thus, will not people simply exchange their clay idols for silver ones, and their wooden idols for gold ones? But if we give up our ancestors' practices, then we can silence the seculars; how is this not the better outcome? Ngg Onglieen's argument is truly an example of "not adjusting them at their lower extremities, but putting their tops on the same level."[27]

At the end of his attack, Ngg Dekphiaw of Dangkarng gave readers an idea of his motivation: "I debate doctrine because I wish to avoid reproach, not because I love debate; I hope that all my fellow believers might broad-mindedly accept my thoughts; this is my heart's desire."[28]

The next issue, No.110, contained a single long paper on the subject of the ancestors, sent in by Mo Efngsefng. In his introduction he took note of the angry turn that the discussion had taken: "I have been reading the discussions

---

24 *Dailaam-Hwsviaa Kaohoexpoix* 108:27-28. For the creation of the bronze snake, see Numbers 21: 4-9. For its end, see 2 Kings 18:4.

25 *Dailaam-Hwsviaa Kaohoexpoix* 108:27-28.

26 Dangkarng – Donggaang (東港).

27 *Dailaam-Hwsviaa Kaohoexpoix* 109:40. The last line is from the *Bexngzuo* (*Menqtzyy* 孟子, *Mencius*). I use James Legge's translation; for the original, see Legge, *The Chinese classics: A translation, critical and exegetical notes, prolegomena, and copious indexes, vol. 2: The works of Mencius*, 2nd edn (Oxford: Clarendon Press, 1895), 423.

28 *Dailaam-Hwsviaa Kaohoexpoix* 109:40.

of portraits in...the *Church News*. They are truly fine work; however, some claims are being advanced rather aggressively."[29] It was his hope that future discussions of theology would be friendlier: "I think that debating this issue is like play-fighting. Just leave others alone; do not try to force them. Taking pictures is fine; so is not taking them. At present, hanging portraits in the hall is nothing about which to quarrel."[30] He also made the point that, theologically speaking, fearing for one's descendants was foolish: "With respect to this issue, we seem to be ignoring God's will. We mustn't speculate about the future; this generation need only worry about the present. As they say, 'Descendants have their own destiny; one needn't work like a horse or ox to give them one.'"[31]

Having taken care of the earlier writers' arguments, Mo Efngsefng went to work to bring the reader round to his own position, that "this practice is beneficial to the church-folk, as it clearly demonstrates to the seculars that we value our ancestors."[32] However, this was not the only positive point about the pictures and Mo listed seven advantages of keeping pictures of the ancestors:

1. Whilst living, we can often look upon our own visage.
2. When we grow old, we can look upon our younger selves.
3. When we die, our descendants can remember our appearance.
4. Those who knew us can see our appearance.
5. The seculars will know that, though we have no ancestral tablets, we nonetheless commemorate our ancestors.
6. If we hang them in a room, then that room will be more attractive.
7. If we hang them in the hall, then our filiality will be obvious.

Mo brought his argument to a close with a short poem, something no other writer had used:

> In the second edition of "Public Opinion," a brother wrote that we can always write on our portraits, and warn future generations not to venerate them; this seems a fine idea. To that effect, I offer the following couplet:
>
> I offer this portrait that you might know my appearance; look on it often after I am gone.
>
> You mustn't worship or venerate it; it is for future generations to treasure.[33]

With this, the discussion came to an end. It may be that nothing further was sent in, or perhaps the *Church News*' editors had simply had enough of the matter. Whatever the case, the June issue of the *Church News* had no "Public Opinion" section. The Zhefng-Japan War got underway soon after, and the

29 Ibid.
30 Ibid.
31 Ibid.
32 *Dailaam-Hwsviaa Kaohoexpoix* 110:51-52.
33 Ibid.

Church News had no more churchgoers' opinions on theological questions until after the War's end.

Some Closing Thoughts

Learning about the experiences and opinions of the Zhefng Empire's churchgoers can be difficult, as the number of their writings that we have is quite small, at least in comparison to the those of American and European missionaries working with these churches. However, church periodicals made for the local churchgoers can help us, as some gave space to readers' letters and papers. One such periodical was the Presbyterian Church of Daioaan's *Church News*. As we have seen, this periodical let readers send in their own pieces of writing, which fitted into the two broad categories of accounts of recent events and opinions on theological questions. Here I have presented examples of each and have said something about what was said in them.

My purpose here has simply been to give an idea of the writings in the *Church News*, not to make any kind of judgement on their qualities, theological or otherwise. But, it seems to me that the existence of this material should itself be of interest to readers and writers of history and theology. It is sometimes said that nineteenth-century Protestant missionaries to the Zhefng Empire kept for themselves complete authority over all things theological. While that may have been true of some churches, in the Presbyterian Church of Daioaan things were different. As we have seen, the missionaries not only let the churchgoers give voice to their theological opinions, but also even provided opportunities for them to do so.

Further, the churchgoers seem to have put these opportunities to good use. Far from letting their leaders – the evangelists and missionaries – be completely responsible for the Church's theology, through questions, discussions, and even arguments in the *Church News*, churchgoers derived a theology based on their own experiences and ideas. For example, the discussion about respecting the ancestors constituted a wide range of opinions, supported by complex arguments based on local believers' reading of the Bible and experiences with churchgoers and seculars. From the outset, the making of theology in the Presbyterian Church of Daioaan was a group effort.

From this discovery, though, come other questions. Were the experiences and theological views of local churchgoers valued by missionaries in the Zhefng Empire's other Protestant Churches, or was this only true of the churches connected with the Presbyterian Church of England? If the first, what was the range of experiences and theological views across the whole group of churches? If the second, why were things different in this group of Presbyterian Churches? Also, did this history of giving everyone a voice, and not necessarily taking leaders as authorities, affect the actions of the twentieth-century Presbyterian Church of Daioaan, as for example, when it very publicly shared its view on was wrong with KMT rule on the island?

There is not enough space to address these questions, and therefore I close with the suggestion that other writers on the history and theology of the Protestant Churches in the Zhefng Empire should look more closely at the periodicals produced for local churchgoers. Through these we can gain insights into the experiences and views of the local Christians, and see a clearer and fuller picture the Zhefng Empire's churches.

Christianizing China for the Sake of China: Li Guanfang and her Republican Dream

Zhou Yun

Despite instability caused by domestic warlords and imperialist powers, Christianity was generally free in Republican China (1911-1949). In fact, the church in China has probably never had as much freedom as during this period. On one hand, this open era allowed in Western missionaries and permitted evangelical revivals. On the other, the imperialist threat stimulated an intensified discourse of nationalism, which often placed Chinese Christians into awkward situations. Although this period was marked by rebellions, anti-Christian movements and the regaining of control over education by the nationalist government from the missionary enterprise in late 1920s, Christianity and nationalism were not without overlaps or connections. We can find debates on attitudes towards nationalism and responses to the national crisis in Chinese church history and the accounts of Chinese Christians.[1] The two ideologies share the same historical trauma and inevitably the development of Christianity in Republican China was influenced by its contact with nationalism.

Lian Xi offers one way to understand the tangled relationship between missions, Protestant Christianity and Chinese nationalism.[2] He cites several prominent Protestant political nationalists and pro-Christian patriots who exemplify disappointment in the search for Christian salvation for China; eventually they turned to other ideologies such as socialism and communism. What Lian presents is in essence a divorced relationship in which common ground between Christian ideals and the challenge of the national crisis could not be found. By exploring within the local Christian community, which had the impetus to transform and distribute this imported religion as an indigenized one by detaching its initially alien image, a methodology emerges for tracing the historical development of Christianity in China. This process was not immune from nationalist sentiment. During difficult times, public advocacy

1 Patriotic signature movement among Chinese Christians. *The Chinese Recorder*, Feb 1936, 123. 'The responsibility of Chinese Christians today', 'The effect of the present national crisis upon the Chinese Church', 'Christians and revolutions in China', *Truth and Life*, Oct 1938. 'What convictions should a Christian have in this great age', *Truth and Life*, Nov 1938. '中国基督徒救国运动之理论与实际', *救国月刊*, 第一卷, 第四五期, Aug 1933.

2 Lian Xi, 'Western Protestant missions and modern Chinese nationalist dreams', *East Asian History*, 32/33 (December 2006/June 2007), 199-216.

was needed to clarify the church's standpoint. This paper examines Christianity and nationalism from the perspective of one local individual – Li Guanfang (1896-c.1937) – by looking at her perception of Christianity. Like other early twentieth century figures such as Deng Yuzhi, Li represents a group of educated Chinese women who obtained social mobility and international experience thanks to their relationship with the missionary enterprise.[3] At the same time, it was specifically as a Chinese Christian that Li chose to promote Christianity as an element in the making a new nation. In her early career she was active in producing literary work for a Christianized China. However, after five years of working in the Christian Literature Society (CLS) she shifted her focus to the social gospel movement and allegedly responded to the national crisis by eventually becoming a Communist.

Li's life reflects the changing social circumstances in which the Christian and Chinese identities were intertwined. Understanding Li's perception of Christianity in relation to religious education, Christianizing the home and national salvation helps us gain a picture of the development of indigenous Christianity. It also adds to our knowledge of female intellectuals in Republican China, who actively engaged in the nation-building discourse with their male counterparts. This paper looks at Li to explore her involvement in the spread of Christian literature and gauge changes in her religious vision over time, and argues that promoting Christianity was strongly associated with national revival in the early twentieth century. In this sense, nationalism was a significant part of the shaping of Christianity in China. This paper draws on materials from Christian women's magazines, Li's theses written overseas and various mission reports.

A Humble Beginning

Although the Treaty of Tientsin (1858) opened China up for Western missions, inland regions remained under the influence of feudalism. Because of long established gender segregation female missionaries founded girls' schools, hospitals and publishing houses, where many Chinese women encountered Western ideas.

Li's childhood exemplifies this transition period. She was the eldest among nine siblings at her home in Lujiang, Sichuan. Before Li's birth in 1896, her father Li Chunfan, taught Chinese to British Bishop Thomas James, encountered the gospel and was baptized. He named his first daughter "Guanfang" (冠芳) specifically to send a two-fold message: in opposition to the feudal patriarchal view, Li's father wanted to raise more daughters and hoped Li could be a leader among his daughters or girls in general (群芳之冠).

3 Emily Honig, 'Christianity, feminism, and Communism: The life and times of Deng Yuzhi', in Daniel H. Bays, ed, *Christianity in China, from the eighteenth century to the present* (Stanford: Stanford University Press, 1996), 243.

Unfortunately, her father's involvement in a lawsuit forced him to run away and the family received no news until 1906 when he wrote a letter saying that he had met Rev. Spencer Lewis of the American Presbyterian Mission (North) and was currently co-translating the New Testament in Nanjing. He asked Li and her younger sister to go to Nanjing Huiwen Girls' School, and thus Nanjing became the place where Li was exposed to an environment that was socially and intellectually Christian.

Miss Laura M. White was the principal of this girls' boarding school from 1907 to 1913 and from 1912 also worked as chief editor of the first Christian women's magazine the *Woman's Messenger,* published by the CLS.[4] Li was among several students chosen to help with its production; her talent, as shown later in her literary work, and perhaps also her close relationship with White, led to her involvement with the CLS.[5] This is the beginning of Li's association with Christian literature work. Li's name first appeared in *Woman's Messenger* in 1914, the year of her graduation from the Huiwen Girls' School. Her work mainly included translating stories and biographies of famous Christian women. One article that illustrates her religious attitudes at this stage was her essay on graduation.[6] Words of gratitude exemplified her humility and willingness to serve God. The low social status of women at that time helps us understand her sense of appreciation. God's grace to her was such that she could not help but kneel down in gratitude. We also learn that her plan was go to normal university for further study, which she did after leaving school.

During her tertiary study at Ginling Women's College, Li carried on her literary work for the *Woman's Messenger*. During this period, Li's work started to feature in the editorial column, indicating a growing recognition and acceptance from her colleagues. Many of her articles addressed matters of equality and religious education.[7] The following extract from an article entitled "How can China achieve equality?" is one such.

> The term "equality" originated from Christianity. It advocates that we are all God's children, although undertaking different roles such as father and son, or master and slave. However, difference doesn't generate hierarchy because God views everyone as being equal. If equality is a wish that current Chinese society holds, the attempt will be far from successful unless everyone accepts Christian education. Those who used to oppress the others would treat people with equality once they believed in Christ. Those who are oppressed, why not safeguard your personality with Christ. If one believes in Christian education, it shall not be

4 Central China Annual Conference of the Methodist Episcopal Church, 1907, 54, 1908, 68, 1912, 18, 1913, 13.

5 Li's memoir of her mother mentioned that she once accompanied White to a popular summer resort in Moganshan in 1916. See *Woman's Messenger*, June 1917, 48.

6 'School Girl's Essay', *Woman's Messenger,* August 1914.

7 '中国社会如何可以平等', *Woman's Messenger*, September 1920; '什么叫做顺命,平等的同胞' *Woman's Messenger*, October 1920; '少年时代之宗教教育', *Woman's Messenger*, March 1921; '我对于基督教全国大会的感言', *Woman's Messenger*, July 1922; '女子的真进步', *Woman's Messenger*, February 1923.

> difficult for him or her to use Christ's moral spirit to fight against the violence exerted by people with power. The oppressed will win eventually by holding onto the truth.[8]

The message implied here was that social problems such as inequality were due to a lack of Christian education, and the latter would help bring about an ideal society where equality would prevail. Influenced by her teacher, Dr. Pirong, Li believed that there was an urgent need for education to become more accessible in China. She was willing, like her teacher, to make the task of educating the general public her life's work. "The only beautiful education in the world is Christ", said Li, and this was her understanding of the ultimate solution to the self-proposed question embedded in the title of this article "How can China achieve equality".

Li worked as a co-editor of the *Woman's Messenger* in the CLS in 1921[9] and two years later returned to Ginling College to complete her B.A.[10] Awarded the McDowell Fellowship ($1,000 for 1926-1927), she went to Boston University to prepare herself for the further literary work to which she felt called.

In Search of a Formula for National Salvation

On August 22nd 1925, the 29 year-old Li embarked on the S.S. Empress of Asia in Shanghai,[11] landing first in Canada and then transferring to the S.S. Princess Kathleen for the voyage sailing to Seattle, where she landed on September 9th. After entering the United States on September 10th Li then traveled to Boston on a vessel called the President Jackson.[12] Before her lay two years of study in the School of Religious Education and Social Service for a Master of Religious Education and in the College of Liberal Arts for a Master of Arts in Boston University. Although the only documents produced in these years were her two master's theses, from them it is clear that during her overseas studies her perception of Christianity was concerned with both individual and nation.

---

8 '中国社会如何可以平等' *Woman's Messenger*, September, 1920. Translated by the author.
9 Thirty-fourth Annual Report of the CLS, 1921, xi.
10 Thirty-sixth Annual Report of the CLS, 1923, 5.
11 Library and Archives Canada; Ottawa, Ontario, Canada; *Passenger Lists, 1865-1935*; Series: *RG 76-C*; Roll: *T-14882*.
12 National Archives and Records Administration; *Immigration and Naturalization Service, Seattle District, Chinese Passenger Arrival and Disposition Volumes, 1903-1944*; Arrival District: *Seattle, Washington*; Arrival Date Range: *Mar 24, 1925-Nov 14, 1925*; National Archives and Records Administration; Washington, DC; *Passenger and Crew Lists of Vessels Arriving at Seattle, Washington*; ARC Number: *4449160*; Record Group Title: *Records of the Immigration and Naturalization Service, 1787 - 2004*; Record Group Number: *85*; Series Number: *M1383*; Roll Number: *109*.

"*Chinese Literature and Christian Religious Education*" for the Degree of Master of Arts[13]

Li's first thesis attempted to understand the extent to which religious education contributes to the aim of modern education as well as the role of literature in religious education. For Li the so-called "education problem" demanded that "everyone shall be educated at least to such an extent that he shall be able to live to the best of his ability, and to conduct himself properly, harmoniously, and, if possible, ideally, in his social community."[14] Rather than explore solutions outside of religion, Li saw her duty was as investigating the role of religious education in modern education, and thus presented the two aims of education as a better understanding of oneself and a relationship with "a Power that is beyond his physical self".[15] She argued that only religious education was capable of meeting these two challenges; to paraphrase her, religious ideals and values were like a nucleus in the "League of Values…that penetrates into the heart of all cultural courses".[16] Failing to teach moral and religious ideals would eventually destroy the "higher selves", the moral integrity, of the next generation and produce a group of "intelligent criminals".[17] Li considered the fundamental task of religious education as the construction of an individual's moral senses.

Li listed the functions of literature in religious education. She claimed that it provides "idealistic images of personality upon personality, of God upon man, and of man upon nature" and "it also gives fresh impulse to the student, and produces scholars of a new type, with strong force and the power to move the world". It promoted the purposeful behavior of youth when they were brought in contact with literature containing idealistic and emotional ideals. She wrote, "it gives sweep to the imagination, depth to thought, and consuming purpose to consecration and service".[18] However, many scholars at that time rejected religion as incompatible with modern science, an attitude echoed in the diminishing classical literary training in educational programs. Li held firmly to her belief in the vital role of literature in religious education. She asserted that "technical knowledge develops life in part [while] literature in religious education deals with life as a whole."[19] From her emphasis on the primary importance of religious and moral education in order that a person could have some idealistic images for guidance in life we can see the long lasting influence of religious literature on Li.

13 In partial fulfillment of requirements for the degree of Master of Arts, 1926, Boston University, College of Liberal Arts.
14 Ibid., 2-3.
15 Ibid., 4.
16 Ibid., 5-6.
17 Ibid., 6.
18 Ibid., 23-24.
19 Ibid., 26.

Unlike some early twentieth century intellectuals, Li's attitude towards Oriental religious literatures was not dichotomous. Rather, she pointed out their similarities with Christianity. Concerning Confucianism, she wrote that its founder believed "that personal and national welfare rest on the moral and ethical basis of each individual life" and that "critical imitation is the most effective method for education".[20] In citing this enduring philosopher, Li made the argument of her thesis consistent with an accepted Chinese historical narrative. Instead of framing her views on the function of religious education as brand new, Li acknowledge their historical origin and thus drew authority from China's long-adored philosophical classics.

The literature of Taoism is different to that of Confucius, and Li wrote that rather "setting up a system of rules and regulations, and adjusting souls to them; he [Lao-tze] sought to develop inner poise, purity, passivity, that is, self-subordination, and perfect obedience to the promptings of Tao."[21] Many Taoist teachings share similarities with Christian philosophy. Li appraised the philosophy of Taoism as spiritually profound and lofty, and suggested linking Taoism with Christianity to salvage Taoist values from traditional mysterious practices and produce high moral character. The application of religious education would prevent people from focusing only on the magical side of the religion and missing its very essence.

Li's discussion of Buddhist literature dealt with some of its idealistic elements. In her analysis of the characteristics of Buddha's teaching, Li explained briefly the reason why Buddhism gained more popularity than any other religion in China. Compared with Confucianism and Taoism, Buddha's moral codes were simple for followers to understand and concrete for them to obey. In this sense, Li felt it occupied an important place in the realm of religious education. Buddhism is similar to Christianity in that a man was "directed to be a saint and enter upon Nirvana, not for his own sake, but in order that he may become a savior of all beings in some future existence".[22] The self-denial and earnest passion for truth were like the missionary spirit in making a person an enlightened personality.

Simply put, Li saw the relationship between these Oriental religious literatures and Christian religious education as harmonious. By offering connections to Oriental philosophy the traditional classics helped de-alienize the image of Christianity. Thus, Li proposed a collaborative approach for the educational institution; the minds of Christians should be broadened to utilize idealistic elements in the various religions. The thoughts of great sages such as Confucius, Lao-tze, and Buddha about God had far-reaching consequences. The giants "all probably thought along specific lines or channels, and not on the organic whole, until Jesus came and revealed Himself, as the Absolute Truth,

20 Ibid., 30-31.
21 Ibid., 47.
22 Ibid., 61.

Life, Way, and Life",[23] and thus non-Christians should constantly ask themselves, "What are the truths, the religious and moral ideals in these religions [Christianity, Buddhism, Confucianism and Taoism]?"[24]

"*The Contribution of Religious Education to the Democratization of China*" for the Degree of Master of Religious Education[25]

This thesis raised the potential contribution of religious education from individual to nation level. The first chapter was a brief summary of Li's other thesis, establishing a historical background and foundation for the chapters that would follow. Li argued religion and government were the two dominant factors in shaping the destiny of Chinese education, one providing moral resources and the other implementing policies to build ideal citizens. In this sense Chinese educational institutions were "the expression of Chinese character", in turn the "reflection of national ideals" that had "their origin largely in religious experiences".[26]

Her chapter two examined the "educational determination" roughly four thousand years ago for a better understanding of the historical development of China's education system. Educational institutions had been mainly in private hands, although the government ran a competitive examination system. Li reckoned educational spirit was democratic. The aims for the students were two-fold: a vocational purpose and the maintenance of the state. Li thought that after 600 B.C. when "a new body of knowledge came into existence in well organized forms in the Confucian and Taoist Classics and other philosophical writings", the ancient system of popular education had vanished without any hope of returning until the emergence of Christianity.[27] The next chapter in Li's thesis discusses modern education in a renaissance China.

In chapter three she examined the causes of and reaction to modern education in China from 1842 until her own time. Despite acting for centuries as a source of moral philosophy for neighboring countries, the modern history of China witnessed its realization of the urgent need to learn from the West. Li asserted that Christianity in this period contributed greatly to the new China. She appraised the role of the Protestant Reformation in building democratic states. The rich inheritance of Christianity consisted of four kinds of contributions it had made (and would continue to make) to China. One was the material gift from missionaries that laid the financial foundation for the initiative of school building. Another gift was intellectual, reflected in the sciences, artistic ideals and various organizations. The third contribution was religious, where Christianity added a theistic element to traditional Chinese

23 Ibid., 70.
24 Ibid., 69.
25 In partial fulfillment of requirements for the degree of Master of Religious Education, 1927.
26 Ibid., 10.
27 Ibid., 36.

humanistic religious thought. The fourth gift was the living Christian missionaries themselves. Perhaps the most outstanding contribution was Christian education through the missionary enterprise. Li valued the mission educational enterprises that took responsibility for the cultivation of the highest scholarship during the persistent domestic instability. Truth from Christian education, together with the traditional spiritual inheritance, functioned as moral guidance to inspire "young people's minds as an intellectual and spiritual ferment". Li that envisioned a great China borne on the wings of Christ's saving power would eventually come.

Li discussed democracy as both a term and a historical phenomenon. On the one hand the term 'democracy' sounded ideal because "it is a majority rule of the people rather than that of one or a few".[28] On the other hand, Li doubted whether it was the best form of government since it had failed to function in China. The collected scholarship of Dr. W. S. Athearn, H. F. Cope, B. S. Winchester, George Albert Coe, Plato, and Aristotle brought new light to Li.[29] For her, the best way to conceive of it was illustrated by her citation of Dr. Winchester:

> "The function of Democracy is not primarily to produce the best government but to produce the best men…[Real Democracy] is something [sic] the resultant of forces [which are within the life of the individual, forces] which are spiritual and religious in their nature."[30]

Since the spirit of democracy endows each citizen with the right to participate in nation building, the proper function of a democratized China (in theory) would thus be the cultivation of "the best men". Li referred to the historical sources of Chinese democracy, such as the various revolutions that had occurred across the land in the first decade of the twentieth century and the nascent political regime represented by the National Assembly in Nanking. The overthrowing of the absolute monarchy of the Qing and the transformation to a republican government demonstrated democracy. Sixteen years of turmoil both at home and abroad had given the Chinese the opportunity to struggle for freedom and self-determination. Li hoped that China, despite all its sufferings, was "organizing, synthesizing and creating… the political reconstruction of the nation… the educational system… formulating religious issues…[and] making social and economic adjustment."[31]

Religious education would be fundamental in the democratization of China, because in such a country each individual has a duty and his or her moral status

28 Ibid., 82.

29 Ibid., 84. Li referred to works by pioneers in religious education. Athearn Water Scott, *Character building in a democracy, a national system of education, religious education and American democracy, Protestant contributions to democracy*; H. F. Cope, *Education for democracy*, B. S.Winchester, *The religious education and democracy*; George Albert Coe, *Social theory of religious education*; Plato, *The Republic*; Aristotle, *Politics*.

30 Ibid., 84. Content in brackets was in the original work of B. S.Winchester, *The Religious education and democracy* (New York: Abingdon Press, 1917), 23.

31 Ibid., 110.

becomes a basic element in constructing the nation. With an appropriate approach to religious teaching, citizens would possess the qualities and attributes needed in a democratic country, "then...ideal democracy will be achieved".[32] Li concluded with the comment that she shared the same prayer as Miss Betty Hu:[33]

> "God, give us a leader who can lead like Moses of old and make every Chinese man and woman real working citizens".[34]

Li's vision echoed that of Hu – she saw leaders like Calvin, Luther, and Knox emerging in China to educate the people with Christian teachings. Li believed that salvation should in some way be embodied as democracy and that religious education would facilitate the best functioning of democracy in China. She highlighted how Christianity could contribute primarily to the cultivation of the individual and secondly to the democratization of China. In this sense, Li's concern was focused on the individual and oriented to the nation.

Broken Cocoon

On May 7th 1928, Li sailed back to China on the ship "Minnesota".[35] She was introduced as a new member at the forty-first annual meeting of the CLS on November 23rd 1928, where she made a "witty and warm-hearted speech". Her comment that she intended to "evolute not revolute"[36] provided some context to her new approach, a combination of her Western experiences and interpretation of China's situation which probably led Li to propose a gradual transformation of the nation's mindset to meet the needs of the time. This echoes the place of religious education that was repeatedly advocated in her theses. Although the CLS expected Li to devote herself to full-time literature work, she was temporarily loaned to work part-time at McTyeire Girls' High School in 1928.[37] From 1929 Li was the editor of the *Woman's Messenger*, her writing centered on the theme of the Christian home, a response to the nation-wide call for a Christianizing home movement, one of six items in the Five Year Movement (1929-1934) of the National Christian Council of China (hereafter, NCCC).[38] However, Li resigned the editorship in 1934 because of her deep interest in and

---

32 Ibid., 128.

33 According to Li, Betty Hu contributed an article 'What can girls expect to contribute toward the Reconstruction of a new China' to the *Chinese Christian Student*, ibid., 133.

34 Ibid., 133.

35 Class: *BT26*; Piece: *873*; Item: *134*.

36 *The Chinese Recorder*, January 1929, 60.

37 Forty-first Annual Report of the CLS, 1928, 9.

38 The initiation of the Christianizing Home movement by the NCCC was based on the prevalent interpretation among leading Chinese Christians that the basic unit of Chinese society was the home. Fundamentally, winning China for Christ required Chinese homes to be Christianized. 中华全国基督教协进会第十届大会报告, July 1935, 46.

strong call to social work.[39] Li was engaged with two major Christian institutions, the NCCC and YWCA (Young Women's Christian Association of China), in addition to the CLS before she went to Fujian in around 1936.

After resigning, Li devoted much of her time to the NCCC. Her name first appeared on the list of new members of the religious freedom committee in 1929.[40] Later Li shifted her focus to evangelistic work in the home, which required traveling and writing. She attended three annual conferences of the NCCC from 1931 to 1935 as a member staff listed under its Home Committee.[41] This committee aimed to Christianize Chinese homes as part of the Five Year Movement, which was a nation-wide revival campaign by NCCC in response to the anti-Christianity movement of the 1920s. When Li was selected as chairman of the committee, she traveled to several places in South and East China to hold meetings and deliver speeches. *Jinsheng Monthly* published one of her speeches on "the Resolution of problems on Christianizing the Home".[42] Li explained that the Christianizing process (基督化) should be integrated and natural, penetrating every aspect of life, and she refuted a narrow interpretation of Christianizing confined to Bible reading and prayer. She was also responsible for preparing Home Work materials on child-raising and parenting in accordance with biblical teaching. Her materials published by the Home Committee of NCCC included "Christian Relationships in the Home", "From Morning till Night", "Ideal Mothers' League", "Three Demonstrations" and "Home Week Song 1934". The goal was to popularize Christian teaching in Chinese homes. The Christianizing Home movement stirred up a series of responses; the Methodist Episcopal Church, which Li was also associated with, issued a program of religious education for its churches in China,[43] while the CLS was also in active cooperation with the NCCC and the *Woman's Messenger* published many relevant articles.

Some intellectual Christians in this movement associated Christianity with a strong nation. Cheng Jingyi, NCCC general secretary, was one of them, and gave a public address entitled "The Christianized Home is the foundation of a strong nation", noted by Li in 1930.[44] Cheng highlighted the fundamental role of the family in a nation with reference to Confucian philosophy. Christians holding this perception exerted a crucial influence, which was magnified by their institutional position and use of modern printing techniques. For Li at least, the previous primary emphasis on religious literature was now refocused to serve the Christianizing Home movement. Yet, in her address to the NCCC

39 Forty-second Annual Report of the CLS, 1929, 6; Forty-seventh Annual Report of the CLS, 1934, 16.

40 中华归主, February 1st, 1929,

41 Eighty-Tenth Annual Meeting Report, 1931, 1933, 1935.

42 金声月刊, 1933, *vols*.3 & 4, 11-19.

43 Program of religious education for the Methodist Episcopal Church in China, 1928-1931.

44 Public addresses of the East China Conference for leaders of the Christianizing the Home Movement (NCCC, December 6-16, 1930; March, 1931).

Conference in 1930, she maintained that "the spiritual manna of religious education could be only obtained through literary work" and that "The success of Sun Yat-sen's revolution was not achieved through military force but through the advocacy of words".[45] When analyzing new non-religious literature, Li expressed her admiration for Communist works and belief that its beauty accounted for its appeal to the people. Such new forces affecting literature made the call for Christian literary work all the more urgent and she stressed its importance in this period of transition. Li also expected more women to get involved.[46] However, Li's focus shifted from individuals to families, a divergence from the ideas in her university theses. Her situation of Christianizing Home between Christian literature and nation-building marked a change in her interpretation of Christianity.

Li was also an executive member of the YWCA from 1934 to 1935,[47] during which she focused on the social gospel. In 1933, she attended the third annual conference of the YWCA, which took its theme as constructing a new society.[48] In her address on the organization's progress, Li stressed her deep knowledge of the YWCA and emphasized a broadened approach in the application of Christian teaching, which was to *reject the dross and assimilate the essence* (去其糟粕，取其精華). Although she did not explain what she meant by dross, judging from her approval of the YWCA's positive social engagement it seems fair to include that she was referring to a lack of interaction between Christianity and Chinese society. The YWCA's desire for social progress marked it out as a good example of the philosophy of engagement. In the opening speech at this annual conference, Li encouraged members of the YWCA to bring together their wisdom to overcome the current miserable situation; she used an ancient Chinese idiom (山穷水尽疑无路，柳暗花明又一村) to urge each individual to find the silver lining in the current cloud. The compelling mission of each Chinese person thus concerned the construction of a new society. Li declared, "with a solemn sense of my responsibility, I pledge myself."[49] The social gospel movement enabled Li to engage in the building of a new society while maintaining her Christian identity; for her the essence of Christianity was defined by its social implications.Christian literature, Christianizing home and the social gospel underpinned Li's activities from 1928 to 1935. She was connected to both the core of Christian community and the periphery of ordinary people. Traveling brought the reality of Chinese society to her to and she showed a growing concern for the building of a new society rather than the cultivation of ideal citizens. Her resentment towards foreign imperialism mobilized her to join in the patriotic protests. This was

45 Ibid., 44-45.
46 Ibid., 43-44.
47 Directory of the Young Women's Christian Association of China, 1934-1937.
48 中华基督教女青年会第三次全国大会记录, August 21-29, 1933, 11.
49 Ibid., 16.

most clearly expressed in her involvement in a patriotic signature movement in December 1935. Li and 27 other Chinese Christians declared:

> We believe that every people has a right to existence and to the preservation of their national integrity. Recent events in North China made it plain that all our sufferings and compromises, all our yielding since September 18 1931, have not only failed to satisfy the insatiable demands of our aggressor, but have almost brought our nation into the depths of an unfathomable abyss. For this reason, actuated by a sense of love for the truth, we feel the imperative need for a united front among all our people in fearless opposition to any attempt to alienate our territory and to any measure calculated to deceive or intimidate us into acquiescence in the surrender of our rights. We love peace, but we love justice more. We are against any action that will lead to unnecessary sacrifice, but we are not afraid to shed our blood for the sake of truth and justice. We pledge ourselves to back up to the utmost nation-wide movement of resistance which has arisen throughout the country.[50]

Another example of Li's patriotism was her 1931 article "How we may help China".[51] Strong, emotional words were used to condemn Japan's violent occupation of China's northern territory. Li proposed a systematic and institutional effort to defend China, stressing that the continuous fight against Imperial Japan was necessary for ethnic Chinese or descendants of the nation. In this rising national crisis, priority was given to the nation rather than home and individual. Li stood out as patriotic *and* Christian.

Communism as a New Identity?

Li left the CLS in 1935 and immersed herself into the social gospel movement. Her name appears less and less in Christian publications and mission reports and it seems that in response to the nation's need she took greater interest in patriotic movements. From around 1936, Li worked as the professor of Sociology in Fukien (Fujian) Christian University. Fujian was then under the rule of the Nationalist Party (Kuomintang or KMT), who gradually encircled and suppressed the Communist Party there. In March 1935, the Fujian government reissued a prohibition on anti-Japanese publications to curtail any further demonstration,[52] which stirred up various forms of protest among intellectuals. The establishment of the Fuzhou National Literature Society and its patriotic periodicals not only mirrored the strong national sentiment in the field of culture but also generated and disseminated a kind of passion which led towards a nationalist movement.[53]

Little of Li's work from this turbulent political environment is available apart from one 1936 article entitled "A Picture of China—from Caterpillar to

50 *The Chinese Recorder*, February 1936, 123. For the original Chinese version, please refer to 新闻报, December 24, 1935.

51 *Woman's Messenger*, November, 1911.

52 刘敏，'抗战中的福州文化界救亡协会', *理论学习月刊*, 2 (1990), 61.

53 福州文化界抗敌后援会 was changed to 福州文化界救亡协会.

Butterfly" (in English).[54] The metaphor originated from prominent Chinese intellectual Liang Qichao and indicated that the future of China was bright while the current great pain was temporary. Li adopted a sociological approach to address the situation in China, firstly analyzing the multifarious causes of China's economic difficulties. From the external perspective, the unequal treaties with foreign powers justified the economic invasion and paralyzed aspects of the Chinese economy such as of agriculture, mining, industry, trade and transportation. Looking internally, warlords and natural disasters caused huge economic losses. Then Li addressed the nation's political invasion as a natural consequence of a colonialized economy which was marked by monopolization, division and joint control. She stated the Chinese people were obliged to build up the nation's political structure. As for the second superstructure, which was religion and morality, Li insisted there was no need for outsiders to meddle in its construction (無須外人越俎代庖). In the end, Li expressed her determination to expel imperialism and spare no effort to save the country in its national crisis.

Li's patriotic position and the KMT's suppression of revolutionaries accounted for her secret arrest and execution in 1937. One memoir narrated Li's unmasking of the corrupt deeds of the KMT in classes and public,[55] while another described her as an underground Communist party member. She was friends with Sun Shuzhen, headmaster of the Fuzhou Wenshan Girls' School,[56] and under her influence Sun encouraged her students to join the anti-Japanese movement. Also, the Fuzhou Evening News recently published an article commemorating Li,[57] which noted that Li was a member of the National Literature Society, some of whose members were Communists. The Society provided Li with the opportunity to work with Communist writers such as Yu Dafu and Lou Shiyi; indeed Lou's introduction helped Li join the Communist Party. After Li's arrest, her comrades made protests to the nationalist government. Everyone believed she was killed by the KMT after her sudden disappearance. Although work on Li concluded after her death in 1937, an item in the magazine *Religious Education Fellowship* provides us with a totally different story: apparently Li was seen in Shanghai in March 1938.[58] This is the last information about Li in the history of Chinese Christianity and definitely no more writing or activities were carried out in her name. Whether or not Li did survive is beyond the scope of this paper.

---

54 协大学生, 1936, vol.12.
55 郭毓麟, '协大四年学生生活的回忆', *文史资料选编*:第五卷, 384-385.
56 邓碧玉, '福州私立文山女中百年校史简介', *文史资料选编*:第五卷, 544-546.
57 '1937年福建协和大学女教授牺牲前后', *福州晚报*, March 16, 2014, A16.
58 Religious Education Fellowship News, Religious Education, June 1938, 30.

Conclusion

Through Li's dramatic life we can gauge how one early twentieth-century Chinese woman perceived Christianity, found her social niche and responded to the nation's struggles. This paper has examined why and how one Chinese Christian woman activist worked to spread Christian literature, and how her religious vision changed over time. At Ginling College Li perceived Christianity as a benefactor who saved her from feudal culture and brought her into the light. Then overseas study provided Li with advanced knowledge and a determination to contribute to Christian literature. Her two theses exhibited her concern to apply Christian literature to the construction of citizens and a democratized China. Li believed a powerful China could be achieved through religious, especially Christian literature. A strong nation would emerge when its citizens possessed character and morality, and for Li Christianity was a mechanism to transform Chinese people's minds. She is quoted as saying, "China needs minds, instead of mines."[59]

On her return to China, Li served as chief editor of the *Woman's Messenger* and with the NCCC and the YWCA. These two organizations exposed her to the debates and movement among leading Chinese Christians. Although committed to the cultivation of character, the national crisis drew Li increasingly into the social gospel movement, connecting Christianity with the constructing of a new China.

After she became Professor of Sociology at Fukien (Fujian) Christian University her activities are rather mysterious. Some claim that her growing influence led to her execution by the KMT and others that she joined the Communist Party. The growing invasion by imperialist powers escalated her sense of urgency about national salvation, as seen in the shift in her writings. Although there is no document clearly stating her position, we can conclude that either she considered herself as a Christian as well as a Communist or that she abandoned Christianity and became a Communist.

Li's disappearance and patriotic articles point to her adopting communism. She selectively promoted Christian teaching and it applied in a secular sense. Facing the threat imposed by imperial powers, Li adopted a collaborative approach in dealing with Christianity and nationalist sentiment. Although she allegedly joined the Communist party, there is nothing in her writings to suggest an antagonistic attitude towards Christianity. Li represented a type of patriotic Christian whose center of belief was the nation, and whose faith was developed by patriotism.

Li's ultimate national concern inserted a flux of ethnic fervor to the indigenous development of Christianity. It oriented the trajectory of Chinese Christianity to constructing a new nation in urgent need of renovation. The highlighted social implications of Christianity promoted the social gospel and consequently downplayed the roles of churches and individual salvation

59 Li, *The contribution of religious education to the democratization of China*, 1927, 131.

advocated by conventional forces in church community. Li's active agency drew Christianity into the whirlpool of national crisis. In this sense, Christianity in China was not solely viewed as the allegedly ally of the imperialist powers but also interpreted as a source for national salvation. The entangled relationship between Christianity and nation presented in this case sheds new light on the Chinese experience of Christianity. Understanding Li's perception of Christianity in religious education, Christianizing the home and national redemption thus becomes crucial in order to make sense of the indigenous development of Chinese Christianity in the Republican period.

Translating the Bible into Chinese: The Contribution of Chinese Translators

Monica Romano

Some Background on the Translation of Bible into Chinese

Early Christian missionaries arriving in China, particularly the Franciscans, Dominicans, and the Jesuits in the sixteenth-seventeenth centuries did not engage in Bible translation. Their limited knowledge of the Chinese language, the perceived difficulty of the task, and lack of such a tradition in the Catholic Church were among the main reasons.[1] Later on, the missionaries either had other priorities or were unable to publish their translation works because of the restrictive policies applied by the Congregation of *Propaganda Fide*.[2] During the nineteenth century, some attempts were made by the Catholic Church to make partial translations of the Bible but all remained unpublished.[3] Among them, some translations were produced by foreign missionaries, such as Jean Basset M.E.P. (1662-1707) and Louis de Poirot S.J. (1735-1813); others were by Chinese translators, namely Thomas Wang Duomo (王多默), who translated the Gospels (1875) and the Acts of the Apostles (1883) into Mandarin, and Francis Xin Fangji (辛方濟), who translated the Gospels into classical Chinese. As a result of this, the Catholic community in China had only partial Bible translations, mostly the New Testament, made from Latin *Vulgata*, up to the second part of the twentieth century. In 1968, the first complete Catholic Bible version in Chinese from the original texts was published – known as the *Sigao Shengjing* (思高圣经). This Bible translation was made by an Italian father, the Blessed Gabriele Maria Allegra OFM, with the help of Chinese scholars of the *Studium Biblicum Franciscanum* of Hong Kong. The *Sigao* edition remains the most authoritative and commonly used Chinese Catholic Bible version because of its accuracy and fidelity.

By contrast, the Protestant missionaries proactively dedicated themselves to translation work as soon as they arrived in China. The first complete Bible versions from the original texts were published as early as the 1820s. After

---

1 Nicolas Standaert, 'The Bible in early seventeenth-century China', in Irene Eber et al., eds, *Bible in modern China: The literary and intellectual impact* (Sankt Augustin: Monumenta Serica Monograph Series XLIII, 1999), 33,35.

2 Ibid., 39.

3 J.O. Zetzsche, *The Bible in China: The history of the Union Version or the culmination of Protestant missionary Bible translation in China* (Sankt Augustin: Monumenta Serica Monograph Series XLV, Monumenta Serica Institute, 1999), 26, n.8.

these earlier attempts, there was a proliferation of individual and joint Bible translation projects led by foreign missionaries, up to the publication of the *Union Version* (*Heheben* 和合本) in three different forms – classical, semi-classical and Mandarin.

The *Union Version* in Mandarin was published in 1919 and has always been considered as the Chinese Bible *par excellence*. Due to its emergence in conjunction with the May Fourth Movement, which raised the status of Mandarin (then called *baihua* 白話) to a literary language, this Bible edition was taken as a model for standard *baihua.*

The two above-mentioned Bible translations – the *Sigao* Bible (or Studium Biblicum translation) and the *Union Version* – are milestones in the Chinese Bible translation endeavour. They were produced under the leadership of foreign missionaries, albeit with the crucial and often overlooked contribution of Chinese people. Over time, Chinese Christians became increasingly involved in Bible translation, even leading the whole work.

Chinese Catholic Bible translators

Starting from the second half of the nineteenth century, the Congregation *de Propaganda Fide* granted permission to publish translations to those bishops that requested it. Up to 1968, versions of the Catholic Bible were all partial (mostly covering the New Testament), used both vernacular and classical languages, and in most cases had the Latin *Vulgata* as the textual basis. Apart from foreign missionaries,[4] a number of Chinese people engaged in the translation work as well. Among them, the Jesuit father Joseph Xiao Jingshan (蕭靜山, 1855-1924) translated the New Testament into Mandarin, which was published in 1922 with the title of *Xinjing Quanji* (新經全集 New Testament). This was the first Catholic version ever published in Mandarin and was later on revised by other Jesuits and re-published in 1948 and 1956. They adopted the Greek text as the textual basis, keeping the Latin *Vulgata* as a reference.[5] The supremacy of the original texts in respect of the Latin *Vulgata* had meanwhile been declared in 1943 by Pius XII in the Encyclical *Divino Afflante Spiritu*.

Probably due to the influence of the May Fourth movement, Xiao used Mandarin instead of the literary language. Additionally, he applied the principles of literal faithfulness and comprehensibility.[6] This translation was largely used by the Catholic Church in China after the Second Vatican Council

4 J.J.F. Dejean M.E.P. (1834-1901), Pierre Bosquet M.E.P. (1874–1945), Marie Louis Félix Aubazac M.E.P. (1871–1919), György Litvanyi S.J. (1901-1983), René Archen S.J. (1901-?), and Édouard Petit S.J. (1897-1985).

5 Zetzsche, *The Bible in China*, 419.

6 The non-Christian translation theorist and translator Yan Fu 嚴復 (1853-1921) defined three translation criteria: faithfulness (xin 信), comprehensibility (da 達) and elegance (ya 雅), or 'xin da ya'. These criteria influenced translation theory and practice for almost half a century, including Bible translation. See W. Zhong, *An overview of translation in China: Practice and theory* (http://translationjournal.net/journal/24china.htm).

(1962-1965) and before it was replaced by the Studium Biblicum version, published in 1968, but authorized in mainland China only in the early 1990s. Xiao's New Testament was reprinted several times in the 1980s, bringing the total number of copies to 280,000[7] and initially combined with the *Sigao* version's Old Testament. It was used for training purposes, including in the seminaries.[8]

There are other two important Chinese Catholic translators. Ma Xiangbo (馬相伯, 1840-1939) translated into classical language a Harmony of the Gospels in 1923 and later on he undertook a proper translation of the Gospels, which was published posthumously in 1949.[9] John Wu Jingxiong (Wu Ching-hsiung, 吳經熊, 1899-1986), a jurist and ambassador to the Holy See, translated the Psalms and New Testament into poetic forms of classical Chinese.[10] Chiang Kai-shek (Jiang Jieshi 蔣介石), who was a Christian, highly appreciated Wu's translation, commissioning him for work on the New Testament.[11] The Psalms, translated from a bilingual version of the Masoretic text, the Latin *Vulgata*, and a French Bible edition were first published in 1946 and finally in 1975 with the title *Shengyong Yiyi* (聖詠譯義 Translation of the Psalms). The New Testament was translated into classical language from English and French editions and published in 1949 with the title *Xinjing Quanji* (新經全集 New Testament).

After the Franciscan Bible was published in 1968, other translations were produced by both foreign missionaries and Chinese people.[12] In 1983, the Sheshan Seminary near Shanghai started translation work on the New Testament under the direction of Aloysius Jin Luxian (金鲁贤, 1916-2013), bishop of Shanghai.[13] Bishop Jin decided to focus on the Gospels and the Psalms, due to their prominence as readings during Mass.[14] He was assisted in

---

7 J. B. Zhang, 'The promotion of the Bible in contemporary China and evangelization', *Tripod,* 27 (Spring 2007) (http://www.hsstudyc.org.hk/en/tripod_en/en_tripod_144_03.html); 卢国龙, ed, 宗教在文化战略中的地位和作用, 中国社会科学出版社, May 2014, 428.

8 Ibid.

9 Wang Weifan, 'The Bible in Chinese', *Chinese Theological Review*, 8 (1993), 80; Zetzsche, *The Bible in China*, 420.

10 D.K.T. Choi & G. K.W. Mak, 'Catholic Bible translation in twentieth-century China: An overview', in C. Yik-yi Chu, ed, *Catholicism in China: 1900-present* (New York: Palgrave, 2014), 109.

11 F. K. H. So, 'Wu Ching-Hsiung's Chinese translation of images of the Most High in the Psalms', in I. Eber, S. K. Wan, K. Walf, in collaboration with R. Malek, *Bible in modern China: The literary and intellectual impact* (Nettetal: Steyler Verlag Monumenta Serica Monograph Series XLIII, 1999), 322, 324.

12 Apart from the Shanghai New Testament translation led by Bishop Jin Luxian, another relatively widespread Bible edition is the Pastoral Bible (*Muling Shengjing* 牧靈聖經), in 1998 in Hong Kong in traditional characters and in simplified script in 2000. The translation work was led by the French Claretian father Bernard Hurault with the help of Chinese translators from Taiwan.

13 M. Romano, *The Chinese New Testament edition of the Jerusalem Bible by the Shanghai Diocese*, paper presented at The LEWI International Conference, Hong Kong Baptist University, June 4-5, 2015.

14 Information provided by a former employee of Shanghai Guangqi Press.

some translation work and proofreading[15] by Lu Shuxin (卢树馨) of Shanghai's Guangqi Press and by other highly educated Catholics. In 1986, the Gospels were published and subsequently – one after the other in separate volumes – the Acts of the Apostles, the Letters of St. Paul, the Catholic Epistles, and the Book of Revelation. In 1994, the whole New Testament was published in one volume with the title of *Xinjing Quanji* (新经全集). The translation was made based on *La Bible de Jerusalem*,[16] and hence also known as the *Yelusaleng Shengjing* (耶路撒冷圣经 The Jerusalem Bible). The translation was based on an earlier Chinese translation in Mandarin produced in 1953 by the *Xuhui* Jesuit Seminary located in Shanghai – the *Xinyi Fuyin Chugao* (新譯福音初稿 First Draft of the New Translation of the Gospels). Its textual basis was the Greek text by Merk,[17] with reference to a "Latin text".[18] After the New Testament, Bishop Jin, again with the help of Lu Shuxin (卢树馨), translated the Psalms.

Since 1995, Bishop Jin has revised the translation again, using as references Bible editions in the original languages and consulting the *Sacra Pagina Series.*[19] Why did Bishop Jin embark on such an arduous task when a complete and reputable Chinese Bible (the *Sigao* Bible) had already been published in 1968? His initiative even raised some criticism and was stigmatized as a waste of energy.[20] When he started the translation work in the early 1980s, the Catholic Church in Mainland China was still using the New Testament translation by Xiao Jingshan, which by then was quite old and based on the Latin *Vulgata*. Therefore, this translation might have been perceived as out-dated and unsuitable as it was not based on the latest exegetical approaches and tools. The *Sigao* Bible, published in Hong Kong and Taiwan, could not be imported into Mainland China.[21] Only in 1990, many years after the *Sigao* first publication, were 50,000 copies of the Old Testament from the *Sigao* Bible printed in Mainland China, to be combined with Xiao's New Testament.[22] Only

15 Zhang Shijiang 张士江, 圣经与中国及福传, *信德 (Faith)*, 2 (2007), 14.

16 *La Bible de Jérusalem* was published in 1973 by the Biblical Institute of Jerusalem directly from the Hebrew, Greek or Aramaic and generally recognized as one of the best contemporary Bible translations from original texts. The *New Jerusalem Bible* is an English translation of it published in 1985.

17 Zetzsche, *The Bible in China*, 421.

18 蔡錦圖 (D. Choi), 天主教中文聖經翻譯的歷史和版本 [The history and editions of Catholic Chinese Bible translations], in 聖經的中文翻譯 [Biblical Translation in Chinese], *天主教研究學報 [Hong Kong Journal of Catholic Studies]*, 2 (2011), 33

19 Commentaries on the books of the New Testament, published by the Liturgical Press, Collegeville, MN. 张士江, *圣经与中国及福传*, 14; 卢国龙, ed, 宗教在文化战略中的地位和作用, 中国社会科学出版社, May 2014, 428-429; *Sheshan Xiuyuanyi* 佘山修院译, *Shengjing Xinyue quanji* 圣经新约全集 [注释重译本] (Shanghai: Tianzhujiao Shanghai Jiaoqu Guangqishe 天主教上海郊区光启社, 2004), acknowledgement page.

20 'Shanghai needs its own Chinese Language Missals, says Bishop Jin', in *UCANews*, 17 January 1991 (http://www.ucanews.com/story-archive/?post_name=/1991/01/17/shanghai-needs-its-own-chineselanguage-missals-says-bishop-jin&post_id=31858).

21 Information obtained from a former employee of Guangqi Press.

22 Choi & Mak, *Catholic Bible translation*, 112.

in 1992 was the complete *Sigao* Bible printed, definitively replacing Xiao's edition.[23] These developments happened just two years before Bishop Jin's New Testament translation was published in one volume and after most of the books had already been published individually over time.

In 1991, Bishop Jin reportedly noted that the *Sigao* Bible was completed some time ago and some wording was out-dated: "The Bible is for today′s people and therefore it needs new translations so as to keep up with the current use of the language and be read more smoothly".[24] This view was shared by other fathers that were involved in the translation of the *Sigao* Bible. Father Theobald Diederich OFM, who joined the Studium Biblicum Franciscanum in 1953, indicated that the translation needed to be renewed because "the language style lasts more or less one generation".[25] Similarly, Father Joseph Fung Che-ho, director of the Hong Kong Catholic Biblical Association, highlighted that "regarding the usage of Chinese language in mainland China, Hong Kong and Taiwan, each has its own language differences in character writing, style, grammar and idiom to be considered in a new translation."[26]

It seems that one of Bishop Jin's main concerns was the lack of a Chinese version of the post-Second Vatican Council Missal and the need to have at least portions of the Bible translated for reading during Mass.[27] In fact, until 1992, the post-Second Vatican Council liturgy – in particular the use of vernacular language – was not authorized in mainland China, including for the Mass, because there was no model for the Missal in Chinese.[28] However, the post-Second Vatican Council liturgy was officially introduced in the regional Sheshan Seminary and the Xujiahui church of Our Lady in Shanghai *ad experimentum*.[29] Additionally, some dioceses in Fujian adopted the Missal in Chinese on their own initiative, using books from Hong Kong and Taiwan.[30] Bishop Jin reportedly indicated that the publication of a new Missal including readings extracted from his translated Jerusalem Bible was to be considered after the completion of the translation work, as some of the wording for Mainland China may be different from that outside the country.[31]

From 1986 to 2004 the Shanghai Diocese printed 598,900 copies of the Chinese Jerusalem New Testament edition.[32] Although widespread in Shanghai

23 Ibid.
24 'Shanghai needs its own Chinese Language Missals, says Bishop Jin'.
25 'Bible Publisher Lauds 25th Anniversary of Chinese Bible Edition', in *UCANews* 30 Sep. 1994
26 Ibid.
27 The issue of the Missal and Bishop Jin's concern about it was also raised by a former employee at Guangqi press and Prof. Rachel Zhu Xiaohong 朱晓红 of the Department of Religious Studies at Fudan University in Shanghai in an email dated March 2015.
28 C. Yik-yi Chu, *The Catholic Church in China: 1978 to the present* (New York: Palgrave Macmillan, 2012), 78.
29 'Shanghai needs its own Chinese Language Missals, says Bishop Jin'.
30 C. Yik-yi Chu, *The Catholic Church in China*, 78-79.
31 'Shanghai needs its own Chinese Language Missals, says Bishop Jin'.
32 Zhang, *圣经与中国*, 16.

and neighbouring dioceses, this version has not challenged the authority of the *Sigao* Bible.

Chinese Protestant Translators

Bible translations published after 1919 were nearly all by Chinese translators and in vernacular language. After the 1970s, a number of translations were produced from Bible versions in modern languages, including Chinese. In addition to some efforts by Chinese translators in the 1930s,[33] a meaningful translation was produced by pastor Lü Zhenzhong (吕振中). Knowledgeable of the biblical languages, his translation represented the hope that a Chinese scholar could produce a Chinese Bible to replace the *Union Version*.[34] The New Testament translation was completed in 1945 or 1946, with the title *Lüyi Xinyue Chugao* (吕譯新約初稿) and printed in Beijing only for private circulation and submission to experts for their advice and correction.[35] In 1952, a new draft translation (*Xinyue Xinyi Chugao* 新約新譯初稿) was published in Hong Kong.[36] According to Prof. Galik, in October 1962 feedback was sought on Lü's translation of selected passages of the Old Testament from consultants in various theological seminaries and other institutions in Hong Kong, Taiwan and abroad.[37] While most agreed that Lü's translation was more faithful to the original texts than the *Union Version* and that a revision of the latter was needed, opinion on whether Lü's translation contained more accurate interpretations than the *Union Version* was mixed.[38] In 1963, while Lü's major scholarly contribution was acknowledged, it was concluded that because of the "style and general semantic principles" he adopted, his translation could not be supported by the Bible Society.[39]

Lü's complete Bible translation (*Shengjing* 聖經) was published in 1970 with the partial support of but not under the aegis of the Bible Societies,[40] which meant that its circulation was limited.[41]

As a textual basis, Lü used an unspecified Hebrew test and the critical edition of the Greek text by Souter (and occasionally by Nestle).[42] Lü applied a

33 Mostly of the New Testament, such as by Wang Yuande 王元德 (1933), Zhu Baohui 朱寶惠 (1936), who also translated the whole Bible (1939), Prof. Zheng Shoulin 鄭壽麟 and Pastor Heinrich Ruck (1939), and Theodore E. Xiao Tiedi 蕭鐵笛 (1967).

34 A. H. J. Murray, 'A review of Lü Chenchung's revised draft of new translation of the New Testament in Chinese', *The Bible Translator*, 4 (1953), 166.

35 R.P. Kramers, 'Some thoughts on revision of the Bible in Chinese', *The Bible Translator*, 7 (1956), 161; M. Galik, 'Lü Zhenzhong: A Chinese translator of the Bible', *Asiatische Studien: Zeitschrift der Schweizerischen Asiengesellschaft*, 54 (2000), 819.

36 M. Galik, ibid.

37 Galik, *Lü Zhenzhong*, 821.

38 Ibid., 822.

39 Ibid., 822-823.

40 Zetzsche, *The Bible in China*, 347.

41 Galik, *Lü Zhenzhong*, 815.

42 Zetzsche, *The Bible in China*, 415.

principle of literal fidelity, keeping the original structure of the biblical languages in the Chinese text, rendering "the same Greek term with the same Chinese term".[43] Compared with the *Union Version*, Lü moved from "easy paraphrase to accurate and exact translation", though with "some sacrifice in point of style" and "conciseness",[44] and even "painstaking honesty and faithfulness, though sometimes to the detriment of Chinese style".[45]

Other translation attempts include the "Contemporary Bible" (*Dangdai Shengjing* 當代聖經), a sort of paraphrase of the *Living Bible* published in 1971. After the translation of the New Testament in 1974, the complete Bible was published in 1979. This edition renders the source text freely, includes explanatory notes, and adopts clear and simple language.[46]

A committee of translators from the Taiwan and Hong Kong Bible Societies produced the first inter-confessional Chinese Bible edition.[47] Based on the *Today's English Version* and with reference to the original texts,[48] the *Xiandai Zhongwen Yiben* (現代中文譯本), also known as *Today's Chinese Version*, applied Eugene Nida's principle of "functional equivalence" or "dynamic equivalence".[49] Its language is clear and simple and is suitable for an audience

43 Jia Baoluo 賈保羅 (R. P. Kramers), 'Ping Lü Zhenzhong Mushi Xinyue xinyi xiugao 評呂振中牧師新約新譯修稿 [Commentary on the revision of Lü Zhenzhong's translation]', in Jia Baoluo 賈保羅, ed, *Shengjing Hanyi lunwenji* 聖經漢譯論文集 [Essays on Chinese Bible translations] (Hong Kong, Jidujiao Fuqiao, 1964), 138; X. Ren, 'A study of the major English and Chinese Bible versions throughout the history of Bible translation', *Asian Social Science*, 4, 7 (July 2008), 52.

44 Murray, *Lü Chenchung's revised draft*, 167; X. Ren, *ibid*.

45 R.P. Kramers, *Some thoughts*, 161; Jia Baoluo 賈保羅 (R. Kramers), 'Zuijin zhi Zhongwen Shengjing yiben 最近之中文聖經譯本 [Recent Bible translations into Chinese]', in Jia Baoluo 賈保羅, ed, *Shengjing Hanyi Lunwenji* 聖經漢譯論文集, 35-36; Liu Yiling 劉翼凌, 'Cong Zhongwen jiaodu kan Yuehan Fuyin xinyiben 從中文角度看約翰福音新譯本 [The Gospel of John in the New Bible Translation from the perspective of the Chinese language]', in Liu Yiling, ed, *Yijing Luncong* 譯經論叢 [Essays on Bible Translation] (Hong Kong: Evangel Literature, 1979), 78.

46 Wu Shengwu 吳繩武, *Renshi Shengjing* 認識聖經 [Knowing the Bible] (Hong Kong: n.pub., 1993), 91; Wu Shengwu, 'Dangdai Fuyin' shuping '當代福音'書評 [The contemporary Gospel], *Jingfeng* 景風, 45 (1975), 36.

47 Thor Strandenaes, *Principles of Chinese Bible translation as expressed in five selected versions of the New Testament and exemplified by Matthew 5:1-12 and Colossians 1* (Stockholm: Almqvist & Wiksell, 1987), 123; Zetzsche, *The Bible in China*, 416.

48 Different scholars expressed different opinions as to whether the translation is 'merely' a translation of the *Today's English Version*, albeit with checks from the original, or uses the original texts more extensively than only for reference.

49 According to Nida's translation theory, the principle of formal correspondence focuses on formal fidelity and attempts to match as closely as possible the formal elements of the source language. The principle of functional or dynamic equivalence is to reproduce 'in the receptor language the closest natural equivalence of the source-language message'.

with junior middle school education.[50] The New Testament was published in 1975 and the complete Bible in 1980, with a revision in 1995.[51]

In 1972 a committee of translators from China and some Southeast Asian countries was formed to work on a new Bible translation in Chinese financed by the American Lockman Foundation.[52] The translation principles that were adopted included fidelity to the original texts both in form and content, clarity and comprehensibility, fluency and simplicity, the adoption of a Chinese-language style, and reference to authoritative previous versions in case of ambiguity of the original texts. The textual basis was the *Biblia Hebraica Stuttgartensia*, the Greek text edited by the United Bible Societies, and the Mandarin *Union Version.*[53] The New Testament was published in 1976 and the complete Bible in 1993 with the title *Shengjing Xinyiben* (聖經新譯本 New Translation of the Bible). Liu Yiling (劉翼凌) – an expert in Bible translation into Chinese and translator of a version of St. John's Gospel published in 1964 – emphasized the superiority of the *Union Version* over this new translation. He considered the *Union Version* almost perfect, "ancestor of the modern Chinese literature in *baihua* (白话)" and "in some points clearer, simpler and more comprehensible than the King James Version".[54] Although he felt that a new translation of the Bible was necessary to keep up with changes in the Chinese language, he did not appreciate any of the new translations produced after the *Union Version.*[55]

Comparative Analysis of Selected Translations

A few relevant passages from St. John's Gospel are selected to illustrate some of the translation features of the different Chinese translations by Xiao Jingshan ("XIAO"), Lü Zhenzhong ("LÜ") and Jin Luxian ("JB").[56] Note that Bible texts

---

50 Ren, *A study*, 52.

51 A Catholic edition was published in 1984, differing only in the terms used for 'God' and 'Holy Spirit', which are notably different between Chinese Catholics and Protestants (respectively *tianzhu* 天主/*shengshen* 圣神 and *shangdi* 上帝/*shengling* 圣灵).

52 Zhao Weiben 趙維本, *Yijing Suyuan* 譯經溯源: 現代五大中文聖經翻譯史 [*Tracing Bible translation: A history of the translation of five modern Chinese versions of the Bible*] (Hong Kong: China Graduate School of Theology, 1993), 120; Zetzsche, *The Bible in China*, 417.

53 J. O. Zetzsche, ibid.

54 Liu Yiling 劉翼凌, *Cong Zhongwen jiaodu kan Yuehan Fuyin xinyiben 從中文角度看約翰福音新譯本*, 45-80.

55 Liu Yiling 劉翼凌, '*Gaiyi Zhongwen Shengjing de yige jianyi* 改譯中文聖經的一個建議 [Advice for a revision of the Chinese Bible]', in Liu Yiling 劉翼凌, *Yijing luncong* 譯經論叢 (Hong Kong: Evangel Literature, 1979), 30-44.

56 For an analysis covering other biblical verses and including other Bible editions see M. Romano, *Issues, trends and cultural adjustments in translating the Bible into Chinese*, paper presented at the 14th Conference of the Italian Association of Chinese Studies, Procida (Italy), 19-21 September 2013, forthcoming.

presented here are the Greek text, English text, *Vulgata*, and English Jerusalem Bible.[57]

John 1:1

GT: Ἐν ἀρχῇ ἦν ὁ λόγος, καὶ ὁ λόγος ἦν πρὸς τὸν θεόν, καὶ θεὸς ἦν ὁ λόγος.
ET: In the beginning was the Word, and the Word was with God, and the Word was God.
VG: In principio erat Verbum, et Verbum erat apud Deum, et Deus erat Verbum.
EJB: In the beginning was the Word: the Word was with *God* and the Word was God.

The preposition *prós* is ambiguous in Greek and can indicate both proximity ("near to") and company ("together with").[58] The Latin *Vulgata* opted for the first interpretation. XIAO renders the Latin *Vulgata* literally, and his version thus reads 物尔朋在天主, reproducing a typical Chinese sentence feature with a location complement. This choice is meaningful because Xiao and the following revisers must have known the translation choice of the *Union Version* published a few years earlier (道与神/上帝同在). The choice of the term *tongzai* 同在, "stay with", follows the second interpretation of the Greek text, as well as the *English Authorized Version* and the *English Revised Version,* which are often followed by Protestant translators in case of ambiguity of the Greek text. The form *tongzai* (同在) is maintained by most of the following translations, including that by Lü and the Studium Biblicum Franciscanum ("the *Sigao*" Bible), possibly because it is a more reliable interpretation. The 1956 revision of Xiao's translation is not changed even if it is carried out based on the Greek text. The Jerusalem Bible does not follow most of the earlier translation choices based on the second interpretation, including its authoritative Catholic predecessor (the *Sigao* version) and the French edition of the Jerusalem Bible, which is known for its highly reputable translation (and uses the word "*avec*"), but rather Xiao's translation, with its typical Chinese sentence structure.

To render the term *logos*, while Lü opted for the term *dao* (道) as consistently done by Protestant translations since 1835, the other two translators introduced relatively new solutions. As found in the previous translation by Li Wenyu (李问渔) in 1897, the XIAO 1922 edition adopted a

57 The Greek text (GT) used as a reference is that edited by the United Bible Societies (UBS), the most reliable and respected Greek edition of the New Testament. As an aid to the reader, the English translation (ET) of the Greek based on the *New American Bible* is provided in the footnotes for reference. The Latin *Vulgata* (VG) and the English version of the Jerusalem Bible (EJB) are also provided as these are the textual bases of XIAO and JB respectively.

58 R. E. Brown, *Giovanni, commento al vangelo spirituale* [original title: The Gospel According to John] (Assisi: Cittadella, 1986), 5; R. Schnackenburg, *Il vangelo di Giovanni, parte prima* [original title: *Das Johannesevangelium*] (Brescia: Paideia, 1973), 295.

transliteration of *Verbum* (*wuerpeng* 物尔朋), which was replaced by the neologism *shengyan* (圣言 "sacred word *avec*") in turn by the following *Sigao* translation. The Jerusalem Bible, however, does not follow its authoritative predecessor and chooses the indigenous term *dao* (道), as done by an earlier reputable translator, Wu Jingxiong, but adds quotation marks to alert the reader that the term does not have the traditional Daoist associations.

John 1:3

GT: πάντα δι' αὐτοῦ ἐγένετο, καὶ χωρὶς αὐτοῦ ἐγένετο οὐδὲ ἕν. ὃ γέγονεν
ET: All things came to be through him, and without him nothing came to be.
VG: Omnia per ipsum facta sunt, et sine ipso factum est nihil, quod factum est
EJB: Through him all things came into being, not one thing came into being except through him.

This verse is a long and complex sentence in Greek and is expressed in the passive voice. The translation by Xiao tends to render the sentence quite literally, hence in its length and complexity: 万物就是藉着他造成的。凡受造的，没有一样不是由他造成的. However, compared to the earlier *Union Version* (万物是藉着他造的。 凡被造的，没有一样不是借着他造的), it removes the use of the preposition *bei* (被) emphasizing the passive, replacing it with more specific terms: *shou* (受) to highlight the receiving role of the creation and *you* (由), indicating some sort of delegation of duty. Xiao also uses the disyllabic term *zaocheng* (造成), highlighting the completeness of God's creative act.

Typical of Lü, who tends to render each Greek term with a Chinese one, his translation is even more complex and sophisticated than the *Union Version*: 万物藉着他而被造；凡被造的，没有一物在他以外而被造. Lü repeats the term *bei* 被 three times to render literally the three occurrences of the passive sense of the Greek text, uses emphatically the word *er* (而), and adds the expression 在他以外 (*outside of him*).

Breaking with previous translations and particularly the complex choices of the *Sigao* Bible (万有是藉着他而造成的；凡受造的，没有一样不是由他而造成的), JB considerably shortens, simplifies and 'sinicizes' the sentence using a parallel structure: 万物由"道"而成，万物非"道"不成. To ensure clarity, the literal translation with the pronoun is avoided, replacing it with the noun "Word" of the previous verses.

John 1:9

GT: Ἦν τὸ φῶς τὸ ἀληθινόν, ὃ φωτίζει πάντα ἄνθρωπον, ἐρχόμενον εἰς τὸν κόσμον.
ET: The true light, which enlightens everyone, was coming into the world.
VG: Erat lux vera, quae illuminat omnem hominem, veniens in mundum.

EJB: The Word was the real light that gives light to everyone; he was coming into the world.

The translation by Xiao is based on the Latin *Vulgata* (那才是真实的光，凡来到这世界的人，他都照临), using a typical Chinese sentence structure, where a long object is anticipated for clarity and emphasis. Lü maintains a close formal rendering of the Greek text: 那真的光，那照亮万人的光，当时正到世界上来呢. He seemingly repeats the demonstrative adjective *na* 那 ("that") to reproduce the Greek article "*to*" occurring twice in the Greek text (Ἦν τὸ φῶς τὸ ἀληθινόν). He also renders the relative sentence literally (那照亮万人的光) and the Greek present participle (using *zheng* 正), indicating a continuing action. These features appear rather convoluted and redundant, and definitely not consistent with a sentence in the "Chinese" style. A typical Chinese feature is introduced through the modal particle *ne* (呢) at the end of the sentence, again denoting an incomplete action. A similarly sophisticated and formal rendering is found in the *Sigao* translation, which renders in translation both the relative sentence and the continued action (那普照每人的真光，正在进入这世界).

JB aims to simplify and reads: "道"是真光，"道"进入世界普照众人. For the sake of clarity, it explicitly connects the action of entering the world not to the light but to the Word, following the English Jerusalem Bible edition, and according to a possible interpretation by which the subject is the *Logos* or *Word*.[59]

John 1:14

GT: Καὶ ὁ λόγος σὰρξ ἐγένετο καὶ ἐσκήνωσεν ἐν ἡμῖν, καὶ ἐθεασάμεθα τὴν δόξαν αὐτοῦ, δόξαν ὡς μονογενοῦς παρὰ πατρός, πλήρης χάριτος καὶ ἀληθείας.
ET: And the Word became flesh and made his dwelling among us, and we saw his glory, the glory as of the Father's only Son, full of grace and truth.
VG: Et Verbum caro factum est et habitavit in nobis; et vidimus gloriam eius, gloriam quasi Unigeniti a Patre, plenum gratiae et veritatis.
EJB: The Word became flesh, he lived among us, and we saw his glory that he has from the Father as only Son of the Father, full of grace and truth.

To translate this well-known verse – *the Word became flesh* – unlike most translations including Lü's (道成了肉身) and Bishop Jin's ("道" 成人身), Xiao makes an explicit and explanatory addition to the textual basis using the verb *jiangsheng* (降生, *jiang* 降, "come down", and *sheng* 生, "be born").

Since the beginning, the translators found difficult the translation of the Semitic term *sarx*, "flesh". In fact, earlier foreign Protestant translators opted for a strictly literal translation (*rou* 肉, meat). Anticipating a recent trend, Xiao

59 Schnackenburg, *Il vangelo di Giovanni*, 322.

avoided the Semitism and simply translated with the word *ren* 人, "person". However, this choice was rejected by the *Sigao* translation, which opted for the term *xuerou* (血肉 flesh and blood), indicating the human body with its emotions and weaknesses.[60] Like the *Union Version*, Lü chooses the Buddhist term *roushen* (肉身 physical body), which simply refers to "the body made of flesh and blood" and does not involve the idea of sin.[61] The Jerusalem translation opts for a "compromise" translation – *renshen* (人身) – to retain both the personal element (*ren* 人) and somehow the Semitic connotation (*shen* 身).

The second sentence of this verse includes the verb "*skeno*" meaning "to camp", "to tent", but also "to live in". While our three translators all opt for a typical Chinese sentence structure with the locative mode, Lü translates with a generic verb (住在我们中间), Xiao with a more formal term and sentence style (居住了在我们当中) and JB (寓居我们中间) with an explanatory translation using the term *yuju* (寓居 make one's home in), referring to a location other than one's native place.

The last sentence of the verse ("full of grace and truth") is rendered by Lü with a typical Chinese language feature (丰丰满满地有恩典有『真实』), like the *Union Version* (充充满满的有恩典有真理), which makes the text more understandable for the reader and for those who hear it preached.[62] Furthermore, Lü, again in line with the *Union Version*, adopts the typical Chinese sentence structure *you* (有)…*you* (有), thus achieving a "beauty, order and homogeneity of the style".[63] On the contrary, the other translations have a literal rendering that is not typical of the Chinese language,[64] with the conjunction *he* (和), including XIAO (充满圣宠和真理) and JB (他充 满圣宠和真理).

Conclusions

The Bible is the foundation of the Christian faith, and the way it is transmitted into the languages of the communities to whom the translation is addressed contributes to a greater or lesser extent to the shaping of local forms of the faith and the understanding of the Christian message. Bible translators are a product of their culture but also of the church groups to which they are affiliated, as well as previous experience on which they can draw. All these factors have

60 *Oxford advanced learner's English Chinese dictionary*, 1997, 558.

61 J. O. Zetzsche, 'Bibel in China (3): Terminologische Einflüsse von Denksystemen nichtchristlichen Ursprungs auf das chinesische Vokabular', *China Heute*, 14 (1995), 48; Zhongwen Shengjing Xinyihui 中文聖經新譯會 [The New Chinese Bible Centre], ed, *Zhongwen Shengjing Xinjiuyiben candu xuanji* 中文聖經新舊譯本参讀選輯 [*A selected Comparison between the New Chinese Bible and the Chinese Union Version*] (Hong Kong: Tiandao Shulou, 1996), 79.

62 Liu Yiling 劉翼凌, *Yijing luncong* 譯經論叢, 45-51.

63 Ibid., 51-52.

64 Ibid.

contributed greatly to the translation choices and outcomes of the Chinese Bible translators, including those focused on in this paper.

Fr. Joseph Xiao Jingshan was a Jesuit living in a period when the Catholic Church still used to discourage Bible translation. If ever undertaken, the translations were made largely from the Latin *Vulgata* – which had primacy in the Catholic Church until just before the Second Vatican Council, which proclaimed the supremacy of the original texts. Xiao's version shows the influence of Latin, as demonstrated by the transliteration of the term *Verbum* in St. John's Prologue in the first edition, which was subsequently combined with a translation and finally replaced by a translation. The negative memories of the Rites Controversy (which bitterly split Catholic missionaries in the seventeenth-eighteenth centuries concerning the proper term to translate "God"), but also previous Catholic experience mainly focusing on the New Testament, prevented Xiao from choosing a local philosophical and religious term such as *dao* (道); this had been used for long time by Protestant translators and by the popular *Union Version* produced by foreign missionaries. However, as a Chinese Jesuit, he adopted literary Mandarin, often choosing sophisticated terms. At the same time, Xiao reproduced typical Chinese sentence patterns and resorted to "explanatory" translation options that made more explicit certain meanings, even if these were not rendered in translation with formal fidelity, but were perceived as helpful or of greater clarity and comprehensibility to Chinese readers.

When Bishop Jin of Shanghai started his translation work decades later, he found that the Catholic Church in China still used Xiao's New Testament, whose language had become out-dated from the translation and exegetical perspectives. Meanwhile, the highly reputable and widely accepted *Sigao* Bible had been translated, but was not admitted into the mainland. However, he continued his translation work even when the *Sigao* Bible was allowed into China and distanced himself from the translation approach and often the results of the Franciscan effort. His desire was probably that it was people from Mainland China themselves who should undertake this task and apparently he believed that the Catholic Church in China needed a better translation, because. Bishop Jin avoided redundancies, cut and broke long sentences typical of biblical language but unusual in the Chinese language, and refused some formalisms found in translations more concerned with literal fidelity to the source text, often at the expense of the translation outcome in the "recipient" language. His translation seems to have undergone a sort of "sinicization" process to suit the features of the Chinese language. As a Chinese translator and perhaps as a bishop as well (but also backed by the choice made by an earlier reputable Chinese translator), he had no fear of opting for local philosophical and religious terms, including the contentious *dao* (道) to translate *logos*. The term *dao* had been systematically rejected by other Catholic translators, both foreigners and Chinese, including his authoritative predecessor translations – the New Testament by Xiao and, most importantly, the *Sigao* Bible.

Pastor Lü represented for some time the hope that the supremacy of the *Union Version* – a major effort of the foreign Protestant missionaries in China and still the most widespread Chinese Bible edition – could be overcome by the work of a Chinese translator. Lü Zhenzhong was acquainted with the biblical languages – something still rare in the 1970s, when a number of translations started to be made from editions in modern languages rather than the original texts. His translation approach is highly accurate and rigorous, and recalls that adopted by Fr. Allegra and the Studium Biblicum Franciscanum. While this achievement is remarkable for a Chinese translator, especially at that time, it is constrained by what is perceived by many as too rigid a literal fidelity, which negatively affects the translation outcomes. However, Lü also greatly benefitted from the long and rich experience of previous translations, primarily the *Union Version*, keeping a number of translation choices and features, especially for key terminology, such as the term *dao* (道).

In engaging with Bible translation, Chinese translators have greatly contributed to the shaping of Christianity in China, bringing in their own linguistic and cultural considerations and sensitivities. They based their work on the objectives of their translation work, carrying this ambitious task within the framework of the church groups they belonged to and both building on and rejecting aspects of the experience they had inherited. In different ways, with different concerns, and achieving different outcomes, they worked hard to render the biblical text into Chinese, positioning themselves along a contextualised continuum ranging from relatively literal translation to more dynamically equivalent approaches.

Part Three

Building the Faith

The Chinese Clergy and Church Autonomy in the Diocese of Kwangsi-Hunan, 1909-1950

Peter Cunich

When the last members of the Church Missionary Society (CMS) left Guilin in September 1950, it did not seem that their departure would mean the end of the Kwangsi-Hunan Diocese of the Chung Hua Sheng Kung Hui (CHSKH, Zhonghua Shenggong Hui), as the Anglican Church was known in China. Although still the smallest and poorest of the CMS-controlled dioceses in China, it had nevertheless made important strides in self-propagation and self-governance since the 1920s. The climax of these developments was the enthronement of Kwangsi-Hunan's first Chinese bishop, Addison K.S. Hsu, on 12 March 1950. After the departure of the foreigners the main parishes in the diocese continued to be served by seven Chinese priests and a large number of lay workers.[1] While it was recognised that the changed circumstances in China represented perhaps the greatest challenge in the diocese's short history, Bishop Hsu was heartened that his workers, both clerical and lay, felt 'a new impetus to go forward and strengthen the Church's witness to Eternal Truth and Love'.[2] A two-week retreat was held for all workers at the diocesan centre in Lingling in August 1950 so that they could gain a comprehensive understanding of the 'New Principles of the People's Government' and form a 'constructive programme to meet future needs'. They wrestled with a range of issues, including the application of dialectical materialism to their work and 'using the new method of constructive and sincere criticism', but the major question was how to 'carry on and extend Evangelistic work under present restrictions'.[3] Despite the difficulties involved in adjusting to the new regime and the renunciation of faith by many young members of the church, there were signs of a renewed strength of purpose in the diocese and each parish had finally become self-supporting. This was achieved partly by all church workers 'plying a trade to contribute to their own support' in addition to their spiritual work 'which must of course have first claim on time and thought'. Even though public ministry was no longer possible, 'it was felt that the work of evangelism

---

1 Percy Stevens, 'Bishop's foreword', *Kwangsi-Hunan Diocesan Newsletter* (hereafter *Newsletter*), 140 (Apr 1950), 3-4. Percy Stevens had stepped down as bishop on 28 Feb 1950, Hsu having been elected at the diocesan synod held soon after the 'liberation' of Hunan and Guangxi by the Communist army in October-November 1949. There were twelve foreign workers in the diocese in 1949.

2 Addison Hsu, 'A new era for the diocese', *Newsletter*, 141 (Jan 1951), 6.

3 Ibid., 7.

should be unceasingly carried on through Christian homes, individual contacts, distribution and loan of Christian literature, [and] through personal letters'.[4] Hsu and his colleagues were 'full of hope' for the future even though links with foreign missionaries had been cut and financial support from the CMS had ceased.

Unlike some other Chinese missions of the CMS, the development of independent church government had been a priority from the inception of the Kwangsi-Hunan mission in 1899.[5] Successive mission leaders had advocated a Chinese clerical and lay workforce to take control of their own church as soon as possible. When the Kwangsi-Hunan diocese was established in 1909, there were only twenty-five baptised Christians in two missions, and three poorly trained Chinese catechists working under the British missionaries. Despite this inauspicious start, the first bishop, William Banister, was determined to give Chinese Christians 'rightful control' over their church. Even before the erection of the diocese, Banister had asserted in a memorandum to the Archbishop of Canterbury that the presence of foreign missionaries in China was 'only temporary' and that the Chinese church must 'one day become purely National with its own clergy and bishops'.[6] Once appointed bishop he developed a diocesan council to act as an 'organ of union' between the members of the 'foreign Society and the indigenous congregations', even though the CMS Parent Committee in London thought this premature. Nevertheless, Banister was adamant that 'in China there will be a deadlock unless the Mission Boards of England and America are prepared to have more faith in their men and responsible leaders, both Native and Foreign'.[7] The Kwangsi-Hunan Mission Conference supported Banister wholeheartedly. When an amended plan for incorporating Chinese into the governance of the diocese and mission was again rejected in 1915, their strongly worded memorandum to the Parent Committee placed on record their opinion that 'a definite wrong is being perpetuated with regard to our Chinese fellow-Christians'.[8]

Bishop Banister had served in the CMS Fukien mission from 1880 until 1897, where he was influenced by John R. Wolfe, an early believer in building up a Chinese clergy within the mission.[9] Banister served as principal of the

---

4 Ibid., 7-8.

5 The mission field and later diocese of Kwangsi-Hunan consisted of the northern, Mandarin-speaking half of Guangxi province and the southern section of Hunan province below Changsha.

6 Lambeth Palace Library, London, Davidson 252, fol.10, 'Memorandum on the New Diocese of Kwangsi and South Hunan', 15 Feb 1909.

7 Gordon Hewitt, *The problems of success: A history of the Church Missionary Society, 1910-1943. vol.2* (London: SCM Press, 1977), 277; Church Missionary Society Archives, University of Birmingham (CMSA), Kwangsi-Hunan, G1. CH5/O/1913/40, William Banister to Baring Gould, 26 Aug 1913.

8 G1.CH5.O/1915/40, Memorandum on the P.C.'s Resolution, 27 Aug 1915.

9 Ryan Dunch, *Fuzhou Protestants and the making of a modern China, 1857-1927* (New Haven & London: Yale University Press, 2001), 19-20. In 1882, Banister and Wolfe had together introduced the 'church council system' in the Fukien mission. See G1.CH5.O/1915/41, Banister to Frederick Baylis, 1 Sep 1915.

CMS theological college in Fuzhou before being transferred to South China as mission secretary, where he encouraged the formation of 'flourishing and self-supporting congregations in Hong Kong and Canton' and established several highly successful educational institutions.[10] To him, developments in the South China mission were more encouraging than in Fukien or Mid-China (Chekiang) where 'the weak spot…is that Christians have been taught to feel …that they are helping the foreigner to set up his Church, instead of feeling that the foreigner is helping them to organize and maintain *their* Church'.[11] In Kwangsi-Hunan he wanted to try one 'last experiment in Church organization' that would make the local church responsible for the mission's work 'from the outset', 'an advance in the direction of Control by the Chinese' that would lead to the development of a 'truly indigenous' church.[12] Central to this was the recruitment of dedicated Chinese clergy to provide leadership for the laity of the diocese.

The main problem with Banister's radical vision was that there were neither Chinese clergy nor even sufficient Chinese assistants working under him to take on the necessary leadership roles. Moreover, the CMS Parent Committee in London had already quashed the Fukien mission's efforts to give Chinese clergy more authority in the provincial church council established in 1883.[13] Although Banister's colleagues in the field protested that London had committed a 'definite wrong' against Chinese Christians who deserved a greater say in the direction of their church, not everyone felt that the bishop's plan was sensible. Thomas Goodchild, who had been in China since 1898 and had transferred to Kwangsi-Hunan from Mid-China in 1910, was also 'a great believer in giving the Chinese responsibility from the first', but his experience of working in a newly established mission outpost at Hengchow (Hengyang) suggested that self-support should be a precondition of self-government:

> …if 'taxation without representation' is wrong, I think that 'representation without taxation' is also wrong. The principle of forming a self-governing church of coolies, who have never had any responsibility of governing in their lives…[is] a mistake. I want these men to take the double responsibility from the first.'[14]

Therefore, building up a group of Chinese leaders, both lay and clerical, would be a priority in the Kwangsi-Hunan mission if Banister's forward-looking policies were to be approved by London. Like the other CMS missions

10 John Holden, 'The Right Rev. William Banister, D.D.', *Newsletter*, 83 (Aug 1928), 820. Banister had introduced with Bishop Hoare the 'church council system' in the CMS districts around Canton in 1902. See G1.CH5.O/1915/41, Banister to Baylis, 1 Sep 1915.

11 CMSA, G1.CH5/O/1913/43, Banister to Baring Gould, 9 Sep 1913.

12 G1.CH5/O/1913/50, memo of a meeting between Banister, Baylis and G.A. Western, 10 October 1913; G1.CH5/O/1913/43, Banister to Baring Gould, 9 Sep 1913; G1.CH5/O/1913/51A, 'Suggested Regulations for the Diocese of Kwangsi and Hunan', c.Oct 1913.

13 Dunch, *Fuzhou Protestants*, 23-24.

14 CMSA, G1.CH5/O/1913/31, Goodchild to Baylis, 14 Jun 1913.

in China, however, this proved difficult to fulfil, especially finding and training young men for ordination.[15]

> Louis Byrde, the first missionary in the Kwangsi-Hunan field, had already made some progress towards this end. Byrde trained five Chinese workers in Guilin as catechists and evangelists before Banister's arrival in 1910, and Frank Child also did similar work in Yungchow (Yongzhou),[16] with variable results, to say the least. Byrde's Mandarin language teacher, Song Tsong-chen, a Moslem initially persecuted after his conversion in 1902, eventually became a catechist and the first lay reader in Guilin. In 1907 Child reported that Song had been 'a very real help in the evangelistic services, ably preaching to his fellow countrymen and often drawing large crowds to his magic-lantern lectures'.[17] By 1911 he had worked as a catechist in three mission stations and had been asked to find premises for a preaching hall in the new outpost at Hingan. He was even showing signs of suitability for the ministry: 'He is a strong all-round man, and with further training and a wider experience may well become a great power for Christ.'[18] Others were less successful. Ma Feng-yuen, a degree holder baptised in 1903, was very effective as a catechist and teacher because of his academic standing, but was dismissed in 1910 because 'his pride and temper, together with the desire for more worldly advantage, [had] gained the ascendancy over him and marred his usefulness as a Christian worker'.[19] In Yungchow, Chang Chien-san was a valuable addition to the staff from 1906: 'a good man and a fluent, thoughtful preacher. Being much older than any other Christian, he was able to give a lead which none of us, foreign or Chinese, can supply'. He had a strong prayer life and was an avid reader, giving his sermons 'the mark of a true Chinese scholar', but he died in 1909 just as he was becoming a leader of the local Christians.[20]

So successful were these early recruits that, by 1910 in the Yungchow district, the country work was done 'entirely by our Chinese brethren', and Louis Byrde rejoiced 'to bear witness to their general zeal'. Three of the workers were particularly talented at their work, but it was recognised that they needed proper training to achieve their full potential. Byrde had already held two examinations for Chinese staff under his direction, but he felt that a more formal training regime was necessary, so in 1910 two workers were sent to the American Church Mission's catechetical school at Hankow.[21] By 1913 the Kwangsi-Hunan men numbered four, supported by a grant from London. Later in the decade, British supporters of the mission made regular donations for the training of catechists.[22] In this way, a rudimentary formation programme was

15 G. F. S. Gray, *Anglicans in China: A history of the Zhonghua Shenggong Hui (Chung Hua Sheng Kung Huei)* (New Haven: Episcopal China Mission History Project, 1996), 23.
16 CMSA, G1. CH5/O/1913/10, Louis Byrde to Baring Gould, 21 Feb 1913; *Extracts from the annual letters of the missionaries for the year 1907* (*Annual Letters*) (London: CMS, 1908), 205.
17 *Annual letters*, 1907, 205.
18 *Newsletter*, 27 (Aug 1911), 43.
19 *Annual letters*, 1910, 374.
20 *Annual letters*, 1909, 437; *Newsletter*, 27 (Aug 1911), 43.
21 *Annual letters*, 1909, 438; 1910, 124-25.
22 Mrs Bourdillon of Bexhill was particularly generous, providing £15 up to 1922; *Newsletter*, 63 (Dec 1922), 382.

started in the diocese for training Chinese workers who might one day be ordained. Fully trained men were also borrowed from other dioceses. Mr Lei, a graduate from the Hankow school, started catechetical work at Guilin in April 1911. He was initially 'a tremendous success', with 'the gift of drawing people in':

> He is a gentleman, with winning ways, tactful, intelligent, well read, versed in things modern, conscious of the backwardness of his own nation and of national defects, and convinced that the Gospel is China's only hope. Moreover he is quite a good preacher, and better still in teaching enquirers and catechumens.[23]

After a year of effective work Lei had to leave when it was discovered that he had interfered in a lawsuit, causing trouble with local officials, a failing not uncommon among men in his position but which the CMS had specifically banned.[24] Another catechist on loan from Bishop Roots of Hankow, Li Chin-chien, went to the difficult station of Hengchow to assist Thomas Goodchild in establishing new work there; by the end of 1912, he was preaching to congregations of forty to sixty people.[25] In order to consolidate the training of Chinese workers within the diocese, Bishop Banister appointed Louis Byrde as Archdeacon of Kwangsi in 1914, with the special role of instructing prospective church workers 'by means of courses of Bible Study'.[26] This scheme was short-lived, as Byrde had to return to England in early 1916 and the scheme was 'disbanded' and not reactivated before his death in 1917.[27]

By the outbreak of World War I, the bulk of the Chinese mission staff in Kwangsi-Hunan consisted of evangelists and catechists, working as indigenous preachers and community leaders and serving in small, often isolated mission outposts scattered across the countryside. Catechists had usually received some ministry training and were accorded a higher status, while an evangelist held 'a less responsible post' and was usually a younger man 'or one who is unfitted intellectually for the higher place'.[28] Catechists were generally admitted as lay readers at special services at which the bishop officiated. By 1916, five of these men had been trained at the Hankow catechetical school to a level where Banister felt able to license them to act as 'quasipastors to certain congregations' in the diocese. Another group of catechists had undergone training under the bishop and Archdeacon Byrde and were also licensed as lay readers.[29] At this time there were still no Chinese deacons or priests in the diocese, but this deficiency was addressed in 1915 when Rev Fang Ling-seng was loaned by Bishop Malony from the Mid-China diocese after a request from

23 CMSA, G1.CH5/O/1911/7(i), Edith Couche to Banister, 13 Sept 1911; John Bacon, 'Advance in Kweilin', *Newsletter*, 29 (Mar 1912), 88-89.

24 G1.CH5/O/1912/72, John Bacon to Baring Gould, 26 October 1912; Dunch, *Fuzhou Protestants*, 28.

25 *Newsletter*, 30 (Jun 1912); G1. CH5/O/1912/73, Banister to Baring Gould, 4 Nov 1912.

26 G1.CH5/O/1914/76, Banister to Baylis, 10 Oct 1914.

27 G1.CH5.O/1916/15, Byrde to Cyril Bardsley, 13 Mar 1916.

28 Percy Stevens, 'A convention', *Newsletter*, 65 (Jun 1923), 434.

29 CMSA, G1.CH5.O/1916/38, Banister to Baylis, 13 Oct 1916.

the Mission Conference meeting in August 1914.[30] Fang was placed in the new mission station at Siangtan (Xiangtan) in early 1915, working as Mr Ibbotson's curate.[31] Bishop Banister was enormously pleased with this development, having been acutely aware that the lack of 'native clergy' created serious manpower problems. When European staff went on furlough, there was often no one to take over their mission stations temporarily.[32] The long-term solution was the recruitment of local men from Guangxi and Hunan provinces.

Bishop Banister recognised that preparing the young men of the diocese for evangelical service within the mission and eventual entry into orders required a superior education to that provided by the CMS primary schools. He therefore established All Saints' middle school to provide promising boys from throughout the diocese with the type of Anglo-Chinese education necessary to produce 'good Christian workers'. Initially located at Hengchow, the school moved to Yungchow in 1922 and served as an important source of recruits until forced to close in 1927. Pupils were encouraged to 'go further with their education', and from 1923 a 'normal training course' was initiated in the hope that the school would eventually provide 'a sufficient number of trained teachers for all our schools'.[33] Students were encouraged into 'witness-bearing' at weeknight street-chapel preaching services, and in late 1924 a group of students set out with Addison Hsu on a two-week 'social study' trip around the Yungchow mission field to help them consider their futures 'in accordance with the need of society and of the Church'.[34] While such initiatives produced many future teachers and catechists, it is not known how successful they were in identifying and encouraging men suitable for priestly training. Addison Hsu, the vice-principal of All Saints' school, would offer himself for the ministry after it closed in 1927, but the role of the diocesan middle school in incubating priestly vocations remains unclear.

By 1915, Bishop Banister had already begun to consider the best means of training aspirants for ordination, but the proposal of the Shanghai General Synod that year to open a theological training college for the entire CHSKH had an immediate impact on Banister and the Kwangsi-Hunan Mission Conference. The missionaries welcomed this development, but suggested that the new institution be located in a Mandarin-speaking region with the educational programme delivered in Chinese. Moreover, they insisted that 'provision should be made for evangelical uses' in the conduct of public worship at the college 'so that clergy may not feel a wrench when appointed to

30 G1.CH5.O/1914/65, Resolutions of the Conference held at Kuling, 3-13 Aug 1914, resolution no.21; G1.CH5.O/1915/3, Banister to Baylis, 2 Jan 1915.

31 *Newsletter*, 42 (May 1915), 94.

32 CMSA, G1.CH5.O/1915/29, Banister to Baylis, 20 Jul 1915.

33 M. C. Ram, 'First impressions', *Newsletter*, 63 (Dec 1922), 403; T. P. Tindall, '"All Saints"' Boys' School, Yungchow', *Newsletter*, 65 (Jun 1923), 435.

34 T. P. Tindall, 'Yungchowfu jottings', *Newsletter*, 66 (Sep 1923), 473; Addison K. S. Hsu, 'A Winter Trip', *Newsletter*, 71 (Mar 1925), 578-81.

an Evangelical charge'.[35] The Kwangsi-Hunan diocese was strongly evangelical in outlook, so it is not surprising that this provision was considered a *sine qua non* for any future CHSKH training college. It would be some years before the CHSKH's Nanking Theological School would be established, so in the meantime Banister proposed using Bishop Roots' American divinity school in Hankow for clergy training. Banister had been impressed by the quality of the Chinese clergy trained in the American theological colleges and universities in China, judging that in almost every instance these men were of equal value to the church as the average young missionary sent out from England or America, while some were of 'outstanding power and ability, who will be fit to occupy the highest offices in the Church'. When Banister attended a China Advisory Council meeting in Shanghai in 1918, it was mentioned that no Anglican mission in China at that time possessed Chinese clergy such as these American-trained priests.[36] Despite the obvious merits of the scheme, Banister's proposal was strongly criticised on theological grounds by Archdeacon Byrde, on furlough in London, but the bishop defended his scheme by pointing out that all branches of the church in China, whether English, American or Canadian, needed to co-operate as far as possible to avoid the costly mistakes made in clerical training in Japan. The only other option available to Banister was a non-conformist theological school in Changsha, but its decidedly anti-Anglican bias made it totally inappropriate for his men.[37]

The first ordinand for Kwangsi-Hunan was Wu Hong-ching, the catechist-in-charge at Siangtan when that mission was given to Bishop Banister as his episcopal seat by the American Church Mission in 1909. Wu later began training at the divinity school in Hankow from 1915 with a studentship provided by the SPCK, and was ordained deacon in 1917. His was exemplary of the new type of priestly training that Banister wanted to introduce for at least some of his Kwangsi-Hunan clergy.[38] The next ordinand, Song Tsong-chen, was trained according to the older style of preparation used by the CMS in Fukien, which emphasised 'field training'. After nearly ten years as a catechist he was accepted as a candidate for orders in 1916, and immediately sent to Hengchow where he completed theological studies under John Holden.[39] Song was the first Chinese converted by Louis Byrde in Guilin; he became a catechist in 1907 and was extremely able as both preacher and businessman on

35 CMSA, G1.CH5.O/1915/37, Minutes of the Third Conference of the Kwangsi & Hunan Mission, 23-27 August 1915, resolution 5.

36 G1.CH5.O/1918/13, Memorandum on the Need and Supply of Chinese Clergymen, c.May 1918.

37 G1.CH5.L1/179, Baylis to Banister, 11 Aug 1916; G1.CH5.O/1916/38, Banister to Baylis, 13 Oct 1916.

38 G1.CH5.O/1916/31, Banister to Baylis, 16 Jun 1916; Wu's ordination to the diaconate is not recorded, but he was ordained priest in Jan 1918, see G1.CH5.O/1917/34, Banister to Baylis, 22 Oct 1917. Banister says he had only two years of training at the Hankow divinity school; see G1.CH5.O/1918/13, Memorandum on the Need and Supply of Chinese Clergymen, c.May 1918.

39 G1.CH5.O/1916/43, Minutes of Extraordinary Meeting of Conference, 9-10 Nov 1916.

behalf of the foreign missionaries.[40] He was ordained deacon in early 1918. Chen Chi-chang was also a long-standing diocesan worker, serving as schoolmaster in Siangtan for several years and helping in spiritual work 'for some considerable time' before being recommended by Banister in 1916 for training at either Boone University in Wuchang or St John's University in Shanghai. He was said to 'know English well, and has manifested spiritual qualifications for higher service in the mission'.[41] Ultimately he studied at the Hankow divinity school, was ordained to the priesthood in 1920 and appointed to Guilin as assistant pastor.[42] Other early priests in the diocese came to the ministry via their roles as catechists, evangelists or teachers. Song Pu-ren (studied at Hankow, ordained in 1920) was one of the evangelists at Yungchow in 1909; Yu Shao-wen (ordained 1921) had come to Hunan as a catechist from Fujian; Su Ren-Ping (ordained 1926) was also a catechist at Guilin over a long period, as was Tseng Kwang-shuen (ordained 1929). Long years of service as evangelists and catechists constituted strong pastoral preparation before these men committed themselves to further study for the ministry. Apparently, their careers seem to have followed the general pattern of CMS missions elsewhere in China.[43] But not all aspirants for orders were successful. Loh San-pei was rejected by Banister in 1916. He read lessons at Sunday services in Guilin and was the secretary of the local vestry, but worked as a government schoolmaster and had been baptised for only three years. Banister felt that he had 'little experience of Christian Service, and does not at present possess the qualifications necessary for a candidate for Holy Orders'.[44] Clearly, great care was exercised in the selection of ordinands, even though they were greatly needed in the 1920s. Some other aspirants for the Kwangsi-Hunan diocese appear to have fallen away during training. Paul Wu, son of Wu Hong-ching, was in his second year of training at Boone University in 1918, but ultimately decided to become a teacher rather than serve in the diocese.[45]

The cost of training ordinands (approximately £100 for a four-year course in theology) was met from several sources, but mostly from the SPCK and private donations.[46] The Parent Committee warned Banister that London could not guarantee the funds necessary for the 'steady, small flow of men' in Kwangsi-

40 G1.CH5.O/1918/13, Memorandum on the Need and Supply of Chinese Clergymen, c.May 1918. G1.CH5.O/1914/7, enclosure E states that Song was baptised on 8 Jun 1902 at the age of 23 years, and confirmed on 13 Nov 1910.

41 G1.CH5.O/1916/44, Banister to Baylis, 17 Nov 1916.

42 G1.CH5.O/1918/13, Memorandum on the Need and Supply of Chinese Clergymen, c.May 1918.

43 Dunch, *Fuzhou Protestants*, 37.

44 G1.CH5.O/1918/13, Memorandum on the Need and Supply of Chinese Clergymen, c.May 1918.

45 CMSA, G1.CH5.O/1918/13, Memorandum on the Need and Supply of Chinese Clergymen, c.May 1918; G1.CH5.O/1919/21, 'The Needs and Claims of the Diocese of Kwangsi and Hunan', c.Jan 1919; G1.CH5.O/1919/22, Bishop Logan H. Roots to Holden, 11 Jan 1919; G1.CH5.O/1920/7, Banister to Baylis, 20 Feb 1920.

46 Paul Wu and Song Pu-ren received grants from the SPCK, while Chen Chi-chang was supported by a Mr Roberts of Sheffield, see G1.CH5.O/1919/21, 'The Needs and Claims of the Diocese of Kwangsi and Hunan', c.Jan 1919.

Hunan who presenting themselves for training.[47] The war years had caused the income of British missionary societies to plunge, the CMS having to reduce its overseas mission activities. Banister saw this as an opportunity, however, because European missionaries were much more expensive to train and support than Chinese 'native missionaries':

> I am convinced that the right policy to pursue, is not to trust to the hope of the Society being able to supply, in any adequate degree, a staff of European Missionaries commensurate with the needs of the work, but to employ here extensively suitable Chinese, even for posts hitherto held by Europeans.[48]

The London committee saw things a little differently. Putting aside Banister's argument about the Society's declining ability to support new missionaries in his diocese, they preferred to avoid setting a precedent whereby junior Chinese clergy worked regularly as curates under senior Europeans and occupied positions 'that a Missionary might and would otherwise occupy'. They also wanted to distinguish between such ordained men and existing catechists 'of long and good standing...who work in just such linked relations with a Missionary'.[49] Banister was not disturbed by this; he told the London committee in 1920 that he would rather develop his diocese 'chiefly by securing well educated native workers' rather than relying on foreign missionaries.[50] The status of newly ordained Chinese priests in Kwangsi-Hunan was left undecided until the middle of 1921, when the urgent need for 'retrenchment' meant that very few European missionaries were allowed to return from England to the diocese.[51] By early 1922, London had decided on 'withdrawal' from some mission stations in Kwangsi-Hunan, and even suggested that a Chinese pastor oversee evangelical work at Hengchow.[52] From this time on there was little discussion concerning Chinese pastors and the Parent Committee accepted them as absolutely necessary for the future of the Kwangsi-Hunan church, working as curates under European missionaries and more independent pastors in their own parishes.

The value of these newly ordained Chinese clergy was immediately recognised by Banister and other European missionaries. Despite the scandal caused by the 'moral lapse' of Fang Ling-seng, who had to leave Guilin in the middle of 1918, other new deacons and priests performed well and provided excellent leadership within Chinese congregations. They obtained on-the-job training under experienced missionaries at mission stations across the diocese, adapting quickly to their new roles.[53] They immediately gained the respect of

---

47 G1.CH5.L1/187, Baylis to Banister, 16 Dec 1916.

48 G1.CH5.O/1918/13, Memorandum on the Need and Supply of Chinese Clergymen, c.May 1918.

49 G1.CH5.L1/246, Baylis to Banister, 19 Jun 1919.

50 G1.CH5.O/1920/9A, Notes of Interview with Bishop Banister, 2 Jun 1920.

51 G1.CH5.L1/285, Baylis to Banister, 23 Jun 1921.

52 G1.CH5.L1/301, Herbert Lankester & G.A. Saywell to Banister, 12 Jan 1922.

53 G1.CH5.O/1918/19, telegram dated 30 July 1918; G1.CH5.O/1918/29, John Holden to Baylis, 18 Oct 1918. It is not clear exactly what this 'moral lapse' entailed.

both Chinese congregations and European missionaries for their devotion to evangelical and pastoral work, and eventually enjoyed a much fuller share in the administration of the diocese. They sat on the diocesan Synod and committees and, by the early 1930s, many had been appointed as 'pastors-in-charge' of the main parishes in the diocese. In 1930, Su Ren-ping was in charge at Hingan, Yu Shao-wen at Chuanchow, Song Pu-ren at Taochow and Ningyuan, and Tseng Kwang-shuen at Kianghwa, while Song Tsong-chen was assistant at Guilin, Addison Hsu at Yungchow, and Chen Chi-chang at Hengchow.[54]

The rapid advance in the role of Chinese priests is perhaps the most startling of the various developments in the Kwangsi-Hunan mission during the 1920s, but was only part of a wider plan to involve Chinese Christians in the governance of the diocese. Although Bishop Banister had been thwarted in his first attempts at ensuring 'Control by the Chinese' in his diocese, he continued to badger the CMS secretaries in London and planned for an eventual devolution of authority. By the time the 1922 National Missionary Conference in Shanghai began to demand 'most insistently' that 'native churches' control their own affairs, the Kwangsi-Hunan diocesan Synod had already moved a long way towards incorporating Chinese members into its decision-making protocols. The foreign missionaries had committed themselves to fostering the growth of an indigenous church 'in every possible way', and this was demonstrated in the composition of the Synod and its committees. The Standing Committee and Board of Finance were elected 'without distinction of race', giving the Chinese 'an increasingly prominent and effective part in the life of the church'. This was not only a valuable training ground 'for those who we hope will in future years be directly responsible for the work, but also...a means of more efficiently meeting the real situation confronting us; for our co-members bring to the task both consecrated ability, and also in many cases a first-hand knowledge far more detailed than we, as foreigners, can ever possess'.[55] Chinese involvement in decisions regarding the 'choice, promotion, or dismissal of workers' had reduced earlier suspicion and dissatisfaction, but it was felt that while missionary leadership was not yet a thing of the past, 'it is manifestly our duty, more and more, to entrust to the people of the land in which we are seeking to build up a church, the position of leadership and responsibility'.[56]

In 1923, the departure of several foreign missionaries on furlough provided an opportunity for two newly ordained priests to have 'practically independent spheres of work' in new parishes carved out of the Yungchow and Guilin mission fields. A *Diocesan Newsletter* editorial noted that, 'It is a matter of the greatest encouragement that we have Chinese clergy worthy to be put into such

54 *Diocesan Newsletter*, 91 (Sep 1930), 2.

55 John Holden, 'Towards self-government', *Newsletter*, 64 (Mar 1923), 408-9; see also his 'Bishop's letter', *Newsletter*, 68 (May 1924), 507.

56 *Newsletter*, 64 (Mar 1923), 410.

places of responsibility' only a short time after ordination.[57] That year also saw the retirement of Bishop Banister, whose successor John Holden was equally committed to devolution. These sentiments were reinforced by anti-foreign protests in 1925, but it was still thought that the Chinese priests did not yet represent a viable nucleus of leadership for the church:

> We are placed in a most perplexing position, for whilst it is undoubtedly true that the presence of Western leaders militates against the rapid spread of Christianity, the fact remains that in very few cases, of which this diocese is certainly not one, is it possible to dispense with that leadership.[58]

In the political atmosphere that dominated China and the diocese until the end of the decade it became increasingly difficult to recruit new clergy, but this was the time at which Addison Hsu became secretary of the diocesan Synod and began to demonstrate his remarkable organisational abilities, giving Holden hope for the future.

In these difficult times some Chinese clergy demonstrated remarkable courage in withstanding the advances of anti-foreign forces in the diocese. Song Tsong-chen led the Guilin Christians in resisting an attempt by another mission to start an independent and entirely Chinese church 'free from foreign influence of any kind whatsoever'.[59] Yu Shao-wen, who had served at the outstation of Ningyuen after ordination to the diaconate in 1921, faithfully ministered there for seven years, during which time brigands made it virtually impossible for foreign missionaries to visit the city. After his narrow escape from death at the hands of bandits in 1927, he was given Chuanchow parish, which turned out to be a poisoned chalice because of severe anti-Christian feeling in the town. While Bishop Holden considered him 'quite self-reliant and independent', qualities needed for a pastor in an isolated mission station, the bishop had to intervene when 'underground opposition' four times prevented Yu from buying property for the church.[60] Song Pu-ren had done 'good work' at Hengchow early in his ministry, 'full of enthusiasm for his new charge', but in 1926 was sent to the dastardly outpost of Chuanchow where the church was looted by students and he was threatened with personal injury if he returned to the town; until his transfer to Taochow in 1928 he could only visit the outlying parts of the parish.[61] Also in early 1928 the unfortunate Tseng Kwang-shuen (later ordained deacon in 1929) was sent to Ningyuan and was making good progress in reviving its shattered Christian congregation when bandits again attacked the city and all the workers were forced to flee. His next posting was the less nerve-wracking CMS public reading room in Yungchow, where the

57 *Newsletter*, 65 (Jun 1923), 423. The two appointees were Yu Shao-wen and Chen Chi-chang. Despite these positive comments, the names of Chinese pastors were not included in the regular lists of clergy published in the *Diocesan Newsletter* until 1926.

58 John Holden, 'The Bishop's letter', *Newsletter*, 74 (Dec 1925), 635.

59 W. R. Cannell, 'Riding the storm', *Newsletter*, 74 (Dec 1925), 646.

60 *Newsletter*, 76 (Jun 1926), 682; 83 (Aug 1928), 819; 85 (Mar 1929), 868.

61 *Newsletter*, 66 (Sep 1923), 462; 80 (Sep 1927), 768-69.

bishop was pleased to report on Tseng's easy interaction with enquirers there: 'Mr Tseng has a very attractive personality. He is also a splendid preacher and a very good pastor'.[62] The Chinese clergy of Kwangsi-Hunan remained utterly loyal to the foreign missionaries during the anti-foreign disturbances that followed the Shanghai incident in May 1925 and the political problems in 1927. They not only prevented the local churches of the CHSKH from breaking away and forming independent Chinese churches, but also welcomed CMS missionaries warmly when they finally returned to the field in 1928. The *Diocesan Newsletter* is replete with expressions of confidence and pride in what they had achieved while the British had been ordered out of China.

Bishop Holden praised these men whom he had asked to work far away from the main missionary centres and who suffered many privations during the unsettled 1920s. It was no doubt partly in recognition of their service that he hastened the devolution process after a meeting of the Synod boards and committees in early 1926 which discussed how the Mission Conference, consisting only of foreign missionaries, would begin to surrender its powers of appointment.[63] It was also during this tumultuous period that Addison Hsu and Chen Chi-chang represented the diocese at the 1928 General Synod of the CHSKH in Shanghai, where Chinese representatives greatly outnumbered foreigners in the House of Delegates and Lindel Tsen was elected chairman. This impressed Hsu, reinforcing his impression that the CHSKH was making great progress towards 'a truly Chinese organisation'. He was excited at the prospect of the church becoming a 'practically autonomous' province of the Anglican Communion, finally realised at the Lambeth Conference in 1930.[64]

The process of devolution stalled, however, during the political upheavals of 1927 when foreign workers were required to withdraw and the synod planned for early 1927 could not be held until January 1928. During the extended absence of the British missionaries, the Chinese workers took charge of the local affairs of the diocese, doing an exceptionally good job in difficult circumstances. Despite their being labelled as 'running dogs' of the 'foreign tyrants' and subjected to insults from incendiary youth and labour groups connected with the Kuomintang, Bishop Holden was pleased to report to the mission's supporters in Britain that, 'the Chinese workers carried on the ordinary pastoral and evangelistic work for the most part without much opposition'.[65] In Ningyuan, Yu Shao-wen was threatened with death by brigands, and 'bound, hung up, and beaten' by a mob because he was 'the representative of the foreigner'. Despite imprisonment and insult, he helped with medical work among his captors and looked after local Christians who had

62 *Newsletter*, 83 (Aug 1928), 842; 87 (Sep 1929), 15.

63 John Holden, 'The Bishop's letter', *Newsletter*, 76 (Jun 1926), 678-79.

64 Addision K. S. Hsu, 'Some impressions of the General Synod', *Newsletter*, 83 (Aug 1928), 823-25; Hewitt, *The problems of success*, 219; Gray, *Anglicans in China*, 42.

65 John Holden, 'The Bishop's letter', *Newsletter*, 80 (Sep 1927), 766-67.

suffered terribly during the sacking of the city.[66] Such acts of stoicism and bravery were seen at all levels among the diocese's Chinese workers.

The trials of 1927 demonstrated more clearly than ever the need to accelerate the handover of power to Chinese leaders. The performance of the Chinese workers in the face of terror and insult had for the most part been exemplary, while the British consul's insistence on a lengthy withdrawal of the foreign missionaries meant that the Chinese church could no longer rely exclusively on CMS leadership:

> It has been made quite plain, if this was not fully understood before, that for the Gospel to find a wider and readier acceptance, it will have to be presented more really under Chinese auspices and through Chinese channels. Anti-Christian feeling has been only a phase of anti-foreignism, and if the Chinese Church, which is ready enough for the assumption of autonomy and control, will also be ready for the sacrifice involved in genuine responsibility (including ultimately that of finance) the future is bright with hope.[67]

At the same time, many felt that 'the burden borne perhaps too long by the workers from the West cannot suddenly be transferred entirely to the shoulders of the Chinese Church without danger of a breakdown'.[68] The situation required careful consideration and skilful negotiation, but the matter was made considerably easier because a slow process of devolution had been 'quietly accomplished' since the days of Bishop Banister 'without pressure or compulsion before the days of intense nationalism'. When the crisis did come in 1927, Kwangsi-Hunan 'was spared the trial of having a body of Chinese Christians and colleagues who regarded us as having kept them from their rightful privileges'.[69]

At the diocesan Synod in January 1928, the Board of Finance became an executive rather than a deliberative body, with full control over diocesan finances, except with regard to the personal affairs of the missionaries. Bishop Holden felt that this 'acid test of sincerity' with regard to diocesan finances had 'thoroughly convinced' the Chinese workers 'that as far as the Western missionaries are concerned, there is no desire to do anything but help forward the movement towards self-government in the Church'.[70] This move forward was acknowledged by Addison Hsu, the most eloquent of the Chinese laymen (and soon to be ordained deacon), as indicative of 'a great willingness for sacrifice and a loving spirit' among the foreign missionaries, 'making as real as possible the control of the Chinese Church by the Chinese Christians':

66 Yu Shao-wen, 'The sack of Ningyuan', *Newsletter*, 81 (Jan 1928), 784-88.
67 Ibid., 784.
68 John Holden, 'The Bishop's letter, *Newsletter*, 81 (Jan 1928), 781.
69 John Holden, 'Bishop's letter', *Newsletter*, 86 (Jun 1929), 3.
70 John Holden, 'The Bishop's letter', *Newsletter*, 82 (Apr 1928), 800.

> This in fact is the real progress of the Church in this diocese, because it cannot be prosperous and stand firmly unless the Chinese Christians are fully conscious of their responsibility and take an actual part in the control of the work.[71]

This development was confirmed by the foreign missionaries at their long-postponed Mission Conference in early 1929, when the process of devolution was completed as the Conference relinquished its right to appoint missionaries to the Synod. The Chinese clergy played a prominent role in writing to all in the diocese to confirm that there would be 'complete equality' between Chinese and Western workers, in which 'not the slightest distinction remains'.[72]

By 1929, the role and status of the Chinese clergy had advanced considerably since the first deacon was ordained in 1917. Ultimately, 14 Chinese were ordained for the Kwangsi-Hunan diocese, eight before 1930 and a further six between 1932 and 1948 (see appendix). From the late 1920s the formation of priests appears to have taken place at the CHSKH's Central Theological School at Nanking, opened in 1921. Several had previously worked as catechists in the diocese: Lu Chen-nam (ordained deacon in 1931) had been a catechist as early as 1919 before studying at Nanking from 1928,[73] and Peng Hua-tsing (ordained 1932) served at Sintien for five years before brigandage there halted his work in 1927.[74] Wan Hsien-tseh spent three years training at Nanking before ordination as deacon in 1936.[75] They were often exposed to considerable danger from communist insurgents who targeted Chinese pastors and church workers in the mid-1930s, especially around Ningyuan and Taochow.[76] As the number of European missionaries declined in the 1930s, Chinese priests took on more of the administration of the diocese. By 1935, Chinese priests in Kwangsi-Hunan outnumbered missionary clergy by two to one, more often than not leading their fellow Chinese as pastors-in-charge of some of the largest mission stations in the diocese. Bishops John Holden and Percy Stevens (1933-50) were unfailingly complimentary in their assessment of their evangelical work.

Bishop Holden's greatest regard, however, was reserved for one of the newer clergy who was not ordained to the priesthood until 1931. Addison Hsu had been known to Holden since 1912 when, as a thirteen-year-old at St Paul's in Siangtan, he was singled out as 'one of the brightest youths possible to meet', top in nearly every subject. His 'smart, clean, winning ways' made him a favourite with both masters and boys alike, and Holden felt that this was just

---

71 Addison K. S. Hsu, 'A Chinese view of the Sixth Diocesan Synod', *Newsletter*, 82 (Apr 1928), 808.

72 John Holden, 'Bishop's letter', *Newsletter*, 86 (Jun 1929), 3; 'Letter from Chinese clergy to the Christians of the Diocese', ibid., 5-6.

73 CMSA, G1.CH5.O/1919/12, Resolutions of Conference, 17-20 January 1919; *Newsletter*, 95 (Oct 1931), 4.

74 *Newsletter*, 81 (Jan 1928), 783-84.

75 *Newsletter*, 116 (Jan 1937), 3.

76 *Newsletter*, 108 (Jan 1935), 4-5.

what the church needed for its future work in the diocese. Ten years later, Hsu returned to Yungchow as a 'brilliant young university graduate' and 'bright Christian' to be appointed vice-principal of All Saints middle school, the training ground for the diocese's future leaders.[77] Even as a layman, his preaching held congregations spellbound, and by 1928 he was 'one of the leading Chinese workers in the Diocese'. He was one of the few Chinese pastors who wrote articles for the *Diocesan Newsletter* and his command of English was said to be flawless. He 'took the lead' in matters of educational policy and acted as diocesan secretary and treasurer for many years. When the time came for ordination to the diaconate in 1929, he was described by Holden as 'outstanding' among the Chinese workers in the diocese; 'To him, more than to any other colleagues, I owe a great debt in the comparative smoothness with which the process of devolution from mission to diocesan control is now taking place.'[78] After spending four years in parish work and assisting both Holden and his successor, Bishop Percy Stevens, Hsu was sent to Ridley Hall in Cambridge for further studies in 1935-36 and for 'parochial experience' at Folkestone in Kent, before returning to China and being appointed archdeacon in December 1936.[79] Consecrated assistant bishop in 1941, he was elected in 1950 as the first and only Chinese bishop of Kwangsi-Hunan. His rapid rise through the ranks was unlike any other clerical career in the diocese. This was undoubtedly due to his prodigious administrative and pastoral skills, his relatively high level of education, and good command of English, which made him quite different from his clerical colleagues. He possessed a skill set that most rank and file Chinese workers in Kwangsi-Hunan had little opportunity of obtaining.

With the ordination of Addison Hsu, Bishop Holden felt that the future of the diocese was secure. He was no doubt thinking of Hsu when he addressed the diocesan Synod about leadership of the diocese in 1931:

> But most important of all is that we should continue to pray that God will prepare the man of His choice who may in due time take his place as the Chinese bishop of this diocese, for I seriously doubt if the Church will really get to grips with the situation till there is effective leadership provided by a consecrated Chinese from the chief place of control.[80]

Holden continued to lobby for the appointment of a Chinese bishop until his translation to the diocese of West China in 1933: 'As you know, it is my very great hope, within a few years, much less than ten I trust, to give way to a Chinese diocesan bishop.'[81] The House of Bishops of the CHSKH ultimately

77 *Newsletter*, 31 (Aug 1912), 133; 65 (Jun 1923), 435.
78 *Newsletter*, 71 (Mar 1925), 578; 88 (Dec 1929), 3-4.
79 Addison K. S. Hsu, 'A farewell letter', *Newsletter*, 114 (Jul 1936), 10-11.
80 CMSA, G1.CH5.O/1932/1, Proceedings and Resolutions of the 8th Meeting of the Diocesan Synod, 6-13 Nov 1931.
81 G1.CH5.O/1932/9, Holden to Gurney Barclay, 6 Jul 1932.

elected Percy Stevens rather than a Chinese to replace Holden in Kwangsi-Hunan, but it was only a matter of time before Addison Hsu would be consecrated assistant bishop in 1941.

Bishop Holden also tried to introduce the female diaconate into his diocese in the early 1930s as a way of involving Chinese women more fully in evangelical work. As early as 1924, a former student of the diocesan school at Siangtan was reported as wishing to become a deaconess,[82] but it was not until the General Synod of the CHSKH approved a canon for the ordination of deaconesses in 1929 that any serious proposals were made for the training of women. Unfortunately, neither of the Chinese women identified for the diaconate were ordained. Miss Liu Ya-hsiu, a teacher from the girls' school at Ta Yong Kiang near Guilin, was sent to the Wuchang Union Theological Seminary in 1931 but does not appear to have completed the course,[83] and Miss Chen Lien-tsing, a teacher at the Hengchow girls' school, died in early 1931 after a building collapse there.[84] Holden's plan to introduce women into the expanding ranks of the Chinese clergy in his diocese was therefore unsuccessful.

In many respects the Kwangsi-Hunan diocese was similar to the other British missions in China, especially in terms of the type of Chinese workers employed and the way they came to have a leading role in the church, but there were also some notable differences. It could be argued that the Chinese congregations of the Kwangsi-Hunan mission were poorer, more remote, and less well educated than most other regions of China at the turn of the twentieth century. This made recruitment of qualified Chinese workers extremely difficult, and one might expect a highly paternalistic approach to mission, where foreign missionaries would control the work for as long as possible in order to guide their Chinese flocks to a fuller understanding of the gospel message. Hewitt noted in 1977 that 'missionary paternalism died hard' within the China missions of the CMS, 'especially when linked to a deep-seated conviction that some treasures of Christian insight and understanding are of a sort that can only be built up over many centuries, and that their embodiment in an alien Western culture does not seriously impair their transmission to other cultures'.[85] There was certainly some spiritual paternalism in Kwangsi-Hunan, but the mission had been blessed by early leaders such as Louis Byrde and William Banister with their commitment to self-government for the new Chinese church they were helping to build, which was certainly deeper than that of the Parent Committee in London. The CMS headquarters delegation to

82 *Newsletter*, 68 (May 1924), 513.

83 CMSA, G1.CH5.O/1931/14, Resolutions of Boards and Committees of Synod, 30 Jul-1 Aug 1931; *Newsletter*, 94 (Jul 1931), 15.

84 *Newsletter*, 93 (Mar 1931), 25. A fuller discussion of the reasons for the failure of the female diaconate in south China may be found in Peter Cunich, 'Deaconesses in the South China Missions of the Church Missionary Society, 1922-51', in Philip Wickeri & Patricia Chiu, eds, *Christian women in Chinese society: The Anglican story* (forthcoming).

85 Hewitt, *The problems of success*, *vol.2*, 212.

the Far East in 1912-13 noted the aspirations of local churches for autonomy and stated that the aim of the Anglican communion was 'to keep steadily to the front the hope of securing and appointing in due course Chinese Bishops, their office and work being for the time undertaken by foreigners, who are paving the way for Chinese successors'.[86] In effect, the granting of that autonomy took a very long time in many parts of China, but in Kwangsi-Hunan the British missionaries were looking forward to the appointment of a Chinese bishop from as early as 1930.

Kwangsi-Hunan was the most recently established China mission of the CMS, and its late start brought it significant advantages. Mistakes made elsewhere were avoided and new ideas more readily adopted, especially when supported by an experienced and autocratic spiritual governor such as Bishop Banister. One of the greatest difficulties in Kwangsi-Hunan, as elsewhere in China, was finding suitable candidates for the ministry, so self-propagation remained a noble aim towards which the foreign missionaries strove as much as they could, but they still had to rely on the limited human resources of the diocese. Perhaps the most intractable problem, however, was achieving an adequate level of self-support, a difficulty not overcome until after the departure of the missionaries in 1950 and the imposition of necessarily pragmatic measures to support diocesan clergy and lay workers in a radically changed political environment. Although it is true that far greater progress was made in the South China mission than anywhere else in the country towards establishing a self-governing CHSKH church after 1912, it must not be forgotten that the South China mission was the earliest formed in China and had far more ordained Chinese clergy and better trained lay workers as leaders, so devolution was achieved far sooner than in the more recently formed dioceses.[87] Although some of the early Kwangsi-Hunan priests proved to be excellent pastors, competent administrators, and demonstrated their willingness to suffer for the faith, it was only in 1931 that Addison Hsu emerged as a Chinese priest eligible for the episcopate. Unlike some other missions where the events of 1927 elicited a hesitant and uncertain response from Chinese workers, those in Kwangsi-Hunan showed a determination that delighted and inspired the British missionaries. In the disturbed Kwangsi-Hunan mission field, the events of the late 1920s provided an opportunity for Chinese church workers, both clerical and lay, to take the lead in administering their own church, while foreign missionaries' respect for their Chinese co-workers grew and they became more determined to give them a fuller share in the government of the diocese.

---

86 Cyril Bardsley & Frederick Baylis, *Report of the CMS Delegation to the Far East, 1912-13* (London: CMS, 1913), 152.

87 Hewitt, *The problems of success*, 224.

Appendix

List of Chinese Clergy in the Kwangsi-Hunan Diocese, 1919-51

Ven. Archdeacon Chen Chi-chang (1920-50)
Rev. Fang Ling-seng (1915-18), seconded from Hankow
Rt. Rev. Addison Ki-song Hsu (1929-51), asst bishop, 1941-51; bishop, 1951
Rev. Liu Han-hsin (1948-51)
Rev. Lu Chen-nan (1931-51)
Rev. Peng Hua-tsing (1932-51)
Rev. Sen Ming-shui (1946-51)
Rev. Song Pu-ren (1920-45)
Rev. Song Tsong-chen (1918-39)
Rev. Su Ren-ping (1926-51)
Rev. Tseng Kwang-shuen (1929-45)
Rev. Wan Hsien-tseh (1936-51)
Rev. Wu Hong-ching (1917-22)
Rev. Yang Chen-chang (1935-51)
Rev. Yu Shao-wen (1921-48)

Dates refer to ordination to the diaconate or first arrival in the diocese as priest, and departure from the diocese or retirement.

An Indigenous CIM Medical Missionary and National Hero: Unveiling Complexities in the Story of Dr. Kao Gin-Cheng

Lauren Pfister and Liu Jihua

The "Golden City": An Unexpected Surprise

While working with Lanzhou University (蘭州大學) graduate student Chen Yanrong (陳妍蓉) on images of Chinese Christian people and communities in northwest China during the first four decades of the twentieth century, we came across an account of a previously little known Chinese Christian medical doctor who by the early 1920s had made a significant Christian impact in the city of Ganzhou (甘州, now known as Zhangye 張掖) in Gansu Province (甘肅) by establishing a communal Christian institution as well as a vital church community.[1] Oddly, no other Lanzhou University colleagues at that time had heard of Dr. Kao Gin-cheng (高金城醫生 Gao Jincheng, 1888-1938),[2] whose surname translates into English as "Tall" and given name means "Golden City".[3] It is not completely strange that academic colleagues in Lanzhou did not know about him, as that is a very considerable distance from the center of Dr. Kao's activities as a "medical-evangelist",[4] but a memorial museum had been

1 Discussed first in Pfister, Lauren F. & Chen Yanrong, 'Following the traces of Christians and Christian communities in Northwestern China from 1920 to 1936', *Chinese Missionary Alliance Seminary Journal* (*Jiandao shenxue yuan xuekan* 建道神学院学刊) 37, 1 (April 2012), 101-136, and subsequently in a revised work by the same authors, 'Notes from local and China Inland Mission sources about Christians and Christian communities in Northwestern China (1920-1936)', in Wong Man-kong, Kwok Wai-luen, & Lau Yee-cheung, eds, *法流十道：近代中国基督教区域史研究* [The religious [law] spread throughout the ten circuits: Studies of modern Chinese Christianity on the basis of regional perspectives] (Hong Kong: Alliance Bible Seminary, 2013), 593-612.

2 This transcription of his name is found in the Rev. Frank Houghton's memorial volume, *George King: Medical evangelist* (London: The China Inland Mission, 1930), 41.

3 From articles providing oral records of Ms. Gou Chongjian 苟崇儉, whose Christian relative established the Jincheng Elementary School in Zhangye City in Kao's name in 1943, published in the Hero Gao Jincheng Memorial Museum booklet. We are informed that Dr. Kao's personal name at birth was Guting 固亭. See 陳金榮 姚興宏 主編 [Chen Jinrong & Yao Xinghong, eds], *祁連忠魂高金城: 高金城和張掖人民營救紅西路軍將士事蹟* [Qilian's faithful Gao Jincheng: An account of Gao Jincheng and the people of Zhangye rescuing the Red Army] (張掖: 高金城烈士紀念館，2012 [Zhangye: The Hero Gao Jincheng Memorial Museum, 2012])，第1頁及第114頁 [pp.1 & 114].

4 The unhyphenated term 'medical evangelists' is first found in Houghton's volume about George King, and we use it with the hyphen to indicate the special nature of this work.

established in his name by 2010[5] and a picture of him and the street front of his community church building in Ganzhou had appeared in a 1925 China Inland Mission (內地會) publication by three notable missionaries.[6] By 2013 Lauren Pfister became thoroughly intrigued at the prospect of studying this person, but even in May 2013 there appeared to be little information from local sources about the man and the Christian community he established. Since then, however, a whole range of new discoveries has encouraged us to pursue this research and start an investigation into the remarkable lives of Dr. Kao Gin-cheng, some of his family members, and the church communities he helped establish in Gansu.

In what follows we link Dr. Kao's life and work to events in Gansu during the Warlord period (1916-1927), the First Chinese Communist Civil War (1927-1937), and the first few years of the Second United Front (1937-1941).[7] We highlight some matters that should be considered in the light of Dr. Kao's disappearance in early February 1938, including later claims about his being murdered by members of local armies associated with a regional Muslim warlord.[8] Before delving into more controversial dimensions of his story, we summarize what is generally understood about Dr. Kao's life, drawing on recollections from his son about his personal life and family members, and information from what we consider reliable sources.

Dr. Kao Gin-cheng's Life and its Significance

Kao grew up in an impoverished family in a small village in Henan Province (河南) and was originally given the name Gin-cheng (Jincheng 金城), also

---

5 As documented in 朱興忠 著, '感受紅色力量 – 高金城烈士紀念館建設紀實', *張掖日報* 2010 年 8 月 8 日第 1 版。[Zhu Xingzhong, 'Sensing the strength of the red: A record of the establishment of the Hero Gao Jincheng Memorial Museum', *Zhangye Daily*, August 8, 2010, first page.

6 Works by A. Mildred Cable (usually 'Mildred Cable') and Francesca L. French (usually 'Francesca French') provide a significant amount of information drawn from long term personal interactions with Dr. Kao, his family, and members of the Protestant Christian community which they helped to establish.

7 We follow the historical periodization of this complex part of twentieth century Chinese history found in Christopher R. Lew & Edwin Pak-wah Leung, *Historical dictionary of the Chinese Civil War* (Lanham: The Scarecrow Press, Inc., 2013).

8 As claimed in great detail in the first essay in the volume produced by the Hero Gao Jincheng Memorial Museum (陳&姚, *祁連忠魂高金城*, 13-15). That essay was originally written by two Lanzhou people, Zheng Renquan & Quan Shiying, whose interpretive position was strongly supportive of a Communist presentation of Dr. Kao Gin-cheng's later years, and published in 1987 as 鄭仁泉 全士英 著, '祁連魂 — 黨的忠誠朋友高金城烈士', *人物* 1987 年第 4 期， 90-101 [Zheng Renquan & Quan Shiying, 'The Soul of the Qilian [Mountains]: The Faithful Friend of the Party, Hero Gao Jincheng', *People*, 4 (1987), 90-101. The museum's memorial volume relies substantially on that article, but was published 25 years later and adds many pictures of Dr. Kao and others (most found in the Zhangye City museum), while also changing some details to strengthen its claims.

taking on the style-name (*zi* 字) Guting (固亭).[9] Because of this, his given name appears in most public documents, but his style name is sometimes used by his relatives. This article employs the name by which he is known publicly, Kao Gin-cheng (Gao Jincheng in *pinyin*).

The question of how serious and authentic a Protestant Christian believer Dr Kao was needs to be answered because a leading article in a publication from the eponymous museum claims that he started to "lose faith" in Christian leaders in the early 1930s and take on a "firm faith" (*jianxin* 堅信) in Communism just months before he disappeared.[10] However, in a letter written to the museum and displayed in the section devoted to Dr. Kao's career and heroic actions, Kao's youngest son Kao Shih-chieh (Gao Shijie, 高士傑, 1927-) marvels at the fact that his father had never become a communist cadre, but willingly provided medical aid to several hundred wounded and needy Western Route Army soldiers[11] (*Xilu jun,* 西路軍).[12] Notably, an article originally written by female Christian family friend and co-worker Zhang Xiuyu (張秀玉) and oral interviews of Kao Shih-chieh conducted by his daughter (Dr. Kao's granddaughter) confirm that at the time his father disappeared this youngest son was living with him and his step-mother was serving in a hospital set up by Dr. Kao in Lanzhou.[13] The son has given us the following account of his father's

9 In at least one Chinese source transmitted orally by the daughter of the founder of the Jincheng Elementary School in Zhangye and in the museum's celebratory volume, the style name is said to be his original name. Those closest to him at different periods of his life – his second wife, Mou Yuguang (1895-1981), and Zhang Xiuyu (1900-1986), who lived in the Christian community in Zhangye and worked under him at the Gospel Hall Hospital – also referred to him by the style name Guting. Notably, Ms. Zhang claims to have grown up in the same village as Dr. Kao and later knew him in Zhangye beginning in 1920 when he served as her medical doctor. From an article written by her and edited later by others, it is obvious that she knew his family intimately, and she and her whole family continued to relate to his children and relatives as documented by photographs in the same volume. For the claim that this is Dr. Kao's original name, see *祁連忠魂高金城,* 114. For an illustration of the use of his personal name see the same volume, p.110. We have learned from his youngest son, Mr. Kao Shih-chieh, that Guting was his father's style name and not his given name (Linda Kao, 25 Oct 2016).

10 Quoting from *祁連忠魂高金城,* 13. These claims appear in the original version of the essay. See Zheng & Quan, *祁連魂 — 黨的忠誠朋友.*

11 The questionable political status of the Western Route army in Chinese Communist history in the period 1936-38 will not be addressed here but could be a matter for further deliberation in the light of the 'schema' and 'cultural script' of Dr. Kao as a national hero. The shaping of heroes by socially reinforced schemas is addressed in the last section of our paper.

12 So significant was this claim that the son, Shih-chieh, followed that Chinese sentence with three exclamation points. The letter is displayed among the exhibits on the top floor of the museum devoted to Dr. Kao. Written on stationery with the letterhead of the New York company with which he was affiliated at the time and dated '4/1/2013', it is addressed to the director of the museum.

13 A narrative written originally by Zhang Xiuyu (known as 'Dr. Zhang' to Dr. Kao's youngest son) contains a reminiscence that was edited and included in the museum's celebratory volume, entitled '*Wo suo zhidao de Gao Jincheng yijia* 我所知道的高金城一家' (The Gao Jincheng family that I knew). Ms. Zhang says that Dr. Kao disappeared on the fourth day of the lunar New Year and she was informed two days later by his son, Shih-chieh, that his father had not returned. This testimony is very significant and includes other details revealed later in this article. For the whole passage see *祁連忠魂高金城,* 110.

religious activities and devotional habits.[14] "There was a park adjacent to their Hospital in Zhangye", where both the father and son lived, and it was the regular pattern of his father to go there "by himself every morning with his [B]ible". Subsequently, there was a regular morning worship service led by Dr. Kao which "included all the family, medical and household staff. Breakfast would follow and then the hospital would open for business." After the hospital closed for the day at around 5 o'clock in the afternoon there was another worship service that lasted only "10 to 15 minutes". Dr. Kao would regularly "talk about some section in the [B]ible" and sometimes a hymn would be sung. In addition to the events involving all those involved in the hospital work, it was their family practice to offer a prayer of thanksgiving (referred to as "grace") "prior to their meals" and at the end of the day father and son would pray "before they went to bed". Shih-chieh was about ten years old in 1937-38, but these routines were deeply etched in his memory because of their consistency and certainly indicate that Dr. Kao was a very serious and disciplined Christian on the eve of his disappearance. In this light, then, and in order to enrich the understanding of Christian dimensions of Dr. Kao's life that may not be appreciated by contemporary Chinese historians and cadres, we offer the following synopsis of the nature of Dr. Kao's Christian experiences. We drew on materials not generally accessible to Chinese speakers because they were published in English, as well as information from his youngest son (now in his mid-90s and living in the USA) communicated to us very recently in correspondence with his granddaughter, Linda Kao.[15]

Having grown up in a poor peasant family, the teenaged Kao Gin-cheng sought work that would allow him to study and came into contact with missionaries from the China Inland Mission.[16] Through their teaching and personal influence, the young Gin-cheng became a Christian believer when he was 14.[17] People recognized that he was bright, and he was offered an opportunity to study medicine through a lengthy apprenticeship starting at age 16.[18] He chose to study with CIM medical educators in a relatively newly established hospital in Kaifeng and completed a twelve-year course of study in eleven years. This was 1915 and, aged 27, Kao was already married to a

14 Recorded by his granddaughter, Linda Kao, and sent to Pfister on 5 Jan 2015. This is the second of seven questions Mr. Kao Shih-chieh responded to in that correspondence.

15 Details of the correspondence with Linda Kao are given at the end of the article.

16 A fairly thorough account of his early life in CIM materials is found in Mildred Cable & Francesca French, *Through Jade Gate and Central Asia: An account of journeys in Kansu, Turkestan and the Gobi Desert* (London: Hodder and Stoughton, 1947), 43-45. See also Houghton, *George King*, 25-27. The museum volume carries details and photographs related to this earlier period of Kao's life; see *祁連忠魂高金城*, 1-5.

17 Protestant Christian sources generally state simply that 'he became a Christian'. It can be concluded that because he had these experiences as a child, he was very open to the children he met in Ganzhou and elsewhere.

18 Christian sources emphasize that this was not his father's desire, and so the possibility of Christian education even before he was offered the opportunity to study medicine produced some conflict within his family.

Christian peasant woman surnamed Wu (武)[19] and had two daughters, an elder one who died young and a younger, named Hsieh-Chieh (雪潔).[20] He was a star pupil and was approached with a number of lucrative career options which were particularly attractive to him as a husband and father of two.[21] Yet it was right at this time that Kao received a personal challenge and request from a young CIM medical teacher whom he had befriended, Dr. George Edwin King (1887-1927).[22] Soon after this, in his evening prayers Kao experienced a dramatic and profound sense of God's will for his life which he immediately shared with his wife. They agreed to move to the previously "uncharted realm" of Gansu Province[23] and soon afterwards Kao went first to the provincial capital of Lanzhou and began working as a medical intern and doctor in collaboration with Dr. George King and others[24] at the newly established Borden Memorial Hospital (博德恩醫院). When he called for his wife and children to join him, a new and transformative stage of their family life began. From that time onward, sometimes together and other times individually, Kao and King made itinerant missionary trips into areas around Lanzhou, coming into contact with many kinds of Chinese people and members of ethnic groups in that vast region; King was particularly drawn to the various kinds of Muslims in the region[25] while Kao found interacting with Mongolian and Tibetan Buddhists especially attractive, challenging and interesting.[26]

---

19 In the document where Mr. Kao Shih-chieh wrote down the Chinese names of all his family members (Linda Kao, 25 Oct 2016), he refers to his mother, Mrs. Gao Wu (高武氏) who added the name of her husband to her birth name in Chinese Christian fashion. He could not recall her given name. Apparently, she came from the same area as Dr. Kao.

20 'Hsieh-Chieh' means 'Snow Clean'. This was learned from their youngest brother, Mr. Kao Shih-chieh (Linda Kao, 25 Oct 2016). He remembers visiting the grave of his elder sister, but could not recall her name (Linda Kao, 27 Nov 2016). According to him, there were six children in the original Kao family. An account written by Zhang Xiuyu, medical doctor and Christian family friend, suggests that Shih-chieh, born in 1927, was probably as much as 15 to 18 years younger than his eldest siblings. For Dr. Zhang Xiuyu's account, see *祁連忠魂高金城*, 107-108.

21 Details about Kao's training in the Kaifeng medical school and elsewhere in eastern China are found in most biographical sketches, whether in Chinese or English, but more thorough and colourful accounts are offered in Houghton, *George King*, 25-26, and the article on Kao in 黃錫培著, *捨命的愛: 中國內地會宣教士小傳* (Petaluma: 美國中信出版社, 2007 年), 184-187 [Huang Xipei, *Sacrificial love: Portraits of China Inland Mission missionaries* (Petaluma: CCM Publishers, 2007)].

22 Christian sources are very clear about this, but although Chinese Communist Party sources can name a number of the foreign medical doctors with whom Kao studied, they are generally not aware of this important relationship with the Scottish Dr. King, who was apparently only one year older than Kao and had been an excellent medical student at the University of Edinburgh. Consult relevant portions of Houghton, *George King*, 40-41, and Mildred Cable & Francesca French, *Dispatches from North-West Kansu* (London: The China Inland Mission, 1925).

23 By the term 'uncharted', Protestant leaders meant places where Protestant missionaries had rarely lived. However, there had been Roman Catholic missionaries in that region of northwest China for more than a century, close to what is now Wuwei city of (武威) in central Gansu.

24 Details for all claims here and below are in Houghton, *George King*, 44.

25 Houghton, *George King*, 45.

26 Cable & French, *Through Jade Gate and Central Asia*.

Over the next few years Kao's leadership abilities became more obvious, and together with George King and others he continued to pray, discuss and plan for evangelistic opportunities that would move him and his family farther northward and westward within the province, where no Protestant missionary had previously resided and worked. By as early as 1917 he had become convinced that the city of Ganzhou would be the right place to initiate a new evangelistic effort to create a vital and lasting Christian community.

In 1919 Kao joined together with a small group of Chinese Christians to form the economic and institutional basis of a new church in Ganzhou, using his medical skills to attract those in need, and within a few years had coordinated with others to purchase land and build a special church community within which he became a well-recognized and much relied on Christian leader, community pastor, and active medical doctor.[27]

It was in the Fall of 1924 that Kao, his family, and the growing primarily Chinese Christian community were joined by a trio of senior female evangelists: A. Mildred Cable (蓋群英, 1878-1952), Evangeline F. French (馮貴珠, 1869-1960), and Francesca T. French (馮貴石, 1871-1960).[28] The "Trio" were competent in Chinese and Uyghur[29] and worked in a large area of Gansu from the mid-1920s until 1935, when the political and military situation in northwest China became so instable that they could not continue their itinerant mission work and left China forever by means of the Trans-Siberian railway. While based in China they kept in touch with the Christian community in Ganzhou, and for several years in the mid-1920s were part of it. Dr. Kao's youngest son, Shih-chieh, recalls these three women very fondly, describing how his mother learned some basic English from them so that she could use it with them at times, even though they were fluent in Chinese. He tells also how his father treated them as "family elders", indicating the level of intimacy they

27 Most clearly explained in a brief chapter in Cable & French, *Dispatches*.

28 These three women had lived and worked in a girls' school in the city of Huozhou, Shaanxi province, for at least twenty years. As CIM missionaries they applied to change from educational missionaries to itinerant evangelists in the Gansu region, which at that time included parts of what is now Ningxia, Inner Mongolia, and Qinghai. It was at the start of their very unusual career as 'The Trio' or 'The Three Righteous Women' that they met Dr. Kao and agreed to join him and his Ganzhou Christian community, which proved to be an immensely significant and creative missionary collaboration. Consult Cable & French, *Through Jade Gate and Central Asia*, and Lauren F. Pfister & Chen Yanrong, "*Following the traces*", 101-136.

29 An overview of the Trio's lives is presented in William James Platt, *Three women: Mildred Cable, Francesca French, Evangeline French: The authorized biography* (London: Hodder and Stoughton, 1964) and Linda Benson, *Across China's Gobi: The lives of Evangeline French, Mildred Cable, and Francesca French of the China Inland Mission* (Norwalk: EastBridge, 2008), and at least one of their volumes has been published in Chinese: 黃梅峰 & 麥慧芬 譯 Mildred Cable & Francesca French 著, *戈壁沙漠* (台北: 馬可孛羅文化，2000年) [Huang Meifeng Mai Huifen, trans., Mildred Cable & Francesca French, *The Gobi Desert* (Taipei: Marco Polo Culture, 2000)]. A number of works written by Mildred Cable and Francesca French directly relay conversations with Dr. Kao as well as other accounts of his life, character, work, and critical situations he faced, and are referred to relatively often in our article.

shared.[30] As we have already seen, it is from writings by these women[31] as well as a memorial volume published in 1930 to honor the medical-evangelist, Dr. George King, who died in a drowning accident in 1927,[32] that we learned about Dr. Kao's character, medical work and the Christian community built around it, as well as his missionary methods.

Although the end of the Warlord period around 1927 saw some intense anti-Christian sentiment that increased difficulties for both foreign missionaries and their Chinese church members through much of the country, Dr. Kao and the Ganzhou community began to thrive with support of the Trio in teaching and evangelism and through engagement with various local and itinerant people who passed through Ganzhou.[33] It was during this period that Dr. Kao faced some of his most difficult challenges, which had to do with false charges against him made by Wu Tongren (吳桐仁),[34] the "governor of the prison" or *zhenshoushi* (鎮守使) in Suzhou (肅州), that he had "led an armed mob to break open the city jail in order to release a certain Moslem prisoner."[35] This occurred when many Christian leaders had been opposed publicly in "successful demonstrations" by "anti-Christian organizations in large cities" and was an opportunity to accuse Dr. Kao of a crime that would lead to his execution.[36] Nevertheless, this outlandish falsehood produced such a sense of public injustice that the case became well known and thus documented in some detail in both Christian and Chinese materials.[37] Dr. Kao was arrested by members of the police force under Mr. Wu's supervision and remained in jail

30 As described in correspondence received from Linda Kao on 7 November 2016.

31 Most of their more than twenty works were produced by two of them, 'Mildred Cable' and 'Francesca French'. We have chosen three with direct reference to Dr. Kao: *Dispatches*, *Through Jade Gate and Central Asia*, and Mildred Cable, Francesca French & Evangeline French, *A desert journal: Letters from Central Asia* (London: Hodder and Stoughton, 1949).

32 See Houghton, *George King*, 75-84, in which the May 1927 tragedy was also described.

33 Accounts of this period are found in Eva French, Mildred Cable, & Francesca French, 'The far North-West: A circular letter (from Liangchowfu, Kansu, April 11, 1924)', *China's Millions* (August 1924), 126-128 (Assumed UK edition); Eva French, Mildred Cable, & Francesca French, 'Progress in the far North West: A circular letter (from Kanchow, Kansu, July 8, 1924)', *China's Millions* (November 1924), 170-172 (Assumed UK edition); *Dispatches*, *Through Jade Gate*, and *Desert journal*, supplemented by Benson's thorough account in *Across China's Gobi* and Platt's *Three women*.

34 The Chinese name of this person was unknown to Christian sources, but is recorded in the museum account found in the next footnote. Very serious but trumped up charges were registered by Wú along with the statements of two other prominent public officials.

35 Cable & French, *Through Jade Gate*, 160, with slight changes (for example, changing 'gaol' to 'jail'). In Chinese the charge was written as *jié jiān zá yù, fàngzǒu fànrén* 劫监砸狱，放走犯人, and is found in *祁連忠魂高金城*, 3.

36 The historical context for the anti-Christian campaigns unleashed in numerous places during 1925 is thoughtfully described in Cable & French, *Through Jade Gate*, 162-163.

37 It became the main topic of chs. 26 & 27, 'Gathering Clouds' and 'The Storm', of Cable & French's *Through Jade Gate and Central Asia*, found particularly in *ibid*., 156-167, and is also discussed with corroborating details in *祁連忠魂高金城*, 3-4.

from 17 February 1926 until the first of June the same year;[38] subsequently, as a prisoner he was required to make the eighteen day trek to the provincial capital, Lanzhou, for the final hearing.

According to the Trio's records, after the initial charges were made and Dr. Kao imprisoned, the provincial governor confirmed that the charges were worthy of "the extreme penalty of the law" but added that if he were proven innocent, the civil magistrate would "personally be held responsible".[39] In fact, the "district judge" refused to "ratify this sentence" against Dr. Kao and the situation became far more ominous,[40] with Dr. Kao remaining in a filthy cell. Dr. Kao requested all his supporters to "refrain from any kind of interference".[41] Needless to say, this was an immensely disruptive experience for all the Christians, and they followed the matter with great concern and many prayers, until they were able to visit Dr. Kao in prison regularly.[42] As things progressed, the two "witnesses" – one a *daotai* (道台, a regional political administrator, "civil magistrate" or "mandarin" of the city), and the other a *nietai* (臬台, regional land superintendent[43]) – both "backed out", claiming that "only fear of torture had led them to give evidence".[44] Once the case proceeded toward its conclusion and Dr. Kao was officially exonerated, Wu Tongren escaped to "Turkestan" (today's Xinjiang) out of fear of being punished for corrupt practices.[45]

After he had endured this persecution, Dr. Kao's character and service as a medical doctor were noticed by the "Christian marshal" in Lanzhou, the

38 Cable & French, *Through Jade Gate*, 161. The length of the incarceration is given as 'forty-two days'.

39 This clever move on the part of the provincial governor is referred to in Cable & French, *Through Jade Gate*, 162.

40 Cable & French, *Through Jade Gate*, 163, clarify the situation thus: 'By the law of China, it is the Civil Magistrate who pronounces the sentence upon the prisoner; nevertheless, it cannot be carried into execution without the additional authority of the District Judge; therefore, when this Official was approached and asked to ratify the sentence upon Dr. Kao, he very indignantly replied: "I refuse to condemn a man whom we all know to be innocent. Every child in the Suchow streets knows that the prison door has never been forced, nor has any prisoner there been unofficially released".'

41 Ibid. Here the Trio admit that they 'duly informed our Lanchow friends of all the facts, urging them, if possible, to use their influence to secure an impartial inquiry'.

42 At first the Christians from 'the Mission Compound' could only pass on food and materials to the doctor through the jailers, and the initial period was full of 'suspense' and 'terrible'. Only after an official enquiry by a 'Special Commissioner' from Lanzhou was ordered was it possible for all the Christians, including the Trio, to visit Dr. Kao in the jail compound. Details in Cable & French, *Through Jade Gate*, 162-164 *in passim*.

43 The initial essay in the museum book identifies these two major political leaders as civil magistrate, Qi Lianyuan (齊連元), and superintendent of land, Zhu Zang (朱贊). It goes on to claim that military leaders Ma Lin (馬麟) and Ma Qi (馬麒) were known for their cruelty and suggests that they were involved, but Cable and French only mention 'two other most important officials of the city' as witnesses. See *祁連忠魂高金城*, 3, and Cable & French, *Through Jade Gate*, 162.

44 Quoting from Cable & French, *Through Jade Gate*, 164.

45 Both sources refer to this intention by the jailer, but it is confirmed as done in the museum essay.

warlord Yü-hsiang (馮玉祥, Feng Yuxiang, 1882-1948). Marshall Feng arranged for him to take up the post of "medical officer in charge of the Red Cross work in his own military hospital" and in other parts of the Republic of China for an interim period, possibly as long as for two years.[46]

As the first Chinese Communist Civil War began to have impact throughout the nation, Dr. Kao and the Christian community in Ganzhou had to endure great cultural pressures, serious threats, and some deeply felt losses. Famine had stricken the area in 1930[47] and the political situation became particularly difficult. In a letter from the latter part of 1930 the Trio did not mince their words about the general situation or the specific problems faced by the Ganzhou Christian community:[48]

> On making enquiries regarding a neighbouring town [near Ganzhou] which we hoped to visit, we found to our horror that, barring twenty survivors, its population had been wiped out, yet so fearful is everyone of espionage that this was not known in Suchow [Suzhou]. Incendiarism, pillage, rape and murder has been the order of the day.

Regarding the city of Ganzhou and its region, they recorded solemn news:

> In early November we reached Kanchow [Ganzhou], which township is in a chastened mood. A few miles outside the city gate we met soldiers carrying the head of a recently executed man, which was to be exposed in his native village as a warning to all. At the present time Islam rules and militarism is rampant. It is the peasant's privilege to feed, warm and clothe a large army, while he and his family are often without food, clothes or firing…The Kanchow Church has passed through much tribulation since the happy days of our first coming there. We are still too close to events, which broke in a storm of persecution on the Church, to measure the effect on the large number who professed and called themselves Christians…[49]

That "storm" had certainly begun with the unjustified arrest of Dr. Kao, and during his subsequent absence of several years other things had transpired. Notably it was in May of the same year that other Chinese doctors and Christian citizens were attacked by Muslim-led armed forces in the southern Gansu town of Qinzhou (秦州), resulting in the death of over 4000 people, including Dr. Wu Baoying (吳寶瑛, 1897-1930)[50] a Christian graduate of Borden Hospital whom Dr. Kao had known.

By the early 1930s, Dr. Kao had also suffered great personal loss through the death of his first wife, probably sometime in 1930 or 1931, and the death of

46 Cited from Cable & French, *Through Jade Gate*, 167. This claim is also confirmed in the original essay by Zheng & Quan, *祁連魂* and in its later version in the museum's celebratory volume of 2012.

47 Consult articles about these problems in *China's Millions*, issues for 1930 and 1932.

48 Cited from *A desert journal*. This volume was first published in 1934.

49 French, Cable & French, *A desert journal*, 152-153 *in passim*.

50 As narrated in a chapter dedicated to Dr. Wu's life, and including details about the impact of that attack on his younger brother, other Chinese Christians, and medical missionaries in the same town at that time. Consult 黃, *捨命的愛*, 198-208.

their eldest son, Ying-chieh[51] after all six of their children had reached maturity. When this son graduated in 1930 from Yenching University (燕京大學), the premier Protestant university in China, he had apparently become enamored of the daughter of a warlord. Their experience of warlords in northwest China made Dr. Kao and his wife unwilling to agree to marriage between the two and their son killed himself in anger.[52] So traumatic was this experience for Mrs. Kao that she was overwhelmed with sorrow and probably died within a year. The deaths of two of his closest family members would have had a profound impact on Dr. Kao, but we learn from his youngest son that that his father remained a very committed Christian leader to the end of his days, in spite of this profound family tragedy.[53] Subsequently the younger children were committed to the care of a Christian family and an orphanage school in the Beijing area, the Fragrant Mountains Charitable School for Young Children (香山慈幼院, Xiangshan Ciyouyuan).[54] Sometime afterwards the widowed Dr. Kao returned to Lanzhou with the intention of establishing a new hospital.

It was under these conditions that in 1934, Dr. Kao married his second wife, the Christian Mou Yuguang (牟玉光, 1895-1981), who had served as head nurse of the Beijing hospital where Dr. Kao had worked as leading medical administrator during the early 1930s.[55] Having set up the hospital, Dr. Kao returned to Ganzhou in the fall of 1934, followed by his wife later. Due primarily to his medical work he had already been in contact with communist cadres in various places including Shanghai and Beijing, but the Second United Front was still three years away and these relationships were not yet part of his normal ties. On returning to Ganzhou, Dr. Kao once again opened up his medical-evangelist ministry in the Gospel Hall Hospital, maintaining the unusual Christian community in what had become an increasingly unstable and violent political milieu. It was during this time that he met various Communist

51 Their Christian friend Zhang Xiuyu mentioned only 4 children, in *祁連忠魂高金城*, 108-109.

52 This account was given by the youngest son, Shih-chieh, who was probably three years old at the time, but remembers the tragedy concretely and with considerable sadness. Communicated in two emails with his daughter, Linda Kao, on the 13 and 27 Nov 2016.

53 It is thus completely understandable that the youngest son, living with Dr. Kao during the last days before his father disappeared, could clearly remember the pattern of his father's personal and communal Christian piety, but nothing about his mother's, because she died when he was very young. Citing correspondence from Linda Kao, received on 5 Jan 2015.

54 The name of this institution was written down after the names of most of his family members, with the additional word 'Beijing' in front of the school name. Found on a single hand-written text sent on 25 October 2016.

55 A note in Zhang Xiuyu's article mentions that in the early 1970s Mou Yuguang joined the Communist Party. See *祁連忠魂高金城*, 112-113. This should be understood as the result of her submission to an intense 'propaganda of integration' campaign towards the end of the Cultural Revolution. See Ellul's appendix, 'Mao Tse-Tung's Propaganda', in *Propaganda: The formation of men's attitudes* (New York: Vintage Books, 1973), 303-313.

military leaders,[56] employing the same kind of flexibility that Christian military leader Feng Yuxiang did in crossing ideological divides.[57]

The cruelty and instability of life in 1930s Republic of China should not be underestimated, and the heroic character of Dr. Kao Gin-cheng and the members of the Christian community in Ganzhou during the period 1924 to 1937 was made manifest in events and difficulties they endured; these suggest that the extraordinary quality of these people's lives should be certainly be highlighted.[58] Kao and others had already shown a Christian expression of heroism that was much appreciated by some residents of Ganzhou but which also provoked rivalry and some animosity against him from some local leaders. The decision to align himself with Communist armed forces associated with the West Route Army or Sixth Route Communist Army, which would pass through the Ganzhou region in 1937 and early 1938, undoubtedly represented a further step of boldness that would mark Kao's destiny. His commitment to work within a local underground cell in Ganzhou supporting the Chinese Communist army, to some degree reflects both the Second United Front (1937-1941) collaboration between the Nationalist and Communist forces to oppose the Japanese[59] and increasing fears about the cruelty of the regionally dominant Muslim political General Ma Bufang (馬步芳, 1903-1975) and his forces. Kao and the Communists met occasionally in the Gospel Hall Hospital in Ganzhou during the Summer and Fall of 1937. Another reason for Dr. Kao's support of these Communist army leaders was the immense losses they had experienced in major battles between the Sixth Route Communist Army and local Muslim-led armies; he hoped that under the new United Front he could help wounded Chinese soldiers from that army regain health. In the end, he and others provided medical support to over two hundred soldiers from various places in the nearby Qilian mountains (祁連山) and villages on the Gansu plains, arranging for them to enter the Gospel Hall Hospital by a back door with a pre-established secret code. The vast majority managed to survive, part of the "great rescue" in which Dr. Kao played a major role, ultimately making him a

56 Some matters are not mentioned in most Christian literature I have reviewed, but highlighted in works by Communist historians and intellectuals.

57 As seen in 王光遠 著, *馮玉祥與中國共產黨*，(北京: 中央文獻出版社, 2004) [Wang Guangyuan, *Feng Yuxiang and the Chinese Communist Party* (Beijing: Central Literature Publishing Society, 2004)]. General Feng's wife became a Communist cadre in the 1930s, indicating the significance of that connection for the general himself.

58 A Chinese novelist of this period, Feng Zhi (馮至, 1905-1993), wrote in German to another (translated into English by Pfister) on 14 September 1933, 'In China one lives a God-forsaken life, and dies the most spiritually impoverished death. Truly in our time brutality and banality reign. My soul relies on things that are vanishing, so that my thoughts are focused on a few good and great deaths [of persons known to him]'. Quoted from the original German in Zhang Huiwen, *Kulturtransfer über Epochen und Kontinente: Feng Zhi's Roman* 'Wu Zixu' *als Begegnung von Antike und Moderne, China und Europa* [Cultural adaptations transcending epochs and continents: Feng Zhi's novel, *Wu Zixu*, as an encounter between ancient and modern, China and Europe] (Berlin: Walter de Gruyter GmbH., 2012), 53, fn.51.

59 As highlighted in helpful detail in *祁連忠魂高金城*, 8-9.

national hero in the eyes of Communist Party historians – this has recently been featured in a regional television series.[60] It was in this complex environment that Dr. Kao disappeared in early February 1938. He was reported missing by his second wife, who received an initial report from Zhang Xiuyu, who had been alerted to his disappearance by his youngest son, Shih-chieh, who was living with him in Ganzhou at the time.[61] Only about a month later, his loss as "a good friend of the Chinese Communists" was finally reported to Communist military leaders;[62] because his death was assumed to have been ordered by enemies of the Communists, Dr. Kao status as a national hero was already firmly established when he was given the official title in the late 1960s.

The Need to Reconstruct Dr. Gao Jincheng's Story: Some Interpretive Concerns

In reviewing relevant materials one cannot avoid coming across problems such as lack of basic information, conflicting accounts, and inconsistent details.

The lack of shared information between Christian and Communist Party sources must be recognized. In writings produced by authors belonging to the CIM or other missionary societies resident in China[63] we have found important accounts of Dr. Kao's earlier years in Lanzhou and Ganzhou. In the writings of the CIM missionary "Trio" we have discovered numerous details derived from their personal dialogues with Dr. Kao over at least two years (from 1924 to 1926) when they were working with him in Ganzhou. None of these details are found in many of the current Communist historians' writings that we have read,

60 Consult 沈擁軍 總編導 劉靜 陳喜平 編導, *大營救 – 背後的真實故事*, 三盤, 十二集 (蘭州: 甘肅電視台文化影視频道，2012 年) [Shen Yongjun, General Director; Liu Jing and Chen Xiping, Writers and Directors (2012). *The Great rescue: The true story behind the events*. Three DVDs, twelve programs (Lanzhou: Gansu Television Station Cultural Film and Television Channel, 2012)].

61 This detail is not mentioned in other accounts that we have read, but is found in the article originally written by Zhang Xiuyu in *祁連忠魂高金城*, 110.

62 As mentioned in the memorial museum volume's leading article, it was Xie Juezai and the local leader of the Eight Route Army, Wu Xiuquan, who reported Dr. Kao's 'sacrifice' to the central authorities. Consult *祁連忠魂高金城*, 14.

63 Note that the historical account prepared by Wang Jin & Yang Huijuan is a more balanced interpretation. See 王勁 楊惠娟, '牧師·醫生·戰士: 記為營救紅軍西路軍英勇獻身的高金城牧師', in *中國宗教*, 4 (2005), 22-25 [Wang Jin & Yang Huijuan, 'Pastor, medical doctor, warrior: remembering Pastor Gao Jincheng, who heroically sacrificed his life in rescuing the Communist Army's West Route Army", *Chinese Religions*, 4 (2005), 22-25], and the Christian account in a Nanjing Christian journal by Kou follows the account in the Hero Gao Jincheng Museum commemorative volume, 寇建國 著, '血灑祁連愛國心 濟世救人榮主名: 記為營救工農紅軍西路 軍英勇獻身的基督徒革命烈士高金城' in *天風*, 5 (2013), 50-52 [Kou Jianguo, 'Blood spilled on the Qilian Range for the love of country, having compassion for the age and saving people for the glory of the Lord's name: Remembering the Christian revolutionary hero, Gao Jincheng, who heroically sacrificed himself in rescuing the workers and farmers of the Communist West Route Army', *Tian Feng*, 5 (2013), 50-52]. By contrast, Huang's article in a Chinese book published in the USA does not include any reference to these interpretive materials. See 黃, *捨命的愛*.

though to its credit the first essay in the museum's tome does at least mention basic details related to Kao's childhood conversion, training under CIM medical mentorship, and role as a medical-evangelist. Similarly, accounts of Dr. Kao's involvement with Communist armed forces in 1937-38 highlighted in writings by cadres and historians[64] are generally not found in most contemporary Christian writings. Notably, they are also not cited in the more recent accounts by the Christian historian Li Yading (李亞丁) or the Christian writer Huang Xipei.[65] Most significantly, a surprisingly comprehensive account of his disappearance in February 1938 appears in the celebratory volume published by the Zhangye museum honoring Dr. Kao's heroic sacrifice and at least one online resource about him.[66] These publications claim that Dr. Kao was murdered by Han Qigong (韓起功, 1886-1951), a subordinate of General Ma Bufang, who also served as a local municipal leader in Ganzhou. Significantly, this claim is mentioned even though Ma was at least nominally supported by the Nationalist government. The details of the murder scene are vividly portrayed in the museum volume; not only are the means of torture and death explicitly stated, but also the impromptu burial place of the body ("in the back garden of the Yamen" in Ganzhou).[67] If these details were true they would constitute a major breakthrough in a murder case that has been a long-standing mystery, specifically because of problems in identifying the manner of Dr. Kao's death and the location of his remains.

---

64 Such as 沒有姓名, '高金城同志生平簡介', in *甘肅社會科學*, 3 (1980) [Anonymous, 'A brief biography of Comrade Gao Jincheng', *Gansu Social Sciences*, 3 (1980)]; 沒有姓名, '懷念幫助我黨營救西路軍的馬德涵，趙守鈺先生及高金城烈士', in *青海民族學院學報*, 1 (1982), 46-48 [Anonymous, 'Mournfully remembering Ma Dehan, Zhao Shouyu, and Hero Gao Jincheng, those who helped our party [by] rescuing the West Route Army', *Academic Bulletin of the Qinghai National College*, 1 (1982), 46-48]; 必信, '瞻仰高金城先生碑誌', *甘肅檔案*, 2 (1984), 30-31 [Bi Xin (Pen-name meaning 'Must Trust') 'Respectfully looking into the Gao Jincheng stele', *Gansu Archives*, 2 (1984), 30-31]; 王存福, '高金城捨生忘死營救西路軍戰士', *四川統一戰線*, 4 (2005), 20-21 [Wang Cunfu, 'Gao Jincheng lost his life rescuing warriors of the West Route Army', *Sichuan United Front*, 4 (2005), 20-21].

65 Consult Huang, *捨命的愛*, which includes a lengthy article about Dr. Kao, but admits even in the title that his birth and death dates are unknown, and uses the incorrect characters 高建成 for his name. See pages 183-197. That account of Dr. Kao's life and work ends around 1931, and does not deal with any historical materials other than Christian ones. While a helpful Chinese summary of those English materials for a wider audience, it contains nothing outside of Christian sources cited. Details of Dr. Kao's life and works in the online article by Li Yading (n.d.) are also limited to Christian sources and Kao's name is written incorrectly. Consult Li Yading, 'Gao Jiancheng (Kao Gin-cheng), 1888-', trans. G. Wright Doyle, in the *Biographical Dictionary of Chinese Christianity*, found online at http://222.bdcconline.net/en/stories/g/gao-jiancheng.php. Chinese version 李亞丁著 (年期不詳) '高建成 Gao Jiancheng 1988-', in *華人基督教史人物辭典*. http://www.bdcconline.net/zh-hant/stories/by-person/g/gao-jiancheng.php.

66 See 高金城 (Gao Jincheng) at the Baidu baike website 百度百科, http://baike.baidu.com/view/1076645.htm (accessed 9 Oct 2016). This entry cites numerous passages directly from the first article in the museum volume without any additional reference. Though it does not include all the details found in that article, it does locate Dr. Kao's mutilated body in the place mentioned in the summary.

67 Consult the end of the first essay in *祁連忠魂高金城*, 14.

There are several significant reasons to doubt the veracity and historical reliability of details of Dr. Kao's final days concerning the dialogue with his captors, the means of torture, and where his body was buried.[68] For example, it is revealing that Kao's alleged murder is not included in the list of Han Qigong's nefarious deeds in a recently published account of Han's life.[69] If the claims made in the museum article were true, one would not expect the same volume to record that in 1982 an official ceremony was held at the Hualin Mountain (華林山) Heroes Burial Grounds to honor Dr. Kao, and that only personal paraphernalia representing him were laid to rest (*yiguanzhong* 衣冠冢) because his physical remains have not been recovered.[70] Added to this are the serious doubts recorded by Zhang Xiuyu, one of those closest to Dr. Kao's family, who in February 1938 received no satisfactory answer from anyone about the disappearance of the medical-evangelist. Her article, edited from an earlier published account, goes on to claim that only in 1950 did Ms. Zhang draw the conclusion (on the basis of other information) that the murderer had been Han Qigong.[71] Added to these doubts is a record made by Isobel Kuhn of a CIM missionary who had lived in the former home of the Kao family in Zhangye since 1948 and who in 1953 was being pressed to admit involvement in Dr. Kao's murder more than a decade earlier![72] All these accounts suggest that the leading article in the museum's celebratory volume does not contain sufficient evidence to confirm how Dr. Kao disappeared and died. Consequently, many questions remain about the claim that Han Qigong and those under his authority tortured and murdered Dr. Kao, burying his remains at the yamen.[73] It is at best a clever speculation, rather than a confirmed or confirmable historical fact.

When there is a diversity of claims between the sources, one feels obliged to resolve these factual contradictions as much as possible, or to indicate where insufficient information remains a problem. Here we consider some significant interpretive problems concerning facts about Dr. Kao.

There is confusion about when Dr. Kao was born; most Chinese sources put the date as 1886, while one later Christian source claims it was 1888. From the

---

68 The vast majority of these claims already appear in Zheng & Quan's, *祁連魂 — 黨的忠誠朋友*, but the version that appears in the museum's volume published in 2012 includes new elaborations of some of those claims, and is augmented by pictures and paintings.

69 This appears on the same website as that on which the former article on Dr. Kao was found. See *韩起功* (http://baike.baidu.com/view/3037165.htm (accessed 9 Oct 2016). According to this article, Han Qigong was born in Qinghai of the Sarlas (or Salas) ethnic minority.

70 See *祁連忠魂高金城*, 107 (photo and caption in lower left corner of page).

71 Also found in *祁連忠魂高金城*, 110-112.

72 See Isobel Kuhn, *Green leaf in drought* (Littleton: Overseas Missionary Fellowship, Inc., 2010), 105-106 (Probably first published in 1954). The date of the murder was given as 1936 instead of 1938, indicating misinformation from local and international sources even at that time.

73 Though the narrative in the memorial museum volume places the blame for Dr. Kao's murder directly upon Han Qigong, the citation of the military court's judgment that led to Han's execution says nothing about any involvement in the battles that destroyed the Sixth Route Army or the killing of Dr. Kao. Compare *祁連忠魂高金城*, 14, 194-196.

materials about Dr. Kao written by the Christians Cable and French, who worked with him in the mid-1920s, we learned more about his early life and have been able to determine the year of his birth as 1888.[74]

More troubling are the different forms of Dr. Kao's name in various contemporary English language sources, as well as one notable later one. For these materials, clarifying the context is very important, because there were many people surnamed "Kao" associated with the CIM and other missionary societies, but we regularly hear about our "Kao" or "Dr. Kao" in the context of Gansu. More specifically, we can be assured that when CIM's *China's Millions* mentions "Kao" or "Dr. Kao" in articles about Ganzhou, this is the subject of our research. We also come across "C. C. Kao" in the important *Chinese Recorder* missionary journal, and from contextual references to Kaifeng and Ganzhou identified him as our "Dr. Kao".[75] Nevertheless, this is not to say that no other "Dr. Kao" in Gansu was mentioned by Christian sources. In fact, a "Dr. J. Hillington Kao" mentioned in the January 1932 issue of *China's Millions* was an American missionary from Pennsylvania who worked in the southern part of the province.[76] Fortunately, on both a calling card[77] (one of the few items left from Dr. Kao's Ganzhou residence) and in the volume dedicated to Dr. George King we find consistent references to "Kao Gin-cheng".[78] In Chinese and English articles by Li Yading and a Chinese article written by Huang Xipei, Dr. Kao's full name is rendered "Kao Gian-cheng 高建成", alternative Chinese characters and romanizations that we take as incorrect.[79] This does not mean that all the issues in identifying Dr. Kao are clearly resolved.[80] Yet, we can confirm that the adult Dr. Kao usually referred to himself as "Kao Gin-cheng" rather than other possible forms.

In the previous section we presented a reconstructed biographical account of Dr. Kao's life that may seem incongruous to some scholars: Dr. Kao was an attested Chinese Christian leader and medical-evangelist, who as a Christian had good reason to sympathize with wounded and dying Chinese Communist soldiers left behind after battles with the local Muslim armies that dominated the region. Dr. Kao appears to have held both of these commitments together during very unstable late 1930s, and his ordination as a medical-evangelist in

74 Consult the account in *Dispatches from North-West Kansu*.

75 See 'All-Kansu United Church Conference', *The Chinese Recorder*, 51, 12 (December 1920), 881.

76 This reference occurs in the context of a long journey from Beijing to Lanzhou, and later writers may have confused the two men. See 'An interview with Mr. Findlay Andrew', *China's Millions* (January 1932), 6.

77 This calling card is kept at the museum and was shown to us by the staff.

78 This form of Dr. Kao's name in found in Houghton, *George King*, 41.

79 As seen particularly in the Chinese version of the article. See 李, *高建成*. These errors were also quickly spotted by Dr. Kao's son, Kao Shih-chieh.

80 A piece by a 'C. C. Kao' dealing with workers' conditions at a Chengdu Christian university might be Dr. Kao's only published article. He *may* have done research there, but we cannot be sure. See C. C. Kao, 'Chengtu campus labor conditions', *The Chinese Recorder*, 55, 8 (Aug 1924), 543-544.

Ganzhou by a group of indigenous and foreign missionaries in 1920 is evidence of this.[81] Many years later, Dr. Kao worked with the Communists as well as local warlord officials to care for the needy, motivated by the hope of forming a "united front" against Japanese aggression. To justify this interpretive position, we offer the following theoretical support.

Revealing the Heroic, Honoring the Religious: The Hero Kao Gin-cheng and his Christian Community in Ganzhou during the Republican Period

Heroes come in various forms and expressions, but normally command respect for their outstanding character, sacrificial commitments, and practical ways of addressing the needs of the "underdogs", commoners, and disenfranchized.[82] However, the public shaping of any hero's story is built upon certain prototypes, standard schemas of expectations for a hero within a particular context. For example, within most Christian communities "saintliness" brings the expectation that even when facing immense difficulties saintly people will be faithful to their divine calling, including dying to save others and martyrdom.[83] If one is doing what is perceived as right and good then dying in the process of serving others can profoundly influence the creation of a hero. As the Danish Christian philosopher Søren Kierkegaard wrote: "The tyrant dies and his rule is over; the martyr dies and his rule begins."[84]

Thus, "cultural scripts" can mould charismatic aspects of a hero's true experiences into forms more suitable for our preferred schemas and less true to the situations that shaped them.[85] Political and religious schemas as well as cultural and ideological tendencies can be at work here and people might avoid unexpected or undesirable elements within a hero's socially confirmed character and extraordinary qualities. "Schemas not only cause us to interpret information about people in ways that fit our expectations, they also blind us to information that doesn't fit the schema…Schemas not only lead us to ignore things that are there but also to see things that aren't."[86]

In the case of Dr. Kao Gin-cheng there could be a two-fold distortion. On the one hand, in the midst of many confirmable facts and historically reliable accounts, Christian summaries of Dr. Kao's life and works capture his Christian heroism in contexts that are not affected by the political complexities of his time, and so leave out references to difficulties he faced in the late 1930s when

81 As documented in *The Chinese Recorder*, 51, 12 (December 1920).

82 A summary of major themes in Scott T. Allison & George R. Geothals, *Heroes: What they do and why we need them* (New York: Oxford University Press, 2011), 58-71.

83 The 'Saint' prototype is set alongside 'the Underdog' and 'The Bad Boy'. Dying in the process of heroic actions is significant in the cementing of a person's heroic status. See Allison & Geothals, *Heroes*, 69-71, 182-185.

84 Quoted in ibid., 186.

85 As discussed in ibid., 189-190.

86 Quoted from ibid., 60.

he made political choices that for many Christian writers would not appear within the "normal scope" of an evangelical medical missionary. This is distortion by omission, and seems like a conspiracy of silence in the face of the difficult choices great moral leaders (including Christians) have to make in order to fulfil their visions. On the other hand, even though important historical details have emerged from Chinese military history and Communist documents related to Dr. Kao's association with Communist military officials in 1937-38, there seems to exist an intention on the part of some to make Dr. Kao into a model "Chinese Communist hero". This might be the case when great effort is spent in creating the scenario of a cruel death under circumstances that no one could observe or record, much less justify through verifiable evidence. This is a distortion by mythification, and appears ideologically questionable precisely because it makes claims that should only be presented as reasonable but unsubstantiated speculation.

None of this is to deny Dr. Kao's heroism, or that of many of his family members, colleagues, and close friends. Indeed, most, if not all of those people would have quickly indicated that his heroic qualities were outstanding and pioneering inspirations for their own expressions of heroism. In this sense Dr. Kao deserves the honors he has been given, but for reasons that challenge some standard ways of perceiving heroes from China's late Republican period. The unusual life of Dr. Kao is a hybrid of the saintly and the underdog prototypes within the general categorization of heroes.[87] He was an evangelical Protestant medical missionary who helped wounded and dying soldiers associated with Communist forces in Gansu. One of the reasons for this, despite Kao's previous association with Nationalist armed forces under the Christian general Feng Yuxiang, was the new United Front that brought both sides together against Japanese imperialist intrusions. Another reason was Dr. Kao's awareness, shared by many in the region, that the faction under Muslim warlord General Ma Bufang was tyrannical, cruel, and destructive. Consequently, there developed a sense of righteousness and compassion for all those who suffered in Gansu, and the Christian medical missionary was all the more concerned for wounded soldiers who lived under the threat of the merciless warlord's armies. Under these conditions, a hybrid hero emerged, the evangelical Christian medical professional determined to rescue a group of very vulnerable Chinese Communist soldiers.

We should add that the heroic aspects of Dr. Kao did not only emerge in the last two years of his life. All that we have revealed about his earlier career in Lanzhou, Ganzhou, and elsewhere indicates many facets of his heroic character and we need to apply our hybrid account of his heroism to all of what we know about him. Dr. Kao's heroism was already evident when he and his first wife made the decision to move to Gansu and become medical-evangelists; his ordination to this role in 1920 confirmed his Christian calling and motivated its

87 This is based on Allison & Hoebels' categorization.

fruitfulness. In addition, his innovative, creative and courageous Christian approach to life had already taken on heroic dimensions by 1926, when he was not only prominently recognized within Mongolian and Tibetan religious circles, but also suffered oppressive injustice from an official in Suzhou and was incarcerated before being exonerated. We also note that before Dr. Kao provided medical help for soldiers of the ill-fated Sixth Route Communist Army, he had also offered his medical skills to Marshall Feng Yu-hsiang's "Christian army." Returning to the Ganzhou Christian community in the early 1930s, Kao and his second wife faced a seriously destabilized situation affected by a major earthquake in December 1930, a subsequent devastating famine, and cruelties inflicted by the Muslim militia. Clearly, Dr. Kao's heroism was already manifest many years before his involvement in "the Great Rescue" during the early period of the Second United Front, a final long-term effort which confirms him as a heroic figure who "went beyond the call of duty" in the final endeavour that led to his tragic disappearance.

Our conclusion may strike some as unexpected. However, we believe this interpretive approach is justified, and can promote further research into the life and work of Dr. Kao Gin-cheng, his family, his Christian community and medical co-workers in Ganzhou, and his undeniable impact on the lives of numerous people throughout the region of central Gansu Province during the 1920s and 1930s. Many Christian readers may be surprised to discover that such a notable Chinese medical evangelist could also be viewed and honoured as a national hero by Communist historians, which agrees with the proverbial wisdom that fact is sometimes stranger than fiction.

We have found a hero replete with the qualities of selfless sacrifice promoted by Communist leaders for Chinese citizens, who at the same time demonstrated the compassionate care for the vulnerable, needy, and oppressed that is characterized in the image of the Christian redeemer. Both of these dimensions of Dr. Kao Gin-cheng's virtuous and heroic life should be recognized and appreciated.

Email Correspondence and Other Sources Consulted

Kao, Linda. 5 Jan, 2015. E-mail providing answers from her father, Kao Shih-Chieh, to questions raised by the authors.

Kao, Linda. 25 Oct, 2016. Correspondence providing a list of the names and relationships of Dr. Kao Gin-cheng's immediate family, including his first wife surnamed Wu (武) and all siblings, as well as others in the extended family. Written by Kao Shih-chieh.

Kao, Linda. 13 & 27 Nov 2016. Two e-mails providing an account of the context of the suicide of Kao Ying-chieh (高英傑) eldest son of Dr. Kao, and his first wife.

'The work at Kanchow', *China's Millions* (Dec 1924), 186. (Assumed UK edition)

'In Kansu' and 'Unevangelized regions', *China's Millions* (Jun 1925), 90. (Assumed UK edition)

'The advance challenged', *China's Millions* (Jul 1930), 115. (Assumed UK edition)

Mann, E. J., 'Forward Work in Kansu', *China's Millions* (Jun 1931), 102-104.

Reynolds, Miss I., 'Advance Challenged in Kansu', *China's Millions* (Nov 1930), 182-183.

Revisionist Women's Work for Women: The Contribution of Native Women Workers in Canton

Christina Wong

The contributions of Western missionaries to Chinese Christianity have been detailed because of the wealth of correspondence and archives. Records of Chinese Christians in the nineteenth century are more limited, however. Robert Morrison is well known but we are less familiar with his language tutor Abel Yun, who was threatened with death by the Qing. Unnamed helpers supported Morrison in translating the Bible into Chinese and developing a dictionary.[1] Like so-called native workers in other parts of the world, Chinese were mentioned only casually in missionary reports,[2] class, gender, and Western hierarchy making female workers almost invisible.

I am interested in native women who worked with female missionaries, shaping education, medical care, and the broader Christian community in Canton. The scarcity of biographies and original writings by such women means that their stories are presented only partially through the writings of missionaries. I will explore the neglected contribution[3] of female Chinese Christians by examining their relationships with three American Presbyterian institutions:[4] the True Light Seminary, the Ming Sum School for the Blind, and Hackett Medical College for Women.

True Light Seminary

True Light was founded by the first single woman Presbyterian missionary Harriet Noyes (那夏理, 1844-1924) in 1872. It was not the first girls' boarding school in China, yet made a significant contribution, producing female Christian leaders in Canton and facilitating the formation of a Presbyterian women's community.

---

1 Daniel H. Bays, *A new history of Christianity in China* (Chichester: Wiley-Blackwell, 2012), 44; Murray A. Rubinstein, 'The Protestant missionary enterprise, 1807-1860', in R. G. Tiedemann, ed, *Handbook of Christianity in China. vol.2* (Leiden: Brill, 2010), 135.

2 Bays, *A new history*, 49.

3 Mary Raleigh Anderson, *Protestant mission schools for girls in South China: 1827 to the Japanese invasion* (Mobile, AL: Heiter-Starke, 1943), 118.

4 Because of the American Civil War, the Presbyterian Church was divided North and South. Both set up foreign mission boards and sent missionaries to China. The Presbyterian Church in the United States of America (PCUSA), also known as the American Northern Presbyterian Church, established its Canton Mission in 1844.

Here I present portraits of two local female teachers at the seminary in its early days and explore the role of women from the True Light community's Liu and Luo families, connected with Luo Liu Xinci (羅劉心慈,[5] 1871-1946).

Recruiting Educated Female Teachers in the Early Days

Before True Light could employ its own trained students as teachers, Noyes recruited several educated local women.[6] As provincial capital Canton was generally amenable to female education, and nearly half of those admitted to the seminary in the 1870s may have completed some studies before enrollment, although most were not well to do.[7] Women learned at home with private tutors or at private girls schools.[8] These well-educated Chinese women were recruited by Presbyterian women missionaries to teach in their schools, even though they intended to seek Christians first. When the seminary was started, there were few educated women in the Presbyterian community but by 1879 their mission schools for girls and women employed twenty-two teachers.

Canton's mission schools for girls depended initially on non-Christian women with a classical Chinese education. Noyes recalled that at the beginning of True Light, two Chinese women applied to teach at the seminary, both arriving in sedan chairs. Noting their fine etiquette and small bound feet – a sign of respectability[9] – Noyes engaged them.

One unnamed teacher came from a family forced into destitution, which is why she took the unusual step of approaching a missionary for employment. She was interested in Christianity and nearly converted after dreaming that God told her, "I alone am the true God".[10] She died years later in a city remote from Canton, refusing any "idolatrous ceremonies at the burial."[11] Noyes assumed her reluctance to convert reflected Chinese gender segregation, which did not allow a *guixiu* (閨秀 cultivated lady) to be baptized publicly by a male missionary. At that time, only ordained ministers could perform baptisms, and

5 This woman was born into the Liu family but married a man surnamed Luo.

6 Liu Xinci, *Zhenguang guangrong jianshi* (眞光光榮簡史) [A brilliant brief history of the True Light Seminary] (Hong Kong: s.n., 1972), 36.

7 Harriet Newell Noyes, 'Native female education', *Woman's Work in China* 2, 2 (May 1879), 139.

8 Noyes' discovered at least thirty girls' schools in Canton and its vicinity in the 1870s. Private girls' schools run by Chinese educated teachers had existed since the 1830s. See Noyes, 'Native female education', 135-37; Harriet Noyes, *A light in the land of Sinim: Forty-five years in the True Light Seminary, 1872-1917* (New York: Fleming H. Revell, 1919), 29.

9 Noyes, *A light*, 23-24.

10 Ibid., 24.

11 Cf. Ibid., 25. At that time missionaries possibly regarded all Chinese burial ceremonies as containing 'idolatrous elements', from Buddhism, Taoism, and Chinese popular religions. In fact, as early as the seventeenth century, Catholic communities already practiced a kind of Chinese burial ceremony free of such elements. For a detailed examination of Chinese Catholics' use of Chinese and European elements in funeral rituals see Nicolas Standaert, *The interweaving of rituals: Funerals in the cultural exchange between China and Europe* (Seattle, WA: University of Washington Press, 2008).

women were excluded from ordination in most of mainstream denominations including American Presbyterian Church.

Teacher Li was another *guixiu* at the school, who had committed the Chinese classics to memory. Luo Liu Xinci described her as well dressed with make-up. Li was blind and was assisted by a younger tutor, who also dressed like a lady from a well-to-do family.[12]

The curricula for True Light's boarding school for girls and training school for women included the Chinese classics, because of the educated *guixiu* teachers and the school's goal of professional training. The curriculum for Bible women focused on biblical knowledge, but that for teachers included the Chinese Classics in addition to basic reading and writing.[13] When recruited as a teacher at 13 Luo Liu Xinci considered herself well-qualified because she had studied and memorized *Sishu* (四書) [The Four Books],[14] *Shijing* (詩經) [The Book of Odes], *Yijing* (易經) [The Book of Changes], *Mingxin baojian* (明心寶鑑) [Mirror of the Clear Heart], *Nüxiaojing* (女孝經) [The Book of Filial Piety for Women], and *Lienü zhuan* (烈女傳) [Records of Chaste Women].[15] These didactic classics promoted female propriety and chastity, as well as spousal fidelity. In the early days of True Light, these social ideals stood alongside Christian teachings advocated by the missionaries. The *Sanzijing* (三字經) [Three Character Classic] was the inspiration for the Christian *Sanzijing* (brief statement of Christian doctrine) and the more advanced Christian *Sizijing* (四字經) (Four Character Classic, basic understanding of the Gospels), textbooks for the mission's elementary schools.[16] The addition of reading and writing, geography and arithmetic, music, and handiwork[17] provided a comprehensive elementary education.[18]

This combination of Western knowledge, Christian education, and the Chinese Classics was found in other mission schools[19] as a strategy to attract

---

12 Liu, *Zhenguang*, 35-36.

13 Lucy A. Crouch, 'China-Canton', *Woman's Work for Woman* 6, 9 (November 1876), 291.

14 Probably *Nüsishu* (女四書) [Four books for women] (Noyes, *Native female education*, 139). The *Sishu* (四書) [Four books], i.e. *Lunyu* (論語) [Analects], *Mengzi* (孟子) [Mencius], *Daxue* (大學) [the Great learning], and *Zhongyong* (中庸) [the Doctrine of the mean] were studied mainly by male scholars. *Nüsishu* was composed of *Nüjie* (女誡) [Precepts for women] by Ban Zhao (班昭), *Nülunyu* (女論語) [Analects for women] by Song Ruoxin (宋若莘), *Neixun* (內訓) [Instruction in the inner quarters] by Empress Renxiao Ms. Xu (仁孝皇后徐氏), *Nüfan jielu* (女範捷錄) [Extracts of female propriety] by Ming Ms. Liu (劉氏). See also Huang Yanli (黃嫣梨), *Nüsishu jizhu yizheng* (女四書集注義證) [Collective commentary on *the four books for girls*] (Hong Kong: Commercial Press, 2008).

15 Liu, *Zhenguang*, 39.

16 H. J. Shaw, '[Letter by] China-Miss H. J. Shaw, Canton, September 23, 1874', *Woman's Work for Woman*, 5, 82-83.

17 Noyes, *A light*, 238.

18 B. C. Henry, *The cross and the dragon, or light in the broad East* (New York: Anson D.F. Randolph, 1885), 261.

19 M. Melvin, 'The curricula of five representative mission schools for girls in China', *Woman's Work in the Far East*, 21, 1 (May 1900), 5-16.

Chinese parents, because the Chinese Classics and Confucian teachings represented a respectable literati class.[20] Similar to True Light, other schools adopted traditional Chinese *nüxue* [女學 women's learning], including female propriety and *nügong* [女工 women's work] like sewing and embroidery. The women from literati families brought continuity between Christian ideals and Chinese women's education.

Luo Liu Xinci and Her Extended Family Members at True Light

I now consider the relationship between Luo Liu Xinci's family and the True Light community. Liu's great-grandmother Lunshen (倫嬸) worked for the Preston missionary family, caring for their sick daughter Margaret (1855?-1863), described by Noyes as the youngest missionary in Canton. Margaret understood that Lunshen was very sad about her impending death, and invited her to become a Christian with the promise of meeting again in heaven. We know little about Lunshen, but know she was baptized in 1863, and became a Bible woman and Presbyterian Church member, serving there and as a hospital visitor.[21] Liu Xinci's parents were also active at the Second Presbyterian Church (founded in 1872); her father Liu Xingxian (劉興賢, d.1883?) was one of its founders and evangelists.

There were few Chinese evangelists and Liu Xingxian served as an itinerant preacher, eventually succumbing to overwork.[22] His wife Liu Yangshi (劉楊氏, d.1885) was a pious and filial widow who cared for her children and parents-in-law, taking on sewing and embroidery to make ends meet. In March 1884, Noyes invited Liu Yangshi and her daughter Liu Xinci to teach, suggesting that the daughter take responsibility for teaching with her mother acting in a supporting role. Liu Xinci had studied at the seminary and was familiar with the Classics for women and the Christian Scriptures, basic requirements for a teacher.[23]

Liu's sister-in-law Luo Sheng'ai (羅聖愛, 1872-1968) taught at the seminary for fifteen years. Through her father's connections with the English Wesleyan Mission, Luo Sheng'ai studied at the *Shuzheng xuexiao* (淑正學校 Shu Cheng

---

20 Gael Graham, *Gender, culture, and Christianity: American Protestant mission schools in China, 1880-1930* (New York: Peter Lang, 1995), 14.

21 FMCR 1863, 193/6/599 (Jan. 13); Noyes, *A light*, 51-52; Harriet Noyes, *History of the South China Mission of the American Presbyterian Church, 1845-1920* (Shanghai: Presbyterian Mission Press, 1927), 18; C. F Preston, 'The Memoranda of Dates and Events Connected with the History of the Canton Mission of the Board of Foreign Missions of the Presbyterian Church of the US of America', *The Chinese Recorder and Missionary Journal*, 7 (May-June 1876), 190.

22 Liu Xinci, 'Naxiali guniang shilüe' (那夏理姑娘史略) [A brief biography of Miss Harriet Noyes], *Zhonghua jidujiaohui Guangdong dahui baogao* (中華基督教會廣東大會報告) [The Report of the Canton Synod, Church of Christ in China], 11 (February 1924), 1-2; Liu, *Zhenguang*, 38; cf. Wen Guofu (溫國府), *Xi Guangdong zhanglao jiaohui lishi* (西廣東長老教會歷史) [Presbyterian Church History in Western Canton] (S.l.: Qiming Gongsi, 1920), 23.

23 Liu, *Zhenguang*, 35, 38-40.

Girls' School), and probably through her relationship with Liu taught upper level elementary classes at the seminary from 1887.[24] Liu recalled Sheng'ai's vow of singleness for the duration of her educational ministry, in accordance with her interpretation of *First Corinthians* 7: 25-28, 37-38. Like the Apostle Paul, she rejected marriage to serve God. Since her home Siyi district did not practice *zishu* (自梳), Sheng'ai tried to convince her father to accept her vow, referring to scripture for support.[25] The Chinese Union Version originates from the English Revised Version and expresses vv. 37-38 as a father permitting "a virgin daughter" to be single for the sake of God. However, modern scholars believe that the passage refers to a man's fiancée.[26] According to Liu Xinci, Sheng'ai told her father that she did not yearn for anyone or anything in this evil epoch. She declined an engagement arranged by her father and held a special ritual, like other Cantonese *zishunü,* to declare her singleness in front of three hundred witnesses who prayed for her. Sheng'ai also represented her vow by tying her hair in a bun, which was associated with Christian chastity rather than local *zishu* customs.[27] After fifteen years at True Light, Sheng'ai moved to Guangxi's Women's Institute of the Alliance Bible School (梧州建道書院女院), the predecessor of Hong Kong's Alliance Bible Seminary (建道神學院), serving there more than 30 years.[28] In 1927 she was also one of the founders of the annual Canton Bible Conference (廣州培靈研經大會), initiating interdenominational cooperation that continues until today. Luo Sheng'ai was initially affiliated with the Wesleyans, worked for the Presbyterians as well as the Christian and Missionary Alliance (C&MA), and started an interdenominational project, which involved her sister-in-law Liu Xinci and

---

24 Liu Xinci married Luo Riming (a.k.a. Luo Shengbao, d.1888) in 1886. Female missionaries made connections between mission boards but I believe that local Christian women made links with other denominations through their extended families. Such would be the case if the marriage of Liu and Luo Shengbao occurred prior to her teaching at the seminary.

25 *Zishunü* (自梳女) [sworn single woman] was a custom in some Guangdong counties. A *zishunü* wore a single bun as a formal statement of her status as an unmarried adult. *Zishunü* worked in the silk industry in Shunde and neighboring counties around the turn of twentieth century and as domestic workers in Hong Kong and Singapore after 1949. For a detailed study, see Janice E. Stockard, *Daughters of the Canton delta: Marriage patterns and economic strategies in South China, 1860-1930* (Stanford: Stanford University, 1989).

26 Scott Nash, *1 Corinthians* (Macon, GA: Smyth & Helwys, 2009), 220-21; Mark Taylor, *1 Corinthians - The New American Commentary, vol.28* (Nashville, TN: Broadman & Holman, 2014), 184-85, 192-93. There are differences between the English Revised Version and current translations like the New International and New Revised Standard Versions. The Church traditionally understood this text as referring to the dilemma of a father concerning daughters of marriageable age. Greek and Chinese culture both assume the right of a father to give permission for a daughter to marry.

27 Leung Ka-Lun (梁家麟), *Jiandao shenxueyuan bainianshi* (建道神學院百年史) [Centenary history of Alliance Bible Seminary (1899-1999)] (Hong Kong: Jiandao shenxueyuan, 1999), 24; Liu, *Zhenguang*, 42.

28 Leung Ka-Lun (梁家麟), *Jing'e leyu wo zhenguang: zhenguang chuangxiao yibai sanshi nian xiaoshi* (菁莪樂育我眞光: 眞光創校一百三十年校史) [Nurturing the young: A delightful tradition of True Light 1872-2002] (Hong Kong: Jiulong zhenguang zhongxue xiaodonghui, 2002), 37, n43.

Presbyterian women leaders Drs. Guan Xianghe (關相和) and Mei Enlian (梅恩憐) (True Light alumni taught by Luo Sheng'ai) during the 1920s.[29]

The torch passed to the next generation, Luo Liu Xinci's adopted and biological daughter, Luo Daozhen Daisy (羅道真, 1900-45) and Luo Youjie (羅有節, 1888-1961), succeeding her as the second and third Chinese principals of the True Light Primary School. Luo Youjie was a significant female leader in the Church of Christ in China (CCC), general secretary of the Canton Young Women's Christian Association (YWCA), women's dean of Lingnan University, chairperson of the Union Normal School for Women (協和女子師範學校). Daisy studied in the US for eight years before serving as principal of the Renji Road primary school. She married He Yintang (何蔭棠, 1898-1987) in 1927 and resigned in order to study for a Masters of Education at Stanford University with him. After graduation, He Yintang was appointed principal of the True Light Middle School in a newly established Presbyterian compound, Baihedong, where Daisy taught English. After the outbreak of the Second Sino-Japanese war, Daisy moved to the US, promoting friendship between the two countries and advocating for China Relief through the PCUSA network.[30]

It is also important to discuss the impact of Luo Liu Xinci in the broader Presbyterian community. Her memoirs emphasize the connection with and the cooperation among the True Light community, other Presbyterian women's work, and the ecumenical network in Canton.[31]

Although the Chinese might see Liu Xinci as a typical *buxiangren* (不祥人 unlucky person) and *weiwangren* (未亡人 widow),[32] her bitter life supposedly a

29 Liu, *Zhenguang*, 42; Xie Yixin (謝以信), 'Zhongguo Guangdongsheng Guangzhou shi peiling yanjing dahui jianshi 37 (Xianggang gangjiu peiling yanjing dahui qianshen' (中國廣東省廣州市培靈研經大會簡史-香港港九培靈研經大會的前身) [A brief history of the Canton Bible Conference-the predecessor of the Hong Kong Bible Conference], http://www.hkbibleconference.org/hk/about-us/share-articles/247-share-articles-01.html (Accessed 17 Sep, 2013).

30 Dorothy M. Fisher, 'Mrs Yam-Tong Hoh', *Women and Missions*, 22, 10 (January 1946), 250; cf., Daisy Law Hoh, 'How secure is your security?', *Women and Missions*, 19, 5 (August 1942), 136-38.

31 Liu, *Zhenguang*. A close colleague stated that Liu Xinci's vocations were education in the first half of her life and evangelism in the latter (Zhao Guanhai, 'Di'erren xiaozhang Luo Liu Xinci xiansheng shengping (第二任校長羅劉心慈先生生平) [Biography of the second Principal, Luo Liu Xinci]', in Liu, *Zhenguang*, 98. In addition to her education ministry at True Light she was involved in her church and the wider Christian community. She was an ordained church elder, voluntary women's secretary of the Canton Divisional Council of the CCC, and board member of several institutions affiliated with the American Presbyterian Mission (Harriet Noyes, 'One of the Staff of True Light Seminary, Canton', *Woman's Work for Woman and Our Mission Field*, 23, 2 (February 1908), 34; Zhao Guanhai, 'Xu san' (序三) [3rd preface], in Liu, *Zhenguang*, 3. In interdenominational work, she was one of the founders and supporters of the Canton City YWCA. See *1932 Y.W.C.A. News: The anniversary number* (Guangzhou: Canton Young Women's Christian Association, 1932). Liu also actively participated in the Canton Bible Conference and the Bible Society (Zhao, *Xu san*, 3).

32 Ibid.

bad omen for those around her, Noyes wrote that Liu's family had good prospects and served the Presbyterian community afterward.[33] Liu worked diligently as teacher, assistant principal and Chinese principal at the seminary for more than forty years. When Dr. Mary Niles was recruiting female students for medical training at the Canton Hospital, Noyes asked Liu to join, but she declined, despite admitting that medical training could relieve people's physical suffering. She reaffirmed her vocation as a teacher, enabling people to grow holistically, intellectually, morally and physically.[34] In 1924, True Light's alumni and students and the Canton Synod of the CCC celebrated Liu Xinci's forty years of teaching[35] and she was awarded an honorable recognition by the Chinese government as well as the PCUSA.[36]

Significantly, Liu did not dwell on the suffering she had endured, although her widowhood was mentioned in a biography at her memorial service.[37] In the hymn "Recall the Lord's Grace" (1929),[38] written on her sixtieth birthday, she expressed self-pity as an orphan and a widow with terms like "abandoned," "alone," and "forsaken".

I have gone through several decades since birth,
[I have tasted] sweetness and bitterness, joy and sorrow.
When I felt humble, the Lord's hand has lifted me up.
Christ gave me strength to do everything well.

When my parents abandoned me, the Lord has helped me.
The Lord has comforted me in life by the Scripture.
God is the orphan's Father, the widow's Judge,
When I was alone and in bitterness the Lord was with me.

Concord:
Praise the Lord, my heart is full of glory,
And praise the Lord my heart is full of blessings and hope,
The Lord has never forsaken this orphan but sent me in peace,
And with grace and mercy to Heaven.

---

33 Noyes, *A light*, 230-32.
34 Liu Zeshan (劉澤挻), 'Luo Liu Xinci Xiansheng lilüe (羅劉心慈先生歷略) [A brief account of Teacher Luo Liu Xinci]', *Zhonghua jidujiaohui Guangdong dahui baogao*, 11 (February 1924), 3.
35 *Zhonghua jidujiaohui Guangdong dahui baogao*, 1924, 11: 21; Liu, *A brief account*, 4; cf., Harriet Noyes, 'Fifty years in the foreign field'. RG 82/4/9 Canton-True Light Seminary Correspondence, 1912-22. Secretary Files: China Missions, 1891-1955, Presbyterian Church in the USA, Board of Foreign Missions (Philadelphia: Presbyterian Historical Society, 1920).
36 In the early years of the Republic of China, Liu Xinci was invited to give a speech to the Canton Provincial Education Commission, the only female attendant in the conference (Noyes, *A light*, 219-20). She received a medal of honor from the Canton Provincial Governor, and was appointed an honorary member of the Board of Foreign Missions, PCUSA (Certificate, Aug. 15, 1917 and Helen Kittredge to Mrs. S. T. Law, Oct. 27, 1937, Personal Collections by Luo Fuhua).
37 Zhao, *Biography of the second principal*, 96-98; cf. RG193/1, PHS.
38 The first version was published in the memorial service program of Luo Liu Xinci (Ref. to RG193/1, PHS).

Alongside the negative terms, Liu remembered "blessings," "hope," "peace," "grace," and "mercy" received from God.

This section has discussed the first two Chinese teachers at True Light and the ministry of Luo Liu Xinci and her extended family. We have seen the combination of traditional teaching for women and the Christian message. We have also traced the development of the Christian community by women in family networks. Lastly, we have witnessed Christian faith against a background of suffering. Something similar is found in the story of the Ming Sum School.

Ming Sum School for the Blind

The early period of the Ming Sum School for the Blind (明心瞽目學校) was connected with the True Light Seminary and the Gubu mission compound. Its founder, Mary W. Niles (賴馬西, 1854-1933), was the first woman medical missionary sent to the Presbyterian Canton mission in 1882. The start of Ming Sum is linked with Niles' adoption of blind baby girl from an "ash heap" at the Canton Hospital in 1888 or 1889. In 1891, she placed five blind girls in Martha Kerr's day school at the Canton Hospital[39] and employed a local blind teacher, Lin Shan,[40] to teach them knitting and an adaptation of the Braille system to Cantonese. Ming Sum's permanent buildings were constructed in Fangcun (芳村) in 1910. The school contributed to missionary service for the blind throughout China and the development of a Braille system for Cantonese.

Niles connected to the True Light community when she first arrived and later became school physician.[41] Harriet Noyes and Liu Xinci supported Ming Sum's ministry, serving on the Board of Directors and as chairpersons. According to Liu, Noyes named the blind educational ministry "Ming Sum," emphasizing that the blind could see by their hearts.[42] This section introduces significant Chinese teachers there, Margaret Zhou Huici (周惠慈) and the blind head teacher Li Xueji (李雪基).[43]

---

39 This day school was started in March 1888. See Martha Kerr, 'Fruits of the hospital school in Canton', *Woman's Work for Woman and Our Mission Field,* 4, 8 (August 1889), 208-09.

40 Mary Niles, 'Blind girls in Canton, China: A problem'. RG82/70/4, Blind, Missions to China, Secretary Files, China Missions 1891-1955, BFM, PCUSA, Presbyterian Historical Society/Box 28, Folder 21, Philadelphia, 5, 8; 'Blind girls in Canton, China', *The Mentor,* 2, 9 (November 1892), 350-51. Typing mistakes or different romanizations have made the recording of Lin Shan's name confusing; see Niles, *Blind girls in Canton, China* RG82 and *Blind girls in Canton, China* Mentor; See also 'Lin Chau' in D. MacGillivray, *A century of Protestant missions in China (1807-1907)* (New York; Shanghai: American Tract Society; American Presbyterian Mission Press, 1907). I standardize her name to "Lin Shan."

41 Liu, *Zhenguang*, 55.

42 Alice M. Carpenter, ed, *Ming Sum: The school of understanding heart, the fiftieth anniversary, 1889-1939* (Hong Kong: Standard Press, 1939), 98; Liu, *Zhenguang*, 56.

43 Technically, Li was not a native assistant in the nineteenth century as she probably starting teaching at the school after the 1910s. From pupil to the head of blind teachers, Li witnessed the development of the school at the turn of the century. She is a very important example of the labor capacity as well as the economic independence of blind students after they trained at the school.

Due to the closeness of Presbyterian women, Margaret Zhou graduated from and taught at the True Light Seminary before later joining the Ming Sum School. From Noyes' we know that Zhou (called Ah Lau as a child) was one of a group of orphan girls who all studied at the seminary. Ah Lau studied under Luo Sheng'ai and became a teacher at True Light, remaining there for 17 years.[44] She learned the Chinese classics and Bible studies, and became a capable teacher, citizen and Christian leader,[45] who remained single because of her commitment to education. In 1897, Zhou was asked to teach at Ming Sum for one semester, at the end of which she planned to return to the seminary. However, thirty pupils with "tears streaming from their poor sightless eyes" petitioned the principal to keep her as their teacher, deep affection which moved Zhou to remain for 33 years.[46]

Another Presbyterian woman missionary at the Ming Sum School, Lucy Durham (1853-1942), taught Zhou how to transfer music scores into Braille. Zhou became a talented music teacher and the first to instruct blind girls in music in China.[47] Blind students were trained as singing teachers for children, which improved their employability.

Zhou accompanied missionaries abroad in 1910, leading her to "enlarge the knowledge of humanity, of the [grandeur] and beauty of the world, and deeper understanding of God".[48] She created the new school campus in Fangcun as a nature study site for blind students, with flowers, vegetables, trees, and a fish pond.[49] She declined an invitation to serve as the president of the Canton YWCA because of her commitment to the school.[50] Over 33 years at Ming Sum, she served as teacher, associate principal and the first Chinese principal.[51]

Another important figure is the blind Li Xueji, of whom we do not know much. She came from a village in Guangdong and probably grew up in a relatively well-to-do family; she recalled being upset that her blindness meant she could not go to the theatre.[52] She became blind at the age of four and would have no future in the village. Li found an opportunity to study at the Ming Sum School at age 13[53] and was under the care of the principal, Huang Xuezhen (黃雪貞, b.1881), the first graduate of the Hackett Medical College in 1903.[54] In a 50th anniversary booklet, Li stated that her studies brought her knowledge and

44 Noyes, *A light*, 98.
45 Lucy Durham, 'Miss Margaret Chau', in Carpenter, *Ming Sum*, 17.
46 Noyes, *A light*, 98-99.
47 Durham, 'Margaret Chau', 17; 'Sketch of some activities in Canton', *The Torch*, 2, 1 (February 15, 1940), 4-5.
48 Durham, 'Margaret Chau', 17.
49 Ibid.
50 Noyes, *A light*, 99-100.
51 Nov. 15, 1926, 27/1/71, GMA; Edomia S. Marshall, 'Forty-six years of healing and teaching in South China'. RG 360/III/2584, Foreign Missionary Personal Files: Mary West Niles (Philadelphia: Presbyterian Historical Society, 1928), 2.
52 Li Xueji, 'What Ming Sum means to me', in Carpenter, *Ming Sum*, 80.
53 Marshall, *Forty-six years*, 2.
54 Carpenter, *Ming Sum*, 38.

independence, and skills such as reading, knitting and making clothes.[55] She also received a massage certificate at the opening of the Ming Sum School building in 1910. Mary Niles described Li as "an apt pupil" who taught massage to eight more blind girls.[56] Li likely worked at the school for more than twenty years until around 1943.[57] She was appointed as head of the blind teachers.[58] Li Xueji was the first Christian in her family and led the rest to convert, including her brother, Calvin, who was linked with the Presbyterians in Canton. Li's story is an example of evangelism of blind girls at Ming Sum.

The Ming Sum story displays contributions by American women missionaries and Chinese teachers. Significant advances were made in educational provision and training for blind girls, as well as their employability and respectability. The story of the Hackett Medical College, discussed next, contains similar elements.

From South China Medical College to Hackett Medical College

The Hackett Medical College was originally called the Canton Woman's Medical College, and was founded by the female medical missionary, Mary Fulton (富馬利, 1854-1927) in 1899. It was the first school of Western medicine for women in China. It is significant that the South China Medical School (affiliated with the Canton Hospital) began to admit True Light graduates from 1879. There is little information about the first women to have medical training,[59] but the Canton Hospital did admit female students.[60]

During practical medical training and after graduation, some became medical assistants at the Canton Hospital and went on house calls to female patients as well as taking charge of the women's ward.[61] The first female medical missionary, Dr. Niles, mentioned that a well-trained physician, Mrs. Ng A Kwan (probably Wu Lin Shi, 吳林氏) performed operations independently and night shift medical consultations skillfully. The 1896 Canton mission annual report confirms 508 home visits by women medical professionals from the Canton Hospital, among which 239 were made by graduates.[62] Nearly half of all medical calls were answered by Chinese medical

55 Li Xueji, 'What Ming Sum means to me', 80.

56 Mary Niles, 'Dedication of school for the blind', *Woman's Work for Woman and Our Mission Field*, 26, 2 (February 1911), 38.

57 In the fragmented records of the Ming Sum School, I found mention of her at the school until 1943, but nothing more after the War of Resistance. See *The Torch*, 4, 1 (1943), 10.

58 Nov. 15, 1926, 27/1/71, GMA.

59 Sara Waitstill Tucker, 'The Canton Hospital and Medicine in Nineteenth Century China, 1835-1900', Ph.D. thesis, Indiana University, 1982, 359; cf. Noyes, *A light*, 85-86.

60 E.g. three females out of a total of twelve in the 1882 class, five out of eighteen in 1886, nine out of twenty in 1890, and nine out of thirty by 1898 (50th ARBFM 1887, 126; William Cadbury & Mary Jones, *At the point of a lancet: One hundred years of the Canton Hospital, 1835-1935* (Shanghai: Kelly and Walsh, 1935), 179-80; Tucker, *The Canton hospital*, 364.

61 Tucker, *The Canton hospital*, 361, 364.

62 Canton Mission AR 1896, 20, AX430/1/10, Oregon U.

female assistants. This section looks at Fulton's descriptions of two medical assistants.

Mary Fulton's Native Workers in the Canton Hospital Era

Mary Fulton received her M.D. from the Women's Medical College of Pennsylvania in 1884. Just after graduation, she was appointed the second medical female missionary to Canton, after Niles in 1882. Mary Fulton's brother, the Rev. Albert Fulton (富利惇牧師, 1849-1934), came to the field four years earlier[63] and her service in Canton was connected with and supported by her brother's work. She ministered for some time with her brother in Guangxi's Guiping (桂平), helped establish dispensaries in Canton city, and founded the Hackett Medical College. Fulton was another single missionary who committed long-term to women's work with the Canton Presbyterian Mission.

Just after Fulton's arrival in 1884, the first medical assistant Mrs. Mei Yagui (梅亞貴) was assigned to support her. Mrs Mei obtained medical training from Dr. Kerr and assisted in the women's ward at the Canton Hospital.[64] She served as an interpreter for Fulton and accompanied her on trips to local villages. When they saw female patients in well-to-do families, Mei shared the Gospel message with the women.[65] Mei and a Dr. Liang Qianchu (梁乾初) were part of the Fultons' Guiping team, which opened a dispensary and hospital.[66] Returning to Canton, in addition to taking over Niles' dispensary at Shisanfu (十三甫 Thirteenth Street),[67] she opened five more dispensaries between 1887 and 1899.[68] During this period, Mei helped Fulton with dispensaries and hospital work.[69] In *Twenty-Five Years of Medical Work in China* Fulton mentions that she and Mei handled some 63,000 cases, extracting 1,300 teeth, performing 2,100 operations and visiting over 600 patients' homes up to 1891.[70]

---

63 'In Memoriam', *Women and Missions*, 3 (1927), 477.

64 Mary Fulton, *Inasmuch: Extracts from letters, journals, papers, etc*. (West Medford, MA: Central Committee on the United Study of Foreign Missions, 1915), 54.

65 Ibid., 25, 32-33.

66 Ibid., 23-24.

67 This dispensary functioned from Feb 1885 to June 1888 (49th ARBFM 1886, 121, 52nd ARBFM 1889, 139), serving around 3,500 patients (Cadbury & Jones, *At the point*, 286).

68 The Sipailou dispensary at Sipailou chapel treated 80,489 patients and the Tongde Street dispensary 4,614. For detailed information see Cadbury & Jones, *At the point*, 155, 287; Canton Mission AR 1894, 4, AX430/1/10, The Alzo John Fisher's Papers, 1922-1957. Special Collections and University Archives, University of Oregon Libraries; Fulton, *Inasmuch*, 63-64; 'Fumali yisheng shilu' (富馬利醫生事略) [Brief history of Dr Mary Fulton], in *Xiage yike daxue sanshi zhounian jinianlu*, n.p.; Wen, *Xi Guangdong*, 21-22.

69 Cadbury & Jones, *At the point*, 155; FMCR 1893, 216/51, Annual Report; 'Fumali yisheng shilu', n.p.

70 Mary H. Fulton, *Twenty-five years of medical work in China* (Philadelphia, PA: The Woman's Foreign Missionary Society of the Presbyterian Church, 1909), 7-8.

In Fulton's memoirs of her ministry in China, *Inasmuch*, she noted that the early life of the efficient Mei Yagui "[wa]s typical of many and many a poor girl in this land." Mei came from a decent family impoverished by gambling debts, and was sold into a disastrous marriage, widowed, and subsequently became a Christian.[71] She later married a Mr. Mei, a Christian returned from Honolulu. Yagui's marriage to Mr. Mei improved her life. Her daughter, Mei Enlian, studied medicine at Hackett College and became part of the first group of female Chinese physicians in Canton. Fulton was most gratified that Mei Enlian married the Christian leader Guan Enzuo (關恩佐, d.1948),[72] with whom she built "an ideal of Christian home" in China.[73] These second generation Christians grew up at the Gubu Presbyterian compound, and were involved in the Presbyterian Church.[74]

In addition to Mei Enlian's medical profession and her husband's influential family, like her classmates at True Light and Hackett College, Mei served as a leader in the Canton YWCA and Hackett College. She was involved in the Christian women's network, which was formed and nurtured by American Presbyterian women missionaries and Chinese Christian women in Canton, including Mei Enlian's mother, Yagui, and Liu Xinci's great grandmother, Lunshen.

Fulton's Native Colleague Luo Xiuyun in the Hackett Era

Mary Fulton's other assistant during the early development of the Hackett Medical College was Dr. Luo Xiuyun (羅秀雲). Local news reported on Luo's operations and the Chinese public was interested in her western medical practice at the turn of the century.

In the "History of Hackett Medical College," Luo recalled her early resistance to medical studies and how Fulton caused a change of heart. Luo lived with a senior medical student, Shi Meiqing; both were probably adopted by a True Light teacher and grew up in that community.[75] Luo hated the smell

71 Fulton, *Inasmuch*, 55.

72 Guan graduated from Columbia University and taught at the Canton Christian College. He later taught at Zhongshan University and was a leader in the Canton CCC for many years (*Lingnan daxue xiaobao* 48 (1948), 2; Zhao Guanhai, 'Guan Enzuo xiansheng zhi wojian (關恩佐先生生平之我見) [I know about the life of Mr. Guan Enzuo]', *GDXHHK*, 31 (October 1948), 1.

73 Fulton, *Inasmuch*, 93-94.

74 1937-38, 92/1/110, GDPA; 1936, 27/1/84, GMA; William H. Dobson, 'Historical sketch of Canton Station and Chinese churches of Presbyterian origin in Canton', in Alzo John Fisher Papers, 1922-1957, AX430/6/13, Special Collections and University Archives, University of Oregon Libraries, n.d., 17; Wen, *Xi Guangdong*, 23; Zhao, *Guan Enzuo*, 2.

75 Noyes recalled that a graduate from True Light Seminary taught at a Canton mission school for girls for more than 25 years. Her two adopted daughters studied at Hackett College. One, Fulton's assistant at Hackett College and its affiliated Woman's Hospital for many years, would be Luo Xiuyun (Noyes, *A light*, 30). In another chapter of 'Medical Students', Noyes mentions the short life of Shi Meiqing, one of the adopted daughters of a True Light teacher (*A light*, 88, 89). Since Luo Xiuyun lived with Shi before her medical studies, Luo might be the other adopted daughter.

of iodoform on Shi when she returned home from the Canton Hospital, but Fulton encouraged her to study medicine, taking her to see patients, operations, and interesting cases to stimulate her interest. Luo said, "Within half a year, it melted my heart, so I decided to study medicine".[76] Luo applied to study Western medicine at the Canton Hospital under Fulton's and later followed her to Hackett College. In the early days college facilities were very limited; students were busy delivering babies but could not access good medical textbooks and lacked opportunity to see major operations.[77]

After her graduation in 1904, staff changes meant that Luo oversaw the woman's hospital and taught at the medical college.[78] Before the nursing school was set up, she also managed operations and performed duties such as sterilizing utensils, keeping the operating room clean, writing nutritional plans for patients, and even counting their clothes before and after washing.[79] Before Luo left Hackett College for private practice in 1916, she had handled more than two hundred operations there.[80] She was a skillful surgeon, who successfully took charge of "forty-five consecutive severe abdominal operations".[81] The removal of a tumor weighing over 24kg by Luo was reported as "Magical Healing by a Female Physician" (女醫神效) in *Shishi huabao* [時事畫報, Pictorial Magazine of Current Affairs], a social reformist (and/or revolutionary) magazine in late Qing Canton.[82]

In an English language article in *Woman's Work in the Far East* Luo discussed how the Western medical profession related to China's national development and Christian service.[83] She described the significance of the newly founded nursing profession and its emphasis on hygiene, key for Western medicine. She also linked nursing to China's prospects; a prosperous

76 J. F. Karcher, Florence Hannum, & Mrs. J. Oscar Thomson, 'History of the Hackett Medical College'. RG82/71/6 Medical work in China, Secretary Files, China Missions 1891-1955, BFM, PCUSA (Philadelphia: Presbyterian Historical Society, 1931), 2.

77 Karcher, Hannum, & Thomson, *History of the Hackett*, 3.

78 Luo Xiuyun, 'Ji fuwu shier nianshi (記服務十二年事) [A record of serving twelve years]', in *Xiage yike daxue sanshi zhounian jinianlu* (廣州夏葛醫科大學三十週紀念錄) [The Thirtieth Anniversary of the Hackett Medical College for Women] (Guangzhou: Xiage yike daxue 夏葛醫科大學, 1929).

79 Karcher, Hannum, & Thomson, *History of the Hackett*, 5; Luo, *A record of serving*.

80 Luo, *A record of serving*.

81 Fulton, *Inasmuch*, 83.

82 'Nüyi shenxiao' (女醫神效) [Magical healing by a female physician], *Shishi Huabao* 14 (1907). Republished by *Jiuyue baitai: Guangdong shengli zhongshan tushuguan cang wanqing huabao xuanji* (旧粤百态: 广东省立中山图书馆藏晚清画报选辑) [Social life and customs in Old *Yue*: Selective collections from late Qing pictorial magazines at the Sun Yat-sen Provincial Library, Guangdong] (Beijing: Zhongguo renmindaxue chubanshe, 2008), 154. For the revolutionary vision of *Shishi huabao*, see Hou Jingwu (侯京吾), 'Tugai difang fengsu: yi guangzhou Shishi Huabao wei zhongxin (1905-1912)' (圖改地方風俗：以廣州(時事畫報)為中心（1905-1912）) [Social Reform Illustrated: A critical study of current affairs pictorial magazines in Guangzhou]. Master's thesis, Guoli Qinghua Daxue 國立清華大學碩士論文, 2012.

83 This was a significant magazine of the American Presbyterian Mission Press in Shanghai. Most of the authors were women missionaries, and so it was unusual for Luo Xiuyun to publish there.

country needs strong people, and to have strong people, there must be nurses. Luo urged nursing graduates to imitate Jesus' humility in serving others.[84] In addition to her medical practice, Luo took charge of a Sunday school with included twenty-one teachers and two or three hundred students.[85]

In Luo's background there was suffering similar to that of Mei Yagui. Several months after marriage her husband left her to return to New York and sent money occasionally. Two years after this, Luo began to study medicine at Hackett College. Yet like Mei, Luo had a more positive second marriage. In 1934, she married a former professor and board member of Hackett College, the Presbyterian Xu Gantang (徐甘棠, 1874-1948?), when she was around fifty years old.[86]

Conclusion

From 1868, women's work in Canton saw growth under the leadership of single missionaries in cooperation with local Chinese women. The first Bible woman was employed in 1865 by Preston[87] and by the turn of the century the Canton mission had expanded to include 21 Bible women and 33 female teachers, working in hospitals, schools for girls, chapels, and in home visitation, in Canton and at provincial outstations.[88] This can be considered the fruit of the True Light Seminary, some of whose female graduates served together with women missionaries.

Although information is scarce and incomplete, I discovered that Liu Xinci, Margaret Zhou, Mei Yagui and Wu Lin Shi were all highly capable and contributed greatly to women's work. According to the writings by American women missionaries, the lives of destitute girls and poor women seemed radically to be improved as American Presbyterian women's work contributed to their social mobility. In addition to education and medical training, some women were offered work as teachers, Bible women, or medical assistants. Local women benefitted from and then contributed to the professional development, economic independence, and marital choices of others. Some functioned as transmitters of *nüxue* to the True Light Seminary. A few chose singleness, following the local *zishunü* custom and the example of single women missionaries. More broadly, these women made Christianity a part of

84 Luo Xiuyun 羅秀雲 (a.k.a. Lo Shan Wan), 'One of China's present needs', *Woman's Work in the Far East*, 31, 1 (March 1910), 27.
85 Fulton, *Inasmuch*, 83.
86 *Xiage xiaoyou sheng*, 14 (1936), 102. It seems that Xu Gantang and Luo Xiuyun were on the board of directors of Hackett College from 1927 (cf. 'New Board of Directors', 1927). When he taught at Hackett College Xu promoted his revolutionary vision, inspiring students like Liang Huanzhen and the instructor Shi Meiqing. By 1917, he was an editor and translator for the Commercial Press (商務印書局). He also served in the Secretariat of the Legislative Council of the Republican government from November 1928.
87 29th ARBFM 1866, 31; cf., FRMC 1867, 197/7/527 (Nov. 22).
88 AR Canton Mission 1896, 44.

life in Canton through their activity in church networks and their association of Western medicine and Christian faith. Rather than passive assistants, these local Christian women of the late nineteenth and early twentieth century were active agents in their own lives and those of others as they helped shape Christianity in their part of China.

Sources Consulted

ARBFM: Annual Report of the Board of Foreign Missions of the Presbyterian Church in the United States of America. 1838-1928.

Canton Mission AR: Report of the American Presbyterian Mission in Canton, China.

FMCR: Foreign Missions Correspondence and Reports, 1833-1911, the Presbyterian Church in the USA." Microfilmed Records.

Ming Sum AR: Ming Sum School for the Blind, Annual Report.

Mingxin xuexiao xiaodonghui jilubu (明心學校校董會記錄部) [Minutes of the Board of Directors Meeting of the Ming Sum School for the Blind], 1919-46. 27/1/71, Guangzhou Municipal Archives, Guangzhou.

'New Board of Directors, Hackett Medical College and Affiliated Institutions' 1927. RG82/28/21 Canton-Hackett Medical College, 1925-1930, Secretary Files, China Missions 1891-1955, BFM, PCUSA, Presbyterian Historical Society, Philadelphia.

Ming Sum Minutes: Mingxin Xuexiao Xiaodonghui Jilubu.

Yijiu sanliu nian renjitang ganbu huiyi jilubu (一九三六年仁濟堂幹部會議紀錄簿) [Minutes of the Secretariat Meeting of the Renji Church]. 27/1/84 (Guangzhou: Guangzhou Municipal Archives, 1936).

Zhonghua jidujiaohui Guangzhou Renjitang zhishihui jiluce（中華基督教會廣州仁濟堂執事會紀錄冊）[Executive Committee Minutes of Guangzhou Renji Church, Church of Christ in China]. 1936-1943. 92/1/110, Guangdong Provincial Archives.

Wang Hengtong: A Native Chinese Christian Teacher's Approach and Practice, 1902-1915

Bai Limin

Wang Hengtong (王亨统, 1868-1928), a native of Yuyao in Zhejiang Province, graduated from the Presbyterian College of Hangchow (Hangzhou Yuying yishu in Chinese) in 1888. By the beginning of the twentieth century he had established himself as a successful Christian teacher and a prolific writer of textbooks which included his *Illustrated Chinese Primer* (Huitu mengxue jiejing 繪圖蒙學捷徑) and *Illustrated Chinese Reader* (Huitu mengxue keben 繪圖蒙學課本). Biographical information on Wang is limited, which is not unusual, as western-centred histories of Christianity in China have largely neglected the narratives of the indigenous Chinese Christians. As a result, we know little about the position, role and contribution of Chinese Christians like Wang in relation to the history of the missionary movement in China and the nation's move to modernization. This study depicts Wang's life and achievements based on information from a variety of sources, including his account of his education at Hangchow College, the forewords to his textbooks written by missionaries and his Chinese counterparts, and missionary records. This narration of Wang's life throws light on the relationship between foreign missionaries and native Chinese Christians, and reveal how these two groups coalesced into a community where both parties underwent cultural and national boundary-transformations. Analysis of Wang's life, his teaching practice and the content of his textbooks in the socio-political context of early twentieth century China provides insights into the contribution made by native Chinese Christian educators toward the establishment of a modern Chinese education system.

Wang Hengtong and Hangchow Presbyterian College

Education was "the first extra-evangelical work that American missionaries undertook in China."[1] Hangchow Presbyterian College, where Wang Hengtong was educated, was originally the Chongxin yishu (崇信義塾) at Ningpo, a boarding school for boys established in 1845, the year after Dr. Divie Bethune McCartee (麦嘉缔, 1820 – 1900) opened the Ningpo Station.

---

1 Gael Graham, *Gender, culture, and Christianity: American Protestant mission schools in China, 1880–1930* (New York: Peter Lang, 1995), 2.

However, missionaries of that time mostly focused on evangelistic work and mission schools were used only to assist this. The school was moved to Hangzhou in 1867. From 1845 to 1867 seven principals ran the school, but none of them were able to commit themselves to the development of the school's curriculum as most were sent to other places for evangelistic tasks. It was not until 1880 when Junius H. Judson (裘德生, 1852–1930) arrived in China and took up the principal's position that the school had the first missionary educator committed to and successful in developing a comprehensive curriculum. In 1888 it became the Presbyterian Mission high school for Central China, and changed its name to Hangchow Yuying High School.[2] The school was upgraded to a "full-fledged junior college" in 1893. In 1897 its name was changed to Hangchow Presbyterian College, known in Chinese as Hangzhou Yuying shuyuan (杭州育英書院).[3]

In 1901 Wang Hengtong described his own education, relating that he began his Chinese schooling at the age of seven and entered Hangzhou Yuying Yishu when he was eleven. He was twenty-one when he graduated from the school and commenced his teaching career.[4] According to the *Catalogue of Hangchow Yuying High School*, a student had to spend ten years completing the two-levels of courses: four years of preparatory courses (*beiguan* 備館), and then a six-year curriculum (*wenhui guan* 文會館). As an 1888 graduate, Wang would have entered Yuying Yishu around 1878-79.

The ten-years of study in the Presbyterian College of Hangchow were significant in Wang's life. In the Preface to his textbook *Dili wenda* (地理问答 *Geography*) Wang Hengtong acknowledged his intellectual debt to Judson and the Hangzhou Yuying High School:

> I studied at Hangchow Yuying High School at a young age, and studied the subjects such as Astronomy, Geography, Physics (*gewu*) and Mathematics under Master Judson, my American teacher. The knowledge I learned through the study of these subjects is all new and interesting. We could easily follow his instruction on these subjects as the textbooks he used contained clear explanations. When we had difficulty in understanding some parts of these subjects, my master would translate English texts into Chinese, and provided us with lectures along with demonstrations until we all understood. His earnest and patient instruction set a high standard and model for later generations in the teaching profession.[5]

2 *Jubilee papers of the Central China Presbyterian Mission, 1844-1894* (Shanghai: The American Presbyterian Mission Press, 1895), 97; Junius H. Judson, *Catalogue of Hangchow High School* (Shanghai: The American Presbyterian Mission Press, 1894), 2-5; Clarence Burton Day, *Hangchow University: A brief history* (New York: United Board for Christian Colleges in China, 1955), 10-11.

3 Day, *Hangchow University*, 6-7.

4 Wang Hengtong, Preface (1901) to the *Illustrated Chinese first reader* (繪圖蒙學課本首集) (Shanghai: American Presbyterian Mission Press, 1904), 1.

5 Wang Hengtong, Preface to *Dili wenda* (地理問答) (Shanghai: American Presbyterian Mission Press, 1901), 1a-b (Author's translation).

His acknowledgement reflected the development of this college and its achievement under the leadership of Judson. The curriculum and the influence of Judson had a lasting impact on Wang Hengtong's intellectual development and laid the foundation for his career as a Christian teacher and textbook writer.

The content of Wang Hengtong's textbooks reflected the curriculum of the Protestant schools in nineteenth-century China. Christian teaching, Confucian classics and science subjects were three components in the curriculum of mission schools. This curriculum developed over a period of three decades. Calvin Wilson Mateer (狄考文, 1836–1908), an influential American Presbyterian missionary educator who arrived in China in 1864, first proposed this three-component formula for the success of missionary schools in 1872. Under his leadership the Tengchow Presbyterian College (登州文會館) in 1881 developed a uniform curriculum which contributed significantly to the formation and development of Protestant missionary education from the mid-nineteenth century onwards.

Prior to commencing at the Hangchow College, Judson visited Tengchow College,[6] which might have inspired him and influenced him to commit to the role of college principal, developing a curriculum modelled on that of Tengchow. There were resemblances between the 1891 Tengchow Catalogue and the 1894 Catalogue of Hangchow. Both included four years of preparatory and six years of advanced studies, and the courses contained three components: Christian teaching, classical Chinese education and science.

The curriculum developed in mission schools also aimed at addressing weaknesses in traditional Chinese education. In Table 1, the first column lists weaknesses in the Chinese education system as perceived by Judson and the second subjects included in his curriculum intended to correct them.

Table 1: Judson's Comparison of Curriculum in Chinese Education and Missionary Schools

Weakness in Chinese Education System	Judson's Curriculum Included
Lacked knowledge of other nations and held overwhelming regard for their own	Geography and history
Failed to provide students with a basic knowledge of nature	Natural philosophy, chemistry, astronomy and anatomy
Ignored most of the arts and sciences	Arts and sciences
An inability for close and patient logical thought and investigation	Geometry, trigonometry and algebra
Lack of taste, imagination and insensibility to beauty and the principles of order and harmony	Music and sports

6 Junius H. Judson, *Reminiscences of J.H. Judson: From the year one to seventy eight*. Unpublished autobiography (1930) held by Burke Theological Library, Columbia University, 14-5.

Note. Adapted by the author from the *Catalogue of Hangchow High School* (Shanghai: American Presbyterian Mission Press, 1894), 1–2.

This brief information on the curriculum at the Tengzhou and Hangchow colleges provides us with useful information regarding the way in which Wang Hengtong was educated. His education was reflected in the textbooks he produced, revised and reprinted over a period of fifteen years, covering history, arithmetic, geography, astronomy and the Chinese language. Although many of these textbooks are now no longer available for us to view, we may still gain insights into them by means of advertisements and book reviews published in the *Chinese Recorder*.

Wang Hengtong and the Christian Community in Shanghai

When the Chongxin yishu was first established at Ningpo, it made its purpose very clear: training Chinese youths to be native ministers in Christian churches, or to become teachers or medical doctors. Upon his graduation, Wang Hengtong became a teacher at the day school of the American Presbyterian Mission Press. The school was located "in the Mission Press Chapel building,"[7] and was "under the auspices of the Shanghai Presbyterian Mission Church."[8] His proximity to the Press may have inspired his writing of textbooks, and influenced his close relationship with it.[9] It was in Shanghai that Wang met and became involved with other Protestant missionaries and native Chinese Christians who were active in education and in the distribution of knowledge through their writings, translation works and publishing.

Wang Hengtong and Foreign Missionaries in Shanghai

Wang Hengtong was initially associated with missionary members from the Shanghai Station of the American Presbyterian Mission, which was opened in July 1850 when Rev. J. K. Wight and his wife arrived there from Ningpo.[10] However, Wight was rather ineffective because of the Taiping Rebellion. In 1859 John Marshall Willoughby Farnham (範約翰, 1829-1917) arrived in Shanghai and established the first Presbyterian Church there, followed by the Lowrie Institute (also known as Lowrie High School). Unlike most missionary members who were often transferred to mission stations in other locations, Farnham conducted his missionary work mainly in Shanghai and remained there until his death in 1917. Apart from his devotion to education Farnham,

7 Robert F. Fitch, Introduction to the *Illustrated Chinese Fourth Reader* (繪圖蒙學課本四集) (Shanghai: American Presbyterian Mission Press 6th edn, 1914), 2.

8 John Alfred Silsby, Introduction to the 2nd vol of the *Illustrated Chinese Primer* (Huitu Mengxue jiejing 繪圖蒙學捷径) (Shanghai: American Presbyterian Mission Press 11th edn, 1913), 2.

9 *The Chinese Recorder*, 32 (1901), 475.

10 *Jubilee Papers of the Central China Presbyterian Mission, 1844-1894*, 38.

was regarded as "the efficient Secretary of the Chinese Tract Society", according to *A Century of Missions in China*.[11]

The Chinese Tract Society helped build a Christian community of both foreign missionaries and native believers, regardless of denomination. This society evolved from the Chinese Religious Tract Society (中华圣教书局) established in 1878; in 1895 it united with the East China Tract Society, founded in 1885, to form the Chinese Tract Society.[12] As shown in Table 2, each volume of Wang's language textbooks contains an English introduction written by a missionary, and most of them (J.M. W Farnham, A. P. Parker, J. A. Silsby, P.F. Price, H. G. C. Hallock as well as Judson, Wang Hengtong's teacher), were involved in the Chinese Tract Society. By 1916 Wang Hengtong was on the Board of Directors and the Board of Trustees, and he and his wife were listed as life members of the society.[13] The Chinese Tract Society acted as a meeting point between Wang Hengtong and the missionaries, and the connections it facilitated help us map the activities of the Christian community in Shanghai and learn about the cross-cultural integration and interactions between foreign missionaries and native Chinese Christians.

Table 2: List of Missionary Members who Wrote an English Introduction to Wang Hengtong's Textbooks

Name and affiliated missionary group	Volume of Wang's Chinese Primer or Reader
Philip Francis Price (畢來思, 1864-1954); Lexington Pres. Church	*Illustrated Chinese First Primer*
John Alfred Silsby (薛思培, ?– 939); American Pres. Church (North)	*Illustrated Chinese Second Primer*
Donald MacGillivray (季理斐, 1862-1931); Pres. Church of Canada	*Illustrated Chinese Third Primer*
Carl Henrik Tjäder (查明道, 1866-); Swedish Mission in China/CIM	*Illustrated Chinese Fourth Primer*
H.G.C. Hallock (赫顯理, 1870-1951) American Pres. Church (North)	*Illustrated Chinese First Reader*
A.P. Parker (潘慎文, 1850-1924); Methodist Episcopal Church (South)	*Illustrated Chinese Second Reader*

11 Donald MacGillivray, *A century of Protestant missions in China* (Shanghai: American Presbyterian Mission Press, 1907), 382.

12 See 'Historical Note' and 'The Religious Tract Society for China, Jubilee appeal' in *The 1921-2 Annual Report of the Religious Tract Society for China* (Hankow: Arthington Press, Religious Tract Society, 1922) for a brief account of the history and development of the society. *A century of Protestant missions in China* also contains a detailed account of the society, and mentioned Farnham as one of the founding members (pp.620-1).

13 *The Thirty-eight of the Chinese Tract Society/The Twenty-second after the Union of East China Tract Society established 1885 with the China Religious Tract Society established in 1878* (Shanghai: 18 Peking Road, 1916), i.

John Marshall Willoughby Farnham (範約翰, 1829-1917); American Pres. Church (North)	*Illustrated Chinese Third Reader*
Robert Ferris Fitch (費佩德, 1873-1954), American Pres. Church (North)	*Illustrated Chinese Fourth Reader*
John Litt Darroch (竇樂安, 1865-1941); China Inland Mission	*Illustrated Chinese Fifth Reader*
Edward Waite Thwing (丁義華, 1868-1943); American Pres. Church (North)	*Illustrated Chinese Sixth Reader*

Among those who wrote introductions to Wang Hengtong's textbooks, many were professional educators. J. M. W. Farnham established the Qingxin Shuyuan (Lowrie High School) in the early 1860s and remained principal until 1888 when John Alfred Silsby succeeded him.[14] A.P. Parker was first the principal of Cunyang Academy (存養書院) and in 1895 he was appointed President of the Anglo-Chinese College in Shanghai (Zhongxi shuyuan 中西書院).[15] Robert Ferris Fitch was a professional educator with an impressive career in missionary education: in 1903 he was principal of the Ningpo Presbyterian Academy (寧波益智書院); in 1913 he was appointed Vice-President of the Hangchow Christian College and in 1922 he became its fourth president until 1931.[16]

Wang Hengtong, the Shanghai Commercial Press, and the Chinese Christian Union

Wang rendered faithful service as a day-school teacher at the American Presbyterian Mission Press and was also a prolific textbook writer for thirteen years; "then for the succeeding thirteen years was with the Commercial Press in various capacities, as sales manager, advertising manager, director, auditor, and latterly in supervising banknote printing, for all of which his keen mind, wide knowledge and inflexible honesty fitted him."[17] He joined the Commercial Press perhaps in May 1915.[18] His services to both Presses provided links to

14 *Jubilee papers of the Central China Presbyterian Mission, 1844-1894*, 53-55,74.

15 Tanya Storch, *Religions and missionaries around the Pacific, 1500-1900* (Farnham: Ashgate Publishing, 2006), 38; A.P. Parker, 'The relation of the association to the cause of general educational in China', *Records of the Second Triennial Meeting of E.A.C.* (1896), 41-2; and also in *The Chinese Record* XXVII, 7 (July 1896), 343-348. Hu Weiqing, 'Chuanjiaoshi jiaoyujia Pan Shenwen de sixiang yu huodong (傳教士教育家潘慎文的思想與活動) [Educational thoughts and practices of missionary educator A.P. Parker]', *Jindaishi yanjiu* (近代史研究) [Modern History], 2 (1996), 244-262.

16 Day, *Hangchow University*, 32.

17 Gilbert McIntosh, 'In Remembrance: Mr. Wang Hang T'ong', *The Chinese Recorder*, 59 (1928), 313.

18 Zhang Shunian 张树年, *Zhang Yuanji nianpu 張元濟年譜* (Beijing: Shangwu yinshuguan, 1991).

both a foreign missionary community and a group of Chinese Christians in Shanghai.

In 1897 George Field Fitch (費啟鴻, 1845–1923)[19] helped a group of Chinese Christians establish the Commercial Press. The group consisted of Xia Ruifang (夏瑞芳, 1871-1914), Gao Fengchi (高鳳池, 1864-1950) and the Bao Brothers – Bao Xianen (鮑咸恩, 1861- 1910) and Bao Xianchang (鮑咸昌, 1864-1929). They all graduated from the Qingxin Shuyuan (Lowrie High School) and were members of the Presbyterian Church.[20] Due to a lack of financial resources, when Lowrie High School was first established Farnham developed a work-study programme which included learning printing technology.[21] With these skills, on graduation Gao entered the American Presbyterian Mission Press, and ten years later was promoted to manager, while Xia and Bao Xian'en worked for China Gazette (捷報).[22]

The first book the Commercial Press published was *Hua Ying chujie* (華英初階) by Xie Honglai (謝洪賚, also Hsieh Hung-lai and H. L. Zia, 1873-1916), the eldest of the seven children of Xie Yuanfang (謝元芳, also written Dzi Yun-fang), a student at the Chongxin yishu (崇信義塾) in Ningpo.[23] At the age of eleven Xie Honglai entered Buffington College, where he was regarded highly by Parker, his teacher and the principal of the college. This intelligent, hard-working model Christian student graduated in 1890. In 1895 Parker took up the position of president of the Anglo-Chinese College in Shanghai and invited Xie Honglai to work there, first as a librarian and then as head of the Science Department in the second year. Together with Parker, he translated a few science textbooks[24] which were listed as teaching materials for missionary schools such as Hangchow Presbyterian College.

Except for Xia Ruifang and Gao Fengchi from Shanghai, most members of this group originally came from the Ningpo region: both Wang Hengtong and Xie Honglai were from Yuyao in Zhejiang, and the Bao brothers from Yinxian (鄞縣). This regional identity and ties with classmates and in-laws linked them

---

19 The missionary couple George Field Fitch and his wife Mary arrived in China in 1870. They lived and worked mainly in Shanghai, Suzhou and Ningpo, and their five children were born in Shanghai and Suzhou. Robert F. Fitch was their eldest son.

20 Bao Zhecai 鮑哲才 is listed as an 1852 graduate of Chongxin yishu at Ningbo and was the father of the Bao brothers. He later became the minister of the Pure Heart Church in Shanghai and naturally his children studied at the Lowrie High School.

21 Shanghai Tongshe 上海通社, *Shanghai yanjiu ziliao xuji 上海研究資料續集* (Shanghai: Shanghai shudian, 1984 reprint), 324.

22 For a more detailed account of the founding members of the Commercial Press, see Wang Jiarong 汪家熔, *Shangwu yinshuguan ji qita 商務印書館史及其他* [The Commercial Press and other relevant information] (Beijing: Zhongguo shuji chubanshe 中国书籍出版社, 1998), 7-12.

23 Judson, *Catalogue of Hangchow High School*, 5 (Chinese version) and 7 (English version).

24 *A century of Protestant missions in China*, 421. Also, Zhao Xiaoyang, *Zhongguo jidujiao qingnianhui zaoqi wenzi gongxianzhe Xie Honglai ji zhushu mulu* 中國基督教青年會早期文字貢獻者謝洪賚及著述目錄 [Y.M.C.A. writer Xie Honglai and the list of his works], Jidu zongjiao yanjiu (Study of Christianity) (Beijing: Zongjiao wenhua chubanshe, 2006), vol.9, 328–345.

together.[25] This group of Jiang-Zhe Chinese Christians in Shanghai in 1902 initiated the Chinese Christian Independent Movement and formed a society called The Chinese Christian Union (中國基督徒會) in the wake of the Chenzhou Incident (辰州教案).[26] This anti-Christian incident made them feel the necessity and urgency of "the independence of the Chinese Christians in the Protestant churches throughout China, in order that they may learn how to support their own churches, and become finally established Churches."[27] This Union had close ties to the Commercial Press: "The yearly budget is more than $600, which is contributed by the officers and members. Most of the officers live in Shanghai, and are connected with the Commercial Press there."[28]

In the spring of 1903 the Union started a quarterly newspaper, "The Chinese Christian" (中國基督徒報), promoting "the importance of building up self-supporting churches" hoping to "help many Chinese pastors to understand the purpose of the Union."[29]

The Independent movement and the search for co-operation among different dominations and between foreign missionaries and native Christians formed a context within which Wang Hengtong and this Christian community undertook their educational work – compiling textbooks and promoting the use of new methods in literacy education while continuing with their publishing business. Through their deeds and activities we see the shared aims, efforts and achievements of this Christian community, and the relevance of their work for China's modernization.

Christian Teacher and Textbook Writer

According to John Alfred Silsby, Wang was first of all a Christian teacher, as he did not forget "his duty to foster the moral and spiritual growth of his pupils" in his teaching of literacy skills. The textbooks he produced were "the result of years of practical experience and painstaking preparation." The textbooks Wang produced, commented Silsby, were "systematic, progressive, interesting and attractive"; they were also "illustrated, clearly printed, and better calculated to help both teacher and pupil" more than any other textbooks Silsby had ever seen.[30]

By the beginning of the twentieth century, Wang had established himself as a successful Christian teacher and a prolific textbook writer; in about fifteen years he produced 37 textbooks. Unfortunately, several of Wang's textbooks

25 For a detailed account of Xie Honglai and his relation to the founders of the Commercial Press, and a brief biography, see Wang Jiarong, *Shangwu yinshuguan*, 20, 189-190.

26 Wang Peiliang 王佩良, '1902 nian Chenzhou jiao'an de zhenxiang' 1902 年辰州教案的真相 (Facts about the Chenzhou anti-Christian case), *Wenshi bolan* (lilun) 文史博覽 (理論), 4 (2008), 10-11.

27 *The Chinese Recorder*, 43 (1912), 287.

28 Ibid., 289.

29 Ibid., 287-8.

30 Silsby, Introduction to the 2nd vol of *Illustrated Chinese Primer*, 2.

can no longer be found. Nevertheless, based on the information from the advertisements on the inner cover-page of his language textbooks, the introduction and book reviews of his textbooks published in *The Chinese Recorder*, newspapers[31] and magazines, we learn that the thirty-seven books included the following:

English and Chinese Primer (繪圖增廣華英初學) 1 vol.
General Descriptive Geography (新輯地理問答) 2 vols.
General descriptive geography (abridged)
A Geography of China (中國近世地理志) 2 vols.
General Descriptive Astronomy (新輯天文問答全集)
General Descriptive Astronomy (天文問答)
The World-Wide Geography for Young People (最新小學地理課本)
A Primary History of Our Country (小學歷史課本) 1 vol.
A Primary Geography of Our Country (小學地理課本)
Primary Physiology (小學生理課本) 1 vol.
Girl's Reader (最新女子國文教課本) 10 vols.
Illustrated Chinese Primer (繪圖蒙學捷徑) 4 vols.
Illustrated Chinese Reader (繪圖蒙學課本) 6 vols.

Among Wang's textbooks, the two series *Illustrated Chinese Primer* and *Illustrated Chinese Reader* were well known and reprinted more than ten times.

Wang's *Illustrated Chinese Primer* was first published in 1902 and was designed in two volumes, each volume containing two separate sections. Later this set of primers was revised and reprinted many times as four volumes rather than two volumes in four sections. The first two volumes focus on words and characters only. "Each lesson contains six new characters, beginning with the simpler forms and progressing to those more complex. The use of these characters is then illustrated in combinations of two, three, and four characters."[32] The third and fourth volumes contain 100 lessons each and the content can be divided into four categories: Christian teaching, *gezhi* (格致) learning (scientific knowledge or natural studies), moral instruction (advice) and children's literature/stories from both Chinese and English sources (including stories of exemplary children). The content in each category is apportioned as follows:

31 An advertisement in *Zhongxi jiaohui bao* (中西教會報), 107 (July 1904), listed Wang's textbooks including *General Descriptive Geography* (2 vols); *General Descriptive Astronomy*, and the new book *A Geography of China*.
32 *The Chinese Recorder*, 33 (1902), 38.

Table 3: Content Categories – Illustrated Chinese Primer (vols.3&4)

Christian teaching	10%
Gezhi learning	48%
Moral instruction	27%
Children's literature/stories	15%

The *Illustrated Chinese Reader* set was first published in 1901 in four volumes. The fifth volume was first published in 1910 and the sixth in 1913. Each volume contains 80 lessons which can be roughly divided into four categories: Christian teaching, *gezhi* learning, useful knowledge, and moral instruction through children's literature from both Chinese and English sources. The content is apportioned as follows:

Table 4: Content Categories – Illustrated Chinese Reader (vols.1-4)

Christian teaching	12.5%
Gezhi learning	60%
Other useful knowledge	12.5%
Moral instruction via Children's literature	15%

The "useful knowledge" category includes basic science and general knowledge Moral instruction refers to encouragement and guidance on study. Children's stories were drawn from both Chinese and western sources, such as Aesop's fables and traditional Chinese primers. Wang Hengtong made the textbook attractive by including a variety of content such as "geography, history, illustration, story, [and] some of the important sayings of our Chinese sages."[33] Both the *Illustrated Chinese Primer* and the first four volumes of the *Illustrated Chinese Reader* were revised and reprinted more than ten times from when they were first published in the beginning of the twentieth century up to the beginning of the People's Republic of China.

Missionary educators' acclaim of Wang's textbooks can be viewed as testament to their circulation and usefulness. For example, A. P. Parker advised that he used Wang's textbooks in his Anglo-Chinese College, and found them very satisfactory. Both students and their parents were delighted with the New Method of learning Chinese.[34] This New Method refers to a progressive teaching-learning process, in contrast to the traditional Chinese rote learning. The method was introduced into China from the West, but as Farnham pointed

33 Wang Hengtong, Preface, *Illustrated First Chinese Reader* (Shanghai: American Presbyterian Mission Press, 1904), 1.

34 A. P. Parker, Introduction to the *Illustrated Chinese Second Reader* (Shanghai: American Presbyterian Mission Press, 1911), 2.

out, Wang "carried out this principle in his series of books with beauty and symmetry."[35]

Carl Henrik Tjader, a member of the Swedish Mission in China, established the Chiechow (Haizhou) Boarding School in South Shansi in 1895 and was the school principal. He said that his school used Wang's textbooks and "found them to be more serviceable, and this new method of teaching the mother-tongue is a vast improvement on the old." He revealed that his students took "quite a delight in these lessons"; and appreciated that Wang Hengtong did not forget "to foster the moral and spiritual growth of his pupils." Noticing that Wang's textbooks were "much thought of by professional teachers" and were "used in all the schools of our mission," he gladly joined other missionary educators in recommending them.[36]

Such testimonies reveal that Wang's primers were used in mission schools beyond American Presbyterian Missions, and were not limited to Shanghai, Ningpo, Hangchow, Suchow and Nanking, the five centres of the Central China Presbyterian Mission. The tone of these testimonies shows that Wang Hengtong was an educational professional and a colleague to these foreign missionary educators who worked in the same area and shared the same practice. Such appreciation suggests a blurring of the boundary between foreign missionaries and native Chinese Christians, who shared collegial bonds as Christian educators and textbook writers.

Wang's Contribution to the Development of Modern Literacy Textbooks: 1901-1904

The uniqueness and the excellent quality of Wang's textbooks embody his liberated fusion of past and present, East and West, traditional and modern, Confucianism and Christianity. The third volume of Wang's primer, as MacGillivary praised, "judiciously combined the new and the old" with a variety of sources: some lessons originated in the "'paragons of filial piety' and other youthful heroes of Chinese lore out of the *Three Character Classic* (三字经), who from time immemorial have been employed in China to stimulate the youthful scholar"; some were "directly out of Scripture while others impart useful knowledge about birds, animals and plants of China after the manner of Western readers."[37]

Such varieties in the content of Wang's textbooks are also attributed to the competitiveness of the textbook market which emerged during this period. While textbooks produced by missionary educators for use in mission schools became available or were even pirated beyond the walls of missionary schools, a few series of new literacy textbooks written by non-Christian educators were

35 Farnham's Introduction to the *Illustrated Chinese Third Reader*, 2.
36 C. Henrik Tjader, Introduction to the fourth volume of *Illustrated Chinese Primer* (10th edn) (Shanghai: The Presbyterian Mission Press, 1912), 1-2.
37 Donald MacGillivary, Introduction to the third volume of the *Illustrated Chinese Primer*, 1-2.

produced in response to waves of reform and enthusiasm for a new educational system. They were:

- *Mengxue keben* (蒙學課本) in three volumes
  Compiled by Chen Maozhi (陳懋治) and other students from Nanyang gongxue (南洋公學). First published 898, revised 1901 and published as *Xinding Mengxue keben* (新訂蒙學課本).
- *Mengxue jing* 蒙學镜 (alt. title *Dushule* 讀書樂) in 12 volumes
  In 1895 Zhong Tianwei established Shanghai Sandeng xuetang 上海三等學堂 and began to compile literacy textbooks in the course of teaching. First published in 1898.
- *Mengxue duben quanshu* （蒙學讀本全書)
  Compiled by Yu Fu, Wu Zhihui, Ding Baoshu and Du Sicheng for Wuxi Sandeng gongxuetang (無錫三 等公學堂) established in 1898.
- In 1902 these authors set up Wenming shuju 文明书局 in Shanghai and reprinted the set of textbooks.
- *Chengzhong xuetang zike tushuo* (澄衷字課圖說) in five volumes
  Chengzhong mengxuetang was established in Shanghai by Ye Chengzhong 葉澄衷 (1840-1899), one of the well-known entrepreneurs in late Qing Shanghai. Liu Shuping (劉樹屏, 1857－1917), first principal of the school, compiled this set of textbooks in 1901.[38]
- *Huitu wenxue chujie* (繪圖蒙學初階) in six volumes
  Du Yaquan (1873–1933)[39] compiled this series at the invitation of the Commercial Press, published in 1903.

These five sets of literacy primers were produced just before the proclamation of the modern school system, so differed from traditional Chinese *mengshu*. From this perspective, Chinese scholars often regard Nanyang gongxue waiyuan's *Mengxue keben* as the first modern literacy textbook compiled by the Chinese themselves,[40] and Zhong Tianwei's *Mengxue jing* as

38 The information about Ye Chengzhong, Chengzhong mengxuetang and Liu Shuping in these paragraphs is largely based on Wang Zhen 王震, 'Ye Chengzhong yu Chengzhong xuetang 葉澄衷與澄衷學堂', Shanghai Wenshiguan wenshi ziliao gongzuo weiyuanhui上海市文史館文史資料工作委員會, ed, *Shanghai defangshi ziliao 上海地方史資料*, 上海社會科學院出版社, 4 (1986), 148-152. Liu Shuping, 'Chengzhong mengxuetang ji 澄衷蒙學堂記', in Zhu Youyu, *Zhongguo jindai xuezhi shiliao* 中国近代學制史料, 1, 2, 829-830; 'Shanghai Chongzheng xuetang chuangban yuanshi 上海澄衷學堂創辦緣始', ibid., 828-9. 'Liu Shuping', in Zhang Weixiang 张维驤, 'Qingdai Piling mingren xiaozhuan 清代毗陵名人小傳', *Changzhou lü hu tongxianghui 常州旅滬同鄉會*, 2, 9 (1944), 27-28.

39 Xie Zhensheng, 'Du Yaquan zhuanlue' [A brief biography of Du Yaquan], *Zhongguo kejishi zazhi*, 3 (1988), 8-14; Yan Nansheng, *Du Yaquan yu Zhongguo jindai kexue jiaoyu* [Du Yaquan and science education in China], Ph.D thesis (Huadong shifan daxue, 2011).

40 Xiao Xiaohong, 'Mengxue keben zhong de jiuxue xinzhi' <蒙學課本>中的舊學新知 (Old and new knowledge in *Mengxue keben*), *Qinghua daxue xuebao*, 24, 4 (2009), 39.

the first literacy textbook in *baihua*.[41] Du Yaquan's *Huitu Wenxue chujie* was also praised as the first set of modern Chinese literacy primers.[42] Such claims were founded on the definition of the concept of the term "textbook" which, by and large, was the term created and used by missionary educators in 1877 when a Committee for School Text and Books was established to organize, supervise and publish textbooks for the use of mission schools. Around the 1898 Reform period the reformers claimed that the low literacy rate was responsible for China's crisis in face of western powers, therefore elementary education was targeted as one of the key areas to reform. With the exception of Du Yanquan's *Wenxue chujie*, which Du compiled at the invitation of Zhang Yuanji (1867-1959), director of the Commercial Press in Shanghai, the other four sets of literacy primers mentioned above were all directly connected with the new schools the textbook writers established or operated.

Wang Hengtong's literacy primers and readers were produced during this period, but few Chinese scholars paid attention to them, perhaps because Wang was teaching at a Church school rather than in the newly established *xuetang* which did not have the ties with the churches. Nevertheless, if we read and compare the non-Christian textbooks with Wang's primers and readers, we see clear similarities in the use of illustrations, the implementation of new teaching methods and the inclusion of western learning and scientific knowledge. Although none of these authors had a similar educational background to Wang, they all acknowledged the use of western sources through translation and translated materials (*bianyi* 編譯). From this perspective we can contend that textbook writers of that period had access to similar or even the same sources. It is therefore not surprising that there was often a commonality between lessons and in many cases the same material was used in these textbook series. For example, the story about Washington's honesty was included in almost every set of literacy textbooks. In Wang's Primer (vol.4), the lesson informs the reader:

> Washington is the founding father of the United States and its democratic system. When he was little he used a small ax as his toy playing at tree-cutting in the front yard, which caused the tree skin to peel off. His father saw the wounded tree and was furious, but he did not know that Washington did this. Washington initially dared not to tell his father the truth, but in the end he confessed to his father: "This was my doing." His father was very pleased, and praised him with a big cuddle: "Thousands of cherry trees would not be as valuable as telling the truth."[43]

This story can be found in many literacy textbooks produced in the late Qing, such as Lesson 69 in the first volume of Nanyang gongxue's *Mengxue keben* (later included as Lesson 73 in the third volume of the revised version), Lesson 77 in the fourth volume of Wuxi Sandeng xuetang's *Mengxue duben*

---

41 Xue Yuliang 薛毓良, *Zhong Tianwei zhuan* 鐘天緯傳 (Shanghai: Shehui kexueyuan chubanshe, 2011), ch.10.

42 *Dadi* 大地, 1994, Nos.1-12, 57.

43 *Illustrated Chinese Primer*, *vol.4*, Lesson 88, 79 (Author's translation).

quanshu, and Lesson 32 in the fourth volume of the *Zuixin chudeng xiaoxue guowen jiaokeshu* (Shanghai Commercial Press, 1903). These lessons vary in description and vocabulary, but share the story line about Washington damaging his father's cherry tree and later confessing, for which he was forgiven and praised. The story possibly originated in *Shaonian Huashengdun xinglüe* 少年華盛頓行略 (Deeds of Young Washington) published in *Chinese Serial* (遐迩贯珍) in 1855.[44]

According to Michael Bentley, knowledge is the "paradigms of what was and what was not to count as worth knowing."[45] In the case of nineteenth-century China, what was worth or not worth knowing about the West or western learning? The popularity of the story about Washington's youth reflects how knowledge and information about the West flooded into China through the publication of translated works, magazines, newspapers and journals, and circulated in late Qing period. Textbook writers of the time compared this information with the existing works and compiled their own textbooks by maintaining what they thought suitable for children and adding what they obtained from all the sources available to them. This demonstrates that missionary educators (including native Chinese Christian teachers) and non-Christian Chinese reformers and educators, to a certain extent, shared the same view of what was worth knowing. The similarities presented in Wang's textbooks and those produced by non-Christian educators are a reflection of how native Chinese Christian educators like Wang contributed to the development of modern literacy textbooks in the beginning of the twentieth century.

Re-shaping the Content of Wang's Literacy Textbooks: 1905-1915

Socio-political changes in China also re-shaped the content of Wang Hengtong's textbooks. When his literacy primers and readers were first published they largely reflected the education he had received at mission school, containing three components: Christianity, Confucian teaching and science subjects. After 1905 the revised versions of these primers and readers changed due to the changes brought about by reforms. As shown in Table 5, there were 16 lessons on Confucianism in the 1904 edition of the *Illustrated Chinese First Reader*, covering the knowledge of Confucian Four Classics. In the 1913 version, however, the section on the Confucian classics was replaced by other topics, except for the lesson on Confucius himself. When China

---

44 *Chinese Serial*, 4 (1855). Pan Guangzhe, *Huashengdun zai Zhongguo: Zhizuo 'guofu'* (華盛頓在中國：制作'國父') (Taiwan: Sanmin shuju, 2006), 1-3. Also, Xiong Yuezhi, 'Huashengdun xingxiang de Zhongguo jiedu jiqi dui Xinhai geming de yingxiang' 華盛頓形象的中國解讀及其對辛亥革命的影響, in Wang Xiaoqiu, ed, *Xinhai geming yu shijie* 辛亥革命與世界) (Beijing: Beijing daxue chubanshe, 2013), 73-92 (relevant information on pp.74-77).

45 Michael Bentley, 'Evolution and dissemination of historical knowledge', in Martin Daunton, ed, *The organization of knowledge in Victorian Britain* (Oxford: Oxford University Press, 2005), 175.

abolished the civil service examination system in 1905 mission schools lost the rationale for the inclusion of Confucian teaching in their curriculum. Thus, the content of Wang Hengtong's primers was shaped not only by the education he received via mission schools but also by rapid changes in China's socio-political environment.

As discussed earlier, a large portion of the content of Wang's books was devoted to the spread of the "useful knowledge", the dissemination of which was considered a significant part of evangelism by missionaries in the late-nineteenth century. Indeed, missionary educators and their publications were very effective in taking such knowledge to people and thus influencing the broader society. Wang was a product of this education and wanted to impart this educational practice to his country's next generation. For example, his *Worldwide Geography for Young People* was compiled as a cure for Chinese people's ignorance of the world.[46]

Table 5: Lessons on Confucianism in the 1904 edition of the Illustrated Chinese First Reader

Lessons	Content
L.8, 14, 20, 26, 38	Great Learning (*Daxue* 大學)
L.24, 44, 53, 69, 78	The Mean (*Zhongyong* 中庸)
L.33	The Analects (*Lunyu* 論語)
L.55	Mencius (*Mengzi* 孟子)
L.12	An introduction to Confucius
L.25, 28, 35	Exposition of Confucianism from a Christian perspective

Wang Hengtong outlines the content of mathematical study in six-year advanced courses presented in the 1894 Catalogue of Presbyterian College of Hangchow, as well as the content of Mateer's *Arithmetic*, by which he emphasized the importance of mathematics.[47]

Did Wang Hengtong's view represent only what was worth knowing from a Christian perspective? Did the learned Chinese, regardless of whether or not they were Christians, hold the same opinion on the study of mathematics? Take Liang Qichao as an example. In his proposal for a new type of education for children Liang advocated that at the age of eight children should start learning mental arithmetic, and then gradually written calculation, basic geometry, algebra, and infinitesimal calculus, such that they could claim to be specialists

46 *The Chinese Recorder*, 37 (1906), 57.
47 *Illustrated Chinese Third Reader*, Lesson 47.

in the area (*chouren*)[48] before reaching the age of fifteen.[49] Liang's proposal resembles that of Wang, the only difference being that Liang did not openly acknowledge the influence of missionary education. Instead, he relied on Chinese tradition, arguing that in original Confucian education the knowledge of numerals and calculation was as important as the skill of reading and writing. He quietly added the content of missionary education to his proposed curriculum. Liang's emphasis on the study of mathematics may indicate the influence of missionary education which not only shaped a young generation of Chinese Christians like Wang Hengtong, but also contributed to the birth of a modern Chinese education system. In this context, we may conclude that both missionary educators and non-Christian reformers had agreed on the value of western learning for the Chinese education system.

The popularity of Mateer's *Arithmetic* also indicates this positive attitude to western knowledge among both parties. This book was used in missionary schools in the late nineteenth century and was listed by Wang Hengtong as a text that children should study. Beyond Christian education circles, from its first publication in 1892 Mateer's *Arithmetic* actually became "almost the first book in demand by Chinese teachers and pupils outside the mission schools."[50] Excluding numerous "pirated" copies in the market, by 1910 the American Presbyterian Mission Press in Shanghai alone had issued 32 editions and sold thousands of copies. The circulation of the book increased the reputation of Mateer "among the scholarly classes outside the church",[51] suggesting a consensus between missionaries, Christian teachers, non-Christian reformers and educators.[52] This occurred at a time in nineteenth-century China when missionaries, Chinese Christian teachers, non-Christian reformers, scholars and educators all compared China and the West in order to discern the secret of the latter's success.

Naturally, there are differences between Christian and non-Christian textbooks. For example, both Wang Hengtong and Du Yaquan's textbooks include a lesson on the five races, conveying the same information but with different comments at the end of the lesson. The comment from Wang's textbook states:

---

48 'Chouren' referred to people knowledgeable in areas of traditional Chinese mathematics and astronomy. For further discussion of the concept see Bai Limin, 'Mathematical study and intellectual transition in the early and mid-Qing', *Late Imperial China*, 16, 2 (1995), 23-61.

49 Liang Qichao, 'Lun youxue' [On elementary education]', in *Yinbingshi heji* (Collected works and essays from the ice-drinker's studio), 12 vols (1936; reprinted Beijing: Zhonghua shuju, 2003), *wenji*, 1:56.

50 Daniel Webster Fisher, *Calvin Wilson Mateer, forty-five years a missionary in Shantung, China: a biography* (Philadelphia: The Westminster press, 1911), 163.

51 Ibid.

52 For a Chinese introduction to the content and various editions of Mateer's Arithmetic, see Li Di 李迪, *Zhongguo shuxueshi dagang, vol.2 of fujuan* (副卷) (Beijing: Beijing shifan daxue chubanshe, 2000), 426-8. There are other Chinese research papers on the topic, but none appear to go beyond Li's work.

> Although there are five races, they are all descendants of Adam and Eve. Confucius said: 'All within the Four Seas are brothers.' I would say that all within the six continents are compatriots.[53]

In Du's lesson Confucius' maxim is also quoted but with a different interpretation:

> Although there are five races, they share the same origin. Confucius said: 'All within the Four Seas are brothers.' We should extend our love to every human being and all species, making sure not to harm amicable relations of people by emphasizing competition.[54]

It is clear that both opposed social Darwinism, but from totally different perspectives.

Concluding Discussion

This study has gathered information from a variety of sources to narrate the life and career of Wang Hengtong against the backdrop of the socio-political, ideological, and intellectual framework of early twentieth-century China. This portrait of Wang as an 'ordinary Chinese Christian' adds to our understanding of the contribution made by Chinese Christian educators towards the establishment of a modern Chinese education system.

Shanghai served as a meeting point where Wang Hengtong was accepted into a Christian community consisting of both foreign missionaries and native Chinese Christians. Wang Hengtong and a group of Chinese Christians devoted themselves to the indigenization of Christianity in the wake of the 1902 Chenzhou anti-Christian incident. Meanwhile, the assistance provided by George Field Fitch toward the establishment of the Commercial Press suggested a reciprocal search for co-operation between foreign missionaries and native Christians. This Sino-foreign cooperation and interchange of ideas formed the framework within which Wang Hengtong and this Christian community undertook their educational work. This examination of Wang's career as a Christian teacher and textbook writer has thrown light on the relationship between foreign missionaries and native Chinese Christians, revealing how these two groups coalesced into a community in which both underwent cultural and national boundary-transformations.

Furthermore, a close textual examination of Wang's literacy textbooks reveals how his contribution to the textbook literature was linked to the shaping of Christianity in early twentieth-century China. From a broad perspective, both missionary and native Chinese Christian educators valued Wang's textbooks as part of the Protestant missionary participation in the building of a new China. Traditional Chinese education focused on the ability to ascend the civil examination ladder which only served the interests of the elite. Chinese

53 *Illustrated Chinese Second Reader*, Lesson 22.

54 Du Yaquan, *Wenxue chujie*, vol.6, Lesson 70, 32b-33a.

reformers in late Qing called for educational reform in order to develop the intellect of people for the prosperity of the country. Christian education aimed to foster a young generation of Chinese people who would be the foundation for a Christian nation. Missionary educators saw the changes brought by late Qing reforms and resolved that missionary education would still "lead the van in this as in other changes, whose final outcome will be a New China."[55] More specifically, Wang employed a new method for teaching Chinese characters in his literacy textbooks that won him praise from both missionary and native Chinese Christian educators. This so-called "new method" refers to a progressive teaching-learning process, in contrast to the traditional Chinese rote learning. As discussed earlier, new literacy textbooks by non-Christian textbook writers emerged during this period, and the use of this progressive method became common practice in textbook composition. However, in the view of Christian educators, Wang Hengtong was a pioneer "in the preparation of this new literature in schools" and it was predicted that more such schoolbooks would be produced "by those who follow where Mr. Wang blazed the way."[56] It was from this perspective Robert Fitch believed that "China in the long run will owe the most for her intellectual and spiritual advancement"[57] to men like Wang Hengtong.

The greatest accomplishment of Wang Hengtong in relation to the indigenization of Christianity was his contribution to the development of new textbooks sensitive to China's deep needs. His work demonstrates how this generation of Chinese Christian educators, along with missionary educators, traversed the cultural borders between East and West, straddled the religious and ideological boundaries between Confucianism and Christianity, and negotiated the Chinese need for modernization and missionary endeavours to propagate Christian faith. This encounter brought about reciprocal influence between missionary educators and Chinese Christian teachers which in turn moulded the content of knowledge in circulation. This study shows a mutual understanding of what comprised "useful knowledge" between Christian missionary educators, Chinese Christian teachers and non-Christian educators and reformers of the time, and contributes to a cohesive account of how Christian education became relevant to the nation building process in late-nineteenth and early-twentieth-century China.

55 Parker, Introduction to *The Illustrated Chinese Second Reader*, 2.
56 Price's foreword to the first volume of *The Illustrated Chinese Primer* (10th edn, 1912), 2.
57 Robert F. Fitch, Introduction to *The Illustrated Chinese Fourth Reader*, 1903, 2.

Part Four

Living the Faith

Identity, Maturity, and Leadership: Chinese Christians and the Negotiation of Otherness at the Boxer Rebellion

Paul Woods

The suffering of Chinese Christians and Western missionaries in Shanxi during a relatively brief period of the Boxer Rebellion is a well known part of the modern history of China and its church. What may be less familiar to many is the extent to which those tragic events revealed the spiritual maturity and leadership of many Chinese Christians at the time. In addition, the external pressure constituted by the Boxers confirmed and accelerated the negotiation of identity and roles among local believers.

This study focuses on what was probably a relatively small group of Chinese Christians in a fairly small geographical area over a rather short period of time: it constitutes a snapshot of the status and experience of the Chinese church at the turn of the twentieth century. Another caveat is that the Boxer Rebellion brought about a peculiar set of circumstances; people were thrust together by suffering, the urge to survive, and possibly by some theological sense of destiny. Almost certainly, the events transpiring around the city of Taiyuan brought about a degree of liminality in which established distinctions and accepted prejudices were reduced or even removed. That said, the suffering, violence, and chaos associated with the Boxer experience probably intensified existing trends in identity negotiation in the Sino-foreign Christian community.

Several chapters in this volume mention the relative abundance of records of the activities of western missionaries and a corresponding paucity of information about their Chinese brothers, sisters, and colleagues. My own study has operated against a similar imbalance of source material, and is thus an attempt at *history from below* or alternative history in that I am trying to gain a portrait of the Chinese from materials written by westerners and mostly about westerners. I consulted several mission histories written just after the Boxer Rebellion: Forsyth's *The China Martyrs*[1] (abbreviated TCM) and *Narrative of Massacres in Shansi*[2] (NMS), Broomhall's *The Last Letters*[3] (TLL) and *The*

1 Robert Forsyth, *The China martyrs of 1900* (New York: Fleming H. Revell Company, 1904).

2 Robert Forsyth, *Narrative of massacres in Shansi, July, 1900. Pamphlet 41 of 'China and the Chinese'* (Shanghai: North-China Herald Office, 1900)

3 Marshall Broomhall, *Last letters and further records of martyred missionaries of the China Inland Mission* (London: Morgan & Scott, 1901)

Jubilee Story of the CIM[4] (JSC), and Edwards' *Fire and Sword in Shansi*[5] (FSS). These books contain direct accounts and excerpts from missionary letters in which reference to and evaluation of Chinese Christians can be found, and thus our understanding of the faith and practice of local believers is relatively well founded and indeed well rounded. For reasons of brevity I shall group comments about the Chinese believers and analysis of them under four broad headings: *presence and identity*, *maintenance and expansion*, *witness and martyrdom*, and *care and sacrifice*, an arrangement allowing a rough division between the circumstances before the Boxer Rebellion and those during it. The subsequent growth of the Chinese churches and partnership between locals and missionaries is beyond the scope of this article.

Background

The Boxers were a short-lived, anti-foreign group within Chinese society at the end of the nineteenth century. A detailed discussion of the movement is beyond the scope of this article, but Tiedemann tells us that frustration with the actions and attitudes of foreigners in China, severe economic and agricultural problems in north China, Chinese ethnocentrism, and the influence of superstition and rumour lay behind its formation.[6] The Boxers (*Yihetuan* 義和團, lit. *Militia of Righteous Unity*) believed that special exercises and patterns of breathing gave them supernatural resistance to injury, and it was from these that their western nickname was derived.[7]

At the time of the Boxer Rebellion Christian missionaries from powerful western nations moved among Chinese people who followed various local religions and philosophies and sometimes saw themselves as weak and powerless. In addition, for many Chinese people, westerners were agents of imperialism and were associated with the opium trade. Even from this obviously simplistic description it is clear that relationships between missionaries and local believers could have fallen into simple binaries, each viewing the other as alien. As the Boxers grew in power they created a climate of fear in which they forced local believers to declare a simple choice of identity: Chinese or Christian. The Boxers could not understand or accept a compatriot who understood him or herself as both, and thus tried to drive wedges between Chinese people.

4 Marshall Broomhall, *The jubilee story of the China Inland Mission* (London: Morgan & Scott, 1915).
5 E. Edwards, *Fire and sword in Shansi: The story of the martyrdom of foreigners and Chinese Christians* (Edinburgh: Oliphant Anderson & Ferrier, 1907).
6 R. Tiedemann, 'Baptism of fire: China's Christians and the Boxer Uprising of 1900', *International Bulletin of Missionary Research,* 24, 1 (2000), 7-12.
7 J. Esherick, *The origins of the Boxer Uprising* (Berkeley, CA: Univ. of California Press, 1987).

Otherness and Hybridity

This article deals with changing relationships between three groups of people: western missionaries, nationalist Boxer Chinese, and Chinese Christians. While the first two groups were as separate as oil and water, Chinese believers found themselves caught in an uneasy interstitial space. For this reason it will be instructive to consider briefly the notions of *otherness* and hybridity.

Mengstie[8] explains neatly that *otherness* is how we define ourselves or our identities as we relate to others, involving a recognition that we are in some way different from other people or groups. Hall reminds us that *otherness* and difference are neutral ideas; there is nothing inherently negative about noting or feeling that we are different – *other* as an adjective – to those around us. At the same time, Canales[9] is clear that acknowledging our own *otherness* and that of people around us invokes a degree of subjectivity.

Hall places this subjectivity in a broader context, claiming that 'identities are…constituted within, not outside representation'.[10] Mengstie agrees, commenting that the construction of *otherness* is carried out according to relationships, culture, politics, and education.[11] This is related to the idea of stereotyping, in which a person or group is represented in our mind by a small number of selected attributes.[12] In addition, stereotypes require boundaries to distinguish between 'them' and 'us', which often reflect power differentials between groups.[13] Cleary, stereotypes, the selection of attributes, and the drawing of boundaries can be associated with negative perceptions and prejudice.[14] Davies goes as far as to state that 'without an "other" to negate, we could not achieve the sense of power and invulnerability that we all, consciously or unconsciously, seek'.[15]

Going a little deeper, Canales introduces us to exclusionary and inclusionary *othering*.[16] In the first, a dominant group uses its power to exclude those it decides do not fit; the second form is where a dominant or powerful group recognises the *otherness* – inherent differences from the mainstream – yet decides to include the *other* on the basis of these differences and without trying to enforce conformity to the mainstream.

---

8 S. Mengstie, 'Constructions of "otherness" and the role of education: The case of Ethiopia', *Journal of Education Culture and Society*, 2, 7-15 (2011), 7.

9 M. Canales, 'Othering: Toward an understanding of difference', *Advances in Nursing Science*, 22, 4 (2000), 16.

10 S. Hall, 'Introduction: Who needs identity?', in Stuart Hall & Paul Du Gay, eds, *Questions of cultural identity* (London: Sage, 1996), 4.

11 Mengstie, *Constructions of 'otherness'*, 8.

12 S. Hall, 'The spectacle of the "Other"', in Stuart Hall, ed, *Representation: Cultural representations and signifying practices* (Milton Keynes: Open University, 1997), 257.

13 Hall, *The spectacle of the "Other"*, 258.

14 Mengstie, *Constructions of 'otherness'*, 10.

15 Julia Davies, 'Cultural dimensions of intersubjectivity: Negotiating "sameness" and "otherness" in the analytic relationship', *Psychoanalytic Psychology*, 28, 4 (2011), 552.

16 M. Canales, Othering, 19.

She notes that exclusionary *othering* often assumes a 'mythical norm'[17] against which outside groups are evaluated and usually found wanting. Those who explicitly or implicitly challenge the imposed norm are portrayed as suspicious or dangerous by the dominant group. For the dominant and excluding group what is significant is not a genuine understanding of the *other* or an attempt to see things from the *other*'s perspective, but their subjective failure to meet the standards the powerful require and impose.[18] On the other hand, inclusionary *othering* makes use of power differentials for 'transformation and coalition building'.[19] This requires us to walk in someone else's shoes and see the world from the *other*'s perspective – what Lugones calls travelling to someone else's world.[20]

Finally, having considered *othering* as exclusionary and inclusionary – negative and positive – it is necessary to look briefly at hybridity. Bhabha talks of negotiation (a word found in the title of this essay), which refuses representations based on binaries and 'social antagonism',[21] dialogue which works in the in-between spaces to build community without being consumed by the mainstream. Because the representation and creation of *otherness* and identity are dynamic, those involved in the process can draw on various aspects of their cultures and heritages, 'the contaminated yet connective tissue between cultures',[22] and use it as they choose.

During the Boxer crisis it would have been all too easy for westerner and Chinese to default to two camps separated by a huge gulf. The motivation for and discovery of this paper is that local Christians and foreign missionaries moved beyond simple binaries of *otherness* and towards some kind of liminal hybridity. In this process Chinese believers showed considerable spiritual maturity and pastoral devotion, especially as the Boxer movement developed. Likewise, western missionaries, who have sometimes been portrayed as paternalist or orientalist in their attitudes to Chinese Christians, emerge from these accounts as vulnerable, trusting, and deeply appreciative of their Chinese coreligionists.

Yet apart from the obvious *otherness* between western and Chinese, and Christianity and Chinese religions, the cause of such intolerance and violence from the Boxers, the events of the summer of 1900 also accelerated the negotiation of *otherness within* the Christian community. At the beginning of missionary work, there is an inevitable distinction between bringers and recipients of the gospel. As seen in several other chapters in this volume,

17 Ibid., 20.
18 Ibid., 22.
19 Ibid., 20.
20 M. Lugones, 'Playfulness, "world"-traveling, and loving perception', in G. Anzaldúa, ed, *Making Face, making soul/haciendo cara: Creative and critical perspectives by women of color* (San Francisco: Aunt Lute Foundation Books, 1990).
21 Homi Bhabha, 'Culture's in-between', in Stuart Hall & Paul Du Gay, eds, *Questions of cultural identity* (London: Sage, 1996), 58.
22 Ibid., 54.

progress in mission work brings inclusion of and handing over to local believers. Thus within the community of believers, including locals and missionaries, there is an on-going negotiation of roles and responsibilities which results in the redefinition and fragmentation of *otherness*.

Historical Context

The close of the nineteenth century was a very difficult period for Imperial China, which suffered from a combination of foreign aggression and (Manchu Qing) dynastic failure. Depending on one's perspective, foreigners of one kind or another were responsible for much of China's weakness and vulnerability. In addition, westerners who brought in a foreign faith and took a dominant role in its propagation looked and sounded the same as those who arrived on gunships, demanded trade on unfair terms, and sold the dreaded opium to the people. Indeed, arrogance and high-handed attitudes, often combined with paternalism and even racism, were not only found among worldly Western businessmen and traders; in some of the Christian books which movingly record the faith and fate of western Christians in China the modern reader detects attitudes which jar.

To be fair, racism and narrow-mindedness were to be found on both sides of what was often a racial and cultural divide. Many Chinese were opposed on principle to Christianity as a western religion. Western missionaries had been persecuted and abused by ordinary Chinese people as well as the government. Rumours about the barbaric behaviour of the western missionaries existed in many parts of China. There were tales of missionaries eating Chinese children at the time of the Tianjin massacre of 1870. Some Chinese people claimed that the western evangelists took local people's eyes and nipples and stored them in ships. In Shanxi it was said that at night missionaries used large fans to blow the clouds away in order to cause drought.

A sensitive situation across China was made worse in Shanxi by the presence and attitudes of the governor Yu Xian (毓賢). Although in recent years some historians have suggested that much of the violence in Shanxi was not ordered directly by him[23] and that before the tragic events of 1900 he actually tried to suppress the growing Boxer movement in Shandong, it is also acknowledged that he lost his position as governor there as a result of western pressure[24] and was ill-disposed towards westerners, and missionaries in particular.

23 Roger Thompson, 'Reporting the Taiyuan Massacre: Culture and politics in the China War of 1900', in Robert Bickers & R. G. Tiedemann, eds, *The Boxers, China, and the world* (Lanham, MD: Rowman & Littlefield, 2007), 65–92.

24 Joseph Esherick, *The origins of the Boxer Uprising* (Stanford, CA: Stanford University Press, 1987).

Chinese Christians and the Everyday: Presence and Identity

The large amount of material in the various books consulted and the brevity of this paper mean that it is impossible to give anything more than a representative sample of the identity, roles, and activities of Chinese Christians at the time.

Forsyth mentions attacks on Christians in the Taiyuan area,[25] and it seems clear that the Boxers and presumably the general population knew which people in a given village or town were Christian. Indeed, the diary of a certain Mr Dixon[26] mentions 'rumours of plans to destroy all foreigners and native Christians'. In Hsin-chou,[27] Chang Chih Kuo was killed simply because of his faith.[28] There had been bad feeling for some time between Christian and non-Christian in villages in the Chia-chwang[29] area, because the believers refused to give money for the maintenance of temples. Tsai Ching Yung was a Shanxi Christian who worked as a house painter. Before his conversion he also painted idols, but stopped this after becoming a Christian, preaching in the open and even in temples.[30]

Numerous lay people were involved in various aspects of Christian ministry. Forsyth mentions Mr Li, known widely in the Hsin-chou region as a Christian bookseller.[31] Si-er-mao, who lived a few miles from the town, was well known as a believer and often shared the gospel with his neighbours. Another occasional bookseller was Wang-hsin,[32] who was familiar to all in his area on account of a conversion which brought an end to his gambling, opium smoking, and other nefarious activities. These Chinese people self identified in public as Christian and had begun a process of renegotiating their standards and behaviour in the light of their conversion, which to some degree marked them as *other* to much of mainstream society.

Chinese Christians and the Ministry: Maintenance and Expansion

Western missions to China had begun along the east coast and had extended inland slightly later. As an inland province, Shanxi would have lagged behind regions reached with the gospel earlier, justifying Forsyth's comment that 'the church in China, especially in Shan-si…is still in its infancy'.[33]

The records we have, written by westerners, reveal the extent of the work done by Chinese colleagues, many of whom served for a long time and were greatly respected by the missionaries. To the modern reader, some of the

25 TCM, 39.
26 Ibid., 49.
27 忻州 Xinzhou. To facilitate reference to early twentieth century accounts the old transliterations of place names are retained.
28 TCM, 57.
29 Ibid., 372.
30 FSS, 179.
31 TCM, 361.
32 Ibid., 379.
33 TCM, 368.

positive sentiments expressed by the missionaries might appear paternalistic, but we must remember that a hundred years have passed since these comments were written, and the western Christians were a product of their time.

Personnel in the Chinese church across the country consisted of various kinds of experienced and valued lay helpers: booksellers and colporteurs, locals who opened their houses or premises for worship, and Bible women from different denominations, church groupings and mission societies. In addition, there were Chinese church workers and evangelists, catechists, deacons, elders, church pastors, as well as pastors responsible for several churches in a district. Foreign missionaries served as 'bishops' supervising more settled pastoral work in a given area or superintendents of pioneer mission efforts. The volumes consulted suggest that most of these roles were represented in Shanxi at the time of the Boxers, with front line mission work a priority in some areas.

It seems that lay people sometimes took the initiative in evangelism and even preaching. Some Chinese workers were completely independent, while others had rather fluid working relationships with western missionaries. It appears that in China as a whole and in Shanxi, ministry by the Chinese was not simply a matter of either working alone or completely under western leadership. Also, the day-to-day work of the Chinese and the western missionaries was sometimes the same. Given that Chinese is a very difficult language to learn for westerners, and that the non-Christian Chinese showed various degrees of allegiance to Buddhism, Confucianism, Daoism, and folk superstitions, it seems likely that foreign missionaries would have relied quite heavily on their local colleagues. From the books consulted, one might gain the impression that Chinese pastors operated more in a maintenance and consolidation mode, whereas missionaries tended to go into virgin territory. Starting new stations far from existing ones and moving to a new location was more likely undertaken by westerners; Chinese evangelists were generally less mobile, presumably because they had families, jobs, and local responsibilities.

The next section presents examples of Chinese serving the church in some kind of professional capacity. The phrase 'native evangelist' is found throughout the books used for this research but it is not easy to establish the exact status of such people, which would have varied across mission societies and even according to the missionaries alongside whom they served, but it is clear that much day-to-day evangelism and consolidation of the church was carried out by Chinese workers.

Forsyth quotes Timothy Richard's description of the evangelist Mr Chao: 'a brave, noble fellow and thoroughly reliable, who has been working there [Shansi] for about 20 years'[34] in the employ of the English Baptist mission. There is also mention of a Lu Hsi-tei, connected with the same group, while

34 NMS, n.p.

Hsu Ching-so, who had been a Christian for 10 years, is described as a member of the CIM in Shanxi.[35]

Some Chinese workers served 'under the guidance' of a western missionary,[36] but the exact meaning of this phrase is problematic. However, at the beginning of a missionary enterprise or during its expansion into new areas, what we might call 'professional missionaries', trained in Bible, theology, and Christian work, would have been most suitable as leaders. At the same time, local Chinese colleagues would understand the culture, local religions, and language much better than their western colleagues. We know from the expressed strategy of Hudson Taylor's CIM and the CMS in Kwangsi (see Cunich in this volume), that some Western organisations sought to work with Chinese colleagues and empower them as soon as was thought reasonable. A summary of the ministry situation in Ching-chou[37] in Shandong may prove helpful, if it is borne in mind that work there began earlier than in Shanxi. Forsyth quotes Baptist missionary Rev. Bruce's description of the organisation of Christian work in the area:

> The total membership is about one thousand six hundred; this number being mostly composed of small groups scattered over ninety stations in various villages and towns within a radius of about fifteen or twenty miles from Ching-chou Fu. These stations are grouped into six pastoral districts, under the spiritual oversight of four native pastors and two elders, with a missionary (myself) exercising general supervision of the whole.[38]

From this distance we cannot be precise about the nature of Chinese leadership. Probably the four pastors were full-time, ordained men, while the two elders had so-called 'ordinary jobs'. The numbers suggest that each local leader was responsible for more than 250 church members in 15 stations spread over a large geographical area. Bruce comments that his role was essentially supervisory, the implication being that day-to-day ministry was in the hands of Chinese people suitable for the task.

Returning to Shanxi, although much less is said, it is again possible to discern the maturity of the local church and the presence of Chinese people at different levels. We read for example of Deacon Heh in Hsiao-i-hsien[39] and Elder Liu of T'ai Ku Hsien, the latter 'a most valued helper'.[40] Southwest of Taiyuan we come across Mr Fei, a native assistant and man of substance.[41] Chao-yung-yao was an evangelist in rural Shansi. Ho Tsuen-kwei was an older man who after becoming a Christian gave up his share in a business and earned

35 Ibid., 2.
36 TCM, 48.
37 青州, Qingzhou.
38 TCM, 400.
39 Ibid., 66.
40 Ibid., 69.
41 Ibid., 71.

a small salary as an assistant to a western missionary. Forsyth quotes a Mrs Ogren talking about the steadfastness of Pastor Ch'u.[42]

By the time of the Boxer Rebellion mission work at P'ing-yao had already developed such that there were outstations in the district and one of them had a church with a local elder.[43] Broomhall quotes from Edith Nathan's last letter, in which she describes Deacon Li as 'in charge at the city [Ta-ning]'.[44] Nathan and her group were also visited by Pastor Ch'u and Deacon Hsu,[45] as discussed later in this article. Although western missionaries are described in more detail, local servants of the Lord are brought close to us as we read their names and some facts about them. They were known and respected by the western missionaries whose accounts we must read to learn about them.

Naturally, one of the most important Chinese colleagues whose name we have was Pastor Hsi (discussed in more detail by Weber in this volume), whose story and service for the Lord go far beyond the scope of a short paper like this.[46] He was ordained superintendent pastor over a large and undefined geographical area around nine years after the CIM began its work in Shanxi.[47] In a fitting show of respect Broomhall comments that the subsequent general director of the CIM, Dixon Hoste, 'continued for nearly 10 years the valued and trusted colleague of Pastor Hsi';[48] in a situation later marked by tragic ethnic and religious *otherness* it is striking that Hoste is described as Hsi's colleague. At the same set of meetings a Mr Sung was ordained pastor of a church while a Mr Ch'u was ordained as pastor of two districts. Various unnamed deacons and elders were also appointed. There are clear parallels between Shanxi and the more established situation in Shandong described earlier.

Chinese Christians and the Boxers: Witness and Martyrdom

Commenting on 'rice Christians', Forsyth notes that the missionaries knew that they worked with tares as well as wheat. Yet in the same breath he commends Chinese Christians for their devotion and willingness to die for their faith.

The books consulted contain many stories of ordinary Chinese believers, men and women, young and old, who refused to deny their faith and were abused, tortured, or murdered. The Boxers were known to begin gently in their inducements to their countrymen, asking them to make a subtle kowtow before an idol or burn a very small amount of incense, yet Forsyth reports how even 'feeble women and little children' stood firm against this kind of pressure.[49]

42 TCM, 184.
43 Ibid., 116.
44 TLL, 34.
45 Ibid., 36.
46 See, for example, Geraldine Taylor, *Pastor Hsi of North China: One of China's Christians* (New York: Fleming H. Revell, 1905).
47 JSC, 167.
48 Ibid., 168.
49 TCM, 347.

One example would be Mr Liu of Taiyuan, who urged the Boxers to kill him first.[50] Perhaps even more noteworthy are the Christians who not only refused to recant but even engaged with the Boxers. In Hsinchou,[51] Mr Si-er-mao refused to kowtow to his tormentors and commented that he was 'a child of God and would not kneel to devils'.[52] When the Boxers ordered Mr Wang of Fan-si-hsien to 'leave the foreign [Christian] sect' he replied that he already had, inferring that it was Buddhism that was the alien religion. This man had fairly long discussions with the Boxers before he was killed, in which he explained the heavenly doctrine and his 'reverence for the Supreme Ruler (Shang-ti)'. Indeed, the Boxers were afraid of him because of the trouble they thought he might cause.[53] Before she was murdered, a Christian woman in the same county challenged her accusers, 'we have left the false and turned to the true; the evil for the good. How have we done any mischief?'[54]

From the perspective of identity, an exchange between some Christian schoolgirls and a government official in a situation extremely hostile to the gospel is most informative. Broomhall records how the girls were brought before the official, who 'said to them, "You follow the foreigners"; they answered, "No, we follow Christ." He then said, "You read the foreigners' book"; to which they replied, "No, we read God's Book."'[55] The foreign missionaries may have been the channel, directly or indirectly, through which Christianity was brought to them, but in the girls' minds there was no equation between Christianity and foreignness. These young people had already achieved a hybridity of Chineseness and Christianity.

Chinese Christians and the Missionaries: Care and Sacrifice

As the crisis deepened and the Boxers began to hunt down western missionaries and murder them, Chinese Christians also paid a heavy price just for self-identifying or being known as Christians. Although they were literally in mortal danger themselves, they cared for the foreigners; their ministry to the westerners can be divided into three rough (and possibly overlapping) categories. The histories from the time contain many examples of local believers providing for, protecting, and pastoring their foreign friends.

Provision

At a time when their appearance marked them out and put them in danger, western missionaries began to run out of essential supplies very quickly. Some

50 FSS, 176.
51 忻州, Xinzhou.
52 TCM, 369.
53 Ibid., 380.
54 Ibid., 381.
55 TLL, 88.

local people were no longer willing to do business with them and as the crisis developed, going out to buy food or water could result in a severe beating or death.

There are numerous records of local believers bringing supplies to the various missionaries in Shanxi. At Taning,[56] Chinese Christians brought food,[57] and the missionary group from Hsinchou relied on the Liu-chia-shan Christians for food and water.[58] Mr Dixon's diary entry for July 13th describes them as having 'given their all for the missionaries'.[59] Another group brought donkeys to the missionaries.[60] In the Ping-yang area four Christians came to bring help to a Mr M'Kie and his companions. A Miss Way observed that, 'they brought us some silver, and one of them took off his thick coat and gave it to Mr. M'Kie'.[61] Finally, a Mr Fei rode along with the missionaries in the Tai-ku area for a while and 'kept the children amused'.[62]

It is clear from these brief examples that Chinese believers identified strongly with their western brothers and sisters in the church. For some of them, giving material supplies to the foreigners brought genuine hardship; for others, providing for the missionaries meant risking their lives. It seems that at some level the Chinese Christians now proactively extended their hybrid space to include the foreign Christians in a form of inclusionary *otherness*. The foreigners were not Chinese but were provided for as family members, as the local Christians travelled to someone else's world.

Protection

Chinese Christians acted as protectors to the western missionaries in a number of ways. Local believers hid missionaries in their houses, farms, or caves on their land,[63] an example of which would be the anonymous group who helped the Pigott family in the Pei-ling-shan area near Taiyuan.[64] Sometimes the Christians came considerable distances to collect the westerners and their belongings and move them to safety.[65] With the Boxers marking out foreigners and Chinese believers as the enemy, and because foreigners were easily identified, local Christians used the limited amount of power and resources which they possessed to include and benefit the westerners.

The western missionaries trusted the Chinese believers completely; although some local Christians did renounce their faith and betray the missionaries, the

56 大寧, Daning.
57 TLL, 37.
58 TCM, 44.
59 Ibid., 52.
60 Ibid., 50.
61 TCM, 145.
62 Ibid., 72.
63 Ibid., 182.
64 Ibid., 35.
65 Ibid., 50.

westerners accepted any offer of a safe haven without hesitation. They took such offers at face value because they assumed that the support and succour from the Chinese would be genuine; when loyalty and allegiance were being challenged by an external force (the Boxers), the missionaries assumed that their Chinese brothers and sisters would continue to identify as Christian.

This sentiment is reflected in a letter from Bessie Renaut: 'China's Christians are splendid. Lui Chia Shan[66] villagers have risked their lives for us, and now have had to flee from their village without food and money'.[67] While those who brought food and water to the missionaries took great risk and gave of their own meagre supplies, Christians who gave shelter to the foreigners arguably put themselves at greater risk. They were harbouring the foreign enemy and taking the other under their own roof, violating the purity of the Chinese household and the binary *otherness* imposed by the Boxers.

In some cases Chinese Christians acted as messengers, taking news between missionaries or from missionaries to representatives of Western governments in safer areas of China. They also acted as intermediaries between their foreign friends and local Chinese magistrates or officials.[68] At Hsiao-I-hsien a group of local Christians attempted to intervene with a local mandarin on behalf of the missionaries.[69]

Pastoring

The clearest demonstration of spiritual maturity in the church in Shanxi is probably the pastoral care exercised by the Chinese believers toward the missionaries. The books consulted record several meetings between local Christians and the western missionaries, along with comment on them by the foreigners. Coming to minister to the western missionaries involved risk and was born of self-identification as Christian, and the way in which the Chinese pastors and other senior Christians spoke and behaved among the western missionaries speaks of a church which although young had matured, such that the pastoral staff took the initiative to offer pastoral care to those arguably more mature in the faith. The Chinese pastors were renegotiating their identity and *otherness* as recipients of and juniors in the faith, resulting in a positive realignment of roles vis-à-vis the western missionaries.

Edith Nathan's last letter describes the situation at Taning in mid-July 1900. The missionaries were in hiding and were visited several times by 'the Pastor'. Nathan writes:

> Our dear old Pastor came. It is so good to have him. His face is full of light and brightness, not born of earth, but from constant looking into His Master's face. He

---

66 If the letters 'u' and 'i' have been transposed then this would be Liu Chia Shan. There are no Chinese characters to refer to in the books.
67 TCM, 64.
68 TLL, 39.
69 TCM, 67.

> told us that in answer to the question, 'Would he protect us?' which we had asked the Mandarin, he had replied, 'I won't undertake the responsibility. If they like to leave they can leave; if they stay they stay. It is not my affair; I will not injure them.' I happened to say to the Pastor, 'We are pitiable!' He said, 'There is One to care for you better than all earthly magistrates.' I felt condemned, for our God is our Heavenly Father, and lives and cares for us. He will save. We think and wonder in what way our deliverance will come; every way seems blocked'.[70]

The unnamed man is described as 'our pastor' by the missionary. The westerners were genuinely pleased to see him, and Miss Nathan's description of his face needs no explanation. This man's demeanour and encouraging words about the 'One to care for you' speak of spiritual maturity, pastoral skill, and experience.

After Nathan and her group had moved to a different location they were visited by a Deacon Li, which brought great joy to both parties.[71] Another pastor and deacon came to visit them, which to Miss Nathan was evidence of the love the Chinese had for the missionaries. After this the group left for yet another destination and headed to some other villages in accordance with their pastor's advice. The group sang and prayed briefly together, at which the 'dear old Pastor piped his eyes', a demonstration of the emotion shared by several of the group.[72]

A final description of two pastors, Chang and Ch'u speaks of their depth of character as perceived and treasured by the writer: 'the two Pastors are such a contrast in every way, both true pillars of grace, but as different as chalk and cheese'.[73] Miss Nathan observed that the two men had very different personalities, yet both were examples of deep Christian character, part of the indigenous shaping of the faith.

Pastoral care needs to be given and received. It needs to be given willingly by capable people who know what they are doing. In this case it was given at great risk to the giver. The pastors came uninvited and presumably expected to be received and heard as ministers. The western missionaries were also in the middle of their own negotiation of *otherness* as they accepted pastoral care and practical advice from local Christian ministers. These events speak of a crossing or redrawing of boundaries of ethnicity, culture, and even allegiance by the Chinese Christians and western missionaries. In a hybridised subset of a Confucian culture it seemed that those who had been students now identified themselves as teachers confident to minster to those who had previously ministered to them.

---

70 TLL, 35.
71 Ibid., 36.
72 Ibid., 39.
73 TLL, 42.

Analysis and Conclusions

Rural Shanxi Chinese Christians had shown themselves to be exactly that: adherents to Christianity who were culturally and socially Chinese. That many of these people were known as Christians before the arrival of the Boxers shows that they had already begun to negotiate their identities; for these people, the idea that 'one more Christian meant one fewer Chinese' would have been incomprehensible. They remained in many ways the same as their non-believing countrymen and yet their faith made them different; there was an implicit *otherness* in their self-understanding vis-à-vis those around them. In a complementary way, they now shared something precious and meaningful with the foreigners, who looked, spoke, ate, and thought differently from themselves. For the Chinese Christians then, *otherness* had become what we might call composite or multifaceted,[74] rather than binary.

To be a Chinese Christian meant dealing with issues of religious belief in a way that meant abandoning Buddhism (for example) and accepting Christianity, yet not becoming a foreigner. It also meant separating the missionary foreigners (even with their inherent weaknesses and blind spots) from imperialists and purveyors of unfair trade and opium. Following Christ in Shanxi involved a new way of life and integrity in ordinary Chinese villages and towns, and looking at traditional values from Confucianism and Buddhism in a critical way, such that the gold was retained and augmented and the dross filtered and removed. Faith does require the redrawing of certain boundaries, changing their shape and making them dotted rather than clear black lines. Many of those who chose to be Christian while remaining Chinese would have been working through issues of culture, morality, and ethnicity on an *ad hoc* basis, as their own knowledge and that of the missionaries would have been limited – the situation at the turn of the last century thus involved *theology*, as well as *history*, from below. The Chinese believers were negotiating *otherness* and constructing their own identities, rejecting the representation of Chineseness and the 'mythical norm' advocated by the Boxers. While many of the Chinese believers discussed in this volume helped shape Chinese Christianity by writing or teaching, it seems that Christians like those in Shanxi operated on an informal and everyday level.

At the time of the Boxer Rebellion, even in an area of northwest China to which the gospel had come comparatively recently, Chinese believers preached, taught fellow Christians, and exercised pastoral care and leadership. From being receivers of the gospel they had become people who maintained, consolidated, and sought to expand the church. In this sense, they had already taken on some of the roles originally the preserve of missionaries. If the relationship of Chinese Christians to the broader society had already undergone

74 See also Paul Woods, *Theologising migration: Otherness and liminality in East Asia* (Oxford: Regnum, 2015).

some degree of renegotiation of *otherness*, then something similar was happening within the faith community.

The arrival of the Boxers brought suffering and martyrdom to many Chinese Christians, as they were forced back into simple binaries and characterisations of *otherness* which they had already put behind them. Before the Boxers, Chinese Christians self-identified as such within a society indifferent and sometimes hostile to them, yet once the persecution came they were forced to declare allegiance in much more threatening circumstances; I am reminded of the man who implied that Buddhism was a foreign sect and the schoolgirls who explained that they followed Christ rather than the foreigners.

Finally, and possibly most moving, is the remarkable kindness and mercy shown to the western missionaries by the local Christians. Those who had previously been pastored *by* now became pastors *to* the missionaries. In an era when some people were described as 'rice Christians', seeking material gain by means of their association with the missionaries, the believers in Shanxi provided for the foreigners, often at great cost to themselves.

With the benefit of more than 100 years of subsequent Chinese church history and growth it appears that what was crystallising in 1900 (and we can take this as a representative sample, albeit one developing in extreme circumstances) was a form of contextualised Chinese Christianity, perhaps more practical rather than theological. Certain aspects of Chinese culture and social mores can be discerned in the behaviour and attitudes of the local believers. Indeed, Tiedemann talks of a 'kind of Chinese folk Christianity' resulting from a 'locally negotiated Christian accommodation to prevailing social arrangements'.[75]

The Chinese are known for their hospitality, and this comes through in the accounts of provision or protection. At the same time, the importance of relationships and *guanxi* can be seen in how the Chinese Christians looked after foreign missionaries known to them. Indeed, Confucian benevolence (仁 *ren*) is extending kindness to those one already knows.[76] One might be reminded of the famous adage at the beginning of the Analects: 'Is it not delightful to have friends coming from afar?'[77] Truly, these were brothers and sisters in Christ, as well as friends.

Two other Confucian concepts are *li* (禮 rites or propriety[78]) and *zhengming* (正名 the rectification of names[79]). Simply put, *li* concerns behaving in the proper way, and under *zhengming* each person has a title and a role, and society works best when people know and perform these appropriately. At the time of

---

75 R. Tiedemann, 'Baptism of fire: China's Christians and the Boxer Uprising of 1900', *International Bulletin of Missionary Research*, 24, 1 (2000), 12.
76 Hwang Kwang-Kuo, 'Filial piety and loyalty: Two types of social identification in Confucianism', *Asian Journal of Social Psychology*, 2 (1999), 163-183.
77 This translation of Analects 1:1 comes from Chan Wing-tsit, *A source book in Chinese philosophy* (Princeton, NJ: Princeton University Press, 1963), 8.
78 Chan, *A source book*, 790.
79 Ibid., 40.

the Boxer persecution Chinese Christianity contained an expectation that its adherents would know the right thing to do and act accordingly. Confucian propriety seems to have been carried over into Christianity in that those serious about their faith felt the obligation to act, bearing witness, expressing concern, or making provision for those around them. Chinese Christianity has long emphasised titles and roles; *pastor*, *brother*, *sister*, *deacon*, *elder*, *evangelist*, and so on are almost obligatory as terms of address. In the period leading up to and during the Boxer Rebellion, those with roles in the church did their best to fulfil them. The needs of the situation, the perceived danger for the missionaries, and the maturity of the Chinese church meant that pastors or deacons felt allowed and even required to minister to all in need, and none were more vulnerable than their western colleagues. This resonates generally with Simon Chan's powerful defence of the validity of Asian hierarchical views and social order within a Christian framework.[80]

Finally, loyalty is important in Confucian thought[81] and it is clear that there was a great sense of loyalty and gratitude to the western missionaries from the Chinese Christians. This is beautifully illustrated in a letter from Pastor Chang Ghi-pen to the families of some female missionaries in Shanxi. Chang wrote:

> Our three beloved lady Missionaries were of one heart and full of zeal. Our native brethren and sisters in the surrounding district were delighted to receive the Gospel from them, and as a result this Church gradually increased.[82]

This article has tried to look briefly at maturity and identity as they relate to the question of *otherness* within a Chinese Christian context. The renegotiation of *otherness* by Chinese Christians, externally (between church and society) and internally (within the Sino-Western Christian community) was a result of deepening Christian faith and a response to the Boxers and the divisions they sought to spread. From the sources available and the cursory analysis here, I conclude that a Chinese form of Christianity was being shaped which was anchored in biblical teaching and traditional Chinese values. The Shanxi experience is a microcosm of a trend in Chinese Christianity which continues to this day in Chinese fellowships around the world.

Chinese Christians were to some degree involved in leading and shaping Christianity in their country before 1900, and the circumstances in northwest China at the turn of the century may have accelerated and amplified changes that were already subtly under way all over China. The Boxer Rebellion was traumatic for Chinese Christians and foreign missionaries, and occurred between the Taiping Heavenly Kingdom (ended 1864) and the Communist victory in 1949. Inasmuch as it challenged Chinese leaders to distinguish between faith and nationality without sacrificing either the firestorm that was

80 Simon Chan, *Grassroots Asian theology: Thinking the faith from the ground up* (Downers Grove, IL: IVP, 2014).
81 Hwang, *Filial piety and loyalty*, 163.
82 TLL, 46.

the Boxer Rebellion may have prepared the maturing church for the challenges it would meet in the middle of the twentieth century and beyond.

The Contribution of Ni Tuosheng (Watchman Nee)

Stephen Williams

Orientation

In 2012, Dongsheng Wu published a study designed to fill the lacuna formed by the absence of a 'single scholarly volume published in English focusing on Nee's teachings of the spiritual life'.[1] He aimed to make Nee's thought lively on the wider academic scene by hooking him up with the mystical tradition of Christian theology. This had dual potential: firstly, it enabled an appreciation of Nee's thought in its solidarity with a central theological tradition and, secondly, it acquitted Nee on the charge of anti-intellectualism. What is called 'anti-intellectual' is really the mystical and that is a different proposition.

Wu has not been alone in giving academic attention to Watchman Nee in the English-speaking world in the last few years. Two contributors to the conference which spawned these essays – Lian Xi and Alexander Chow – have also treated Nee in ways different both from each other and from Wu. Xi has discussed him in the context of popular Christianity in China in the twentieth century.[2] Chow has incorporated the study of Nee into a proposal that we draw on the resources of Eastern Orthodoxy in order to equip theologically the Chinese churches in the third millennium.[3] Although I do not discuss these works in this essay – they are not monographs on Nee – they are evidently important when it comes to any comprehensive assessment of the contribution of Watchman Nee. My aim in this essay is anything but a comprehensive assessment. Considered in their own right, the ecclesiology and eschatology discussed by Xi and Nee's relation to other strands of twentieth century theological thought in China, as discussed by Chow, deserve our attention no less than does Wu's essay. However, it is Wu's monograph which has provoked the observations which follow, so my decision about which theological waters to chart is determined by the point of entry provided by the springboard of his work.

In aligning Nee with the mystical tradition in Western theology, Wu may well be right. Further, the alignment may be significant. 'What', asked Nee, 'is the highest attainment in Christianity?' He answered: 'That of complete union

---

1 Dongsheng John Wu, *Understanding Watchman Nee: Spirituality, knowledge, and formation* (Eugene, OR: Wipf & Stock, 2012), 2.

2 Lian Xi, *Redeemed by fire: The rise of popular Christianity in modern China* (New Haven, CT; London: Yale University Press, 2010), ch.7.

3 Alexander Chow, *Theosis: Sino-Christian theology and the Second Chinese Enlightenment: Heaven and humanity in unity* (Basingstoke: Palgrave Macmillan, 2013).

with God and total loss of self.'[4] This sounds mystical. Yet, whatever the merits of Wu's study or the plausibility of some of its broad conclusions, the argument is not persuasive for three reasons.[5] Firstly, the connections with mysticism, as described, are too broad. Wu draws on the writings of a contemporary Anglican theologian on mysticism in order to make his point, but the connections between Nee and mysticism, as mediated through this theologian, are often of an extremely general kind. Generalisation need not undermine a case, but it leaves open the question of just how significant the case is.

Secondly, however successfully the connection is established between him and the mystical tradition, Nee is not automatically exonerated from the charge of anti-intellectualism. Statements are made in Nee's most detailed study, *The Spiritual Man,* which cannot be stripped of their anti-intellectual garb; consistency aside, what Nee says here about the mind dangerously demotes it when he associates it with soul, separating spirit from soul and leaving spirit as the sole organ for receiving revelation.[6] Indeed, to demonstrate an affinity with the mystical tradition is not, *per se*, to defuse the charge of anti-intellectualism, for critics of mysticism may ask whether those elements of the mystical tradition into which Nee is plugged may themselves exemplify anti-intellectualism.

Thirdly, Wu's attempt to defend Nee's tripartite anthropology – that humankind is constituted of body (the outermost man), soul (the outer man) and spirit (the inner man) – is unsuccessful. Since this scheme formally grounds Nee's theological thought, a serious defect at this point would, *prima facie*, seem to vitiate the whole product. Actually, I shall later suggest that a tripartite scheme as such, even if mistaken, is not as damaging as we may fear. At this juncture, my interest is confined to Wu's argument. Wu tries to defend the theological credentials of tripartism in a modified form on the foundation of what he calls 'recent biblical scholarship', but if we look at his sources and their dates, the case is problematic.[7] If we ask where the 'heart' belongs within

4 *The latent power of the soul* (New York: Christian Fellowship Publishers, 1972), 53.

5 I have reviewed Wu's work in *Evangelical Quarterly*, 87, 2 (2015). Despite the criticisms I made here, I appreciate the author's thorough scholarship.

6 Intuition, says Nee, 'is totally counter to our mind', *The Spiritual Man*, vol.2 (New York: Christian Fellowship Publishers, 1968), 72. The thoughts of the mind are from us, not from God. The mind instructs us only in mundane affairs; it is intuition which teaches us in affairs of the spirit (74). 'To perform God's will a Christian need simply heed the direction of his intuition. There is no necessity to ask others, nor even to ask himself' (74). If theological research and reasoning were needed, 'only Christians with good minds and education would escape deception' (75). 'The difference between knowing intuitively and knowing mentally is immeasurable. Upon this very distinction hangs the outcome of spiritual success or defeat' (81). In basing my interpretation of Nee on English translations, I rely entirely on Wu's observations on translation: see *Understanding Watchman Nee*, 36, n.88; note also 85, n.6. Vigilance is required when we bear in mind how Chinese context may inform Nee's meaning.

7 *Understanding Watchman Nee*, 118-122. The one Pauline text which makes an apparently tripartite distinction (1 Thess. 5:23) is untypical and usually held not to provide a rigid anthropology any more than the command to love God with heart, soul and mind (Matt 22: 37) provides a tripartite scheme. (In this dominical saying, soul and mind are directly related to God,

the tripartite scheme, Wu's answer is that it 'includes both the spirit's conscience and the soul's mind', but how is this a coherent possibility, given Nee's constant and clean separation of spirit and soul?[8] My point is not that it is categorically impossible to defend tripartism on a biblical basis or to deny absolutely its potential usefulness in constructive theological anthropology. It is simply that, at best, tripartism is biblically precarious and anyone who wants to ground a substantive theological anthropology on an informed biblical basis makes a hard rod for his own back.

Yet, reflection on how this anthropology is put to work in Nee's thought enables us to start working our way towards a positive appropriation of his theological legacy. Preliminarily, we note two things. Firstly, tripartite anthropology does not of itself entail negativity towards the soul and require that we understand 'soul' as a faculty of the natural person who is annihilated, complete with it, in Cross and regeneration. One can maintain the anthropology without espousing this negativity. Secondly and conversely, it is possible to adopt an anti-intellectual negativity towards the natural person without the apparatus of tripartite anthropology. Bearing this in mind, we notice what happens in Nee's best-known and most influential work in the English-speaking world, *The Normal Christian Life*.[9] Although Nee retains his tripartite anthropology in this volume, it emerges explicitly only late in the book (chapter 12), by which time the author has communicated his message without clearly adverting to it and certainly without relying on it. Nee's message about the normal Christian life is embedded in an exposition of Romans 5-8. In these chapters, Paul does not flag up a tripartite anthropology and Nee does not foist one upon him. While Nee's characteristic distinction between the natural and the spiritual holds strong, he can go a long way in describing the normal Christian life without a tripartite anthropology. Between *The Spiritual Man*, completed in 1928, and *The Normal Christian Life*, based on addresses given in Europe shortly before the outbreak of the Second World War, Nee attained a spiritual insight to which he gave theological expression in this latter volume and, broadly speaking, this insight (whatever we make of it) eclipses any scheme of tripartite anthropology.[10] I wish to discover what we can positively draw out of Watchman Nee for third millennial Christianity so I turn now to

something which Nee denies is possible, for that is solely the prerogative of spirit.) The text in Hebrews which distinguishes soul and spirit (4:12) is normally not taken as a division of two distinct and very different faculties in the human person, though it is hard to say dogmatically what distinction is in mind. These two texts are crucial for Watchman Nee as is their grounding in the Genesis text which speaks of God's formation of man (Gen. 2:7). This text is seldom taken trichotomously: the 'living being' which man became is does not denote a faculty of 'spirit' apart from the dust of the ground (body) and the breath of life (soul). The living being is an embodied soul or an ensouled body.

8 *Understanding Watchman Nee*, 147.

9 Watchman Nee, *The normal Christian life*, 3rd edn (London; Eastbourne: Victory Press, 1971).

10 See Nee's reference to this insight in *Sit, walk, stand* (London; Eastbourne: Victory Press, 1962), 30.

two areas where we surely need to take him on board, disagreements notwithstanding. Constraints of space mean that, unfortunately the second will be treated more briefly than the first.

Romans 6

What follows will appear to be a digression, but the reason for it will become clear. During the visit to Europe when he delivered the addresses which eventually became *The Normal Christian Life*, Nee attended for the first time the Keswick Convention. The theological outlook broadly characteristic of Keswick has been controversial in the evangelical world. Over a century after the first Keswick Convention in 1875, one of the leading evangelical theologians of the second half of the twentieth century, J. I. Packer, was urging his readers not to succumb to its teaching on holiness.[11] He had done so before and would do so again. 'Keswick teaching in all its many modes and forms takes its rise from what Paul says in Romans 6: 1-14' about Christians being dead to sin, the old body having been crucified with him; therefore, we are to yield ourselves to God.[12] A landmark in the teaching which emanated from Keswick was reached in 1965 when John Stott gave Bible readings there on Romans 5-8. Stott's international status as an evangelical leader in the last decades of the twentieth century and into the beginning of the next was unexcelled. He decisively rejected that reading of Romans 6 which interpreted death to sin as insensitivity to sin, just 'as a corpse is to external stimuli'.[13] He proffered a fresh one; as a matter of principle, he argued, our interpretation of the teaching that *Christians* are dead to sin must be ruled by our understanding of the statement that *Christ* died to sin (Romans 6: 10). The sense in which Christ died *to* sin was that he died *for* sin.[14] Returning to Romans almost thirty years later, Stott took the same line, admitting that he had come across only one commentator who shared his interpretation of this phrase.[15] In the course of this volume, he made a remarkable statement about the enduring effect on him of his struggle with Romans 6.[16]

John Stott's stature and biblical faithfulness was and is such that those who agree with him in rejecting the interpretation which he rejected must also

11 *Keep in step with the Spirit* (Leicester: IVP, 1984), 145-164.

12 Ibid., 146.

13 John R. W. Stott, *The message of Romans* (Leicester: IVP, 1994), 10.

14 *Men made new: An exposition of Romans 5-8* (London: IVF, 1966), 43.

15 *The message of Romans*, 172.

16 'I confess that, ever since I became a Christian fifty-six years ago, I have enjoyed what could be termed a 'love-hate' relationship with Romans, because of its joyful-painful personal challenges. It began soon after my conversion, with chapter 6 and my longing to experience that 'death to sin' which it seemed to promise. I toyed for many years with the fantasy that Christians are supposed to be as insensitive to sin as a corpse is to external stimuli. My final deliverance from this chimera was sealed when I was invited to give the Keswick Convention 'Bible Readings' on Romans 5-8 in 1965…', *The message of Romans*, 10.

consider seriously his positive proposal. However, it is not surprising that he found himself virtually unsupported exegetically, since interpreting 'die to' as 'die for' appears to place a linguistic and, consequently, exegetical strain on the text. The principal reason that Stott adopted his interpretation was that he could see no other alternative to the one which he rejected. In the later study on Romans, he cited, although rejected, one further interpretation: '...Christ so completely identified with the old era that sin had authority over him, although he never succumbed to it...by his death he gained freedom from its rule...Christ 'died to the realm and to the rule of sin' and we are 'dead to sin' in the sense that we are 'no longer under its rule', being 'out of the territory and the jurisdiction of sin'...'[17] Here, he was quoting Martyn Lloyd-Jones and so we complete a trio of references to influential twentieth-century British evangelicals.

In the preface to his published sermons on Romans 6, Lloyd-Jones averred that he had refused to preach a series of expository sermons on Romans until he had understood chapter 6 and that he had agreed with no interpretation of that chapter offered by any commentator or preacher that he had ever read.[18] What emerged when Lloyd-Jones came to his independent conclusions was startling. Giving short shrift to the Perfectionist teaching that 'we are dead completely to the influence, to the power, and to the love of sin' (16), he nonetheless held that we have died to the 'reign and to the rule of sin' (21). What is startling is the interpretation which Lloyd-Jones placed on this principle. When he proceeded to say that the Christian is 'out of the power of sin' (24) as well as out of its realm, the formal theological distance between his and a 'Perfectionist' interpretation apparently diminishes. Satan cannot touch us, says Lloyd-Jones, so '[e]very Christian who falls into sin is a fool' (27). The tension in this claim is palpable. After all, 'I...am entirely and eternally outside the realm of sin's influence' (74). Yet, 'whether you have sinned or not, you are in Christ...sin does not affect you as a person' (92). Lloyd-Jones reached an expository extreme in the extraordinary claim that sin cannot even tempt us (93). 'Sin in the Christian...is just a nuisance...only a nuisance...only an annoyance, and nothing more than that' (291).

It may be impossible to rescue Lloyd-Jones from the charge of contradiction in his exposition. Be that as it may, we must attend to the meaning which he attached to 'I', 'me', the 'self'. Lloyd-Jones drew the sharpest possible distinction between self and body. The self is untouchable, but the body is touchable. The body is not only touchable; it can experience alien domination. 'It is impossible that sin should reign in us who are Christians, but what is possible is that sin should reign in our mortal body' (152); indeed, if unchecked, 'it will dominate our bodies' (153). Lloyd-Jones was in deepest

17 *The message of Romans*, 172, n.111.

18 D. M. Lloyd-Jones, *Romans: An exposition of chapter 6: The new man* (Edinburgh: Banner of Truth, 1972), xi. From now on, page references to this volume are given in the text.

trouble here. He was propounding a dualism not only incredible – for how can sin be merely a nuisance if it reigns in my body? – but also highly dangerous: the body can be dominated by sin, but the self is eternally secure, out of harm's way. Only one thing explains this conclusion: Lloyd-Jones saw no alternative. He found himself in the same straits as did John Stott, but emerged with a different interpretation.[19]

Why this digression? The point is that, in resisting some traditional Holiness interpretations of Romans 6, evangelical leaders have got themselves into deep water when propounding an alternative and have been more successful in indicating how Romans 6 should *not* be interpreted than how it *should* be. Watchman Nee, whatever putative weaknesses arise from his attachment to the broad Holiness tradition, struck out along lines in some ways more exegetically persuasive than did either Stott or Lloyd-Jones. We can say this even if we should not go the whole way with him and, in fact, view the daily Christian life in a way closer to the other two (for all their mutual differences). If we have problems with Nee on Romans 6, we shall find him in good company. All I seek to do in what follows is to indicate some of the things which Nee says and indicate something of their *prima facie* merit, offering neither a comprehensive explanation of his position nor a claim that he was original. It neither defends all that he says nor even operates on the assumption that Nee's theology coheres satisfactorily. I simply observe why we need him in the conversation.

Nee wanted to work out a theology which was both christocentric and staurocentric (cross-centred). Its strong christocentric expression was that, as '[t]he Son of God died instead of us for our forgiveness', so 'He lives instead of us for our deliverance'.[20] Its strong staurocentric expression is that our theology must not be merely a theology of the blood shed, which avails for forgiveness and cleanses conscience, but also one of the self dead, which is the hinge on which the normal Christian life is meant to turn.[21] Nee adumbrates neither a theology which terminates with forgiveness nor one which leaves the cross behind when it proceeds to pneumatology. If we stop at the forgiveness of sins, we shall neglect to deal with the power of sin.[22] What he said in his day is apparently true of many in ours: 'At the beginning of our Christian life we are concerned with our doing, not with our being; we are distressed rather by what

---

19 What Lloyd-Jones says has to be read in the light of David Wright's observation that 'he was given to overstatement', quoted in Andrew Atherstone & David Ceri Jones, *Engaging with Martyn Lloyd-Jones: The life and legacy of 'the Doctor'* (Nottingham: Apollos, 2011), 23.

20 *The normal Christian life*, 9. '*...The life we live is the life of Christ alone...*What God offers us is an 'exchanged life', a 'substituted life', and Christ is our Substitute within,' 121-22. On the occasion of this anniversary conference, we note that Nee does not at this point refer to Hudson Taylor's 'exchanged life'. Although he does so earlier, his quotations from Hudson Taylor fall a little short of the starkness of his own view of Christ's life substituted for ours (38-39). From now on, references to *The normal Christian life* are placed in the text.

21 Nee distinguishes between the blood which deals with sins and the Cross which deals with self.

22 In the broader context of distinguishing between 'sins' (forgiven) and 'sin' (a power), Nee made the theologically apt observation that '[m]an's thought is always of the punishment that will come to him if he sins, but God's thought is always of the glory man will miss if he sins '(73).

we have done than by what we are' (25). Nee was resolved not to dilute the strength of Paul's words: 'crucified with Christ' (Rom 6: 6) or 'dead to sin' (6: 11). The death of Christ is inclusive of us.[23] 'As the last Adam, Christ is the sum total of humanity; as the second Man He is the Head of a new race' (32). Jesus Christ bore us, not only our sins, on the cross. It is futile to *reckon* ourselves dead to sin without *knowing* it to be so by the illuminating revelation of God, but such illumination is of our spiritual understanding, not anything that we must feel.[24]

Far from saying that the death of the self entails the absence of sin, Nee averred that 'we are not told that sin as a principle in us is rooted out or removed' (47). God's way with us is to separate ego from body; sin continues to work away in the body, but the distinction between the ego and the body means that 'we are knowing deliverance from its power in increasing measure day by day' (48). Deliverance is a case of truth impacting experience: '...*Our experience is coming progressively to tally with that Word*' which tells us that we are dead (53).[25] Yet, Nee can also apparently emerge at the same place as Lloyd-Jones later would: 'Sin, the old master, is still about, but the slave who served him has been put to death and so is out of reach and his members are unemployed' (47). This is the outworking of the logic of Nee's basic position: 'What is 'in Christ' cannot sin; what is in Adam can sin...' (49). If this appears to come close to a dualism which, in the case of Lloyd-Jones I judged fantastic, we need to reckon with two things. The first is the important fact that Nee refused to believe that in the normal Christian life, sin is absent from the believer and that he insisted on progressive deliverance.[26] The second is Paul's own language. In addition to what he says in Romans 6, he tells the Colossians that they have died (3:3). In neither case does Paul leave it there: dead Colossians are to put to death what is earthly in them (3:5) just as dead Romans must not let sin reign in their mortal bodies (6:12). I have deliberately not referred to those things in Nee's exposition with which I beg to disagree or about whose complete exegetical consistency I am worried. However, where there are shortcomings, we should sympathise with the problems facing anyone who tries to get to grips with Pauline language in Romans 6, and it was the purpose of my description of Stott and Lloyd-Jones to elicit a measure of sympathy for any struggling evangelical fellow-interpreter.

---

23 The temporal aspect of this claim apparently required clarification: see 35, n. 1.

24 Early in *The normal Christian life*, Nee established the primacy of believing over feeling (15) but maintained a healthy view of the positive place of experience (e.g., 53). It is no exaggeration to say that '[e]nlightenment is deliverance, and seeing is...freedom', *The release of the Spirit* (Bromley: Send the Light Trust, 1968), 80. In *The latent power of the soul*, Nee distinguished between 'feeling' and 'sensing in the Spirit' (51).

25 'When I have died my old master, Sin, still continues to live, but his power over his slave extends as far as the grave and no further' (109).

26 I am not suggesting that this is absent from Lloyd-Jones' thought; in a digression, my diagnostic account of him is necessarily incomplete.

It seems easier to identify difficulties in Nee's conceptual scheme for interpreting Paul and its application (which I have not considered) than it is to provide a compelling alternative.[27] However, other difficulties emerge when we attend to Nee's persistent conviction that life in the Spirit cannot incorporate anything from the 'natural' man. As a matter of principle, 'nothing of the old creation, the old kingdom or the old world can be transferred to the new' (58). Nee believes that we are mistaken in attempting to consecrate 'our 'old man' with his instincts and resources, his natural wisdom, strength and other gifts, to the Lord for Him to use' (67). In truth, 'without passing through death I have nothing to consecrate, nor is there anything God can accept, for He has condemned all that is of the old creation to the Cross' (68). Nee does not refer to tripartite anthropology here and his point can be made without it, even if its shadow eventually falls across this exposition. Tripartism aside, Nee supposed that 'the natural' was, without remainder, 'the fallen'.

The difficulty with this position surfaces in the following example. We are not, said Nee, to apply to the study of the New Testament those innate powers of ours which we once applied to the study of history, geography or science (155). To do so would be a case of false consecration. Nee here confuses the natural capacities of a *person* with the spiritual energy of a *nature*. As human beings, we all have in common a sinful *nature* and need to become a new creation. Simultaneously, we are distinguished and individuated as *persons* by (amongst other things) different intellectual abilities. These abilities are tied not to a nature, but to a person and to persons considered not according to their generic, shared spiritual condition but according to their distinctive mental constitutions. If we do not adopt a tripartite scheme or adopt it without understanding it as Nee does, we should say that the new creation entails not the abolition, annihilation or crucifixion of our individuated abilities, but just the creation of a new self whose person, including those abilities, is no longer governed by the sinful nature. Nee's dualistic separation of nature and grace either generates or is the product of an antithetical way of thinking. This outlook must be challenged.

Nevertheless, Nee rightly perceived the dangers of operating out of a centre in the unrenewed self rather than in God and the new self. In evaluating what he says, we need both a firm grasp of the social context in which he operated (lacking in my account) and suspicion towards our native, unsanctified self-reliance. I enter into Christ's death, says Nee, but 'His resurrection enters into me': the key is 'Christ in me' (64). What Nee said about the substitution of the risen Christ for us may be contentious, but when he challenges the widespread practical belief that '[w]e know we can receive forgiveness only by entire reliance on the Lord; yet we believe we can obtain deliverance by doing

---

27 For what it is worth, my interpretation runs along the same lines as someone like Douglas J Moo, *The epistle to the Romans* (Grand Rapids, MI: Eerdmans, 1996), 379.

something ourselves' (116), he has hit on a neglected truth, as far as it goes. In emphasizing resurrection, Nee does not move away from the Cross.

Given both the exegetical tradition and the theological inheritance of the Western churches, are we not, at our present stage of church history, bound to tread cautiously and humbly when we interpret Romans 6?[28] Obviously, we can get things badly wrong. Equally obviously, Paul meant something radical and vital when he used language about the death of the self. If we demur from some of Nee's exposition, we should keep in the forefront of our minds just how much twentieth century evangelical leaders, their influence extending into our third millennium, struggled with Romans 6. We surely all need each other on this one.

Creation

With regrettable brevity, we now move onto a second area. Since Darwin and with the establishment of neo-Darwinism, it has been widely supposed that Christian belief in the world as a divine creation and belief in humanity as created and fallen, have been discredited. Adam and Eve are depicted in the Christian tradition as the biological parents of the human race, created perfect; the fall was our world's lapse from a state of perfection to a state of sin, strife, sorrow and sickness unto death. On a Darwinian or neo-Darwinian view, humanity evolved by natural selection from non-human forms and strife, sickness and death preceded the emergence of humanity.[29]

It would be surprising if we unearthed something in Nee's thought which has any significant bearing on the contemporary debate and, indeed, we do not discover anything directly (at least as far as my limited knowledge allows me to judge). However, Nee made remarks about Adam and creation which put him at odds with traditional accounts and in touch with some modern theological emphases. Consider the following remarks in *The Normal Christian Life*.[30] While interpreting our sin in Adam largely in line with the Western tradition (26-29), Nee also stated that Adam was created 'neither sinful nor holy'; he was, 'to so speak, created morally neutral' (77). He was innocent – perfect in the sense that he lacked imperfection, but not perfect in the sense that he was complete (151). Perfection in that (complete) sense could only come as a result of obedient co-operation with God. Adam was incomplete and in that sense imperfect so long as he had yet to attain his destiny. His eschatological future

28 Of course, if we take on board Alexander Chow's recommendation that we look east (in Christian terms), Romans may not look quite the same.

29 Neo-Darwinism is not the only evolutionary scheme on the market; for an introduction to Meta-Darwinism, see T. B. Fowler & Daniel Kuebler, *The evolution controversy: A survey of competing theories* (Grand Rapids, MI: Baker Academic Press, 2007).

30 Nee makes remarks both in this work and *The latent power of the soul* which I simply ignore, so what follows is not a recommendation that we take up Watchman Nee on Adam *tout court*.

was in view when he was divinely created, so creation has an eschatological orientation.[31]

Here, Nee strikes out in a promising direction with respect to the theology of creation. The significance of his trajectory as a contribution to contemporary thought should not be exaggerated: Nee was not dealing with the crucial question of Christianity and Darwinism. However, the eschatological incompleteness of creation is something with we must reckon when we do deal with that question. The Hebrew word for 'good' in the Genesis account of creation is best understood as signifying something like 'fitness for purpose'.[32] Adam and Eve are given a task to accomplish; of humankind, it is said that we must 'fill the earth and subdue it' (Gen 1: 28), while Adam in particular must work and keep the garden of Eden (Gen 2: 15).

In emphasizing the eschatological future envisioned when we view Adam in proper perspective, Nee forges a theological connection both with early Christian thought (Irenaeus) and with later twentieth century Christian thought (Moltmann and Pannenberg). Irenaeus is widely acclaimed as the proponent of a view of Adam and the fall which differs from the Augustinian. According to Irenaeus, Adam was not created perfect, though that is not to say that he was created flawed. He was innocent and needed to grow.[33] Students of Irenaeus acknowledge the challenges of interpreting him.[34] (Bearing Nee in mind, we note that an accurate exposition of Irenaeus' tripartite anthropology is also an interpretative challenge.)[35] Pannenberg frequently occupies himself with Irenaeus in his account of creation and anthropology.[36] Moltmann has less explicit interest in Irenaeus here, but is keen to establish the eschatological orientation of creation.[37]

I neither underestimate the theological distance between Nee and Pannenberg or Moltmann nor assimilate Nee's relatively unsophisticated thought to the structures of Irenaean theology. Yet, Nee's standpoint here is not without significance for an enterprise such as that of Alexander Chow, which is to bring Nee into some kind of positive, if rather minimal, connection both with

31 Although Nee does not develop an eschatological theology of creation in *The normal Christian life*, it is implicit in what he says.

32 See, e.g., Gordon J. Wenham, *Genesis 1: 1-15* (Waco, TX: Word, 1987), 18 on Genesis 1: 4.

33 Irenaeus, *Against heresies* IV. 38, in *The Ante-Nicene Fathers*, vol.1 repr. (Edinburgh: T&T Clark/Grand Rapids, MI: Eerdmans, 1996).

34 Both Eric Osborn, *Irenaeus of Lyons* (Cambridge: Cambridge University Press, 2001) and Denis Minns, *Irenaeus: An introduction* (London/New York: T&T Clark International, 2010) give helpful introductions to pertinent questions.

35 However, there are tripartisms and tripartisms. For Nee, the characteristic of humans 'is neither spirit nor body but soul' (*The latent power of the soul*, 11), a proposition different from those patristic anthropologies which identified spirit or mind as the distinguishing feature of humans. This debate is complicated by the fact that it is carried out in the vocabulary of different languages.

36 Wolfhart Pannenberg, *Systematic theology*, vol.2 (Edinburgh: T&T Clark/Grand Rapids, MI: Eerdmans, 1994), 136-275.

37 Jürgen Moltmann, *God and creation* (London: SCM, 1985) and *The future of creation* (London: SCM, 1979).

the Eastern Orthodox theological tradition and contemporary theological possibilities. Few theological tasks are more important for us today than the propagation of a credible theology of creation. While I cannot comment knowledgeably on the contemporary Chinese theological scene, it appears that tackling this question is a matter of general importance anywhere in the world where serious theological thinking is going on. At the very least, those who question the holy perfection of Adam at creation will find in Nee a theological ally, not a popular foe.

'Moral neutrality', to take up Nee's description, is a suggestive notion and some who will agree with him on the eschatological orientation of Adamic creation will baulk at such language. Yet, it invites serious consideration. The Genesis account of Adam is extremely compressed and subsequent biblical allusion to him elaborates this account minimally, virtually confining itself to its soteriological significance. Before deciding whether Adam is more appropriately described as 'morally neutral' than as 'holy', we should need to do two things.[38] The first is to analyse exactly what morality might amount to in a situation where humankind is unacquainted with good and evil. The second is to provide a phenomenological and conceptual account of what moral *neutrality* might mean. Nee did not doubt Adam's created goodness, but believed that it was consistent with moral neutrality. Where such a belief is combined with the realisation that 'good' is not a moral quality when applied to non-human creation, our theology of creation takes a different shape from that familiar to people in evangelical circles.

The sum of the matter is this: in terms of academic weightiness, we cannot expect Nee's contribution in the form in which he made it to feed into contemporary intellectual discussion in China at a high level. However, we must not only ask what cultural weight should be attached to academic weightiness, but also recognise that dedicated Christians on the ground and their Christian leaders are the salt of the earth and will often have important but perhaps unwitting theological insights as they pursue the life of discipleship.[39] Of course, there is a cloud over Nee's personal reputation in this respect and I make no comment on that.[40] Doubtless, the matters which arise in this connection cannot simply be ignored when we consider appropriating the theological legacy of Watchman Nee. Yet, whatever is the truth in these matters and whatever our disagreement even with theological tenets which are quite fundamental in Nee's thought, we must be willing to learn from his written word. Watchman Nee has something to teach us, whether or not it is original

38 In this context, 'holiness' refers to an internal human moral quality and not an external divine setting apart.

39 To avoid misunderstanding, let me underline that I am certainly not hinting at a demeaning view of the academic enterprise.

40 Both Dongsheng Wu, *Understanding Watchman Nee*, 48-49 and Lian Xi, *Redeemed by fire*, 177, touch on this.

and something which we can learn from elsewhere. He has been influential and may remain so. That suffices to justify our attention.

Conclusion

Only those who know China are entitled to speak into the situation there with the expectation that they should be heard. What the outside observer (like myself) looks out for and desires is the possibility of an authentic Christian theology informing the life of churches there and through the churches, society – a theology capable of fruitful interaction with a number of Chinese strands and traditions. In large measure, the possibility of fruitful intellectual engagement may be purely theoretical: I note Lian Xi's conclusion on Christianity as the religion of the masses in the Chinese future.[41] Perhaps, then, Nee's psychological observations will have nothing to do with native neo-Confucian wisdom, his interest in praxis little to do with Daoist philosophy.[42] There are potential conversations here which may just pass him by.[43] But what of the significance of Watchman Nee on creation or on Romans 6? If Darwinism poses a challenge for both theological reflection and apologetics, Romans 6 poses one for both theological reflection and the Christian life. The gospel as truth will little avail us while we neglect the gospel as power, and Western theologians are surely far too prone to muse over truth at the expense of eagerly seeking power in its spiritually positive, not self-servingly debased, sense. If we need to hear and heed Watchman Nee today, amongst the reasons why is that he directs our minds to the centrality of Paul's teaching on selfhood, death and resurrection. To understand Paul on this is to possess a key to the secret of true spiritual power.

41 See *Redeemed by fire*, 'Afterword'.

42 On another plane, Lian Xi connects Nee with Daoist mystics (*Redeemed by fire*, 10).

43 E.g., such as those of Hans Küng & Julia Ching, *Christianity and Chinese religions* (London: SCM, 1993).

"Abolish this Great Evil": Chinese Christians' Opposition to Opium Trafficking

Charles Weber

The movement to abolish opium use and trade in China can be seen as a remarkable example of cooperation between Chinese and British Christians, which stretched across two continents and two very different cultures. The details and history of the movement are complex, yet it is clear that Chinese Christianity, represented by individuals and organizations, played a pivotal role in the abolition of the great evil of opium. This paper looks at three individuals, Pastor Hsi Shengmo, Yan Yongjing, and Tang Guo-An, as well as grassroots activity and Chinese founded pressure groups.

While the history of opium in China can be traced back more than a thousand years, its "massive consumption…as an addictive drug" essentially commenced in the early nineteenth century. China's opium control efforts date from its first imperial edict for opium suppression in 1729, through Commissioner Lin's destruction of foreign opium and the Taipings' prohibition on the drug. Nevertheless, opium imports, usage, and production increased significantly in the nineteenth century, accompanied by British pressure to legalize the trade in which British India was a major producer and the British East India Company a significant exporter of opium to China and Southeast Asia. Under foreign pressure, China legalized the opium trade in 1858.[1]

Recent studies have argued that the "most consistent and ultimately the most influential source of opposition" to the use and trade of opium in China was the missionary objections.[2] "The vast majority of missionaries in China were outspoken opponents against opium and opium trade in China" both from "a moral point of view and from the concern of converting the Chinese." This concern increased throughout the nineteenth century and the "missionaries' anti-opium campaign and activities intensified after 1890."[3]

In the second quarter of the nineteenth century and through the late Qing era, an impressive anti-opium network developed, encompassing refuges for opium addicts in towns and cities throughout China, churches in the country, mission

---

1 See Zhou Yongming, *Anti-drug crusades in twentieth-century China: Nationalism, history, and state building* (Lanham, MD: Rowman and Littlefield Publishers, Inc., 1999), 11-13, and Jeffery Miron & Chris Feige, *The opium wars, opium legalization, and opium consumption in China* (Cambridge, MA; National Bureau of Economic Research, 2005), 1-3.

2 Timothy Brook & Bob Tadashi Wakabayashi, eds, 'Introduction', *Opium regimes: China, Britain, and Japan, 1839-1952* (Berkeley: University of California Press, 2000), 38.

3 Zhou, *Anti-drug crusades*, 22-23.

agencies and missionaries involved in China, Chinese anti-opium societies, the imperial Chinese government, the British Parliament, churches in Britain, and the anti-opium societies they sponsored locally and nationally. These various aspects of the movement were informally linked but together played an important role in opposing opium trade and use. The social and political activism of Chinese Christians contributed significantly to this anti-opium network.

On the British side, anti-opium efforts were spearheaded by two main agencies. The earlier one, *The Anglo-Oriental Society for the Suppression of the Opium Trade* (the "Anglo-Oriental" was soon dropped from its name), was founded in 1874 by Edward Pease, a prominent banker, with the Earl of Shaftsbury as its first president. Its journal, *The Friend of China*, promoted its efforts to educate the British public regarding opium use and trade while applying pressure to Parliament to make the opium trade illegal. By the late 1880s the movement was languishing and J. Hudson Taylor and Benjamin Broomhall of the China Inland Mission in 1888 formed *The Christian Union for the Severance of the Connection of the British Empire with the Opium Traffic*. Taylor spoke passionately for The Christian Union's purposes when he opposed "the incalculable evils, physical, moral, and social, which continue to be wrought in China through the opium trade". He further observed that, "the opium traffic is doing more evil in China in a week than Missions are doing good in a year, and consequently, one feels that this is a profoundly important question, and one that must be dealt with in the sight of God."[4] The journal of the Christian Union, *National Righteousness,* was edited by Broomhall as was the British edition of *China's Millions*, the main journal of the CIM; both published material critical of opium. As editor for both, Broomhall was responsible for the publishing of two of Britain's strongest anti-opium journals, placing him in the vanguard of the movement. Both the SSOT and The Christian Union were cordial, complementary, and cooperative in their anti-opium efforts, facilitating the network of anti-opium agencies and actively seeking input from the situation in China.[5]

It should be noted that the anti-opium movement in China was predominantly a Protestant cause. Catholics were involved with parish work, education, orphanages, and hospitals; some of their hospitals did treat addicts

4 James Johnston, ed, *Report of the Centenary Conference on the Protestant Missions of the World held in Exeter Hall (June 9th-19th), London, 1888, vol.1* (New York: Fleming H. Revell, 1889), 471, 131.

5 By 1891 the Christian Union was supported by over 3000 members (more than 6000 by 1893) as well as by the YMCAs throughout the United Kingdom, by the supporters of CIM, and by fifteen denominations including the Church of England, Church of Scotland, United Presbyterians, Free Church of Scotland, Presbyterian Church of England, Presbyterian Church of Ireland, Congregational Churches, Baptist Churches, Society of Friends in Great Britain and Ireland, Welsh Calvinistic Methodist Churches, Bible Christian Denominations, Wesleyan, Primitive Methodist, Methodist New Communion, and United Methodist Free Churches. *National Righteousness*, February 1891, 8.

but separate refuges were rare. An explanation of their lack of preoccupation with anti-opium activity compared to Protestants is given by Jean-Paul Wiest, who in his *Maryknoll in China* observes that the "Protestant zealous drive against opium" antagonized many Chinese people and leaders who viewed the criticism as an attack on Chinese governance. Wiest quotes a missioner, Father Philip Taggert, saying, "the foreigner...introduced this curse and it is the foreigner who still keeps the country supplied with the bulk of this drug. I wonder how the Southern Baptists or northern Presbyterians would feel if a crowd of Chinese flocked to America and started to enforce the laws of the United States over the heads of the duly appointed officials of that county."[6] Thus, the anti-opium cause seemed too disruptive, especially as spearheaded by foreign missionaries, and brought unnecessary criticism of the Christian community in China. Therefore, when missions or missionaries are mentioned in this paper, it is Protestants who are referenced.

The British anti-opium societies drew extensively on the testimonies of missionaries and Chinese government officials. Right "from its inception, *China's Millions* had highlighted the opium scandal, with frequent articles and letters from CIM missionaries and staff... [and] of social and personal conditions in a China plagued by opium."[7] Through his editorship of both *China's Millions* and *National Righteousness*, Benjamin Broomhall was effective in giving the Chinese a voice in the anti-opium crusade, presenting to the British public and political leadership the testimony of both ordinary Chinese and officials who uniformly blamed Christianity and Britain for opium's deleterious effects on their people and government. The remainder of this paper will focus on examples of indigenous Chinese efforts to abolish the trade in and use of opium.

Pastor Hsi and the Opium Refuges

The most prominent Chinese anti-opium campaigner, especially from the CIM's perspective, was the legendary Pastor Hsi (Xi Shengmo, 1830-1896; born Xi Liaozhi). The life of Pastor Hsi and controversies surrounding him are well recounted elsewhere. Nevertheless, a few biographical facts serve to highlight his strategic role in fostering an indigenous Christianity in China through his evangelistic and anti-opium work – both of which were integrally linked. His accomplishments as recounted in CIM materials and in the books by

6 Jean-Paul Wiest, *Maryknoll in China: A history 1918-1955* (Armonk, NY: M.E. Sharp, 1988), 331. See also Joyce Madancy, *The troublesome legacy of Commissioner Lin: The opium trade and opium suppression in Fujian Province, 1820s to 1920s* (Cambridge, MA; Harvard University Asia Center, 2003), 267.

7 A.J. Broomhall, *Hudson Taylor and China's open century, Book 7* (Sevenoaks: Hodder and Stoughton, 1989), 67-68.

Mrs. Howard Taylor (nee Geraldine Guinness) probably make him the best-known Chinese Protestant of the latter nineteenth century.[8]

Before Hsi's conversion, he was known as the son of a literary family of traditional medical doctors in Shanxi, a student of the Confucian classics who passed the first of three levels of the examination system, part of the landowning gentry, an opium sot, and a member of the Daoist Golden Pill society. Through contact with David Hill (British Methodist) and Timothy Richard (British Baptist), he overcame his opium habit through prayer, Bible reading, and the work of the Holy Spirit and converted in 1879. The next year he was baptized by CIM missionary Joshua Turner. His education, energetic personality, devout prayer life, practice of fasting, fervent belief in the Bible, and manifestation of spiritual gifts soon brought him the status of a spiritual leader. He believed in the reality of evil spirits and in faith healing. Upon conversion, he dedicated his life to the cure of opium addicts and he took the name Shengmo or "Overcomer/Conqueror of Demons." From this time "he was as a man set apart, with an apostolic sense and conviction of being chosen by God for some special service," for whom only "after years could the full purpose of God be unfolded."[9] In 1886 Hudson Taylor in recognition of Hsi's abilities ordained him as "watcher over and feeder of the sheep of God" and as "pastor-in-chief" of three CIM districts in Shanxi Province near his hometown of Pingyang.[10]

In a recent biography, Wright Doyle cogently summarized Hsi's talents and contributions by stating:

> His powerful personality, brilliant intellect, knowledge of the Bible, preaching ability, organizational and leadership skills, and especially his implicit faith in a prayer-answering God all combined to create a movement that led to healing and deliverance for many opium addicts and the formation of churches that developed out of the opium refuges he founded and staffed with former addicts.[11]

Albert Lutley observed in 1902 in *China's Millions* that Hsi "accomplished one of the greatest works that any man has been privileged to do in China, and who became perhaps the most remarkable man of God the church in China has produced."[12]

Hsi's refuge work became the focus of his life and helped to focus the CIM's anti-opium crusade.[13] "By 1890, the CIM had a variety of refuges in eight or nine provinces" and "they ranged from professional medical wards [in

8 Alvyn Austin, *China's millions: The China Inland Mission and late Qing society, 1832-1905* (Grand Rapids, MI: William B. Eerdmans, 2007), 172.

9 Mrs. Howard Taylor, *Pastor Hsi's conversion* (London: Morgan and Scott, 1907), 72.

10 Broomhall, *Hudson Taylor, Book 6*, 407, and Lian Xi, *Redeemed by fire: The rise of popular Christianity in modern China* (New Haven CT: Yale University Press, 2010), 28.

11 G. Wright Doyle, ed, *Builders of the Chinese church: Pioneer Protestant missionaries and Chinese church leaders* (Eugene, OR: Pickwick Publications, 2015), 12.

12 *China's Millions*, March 1902, 31.

13 Austin credits J. Hudson Taylor with establishing the first missionary 'opium asylum' in Ningpo in 1859. Austin, *China's millions*, 76 and 245.

hospitals], to refuges run by Chinese keepers nominally under missionary control, down to primitive shelters run by Chinese Christians."[14] By 1890 Hsi alone had opened forty refuges for both men and women in four provinces, supervised by about two hundred men and women and treating between two and three thousand addicts each year. His refuge work has been termed "innovative,"[15] creating "centres of spiritual blessing."[16] In fact, Taylor entitles one of her chapters, "The Refuges as Mission Stations".[17] The refuges, which Hsi termed "Heavenly Invitation Offices," were usually supervised by two recovered addicts, one a preacher and the other an administrator. An addict would stay for a few weeks and be involved in prayer, hymn singing, Bible reading and memorization, as well as hearing twice-daily sermons. Literature and Bibles were distributed. The result was the establishment of churches often composed mainly of these recovered addicts. The addicts were prescribed special medicines, Hsi claiming that the formulas for the pills he concocted were given to him by God and combined Western and traditional Chinese elements. The selling of the "the Life-giving pill, the Life sustaining pill, and the Health-restoring pill"[18] provided income and self-sufficiency for the refuges. Hsi supervised these refuges by establishing specific regulations for their operation and holding annual conferences for their keepers, the result being that they "grew into regular mission stations."[19] They also gained the support of their communities because of their sincere dedication and contribution to the welfare of the community.

In his own home, called "The Middle Eden", Hsi established a communal setting where "affairs moved with great regularity" according to regulations set by him.[20] His household was "both a Refuge and a Gospel Hall"[21] and his wife ran the domestic affairs of fifty to sixty people while also taking responsibility for mixing the medicine compounds. In addition, even though it was not culturally appropriate, she departed from her home and husband to "devote her life to the rescue of opium-smoking women."[22] By his death in 1896, it is estimated that his refuge work had resulted in seven hundred persons being baptized. In addition, Hsi was said to have "episcopal authority" with "four subordinate pastors" exercising control over a wide area with fifteen to twenty "other brethren…set apart to the supervision of local centres."[23] Thus Hsi's

14 Ibid., 247.
15 Lian Xi, *Redeemed by fire*, 8.
16 Mrs. Howard Taylor, *Pastor Hsi: Confucian scholar and Christian* (London: China Inland Mission, 1954), 184.
17 Ibid., 248.
18 Broomhall, *Hudson Taylor, Book 6*, 401.
19 Taylor, *Pastor Hsi: Confucian*, 248-250.
20 Ibid., 258-262.
21 Ibid., 258-263.
22 Ibid., 245-246.
23 Mrs. Howard Taylor, *Pastor Hsi (of North China): One of China's Christians* (London: Morgan and Scott, 1905), 351.

combination of traditional medicine, employment of Chinese workers, "Chinese folk religion, visions, healing, exorcism, and opium refuges formed a matrix of evangelism," clearly under his sole control. In this regard, he exemplifies the processes of indigenization, contextualization, and enculturation.[24]

Another legacy of Hsi was his contribution to Chinese hymnody. Over 20 years after his death, it was observed that it was "through his hymns that Pastor Hsi is most widely known...throughout North China."[25] His hymns "were deservedly popular," employing original lyrics from his own poetry and tunes of "native origin." His biographer noted that "like the Psalmist" he weaved "all the vicissitudes into songs of praise and prayer" which "flowed from his pen in simple, often beautiful verse." This indigenous Chinese hymnody was directly meant for his refuge work because the music was related to and intended for the twice-daily worship in the refuges where Hsi himself sang fervently in a high-pitched voice. Music was integral to the refuge work as "nothing cheered the patients in the Refuges so much or was so speedy a cure for anxious care."[26] As expected, anti-opium messages were part of these hymns, and one famous Hsi hymn, "A Song of Opium Woes," consisted of ten stanzas each enumerating one deleterious consequence of opium usage such as reproach to ancestors, spiritual death, poverty, loss of respect, physical emaciation, and abandoning one's "spirit to eternal death."[27] Thus Hsi's anti-opium work also contributed to the development of a Chinese worship style through his hymns and expression of local cultural values.

Hsi had a lifelong antipathy to foreigners, whom he blamed for humiliating China and introducing the opium curse. He "had often chafed at having to collaborate with foreigners" and his ministry "was mostly independent of foreign supervision and certainly not under foreign control."[28] But his sincerity, spirituality, dedication, and success mostly gained the trust and support of his missionary colleagues. As early as 1882, one CIM missionary observed that Hsi "'seems very independent of the opinions of the foreigners, and fortunately he seems to put the Bible where it should be.'"[29] However as Hsi's work progressed it did generate criticism from foreign missionary colleagues who felt that the refuges were too scattered and difficult to supervise, that his staff was not always dependable, and that his work was financially precarious. In addition, some felt that "his power over the native Christians" was so strong that their personal loyalty to him could be a threat to the local church, and that the refuge work gave him too "much influence among native Christians" and

24 Austin, *China's millions*, 10.
25 Albert Lutley, 'Forward', in Francesca French, *The songs of Pastor Hsi* (London: Morgan and Scott, 1920), vii.
26 Taylor, *Pastor Hsi (of North China)*, 124-125 and 206-207.
27 French, *The songs of Pastor Hsi*, 39-42.
28 Doyle, *Builders of the Chinese church*, 166 and 12.
29 Austin, *China's millions*, 265.

was thus "dangerous".[30] Some in the mission community questioned "the whole Refuge system," suggesting that if it were to be maintained it should be "under the direct control of the Mission." Despite Hsi's tensions with some CIM colleagues he was able to cooperate with missionary D.E. Hoste, who allowed Hsi the independence he desired; in Hoste's own words, "in all matters connected with Church and Refuge... [we were] united in prayer and consultation...."[31] Through this arrangement Hsi was able to maintain his autonomy. It did not hurt that "as years went by, his masterful character grew more and more mellowed and softened."[32]

Hsi's work gave credence to the view of the mission and the British anti-opium societies that opium was the main detriment to the evangelization of China. The refuge work began by Hsi continued to prosper after his death, as his wife ministered to women addicts. The annual meetings of refuge workers went ahead, and the *Native Opium Refuge Society* was formed in 1903 for mutual encouragement and to expand the refuge network.[33] In 1902 missionary Albert Lutley, superintendent of the CIM work in Shanxi, estimated that around twenty thousand men and women passed through the refuges and although many returned to opium use, the refuge endeavor "has not only been the means of removing prejudice and preparing the way for the Gospel, but itself has been one of the most efficient methods of spreading an intelligent knowledge of truth and probably not less than one thousand converts have been admitted into the Church by baptism" who were introduced to the Gospel through the refuges.[34]

Perhaps another way to view Hsi is as a leader in a proto-nationalist movement which foreshadowed the emergent Chinese nationalism of the early twentieth century. After all, his work was solely under Chinese control in its financing, organization, and expansion, and combined a strong social and regional cause with political implications and a religious ideology. It was a grassroots Chinese enterprise led by Hsi and his successors after his death. For Hsi "the shame and suffering [of his own opium addiction], the enslavement of his nation, of his emperor and imperial court, viceroys, governors, and magistrates, fired his determination to do all he could to free all who would accept his help, and to complete their liberation by binding them to Christ."[35] The full scope of his anti-opium preoccupation and refuge work illustrated his desire to see a "China for the Chinese." Its organization, funding, evangelization work, and continuing leadership were Chinese.

30 Taylor, *Pastor Hsi: Confucian*, 235-237.
31 Broomhall, *Hudson Taylor, Book 7*, 245. Hoste was one of the 'Cambridge Seven' and a colleague of Hsi in Shanxi from 1885-96.
32 Taylor, *Pastor Hsi (of North China)*, xxi.
33 *China's Millions* (North American Edition), November 1906, 125-127.
34 *China's Millions*, March 1902, 31-32.
35 Broomhall, *Hudson Taylor, Book 7*, 65.

The Grassroots Movements

Hsi's ministry was geographically confined to the interior, northwestern part of China, the southern part of Shanxi province and the edges of some neighboring provinces. But the anti-opium movement among Chinese Christians was much more widespread; a report in the *Chinese Recorder* of 1891 stated that, "the Christian Church in China is practically an anti-opium society,"[36] a view reinforced by the "perfectly unanimous" opinion of the Chinese Church that to qualify for membership a Chinese person must be neither a user of opium nor involved in its sale or production. At the Protestant missionary conference of 1890 in Shanghai, a resolution was passed calling in part for "missionary and native churches...to form native anti-opium societies at all mission stations, [and] for the establishment of Opium Refuges for the cure of those addicted to the habit." Furthermore, the resolution called for a broadening of the scope of these societies by specifying that they "should be formed under the auspices of the officials and gentry in every province and district."[37] Such action would take the anti-opium societies beyond the confines of the church and into society under local leadership. In addition, the conference formed a *Permanent Committee for the Promotion of Anti-Opium Societies* and in 1896 at Suzhou a nationwide *Anti-Opium League* was proposed, which had its first meeting in Shanghai in 1897. However, this increase in anti-opium rhetoric was juxtaposed with the fact that opium consumption in the latter nineteenth century was "a problem of alarming, even epidemic proportions in China." The anti-opium campaigns served to support Chinese reform movements seeking to "ward off foreign insults and humiliation" and contribute to "the formation of Chinese nationalistic consciousness."[38] In 1898, Hampton DuBose, the president of the newly formed *Anti-Opium League,* wrote to the *Chinese Recorder*, calling for public, anti-opium meetings "throughout the provinces" and in the port cities for foreigners and soliciting the support of the "official class" and the "gentry". For him, Ningpo was a model, where the anti-opium society was "a very efficient organization" where "both Christian and non-Christian" are involved.[39] Indeed it has been argued that the strength of the anti-opium movement "in any particular area had more to do with the support of local officials and non-Christian reformist elites" than the activism of the "missionaries and their converts."[40]

Starting in the latter 1890s there developed a growing convergence "among diverse elements in both Britain and China."[41] In Britain, there was Christian

36 *Chinese Recorder*, August 1891, 373.

37 *Records of the General Conference of the Protestant Missionaries of China, Shanghai, May 7-20, 1890*, 335.

38 Zhou, *Anti-drug crusades*, 23, 18, and 21.

39 *Chinese Recorder*, April 1898, 190.

40 Madancy, *The troublesome legacy*, 298-299.

41 Kathleen Lodwick, *Crusaders against opium: Protestant missionaries in China, 1874-1917* (Lexington, KY: University Press of Kentucky, 1996), 71.

opposition from anti-opium societies, church groups, medical professionals, and some politicians; on the Chinese side there were Chinese Christians, foreign missionaries, Chinese officials and merchants who understood the deleterious influence of and moral laxity associated with opium usage, as well as emerging nationalists who wished to see their nation reclaim its greatness on the world scene. Unfortunately, the Boxer Rebellion stymied this collaboration through its disruption of the Qing government and its attacks on western missionaries and national Christians and their institutions. In fact, in a letter to the *Chinese Recorder* in 1901 one person blamed the excesses of the Boxers on the opium trade, which resulted in the "decay of the official class in China, the demoralization of large numbers of people, and their active aversion to foreigners" and further opined that "the opium vice has impoverished the Chinese in mind, in character, in estate, and in development."[42]

Indigenous Organizations

After the Boxer movement, the anti-opium cause was rejuvenated and became a "very visible manifestation of the spirit of reform and combined anti-imperialist sentiments with a desire to strengthen the Chinese body, physically and metaphorically."[43] The period 1906 to 1911 was marked by "one final effort to undo the great harm done by opium,"[44] during which the "rising of anti-opium rhetoric echoed the rising of nationalism among the general public."[45] In fact, "there were few issues of greater symbolic weight in the formation of modern Chinese nationalism than the opium trade."[46] The newly created coalition included intellectuals educated in Western curriculum in China or abroad, professionals such as doctors, lawyers, and engineers, Chinese Christians and missionaries, industrialists and merchants, and even Qing officials, although these feared that anti-opium feeling would turn into anti-government sentiment.[47] In his insightful study of the *Fuzhou Anti-Opium Society* in 1906 Ryan Dunch argues that the Society's leaders were not opposed to missionaries or Western learning and culture, resulting in a "conjunction of the reformist zeal of the Society's supporters and the long-held moral activism of the missionaries and Chinese Protestants." Furthermore, he asserted that the "Fuzhou Protestants thought they knew what would save China. They envisioned a strong and confident China, regenerated through Christianity, built upon an uplifted citizenry educated to the moral duty of patriotism, taking its

42 *Chinese Recorder*, October 1901, 527.
43 Madancy, *The troublesome legacy*, 2.
44 Carl Trocki, *Opium, empire and the global political economy* (London: Routledge, 1999), 128.
45 Zhou, *Anti-drug crusades*, 32.
46 Ryan Dunch, *Fuzhou Protestants and the making of modern China, 1857-1927* (New Haven, CT: Yale University Press, 2001), 49.
47 Zhou, *Anti-drug crusades*, 32.

place confidently in a world community of nation-states progressing toward a bright global future."[48]

The strong stance and organization in Fuzhou may have been unusual. Although in 1908 the *Chinese Recorder* reported that in 1907 the anti-opium cause "made tremendous strides as a popular movement," on the basis of a survey it concluded later in the year that the movement's success was patchy and weakest in the western and southwestern provinces.[49] In 1908 *China's Millions* also reported that anti-opium effort was sporadic, strong in some places and apathetic in others.[50] Indeed the highpoint seems to have been the year 1917, which *China's Millions* said, "will be remembered in [China's] history as the one which witnessed the end of the opium trade."[51] In the same year an article in *China's Millions* was entitled "China's Great Moral Victory: The Closing Chapter of the Terrible Opium History"[52] However, as the nascent Republican government faltered in the 1920s, the anti-opium movement lost momentum as interest in suppression waned, warlords gained power, and governing bodies realized the advantage of revenue from taxing opium.[53]

During the period of transition and growing anti-opium sentiment, Chinese Christians emerged as international leaders. Two Chinese Protestants, Yan Yongjing and Tang Guo-an, made specific contributions to the anti-opium cause.

Yan Yongjing: International Anti-Opium Statesman

Yan Yongjing was born in Shanghai and educated there in the American Episcopal Church Mission, after which he went to the United States for further education, culminating in an M.A. degree. Returning to China in 1861 he held a variety of jobs and remained active in his church and was ordained in 1870. In 1879 he became a founder and first headmaster of St. John's College (Shanghai). Yan was a social activist and he took leadership in the anti-opium movement after the 1890 Missionary Conference in Shanghai. He was then invited to Britain by the anti-opium societies as a voice of the "Shanghai Chinese Christians" to make known "on their behalf the evils from which they and their countrymen suffer through the opium traffic."[54] In 1894, he went to London and stayed with CIM's Benjamin Broomhall. During his seven-month trip, he visited fifty-two cities, spoke to one hundred and twelve meetings of which forty-nine were on the opium issue, testified before the *Royal Opium Commission*, and addressed the annual meetings of the CIM, the Church

48 Dunch, *Fuzhou Protestants*, 54 and 201.
49 *Chinese Recorder*, January 1908, 10 and March 1908, 143.
50 *China's Millions*, 1908, 140-141.
51 *China's Millions*, 1917, 64.
52 *China's Millions* (North American edition), May 1917, 69-70.
53 Madancy, 'Unearthing popular attitudes toward the opium trade and opium suppression in late Qing and early Republican Fujian', *Modern China* (October 2001), 458.
54 *Chinese Recorder*, December 1894, 606.

Missionary Society, the Baptist Missionary Society, and the London Missionary Society, among others. Perhaps his most well-known and challenging statement was, "If the Christian Church of Great Britain can do nothing, then China is ruined."[55]

China's Millions published Yan's address to the CIM, entitled *"From the Chinese Standpoint."* Broomhall introduced Yan as one who spoke against the "great evil of opium smoking, which brings so much sorrow and desolation to the people of China – an evil for which we people are so largely responsible" and sought "to bring to an end the connection of our country with that traffic which has inflicted such evil upon the people of his land."[56] In his speech Yan identified himself as "a fellow Christian worker" and praised the mission for sending its missionaries to "remote districts far away from civilization, far away from European influence." He praised the CIM missionaries for siding with his "own countrymen" in condemning the opium "evil" as a vice and "great obstruction" to the progress of the Gospel…[and] the advance of the salvation of Christ." He noted the irony of Britain supporting the opium trade at the same time as sending the Gospel.[57] When Yan returned to China, he was selected to serve on the Executive Committee of the recently organized *Anti-Opium League*. From this platform and as a leading clergyman, he would help to shape Chinese "public opinion that led eventually" to the opium reforms in China and diplomatic agreements between China and Britain in the early twentieth century.[58]

Tang Guo-An: Christian Patriot

Another prominent spokesman for China who was influential about a decade later than Yan Yongjing was Tang Guo-an, whose criticism of the opium trade in the early twentieth century was closely linked with the cause of Chinese nationalism and the view that mission Christianity needed reform. Tang was born in Macao in 1858 and educated in the United States; after returning to China he became a businessman and in 1900 became involved in the leadership of the YMCA where he advocated for moral and social reforms. In 1907 he joined the Chinese Foreign Office and promoted policies that would strengthen China's autonomy. His international presence was manifested in his representation of China at the 1909 Opium Conference in Shanghai, the Edinburgh World Missionary Conference of 1910, and the Opium Conference

55 Ibid.
56 *China's Millions*, 1894, 103.
57 Ibid.
58 Carol Hamrin, 'Yan Yongjing and Yan Huiqing', in Carol Hamrin, ed, *Salt and Light*, vol.2 (Eugene, OR: Wipf & Stock, 2010), 15-40. Hamrin's chapter is insightful on Yan's life and legacy.

in The Hague which concluded in 1912. He became the founding president of Tsinghua College in 1912.[59]

Tang continued the harsh criticism of opium trade and usage voiced by both his Chinese compatriots and his British anti-opium allies. In fact, at the Shanghai Opium Conference, he expressed his indebtedness to both Benjamin Broomhall and J. Hudson Taylor. His public statements are full of typical expressions such as the "opium evil", "gigantic social evil", the "curse of opium", and "opium demon". But Tang also emphasized a newer approach which reflected the growing Chinese nationalism of the post-Boxer era and coupled it with an appeal for moral reform based on Christian ethics. He desired that the emerging Chinese patriots should be Christian in their beliefs and ethics[60] but was also critical of the missionary enterprise and wanted to see it play a more constructive role in China. His views were cogently outlined in a series of five monthly articles published in the *Missionary Review of the World,* September through December of 1905, entitled "*Obstacles to Christian Missions in China.*" In one installment he asserted that, "among the many acts of injustice which China has suffered and is still suffering at the hands of Christian powers, the opium trade is the most glaring instance" and therefore opium is "a great stumbling-block to the progress of Christianity in China."[61] In addition he called for reforms of missionaries, missionary societies, and native Christians with the "hope of seeing Christianity soon established as the national faith in China."[62] He hoped for a "mighty revival in national righteousness, reaching into every avenue – political, social, and commercial.[63]

China's Millions and *National Righteousness* both published speeches by Tang from 1910, the first entitled, *"China's Fight with Opium"* and the second, *"A Chinese Statesman on Opium and China."* Tang used firm language to reflect the growing connection between anti-opium and nationalist sentiment: "the popular heart is nervously pulsating with the impetus of the anti-opium movement. The entire country is filled with the spirit of anti-opium reform. The popular sentiment has never been so aroused over a single moral and social question. The Chinese press, the anti-opium societies, the students' associations, and our local self-government assemblies are all putting up the universal cry: 'Away with opium! Banish it from our borders!'" He also gave special credit to the Fuzhou anti-opium societies and their network throughout the province, which were very active at this point. He concluded the speech with the statement most closely identified with him:

> Therefore, for the sake of your national righteousness, for the sake of your national fame, for the sake of humanity at large and of the Chinese people in

59 For further information, see Carol Hamrin, 'Tang Guo-an: Pioneering China's rights recovery movement', in Carol Hamrin, ed, *Salt and Light*, vol.1 (Eugene, OR: Wipf & Stock, 2009), 30-49.
60 Ibid, 37.
61 *Missionary Review of the World*, September 1905, 688-89.
62 *Missionary Review of the World*, December 1905, 924.
63 *Missionary Review of the World*, 1909, 70.

> particular, and for the sake of our Lord Jesus Christ in whose sight we are all His children, and who has taught us to love others as ourselves, we invoke your continued co-operation in this opium question until the last shipment of Indian opium has been landed in China, until the last opium pipe has been burnt, and until the last acre of poppy shall have been uprooted and the opium evil has disappeared, not only in China, but throughout all the world.

In this way Tang confronted both the challenges and optimism of an emerging China wanting to take "its proper place in the comity of nations" as a proud and independent country.[64] Carol Hamrin provides an excellent summary of Tang's legacy:

> The continuity of reform ideas and efforts provided a hidden current of progress beneath the surface waves of political turbulence. Motivated by love of Christ, family, and country, Tang's part in the development of railways and shipping, the ending of the opium trade, the recovery of China's sovereign rights, and the founding of modern education constitutes a major contribution.[65]

The Broader Church Community

Christians in the anti-opium movement also drafted petitions and open letters expressing their views, especially to government officials and the public. Missionaries did this, but at critical points Chinese Christians did too. Three letters from 1890 will prove instructive. In March 1890, *National Righteousness* published in both Chinese and English an *"Appeal from the Chinese Christian Churches at Canton to the Churches in Great Britain Against the Opium Traffic,"* "signed by representatives of all our Churches-beseeching your Churches, pastors, and teachers to combine your strength, in devising some efficient means to remove this curse of opium." It enumerated the detrimental impacts on China including: "dissipation of the wealth of the land," "the gradual destruction of the industries and trade of the country," "physical deterioration" of the people, and destruction of the "character and manners of the people." The letter continued to specify "obstacles" to Christian endeavors:

> Your missionaries come with the real desire to benefit the people, but those who see them maliciously declare that opium and missionaries are alike English productions, and they suspect the missionaries of secretly doing evil...Your Christians with singleness of heart, are zealous in many good works, but while opium remains they are all like much water poured out.

This letter concluded by expressing the desire that opium be abolished so "that the Chinese may be released from this yoke of bondage and the obstacles to the preaching of the Gospel be removed...help England and China to abolish this great evil." This reflected and reinforced the views of other Chinese

---

64 *China's Millions*, February 1910, 19-20, and *Missionary Review of the World*, October 1910, 12-15.

65 Hamrin, *Salt and Light*, vol.1, 49.

opposing opium and the anti-opium constituency in Britain. The letter continues by implicating British Christians in the opium trade and presenting the Chinese view that "when your Government plants and sells opium to minister to the evil propensities of the Chinese, you are partakers with them." This open letter was signed by Chinese leaders of six mission churches representing 2,430 communicants.[66]

Another appeal was a petition dated August 2, 1890, from *"The Pekin Anti-Opium Society to All Lovers of Virtue in Great Britain."* In stark terms it specified the crisis at hand. Opium was identified as "an evil ulcer, daily spreading and putrefying, infesting the whole body...destroying body and soul." It claimed that, "there is no virtuous or benevolent Chinaman who is not sick at heart at the ruin of opium." So while condemning the "evil poison of opium," the letter also praised Britain as a "noble country" with a "benevolent heart" which had stopped the slave trade, and questioned the contradiction of allowing the opium trade. There is a pointed reference to missionaries, stating that "frequently men" say about them, "Your words exhort us to virtue, but your heart conceals poison, since you kill us with opium and carry our money to your country." The letter concludes with an appeal for "united strength [to] stop the curse, cast out from China this giant evil, and prohibit the traffic." The letter was signed by the committee of the *Pekin Anti-Opium Society*.[67]

A third appeal, dated May 1890, was addressed from "The Christian Women of Tung Chow, North China...to the Christian Women of England." It enumerated the "evils of opium" which have "caused untold injuries to the bodies, the homes, the country, and the State." It specified the physical deterioration and lack of purpose of the addict. Furthermore, the addicts were charged "as a class" with being "vicious in heart, wicked in deed, evil in thought, impure in word, false and crafty in intercourse with others" and having lost "the will to do right." These Chinese women appealed to their "sisters in England" concerning the "awful desolation which opium brings into their homes." They thanked them for listening to their description of the "evils of opium" and then "earnestly" beseeched them "to use the utmost efforts of your hearts to arrest this trade." They concluded by expressing the hope that through the efforts of English Christian women "the humanity of England will be manifested, the great evil of China will be removed, and the holy Name of God will be glorified."[68] While the legal termination of the opium trade was still a quarter of a century away, the effort involved many parts of society, including both Chinese and English women.

---

66 *National Righteousness*, April-June 1890, 10-11. The Chinese version is on page 9.
67 'Britain's crime against China' (London: Dyer Brothers, 1891), 24-26.
68 Ibid., 29-30.

Conclusion

By 1916 "China was practically free from opium"[69] due to the concerted efforts over many decades of anti-opium forces and the strengthening of international governmental actions such as the Chinese imperial anti-opium decree, the Sino-British agreements to stop the trade, and the opium conferences in Shanghai and The Hague. Integral to all of this were the persistent actions of religious anti-opium forces across a broad geographical and social spectrum. In China these ranged from a system of refuges developed by Pastor Hsi in rural China and sustained by his successors and publicized in the British religious press, through the Protestant churches and mission agencies in China that uniformly condemned opium, to Chinese anti-opium societies and religious leaders appealing to their own society and government and the British public. In Britain, churches, mission societies, and religious leaders campaigned and pressured the British Parliament. In this extensive, international network, Chinese Christians were instrumental in promoting the anti-opium cause both in China and to the broader international community. The anti-opium cause was a matter of the heart on many levels and Christians in Britain and China collaborated in abolishing the opium trade and usage. The China Inland Mission under Broomhall and his journals, *China's Millions* and *National Righteousness*, along with the anti-opium societies like the *Christian Union* and the *Society for the Suppression of the Opium Trade* promoted the issue in Britain but also sought input and expert testimony from Chinese Christians. Chinese church leaders like Yan Yongjing and Tang Guo-an gave direction to the Chinese Christian community but also stated their own views on opium and other related matters outside of China. On occasion petitions were also used to express Chinese grievances to the Christian community, especially in Britain. Indigenous Chinese Christians contributed moral and socio-political input into Chinese society through their activism related to the crusade against anti-opium and its related evils.

69 *China Mission Year Book*, 1925, 331.

Part Five

Commending the Faith

Torn Between Two Worlds: Rev. Shoki Coe, Domesticity and the Taiwanese Self-Determination Movement

Niki Alsford

> I am now living on "borrowed time". It is in "borrowed time" that I am now trying to write a memoir of "my" existence, which began in 1914 and may end any time. Is there a point in my trying to do this? It all depends on the philosophical and, for me, especially, the theological question "Is there any meaning at all in time and history?
>
> Shoki Coe (1988)[1]

> Unborn generations will think it strange that the vastness, the completeness, the pervasive force of missionary enterprise, made so small an impression on the public mind […] Like leaven, [the Christians] are hid among the people. They are the scattered lights of a country-side. In this village, where we stand, there is but one Christian. Yonder, half a mile to the north, live thirty worshippers; in a village two miles south, about a dozen; in that hamlet, half a mile to the east, are two Christian families.[2]

These words were written by Campbell Moody, a missionary of the Presbyterian Church of England (PCE), who arrived in Taiwan on 18 December 1895.[3] His arrival coincided with a moment of great change not only for the mission enterprise but also for the island and its peoples. Only two months prior to his arrival had the Japanese formally declared the island pacified following its incorporation into the Japanese Empire as a condition of the Treaty of Shimonoseki.[4]

The growth and future influence of the Presbyterian Mission were largely underestimated by Moody. Following the 2-28 Incident (二二八事件), according to Murray Rubinstein the church defined itself "as the self-anointed conscience of the Republic of China".[5] Broadly speaking, this transformation

---

1 Shoki Coe, *Recollections and reflections* (Taipei: Formosan Christians for Self-Determination, 1993), 263.

2 Campbell Moody, *The saints of Formosa: Life and worship in a Chinese church* (London: Oliphant, Anderson & Ferrier, 1912; reprinted in Taipei, Ch'eng Wen Publishing Company, 1971), 13-14.

3 Niki J.P. Alsford, ed, *Chronicling Formosa: Setting the foundations for the Presbyterian mission, 1865-1876* (Taipei: Shung Ye Museum of Formosan Aborigines, 2015), 499.

4 Harry J. Lamley, 'The 1895 Taiwan War of Resistance: Local Chinese efforts against a foreign power', in Leonard H.D. Gordon, ed, *Taiwan: A study in Chinese local history* (New York: Columbia University Press, 1970), 55.

5 Murray Rubinstein, 'Mission of faith, burden of witness: The Presbyterian Church in the

from "missionary enterprise" into "self-anointed conscience" occurred after an absence of mission during the war years (1940-45) but also as a reaction to a new political, cultural, and spiritual climate that followed the Chinese Nationalists' loss of the mainland to the Communists in 1949. Collectively these two important moments would coalesce in the decision by church elders and pastors to "bind themselves to the cause of Taiwanese selfhood," and more specifically to the peoples' "sense of ethnic and provincial identity".[6] This collective binding was perhaps first evident in the efforts to "rescue" Peng Ming-min (彭明敏), a noted democracy activist and advocate of Taiwan independence.[7]

It was through "exiled church leaders" that the beacon of self-determination was carried. Known as Formosan Christians for Self Determination (FCSD) (*Taiwan renmin zijue yundong* 台灣人民自決運動), this band, which included Shoki Coe, Dr Ng Bú-tong (黃武東, *Huang Wudong*), Lim Chông-gī, (林宗義, *Lin Zongyi*), and the Rev. Dr. Sòng Chôan Sēng (宋泉盛, *Song Quansheng*), advocated for Taiwan in international settings.[8]

This paper looks at the history of one of them: Shoki Coe (1914-1988). However, rather than simply explore a biographical history of Coe, which has already been carefully done by both Shoki Coe and Boris Anderson in his memoirs, and by Jonah Chang in *Shoki Coe: An Ecumenical Life in Context*, this short essay will examine how Shoki (whether consciously or not) was torn between two worlds: those of domesticity and his contribution to the self-determination movement. Since the Presbyterian Church of Taiwan (*Tâi-oân Ki-tok Tiúⁿ-ló Kàu-hoē* 台灣基督長老教會) in 2015 marked its 150th anniversary of the arrival of the PCE on their shores, this paper seeks to (re)explore Shoki's importance in creating an indigenously pastored church and any relevance he may still have on the continuing question of a Taiwanese selfhood.

The Foundations of a Presbyterian Mission

In discourse on the history of Christianity in China, the voice of the Chinese Christians is often silenced as the voice of the missionary is louder. Difficulties in locating primary material on these subalterns have often been overlooked due to the plethora of mission archives pushing them to the periphery. This is in

evolution of modern Taiwan, 1865–1989', *American Asian Review*, 9, 2 (1991), 88.

6 Ibid., 88.

7 Yoshihisa Amae, 'Pioneers in Taiwan's human rights and democracy: The role of the foreign missionaries of the Presbyterian Church in Taiwan', in Linda Gail Arrigo & Lynn Miles, eds, *A Borrowed voice: Taiwan human rights through international networks, 1960-1980* (Taipei: Social Empowerment Alliance, 2008), 176. On Peng Ming-min, see Peng Ming-min, *A Taste of Freedom* (New York: Holt, Rinehart and Winston, 1972); Christine Louise Lin, 'The Presbyterian Church in Taiwan and the advocacy of local autonomy', *Sino-Platonic Papers*, 92 (1999), 35-44.

8 Zhang Canhu 張燦鍙, *Taiwan duli yundong sanshinian, 台灣獨立運動三十年* [Thirty years of the Taiwan Independence Movement] (Taipei: Avanguard, 1991), 447.

no way meant to imply that foreign missionaries played no part, but to a periphery social historian working on Taiwan, the focus on an indigenous contribution is gratifying. What is more it is an honour to contribute to such important subject matter. Building on this, this section explores how the growth of the mission propelled the church to train indigenous clergy.

On 26 May 1865, James Laidlaw Maxwell, a young Scottish medical missionary, took up the task of establishing the first Protestant Church on the island since the Dutch in the seventeenth century.[9] In spite of initially friendly greetings, Maxwell recounts that just two months after their arrival he, along with Carstairs Douglas, Niû-á (*niang zai,* 娘仔, Aunty), Ngó-á (*unknown*), and Gaw Bûn-sui (*Wu Wenshui,* 吳文水) began to face hostility from the local population:

> Having shut, bolted, and otherwise secured the door, against which the crowds kept pressing, we commended ourselves, our helpers, and those who had stood by us since the riot commenced, in prayer to God, and waited patiently as we could for some news.[10]

In spite of the fact that they believed that there were sympathisers among the crowds, this incident forced them to relocate to Takao (present-day Kaohsiung).[11] By 12 August 1866 the PCE had baptised their first eight converts. The challenges endured by this small mission in its earlier years, instead of deterring them, in many ways strengthened their resolve.

With church activities expanding in the south, the FMC of the Canadian branch of the Presbyterian Mission sanctioned the appointment of George MacKay from Ontario to begin work in northern Taiwan.[12] Henceforth, the River Dajia (大甲) in Taichung became the dividing line between the two missions.[13] MacKay's first discernment of the island's inhabitants was distinctly bitter. His portrayal of the North in 1875 recounts:

> The Gibraltar of heathenism in North Formosa … [where] the citizens, old and young, are daily toiling for money, money – *cash, cash.* They are materialistic, superstitious, dollar-seekers. … [A]t every visit, when passing through the streets

9 Edward Band, *Working his purpose out: The history of the English Presbyterian mission 1847-1947* (London: Publishing Office of the PCE, 1947; reprinted Taipei, Ch'eng Wen Publishing Co., 1972), 76.

10 Donald Matheson, *Narrative of the mission to China of the English Presbyterian Church* (London: James Nisbet & Co., 1886), 58.

11 George Williams Carrington, *Foreigners in Formosa 1841-1874* (San Francisco: Chinese Materials Centre, Inc., 1977), 254.

12 William Campbell, *Sketches from Formosa* (London: Marshall Brothers Ltd., 1915; reprinted by SMC Publishing Inc., 1996), 153; Harold Otness, *One thousand Westerners in Taiwan, to 1945: A bibliographical [sic] and bibliographical dictionary* (Taipei: Institute of Taiwan History, Preparatory Office, Academia Sinica, 1998), 103; Band, *Working his purpose out*, 90; and Alsford, *Chronicling Formosa*, 12.

13 Also referred to as Tai-kah khe. See Lin, 'The Presbyterian Church in Taiwan', 9.

> we are maligned, jeered at, and abused. Hundreds of children run ahead, yelling derisive shouts; others follow, pelting us with orange-peel, mud and rotten eggs.[14]

Notwithstanding these early impressions of the district, by 1893 MacKay was being paraded through its streets in a sedan chair as an honoured member of the community, a change perhaps reflecting his adroit leadership and willingness to compromise. As Murray Rubinstein has argued, British missionary pioneers actively sought the establishment of an *indigenous* church – one that could identify with the local community, delivering necessary social services as well as gospel preaching.[15] The mission began to contextualise its congregation around the themes of "independent, [and] self-supporting", where they "laid great stress upon [the] training [of an] indigenous clergy."[16]

MacKay, a strong advocate of this practice, believed that that the work and success of the mission should reflect an "idea of a native ministry"[17] and argued that "mission lay not in foreign workers"[18] but in the training of "evangelists, teachers, preachers, and pastors."[19] MacKay also alluded to practical and financial reasons for training a native ministry:

> One reason for a native ministry…is that is by far the most economical, both as to men and money. Natives can live in a climate and under conditions where any foreigner would die, and they can be hale and happy where I would tremble with chills and fever. And the cost of a native preacher and his family is so much less, that the contributions of the churches can be made to support a very much larger staff than if foreigners alone were employed.[20]

The outcome of this was, as argued by Robert Bickers, "that [the] missionaries found themselves generally working with, rather than over, Chinese Christians."[21] The integration of the mission into local life addresses a transnational interconnectivity that is central to how Shoki Coe mobilised foreign support for Taiwan during martial law. It simultaneously reflected upon both the *local* as well as the *global*. The amalgamation of this is represented in the narrative of early converts and is arguably best illustrated in the history of Gaw Bûn-sui who died in 1879.[22] Known simply as 'Elder Bun', he worked tirelessly with Maxwell (arriving with him from Amoy) to establish the

14 George Lesley MacKay, *From far Formosa* (London: Oliphant Anderson and Ferrier, 1896; reprinted by SMC Publishing Inc., Taipei, 2002), 164.
15 Robert Gardella, 'From treaty ports to provincial status, 1860-1894', in Murray Rubinstein, ed, *Taiwan: A new history* (Armonk, NY: M.E. Sharpe, 1999), 169.
16 Rubinstein, 'Mission of faith', 70-72.
17 MacKay, *Far from Formosa*, 285.
18 Ibid., 285-86.
19 William Campbell, *Handbook of the South Formosa Mission* (Hastings: F.J. Parsons, Ltd., 1910), 52.
20 MacKay, *Far from Formosa*, 286.
21 Robert A. Bickers, 'To serve and not to rule: British Protestant missionaries and Chinese nationalism', in Robert A. Bickers & Rosemary Seton, eds, *Missionary encounters: Sources and issues* (Richmond: Curzon Press, 1996), 236.
22 Alsford, *Chronicling Formosa*, 15.

mission.[23] William Campbell, who spent three years with him, wrote that he presided as chapel-keeper and "speedily became the missionary's right hand."[24] What is more, "he became the constant referee in all matters of difficulty which arose amongst native brethren" and "was ever ready to speak of Christ – in the chapel, on the streets, in the Hospital, but most of all to individuals."[25]

To understand further how the practice of a "native ministry" characterised the mission on Taiwan, the following section will examine Shoki Coe's early life.

"Man Without Country", "Homeless Guru": The Life of Shoki Coe[26]

Shoki Coe was born 20 August 1914 in Changhua (central Taiwan), Shoka in Japanese. His grandfather Ng Leng-kiat (黃能傑), born in 1852, was the first in his family to convert. Ng (Romanised in Japanese as *Ko*) had been a practising Taoist priest and often spoke about his vow to commit his firstborn to the ministry. When his first son died in a shipwreck that promise was transferred to his second son, Shoki's father.[27] Jonas Chang argues that it was perhaps the influence of the early missionaries that had most impacted Ng's life. When Maxwell arrived Ng was only 12 years old but already a priest.[28] The first recorded contact with the mission was in 1885 during his enrolment in the Gospel College (now the Tainan Theological College) at the age of 32.Shoki Coe lived exactly half of his life in Taiwan. Less than a year after he was born the family moved to Chiayi, where his brother Eng-hui (黃永輝) was born. Shortly after, they moved again, this time further south to Tainan. Here Shoki's father was appointed housemaster of a preparatory school attached to the Boy's Middle School (Chang Jung Boys' School, *changrong zhongxue* 長榮中學) at the request of Edward Band.[29] In 1920 when the prep-school closed they moved house but remained in Tainan. For the next seven years this "was the neighbourhood in which [he] lived and played [...] it was [his] world and [he] knew it intimately."

It was Christmas 1924 that altered Shoki's perception of life inside a home. He recounts:

> We [Shoki and Eng-hui] did indeed have a glorious time. On Christmas eve, we two brothers sang some of the carols we had learnt at East Gate Sunday School to

23 Band, *Working his purpose out*, 107; Also, Niannian buwang wenge, 念念不忘文哥 [Brother Wen that cannot be forgotten] *Taiwan Church News*, 2024 (16 Dec 1990).
24 Campbell, *Sketches from Formosa*, 366.
25 Ibid., 366; and Alsford, *Chronicling Formosa*, 15.
26 'A man without country' was said by Desmond Tutu and 'a homeless guru' by Kosuke Koyama (Dean of Southeast Asian Graduate School of Theology), see: Jonas Chang (trans., Ching-fen Hsiao), *Shoki Coe: An ecumenical life in context* (Geneva: WCC Publications, 2012), xvii.
27 Ray Wheeler, 'The legacy of Shoki Coe', *International Bulletin of Missionary Research*, 26, 2 (2002), 77.
28 Chang, *Shoki Coe*, 3.
29 Coe, *Recollections and reflections*, 9.

> the applause of a packed church, and recited our Bible portions so well that the village folk were full of admiration. In short, as our auntie told us to our delight, we two brothers "had become the bright stars of the evening". But a day or two later, all was changed.[30]

Following the boys' return to Tainan, Eng-hui fell ill. He died 10 days later.

> He was still smiling when I visited him that afternoon from school, but by the time I went back there to join father about nine o'clock, he lay completely still and peaceful, as if all pain was gone. He was dead.[31]

Later that night, Shoki recalls being startled as he woke to find his mother beside him. "Mother drew me close to her and wouldn't let me move". With the sudden realisation that following morning that his brother was no longer with him, Shoki describes the feeling as:

> [A] blow [that] seemed somehow to come from within…no, no, even after more than sixty years have passed, I still don't know how to describe it…it was as if something had gone dead inside me.

Six months later Shoki's mother Kim Lim *Qin Lin* (親林) died.

In his *Recollections and Reflections* Shoki Coe quickly moves to discuss his life as "not completely taken up with family matters, or even with family and school interests." He goes on to say that he began to contemplate the bigger world and how that, as a Taiwanese, he felt that Taiwan "had a certain place in the world of nations." However, before engaging with Shoki Coe's *reflections* on self-determination for Taiwan, this chapter will explore his domestic life.

Two Countries, One God, Many Families: Domesticity and Shoki Coe

The separation between public and private spheres in the life of Shoki Coe reveals a kind of fluidity. In many ways it did take on a gendered form, yet without an absolute separation. Coe's wife Winfred (née Saunders) is perhaps most illustrative of this as she was active beyond the domestic sphere. She was born in Bristol on 17 August 1913, one of nine children of an employee of the Great Western Railway. She attended Colston High School (then Shrewsbury) before joining the London Missionary Society (LMS).

The model of "woman at home" may have shaped the social relations of many across time and space,[32] but things were slightly more complicated in Winifred's context. When the two met in London in 1943 she was training to become a missionary. On 12 August 1946 they were married, proclaiming that "in Christ there is no East and West". Yet the very need for such a message betrays the hidden prejudice in society towards mixed marriages. In early twentieth century Shanghai, for example, marriages with ethnic Chinese were

30 Ibid., 17.

31 Ibid., 17-18.

32 Deborah L. Rotman, 'Separate spheres? Beyond the dichotomies of domesticity', *Current Anthropology*, 47, 4 (2006).

feared, the resulting "Eurasianness" frequently condemned for "contaminating the race and diluting the boundaries that were believed necessary for the maintenance of a segregated colonial environment."[33] Yet in spite of the Nazi atrocities being reported in England at the time, this prejudice continued unabated. Andrew Coe (the youngest son) believed that his grandparents (the Saunders family) disapproved of the marriage; Shoki refused to be drawn into a conversation about it when asked and Winifred was completely unforthcoming (though she remained in touch with all her brothers).[34]

Their marriage was not received well at first by the mission committees either. Boris Anderson writes that "some were fearful that [their marriage] would make it harder for Shoki to settle back in Taiwan, and were uncertain too whether Winifred would be able to adjust happily to life as the wife of a Taiwanese pastor and daughter-in-law in a large Taiwanese family."[35]

Prior to their marriage Winifred's career had, like Shoki's, been interrupted by the outbreak of war; unable to leave for China, Winifred took up work as a "Church Sister". Matters became more difficult for Shoki following the signing of the Axis Treaty between Germany, Italy, and Japan on 27 September 1940. As a Japanese passport holder, Shoki not only had difficulty finding work, but also found that remaining in the UK was becoming increasingly complicated.

Coe and Rev. W.E. Montgomery (then principal of Tainan Theological College) were invited to attend a meeting of the Overseas Mission Committee (OMC) on 14 April 1940. The atmosphere was tense as they had to prepare for the evacuation of all foreign missionaries from Taiwan who were ordered to be repatriated by the end of 1940.[36] The committee unanimously agreed to keep Shoki in England; being neither a missionary nor a British subject, there was no channel from which he would receive "a call that would lead to ordination" and thus the OMC appointed him a mission educator.[37]

Shoki Coe had just completed an assignment at the Presbytery in Newcastle and was at a speaking engagement in Edinburgh when, following the Japanese assault on Hong Kong just eight hours after their attack on Pearl Harbor and their landing at Kota Bahru in Malaya, he became an enemy alien and lost all freedom of movement as Britain declared war on Japan. Church leaders in Edinburgh urged him to travel south to London. Shortly before leaving Scotland, Coe was questioned by the transport police, but fortunately for him

---

33 Mark Gamsa, 'Mixed marriages in Russian-Chinese Manchuria', in Dan Ben-Canaan, Frank Grüner, & Ines Prodöhl, eds, *Entangled histories: The transcultural past of northeast China* (Heidelberg: Springer, 2014), 53.

34 Andrew Coe, Shoki and Winifred and some of their families! SOAS (5 November 2015).

35 'Boris Anderson, Marriage and Family, 1944-1974', in *Recollections and reflections,* 103-104.

36 PCE/FMC/6/01/62, Letter from the Rev. E. Band to the Rev. T.W.D. James (6 December 1940). This was also similar for missionaries in occupied areas of China and Korea. See Archie R. Crouch et al., *Christianity in China: A scholars' guide to resources in the libraries and archives of the United States* (Armonk, NY: M.E. Sharpe, 1989), 197; and Norman E. Thomas, *Classic texts in mission and World Christianity* (Maryknoll, NY: Orbis Books, 1995), 290.

37 Chang, *Shoki Coe*, 61.

Mr MacDonald (whose houseguest Shoki was while in Edinburgh) used his own name to book a berth on the night train.

Finding a place to stay was not difficult for Coe. Since his initial arrival in England he had been acquainted with the Landsboroughs of Redhill, Surrey, who functioned as Coe's guarantors. They had not long retired from mission work in Taiwan,[38] and their son David had been born in Changhua and served as officer in charge of the medical department at Chuanchow General Hospital in Quanzhou.[39]

In London Coe found full-time employment teaching Japanese at the School of Oriental and African Studies (SOAS) and occasionally worked with the BBC World Service. Rumour has it that he was also tasked to assist in cracking Japanese encryptions at Bletchley Park, although there is no record of him serving in this capacity.[40]

In early 1947 Shoki, Winifred, and their son David left for Taiwan, each with their own excitement and apprehensions. For Shoki this had been 11 years in the waiting. He was apprehensive since his "native land [had] at last been liberated from 50 years of Japanese imperial rule"[41] For Winifred this was to become a new land, a new home. As for David:

> It was more the excitement of sailing in a big ship with so many soldiers about. For ours was a troop-ship with over 2,000 soldiers and a few civilians.[42]

Their optimism and excitement suffered a setback when the ship landed in Hong Kong. Shoki became reacquainted with Chhoa Ai-ti (a former classmate from Tainan) who had travelled down from Shanghai "to warn him not to return to Taiwan".[43] Chhoa had returned to Taiwan in 1946 and witnessed first-hand the horrors of the 2-28 massacre. Coe was not dissuaded and on 27 September 1947, they arrived in Keelung and were greeted by Shoki's sister A-Siok (Ng Siok-eng 黃淑英). To further understand how the events of 28 February affected not only Shoki Coe's political activism but also his theology, it is important to see how the church functioned as a channel through which he was able to express his feelings. Building on this, the following illustrates the connectivity between the PCT and Taiwan self-determination, and how Shoki through his own reflected experiences became a leading spokesperson for the cause.

---

38 See Marjorie Landsborough, *Dr Lan* (London: The Presbyterian Church of England Publications Committee, 1957); Marjorie Landsborough, *In beautiful Formosa* (Taipei: Ch'eng Wen Publishing Company, 1972); and Liu Zhaoren 劉昭仁, *Taiwan renyi di shenying, 臺灣仁醫的身影* [Following the footprints of compassionate doctors in Taiwan] (Taipei: Showwe, 2006), 24-33.

39 T.J. Liu, *Oral history of Dr. D. Landsborough IV* (Taipei: Institute of Taiwan History Preparatory Office, Academia Sinica, 2002), 305.

40 A Roll of Honour listing signals intelligence personnel can be found at http://rollofhonour.bletchleypark.org.uk/search (accessed 27 May 2015).

41 Coe, *Recollections and reflections*, 107.

42 Ibid., 107.

43 Ibid., 108.

The Long Journey Home: Heavy Responsibility and Self-Determination

The two months between the Japanese Emperor's broadcast on 15 August 1945 and the arrival of Chinese Nationalist (Kuomintang, KMT) troops in late October were a period of uncertainty, but most accounts suggest that the Taiwanese welcomed the reintegration of the island under Chinese rule with only a minority calling for independence or UN trusteeship.[44] Disillusionment began in earnest in October with the arrival of Nationalist troops; George Kerr (a United States Diplomat) witnessed the disbelief with which many Taiwanese beheld the condition of the arriving soldiers compared to the departing Japanese.

> Word soon spread, and lost nothing in telling. Formosans [Taiwanese] along the way laughed at the shambling, poorly disciplined, and very dirty Chinese troops. It was evident, they said that the 'victors' ventured in Formosa only because the United States stood between them and the dreaded Japanese. Much evil and many individual tragedies were to spring from these expressions of open scorn, for the mainland Chinese were losing face, dearer than life itself.[45]

These "individual tragedies" climaxed in the 2-28 Incident,[46] probably best represented in Hou Hsiao-hsien's (候孝賢) film *City of Sadness,* This incident is not only "historically relevant" to modern Taiwan as argued by authors such as Robert Edmondson and Stefan Fleischauer;[47] it is perhaps the origin of the desire for self-determination for many Taiwanese and in particular for the Presbyterian Church of Taiwan, PCT.

The PCT, according to Murray Rubinstein, "looked upon themselves as a Taiwanese church that represented Taiwanese, Hakkas, and mountain people."[48] Since the KMT had shown itself hostile to Taiwanese aspirations following the 2-28 Incident, the PCT stridently opposed the government.[49] Although individual members of the church suffered as a result of the White Terror, the KMT were in no position to take on the church as a whole for fear of foreign intervention. It is perhaps because of this degree of safety that a number of the Tangwai or opposition movement (*dangwai* 黨外) were able

---

44 Denny Roy, *Taiwan: A political history* (Ithaca, NY: Cornell University Press, 2003), 58; and Dafydd Fell, *Government and politics in Taiwan* (London: Routledge, 2012), 13.

45 George Kerr, *Formosa betrayed* (Boston, MA: Houghton Mifflin, 1965), 73-74.

46 Lin Wenqi 林文淇, '"Huigui", "zuguo", "ererba": Beiqing chengshi zhong de Taiwan lishi yu guojia shuxing, 回歸、祖國、二二八: 悲情城市中的台灣歷史與國家屬性 ['Return', 'Motherland', '2-28': Taiwanese history and national identity in *A City of Sadness*]', *Dangdai 當代*, 106 (Feb 1995), 94-109.

47 Robert Edmondson, 'The February 28 Incident and national identity', in Stephane Corcuff, ed, *Memories of the Future: National identity issues and the search for a new Taiwan* (Armonk, NY: M.E. Sharpe, 2002), 25-47; Stefan Fleischauer, 'The 228 Incident and the Taiwan Independence Movement's construction of a Taiwanese identity', *China Information*, 21, 3 (2007), 373-401.

48 Murray Rubinstein, *The Protestant community on modern Taiwan: Mission, seminary, and church* (Armonk, NY: M.E. Sharpe, 1991), 29.

49 Lin, 'The Presbyterian Church in Taiwan', 29.

channel their objections through the church. Most notable among them was Peng Ming-min.[50] In his memoirs he writes:

> I was now often asked to talk to church groups. Hitherto I had been too preoccupied with academic affairs and had not shown much interest in the local Christian community although members of my family were extremely active in it. My late father, my mother, and my sister were officers in the Presbyterian church, an uncle was a pastor, and a cousin would soon become president of the Taipei Theological Seminary. Given my academic background and connections, my appearance at church-sponsored meetings usually drew a considerable audience.
>
> At one of these public meetings, early in 1962, I addressed an audience at the Tainan Theological College. This is the only school in Formosa where all instruction is carried on in the local Formosan dialect (Hollo) [*sic*]. I therefore chose to speak in Formosan rather than in the official Mandarin Chinese, and I found myself discussing the problem of Formosan self-determination, speaking more bluntly than ever before in an open meeting.[51]

It was perhaps the arrest of Kao Chun-ming (高俊明, general-secretary of the PCT) following the Kaohsiung Incident on 10 December 1979 that not only brought the entire Presbyterian Church in Taiwan into the maelstrom of democratisation but also crystallised the KMT's view that it was a political entity.[52] What is more, the rallying of "exiled church leaders" and the initiation of the Formosan Christians for Self Determination, on 20 March 1973, by Shoki Coe, Dr Ng Bú-tong, Lim Chông-gī, and the Rev. Dr. Sòng Chôan Sēng, began to strengthen the Taiwan cause internationally.[53]

Like Peng Ming-min, Coe also questioned his identity in the wake of martial law and in particular his position as a "Chinese Christian":

> I began by saying that I knew I was 'A Chinese' – or thought I did – and that was one of the reasons why, six years previously, I had gone back from England to Taiwan; but after having been back there all those years and lived under the Chiang regime's martial law, I had begun to wonder whether I was really a Chinese, or just a Taiwanese.[54]

The following section will take this notion of identity further to explore whether these 'historic moments' shaped Coe's theology.

---

50 On PCT as a sanctuary for Tangwai activists, see Amae, 'Pioneers in Taiwan's human rights', 194-196.

51 Peng, *A taste of freedom*, 123.

52 Chang, *Shoki Coe*, 133; Also Lu Hsiu-lien & Ashley Esarey, *My fight for a new Taiwan: One woman's journey from prison to power* (Seattle: University of Washington Press, 2014), 137; and Hu Huiling 胡慧玲, *Shizijia zhilu: gaojunming mushi huiyilu*, 十字架之路: 高俊明牧師回憶錄 [Walking with the cross: The memoir of Rev. Kao Chun-ming] (Taipei: Wangchunfeng chubanshe, 望春風出版社, 2001). It was not until the late 1960s that the PCT developed a strong democratic theology. Kuo contends that prior to this church members 'followed the obedient political teachings of John Calvin, who proposed that Christians take a submissive stance toward the government, even if the government is a tyranny'. See Cheng-tian Kuo, *Religion and democracy in Taiwan* (Albany, NY: State University of New York Press, 2008), 39.

53 Chang, *Shoki Coe*, 126.

54 Coe, *Recollections and reflections*, 172; and Lin, 'The Presbyterian Church in Taiwan', 42.

The transnationality of Coe's identity became clear in his account of leaving Hong Kong for Taiwan in 1947. Coe discusses the impact that both the end of the Second World War and the ensuing civil war had on the colony. Coe recalls an endless stream of refugees crossing the border. According to him, had it not been for David Landsborough who had 'shielded' him from the crowds that were trying to board the ship but were being held back by "the whistling sound of police whips", he would never have made it.[55] At this moment Coe felt both familiarity and difference. He anticipated a problem with the police because he looked similar to the refugees, whilst at the same time he felt different. At this moment he identified more with Landsborough, an antagonism which continued to persist after his arrival in Taiwan.

On 3 May 1949, Michael (the second son and first of three to be born on the island) was born. It was the start of a complicated period for both Shoki and Winifred which culminated in her returning to England with the children a decade later; it was not until 1965 that Coe was reunited with his family. The difficulties began when Shoki and Winifred visited the Registry Office in Tainan to register Michael's birth. The following month they received a letter stating that unless Winifred 'naturalised' they could not legally register their son as this "was an official ruling from the Ministry of the Interior."[56] The problem was that 1949 was a critical year in the history of the KMT; with the capital officially moving to Taipei on 7 December, it had been only a year since the Temporary Provisions Effective During the Period of Communist Rebellion (動員戡亂時期臨時條款) came into effect which established martial law on Taiwan and curtailed civil liberties.[57] Winifred Coe was strongly advised by staff at the still-active British Consulate in Tamsui[58] not to relinquish her UK citizenship. The Consul accepted the birth certificate (signed by David Landsborough and Gretta Gauld) and inserted Michael's name into Winifred's passport, a process which was repeated when the other children were born.

Problems continued when Shoki needed to apply for a passport (then only valid for a year) and was listed on the document as being a 'bachelor' rather than 'married'. He subsequently began receiving letters from the government instructing him to register the children as "Chinese citizens". These letters continued to arrive unabated until Winifred and the children had left Taiwan and only then did they cease completely. It was in 1966 during the General Assembly that:

> A rather 'notorious' minister got up to move an emergency resolution the purpose of which was to censure me for having lived with a woman without marriage and for having four illegitimate children by her!!! He was apparently shouted down, or

55 Coe, *Recollections and reflections*, 108.

56 Ibid., 134.

57 See e.g., Roy, *A political history*, 76-94; and Joseph Wong, 'Deepening democracy in Taiwan', *Pacific Affairs*, 76, 2 (2003), 241.

58 Britain switched recognition from the ROC to the PRC on 6 January 1950. In spite of this Britain maintained a consulate office in Tamsui until 1973.

removed. How a minister could sink so low is beyond my imagination. He must have got the information from somewhere that I had been travelling with a passport which described me as a 'bachelor'.[59]

Infiltration of the PCT was not uncommon and a number of pastors who had expressed opposition to the KMT were forced to sign "a confession of guilt."[60]

As a result of this, Coe's concept of the role of the church changed. In June 1964 he initiated a plan for the "Religious and Social Survey of Taiwan", in which he identified that the two decades since the end of the Second World War had seen a period of massive upheaval for Taiwan. It had been "plunged into the maelstrom of industrialisation, population growth, and involvement with international affairs so characteristic of the mid-twentieth century."[61] In addition, the PCT was approaching its centenary and its celebration would be multi-denominational, under the theme "Into the Second Century Together". A survey committee was formed, whose primary focus was "Total Community in Taiwan," meaning that it sought to survey the following areas: (1) Demographic considerations, (2) the religious and cultural situation, (3) the family and social relations, (4) economic, occupational, and political factors, and (5) health, education, and welfare. Furthermore the survey would seek to identify the "relevance of the Christian mission to the human situation", evaluate the present situation, and recommend future goals. With these new considerations in mind, Coe coined the term "contextualisation",[62] which for him was an interplay of Scripture and the changing context in which it must be interpreted.

In *Recollections and reflections* Coe discusses having asked a critical question publicly:

> I am amazed that there is so much talk about Nationalist China and Communist China, but nothing about what the people in Taiwan hope for their future and the future of Formosa, their homeland. My question is: 'Is a two-China policy a real option? I know the Nationalists in Taiwan wouldn't accept it, though I don't know what the Communist reaction would be.' Why not one China and one Formosa, like one India and one Ceylon?[63]

The publication of his "One China, One Formosa" policy in the work of D.T. Niles (a Ceylonese pastor) and his pro-Taiwan independence stance saw him in virtual exile after returning to England in 1965. Yet this exile, according to Jonas Chang, enabled both Shoki and Winifred to organise ecumenical and political movements from abroad.[64]

Shoki Coe chose a church in Bromley, Kent for his Theological Education Fund office as it was close to Seaford, where Winifred and the children had

59 Coe, *Recollections and reflections*, 135.

60 Lin, 'The Presbyterian Church in Taiwan', 45.

61 PCE/FMC/6/01/87. Plan for the Religious and Social Survey of Taiwan (June 1964).

62 Wheeler, 'The legacy of Shoki Coe', 78.

63 Coe, *Recollections and reflections*, 173.

64 See Chang, *Shoki Coe*, 121-134.

settled. There both Shoki and Winifred sought to "indigenise" the church, a "missiological necessity" for Coe, whereby the "gospel moves from cultural soil to another and has to be retranslated."[65] This is most interesting in the context of Shoki's transnationality, and the expression 'contextualisation' is more fitting than 'indigenisation':

> Indigenous, indigeneity, and indigenisation all derive from a nature metaphor, that is, of the soil, or taking root in the soil. It is only right that the younger churches, in search of their own identity, should take seriously their own cultural milieu. However, because of the static nature of the metaphor, indigenisation tends to be used in the sense of responding to the gospel in terms of traditional culture. Therefore, it is in danger of being past-oriented. Furthermore, the impression has been given that it is only applicable to Asia and Africa, for elsewhere it was felt that the danger lay in overindigenisation, an uncritical accommodation such as expressed by the cultural faiths, the American Way of Life, etc. But the most important factor, especially since the last war, has been the new phenomenon of radical change. The new *context* [own italics] is not that of static culture, but the search for the new, which at the same time has involved the culture itself.[66]

This lengthy quote is important for a number of factors, not least because it is within this text that Shoki merges theology with activism. In Andrew Walls' essay "The Gospel as Prisoner and Liberator of Culture", he sees the 'indigenising principle' as rooted in the gospel but in tension with the pilgrim principle.

> Along with the indigenising principle which makes faith a place to feel at home, the Christian inherits the pilgrim principle, which whispers to him that he has no abiding city and warns him that to be faithful to Christ will put him out of step with his society; for that society never existed, in East or West, ancient time or modern, which would absorb the word of Christ painlessly into its system…[67]

In *Recollections and reflections* Shoki Coe begins with the phrase "Oikoumene" (from the Greek οἰκουμένη or *oecumene*, lit. 'inhabited') followed by "in Christ there is no East or West" (a Coe family phrase). If one takes this and his 'nature metaphor' into consideration it is clear that Shoki links the concept of 'habitation' with milieu. What is more, this social environment is not static and must be understood in terms of its context (contextualisation). It is here that Shoki expresses his political activism.

There is general agreement that it was at "the Bye" in Seaford, the Coe family home, that this interconnectivity of theology and activism was best expressed.[68] Jonas Chang writes that the family home doubled as a hostel with a

---

65 Coe, *Recollections and reflections*, 270-271.

66 Ibid., 271.

67 See Jonathan Parnell, 'Andrew Walls on two principles of the gospel in culture', *Desiring God* (22 Oct 2010), http://www.desiringgod.org/articles/andrew-walls-on-two-principles-of-the-gospel-in-culture (accessed 30 June 2015).

68 Zhang Reixiong 張瑞雄, *Taiwanren de xianjue: Huangzhanghui*, 台灣人的先覺: 黃彰輝 [*The pioneer for the Taiwanese: Shoki Coe*] (Taipei: Wangchunfeng chubanshe 望春風出版社, 2004), 318-326.

room always set aside for visitors. "They might not provide big meals like Taiwanese and Americans who were accustomed to entertaining guests, but they did provide proper English family meals for visitors with sincere hospitality."[69] Collections of photos, both within and without the family's archives, show the 1930s detached property as a backdrop to every visitor. The sheer number of photographs demonstrates clearly the importance that Shoki attached not only to the Taiwan Presbyterian ministry but also to those involved in Taiwan self-determination.

Yoshihisa Amae argues that the "torch of Taiwanese self-determination lit by the PCT was carried on by the exiled church leaders". In March 1976, Shoki Coe, C.S. Song, Y. Chao (*Zhao Youyuan* 趙有源), Daniel Beeby, and Boris Anderson were invited to testify on the 'Taiwan situation' before the UK parliament.[70] Moreover, Amae contends that the 1970s was a period in which exiled leaders and missionaries "felt that the Taiwanese church needed to speak on behalf of the 'voiceless' native Taiwanese who have been deprived of their political rights and basic freedom."[71]

On 28 July 1987, thirteen days after Chiang Ching-kuo ordered the lifting of martial law, Shoki Coe arrived back in Taiwan.[72] Whilst in Taipei, Coe stayed with his former student Kao Chun-ming who had served four of his seven years' imprisonment for hiding Shih Ming-teh (施明德) and his then-wife Linda Arrigo.[73] Having heard that Coe was staying with Kao, leaders of the newly formed opposition Democratic Progressive Party (DPP) "made a special trip to see this forerunner of the Taiwan democratic movement."[74]

In 1988, both Shoki and Winifred passed away. To the PCT he is "a rare and precious person."[75] In the field of bible translation and interpretation he is best known for coining the term "contextualisation" as a process of interpreting the social environment in which a text is understood or an action carried out. His contribution to missiology, according to Wheeler, offered "a model that moved significantly beyond indigenisation".[76] For Coe, the hermeneutics of the political situation of Taiwan was contextualised in biblical texts. It attempted to present the gospel in culturally relevant ways by recognising the differences that exist between biblical and contemporary contexts. In so doing it observed indigenous expressions of the gospel. It met local goals and worshipping

69 Chang, *Shoki Coe*, 135.
70 Amae, 'Pioneers in Taiwan's human rights', 190.
71 Ibid., 180.
72 On 4 June 1991, Lee Tung-hui 李登輝 abrogated the arrest warrants of 7 people living in exile including Peng Ming-min. Peng returned to Taiwan on 1 November 1992. See Shih-shan Henry Tsai, *Lee Teng-hui and Taiwan's quest for identity* (New York: Palgrave Macmillan, 2005), 183.
73 Ibid., 244.
74 Chang, *Shoki Coe*, 142. On the election of Kao into the DPP, see Shelly Rigger, *From opposition to power: Taiwan's Democratic Progressive Party* (Boulder, CO: Lynne Reiner Publishers, Inc., 2001), 23.
75 Ibid., 151.
76 Wheeler, 'The legacy of Shoki Coe', 79.

patterns. His conviction about contextual ministry was set by his own experiences. In Taiwan the pace of urbanisation, the political struggles, and the ethnic differences found throughout the island influenced the identity of the church. For Coe the indigenisation of the church was not simply to accommodate difference, but meant rather that through contextualising the gospel the ultimate aim was to 'transform the cultural context itself.'[77]

Outside of Taiwan missiology, for scholars on Taiwan's democracy and identity,[78] Shoki Coe gets but a passing mention, footnoted only as among those who championed the cause of independence. Lim Iong-iong's documentary "Is Time Still on Our Side" (時間還站在我們這邊嗎?) reflects on Shoki Coe's "great disappointment" as self-determination was never realised in his lifetime, and the Taiwanese continue to battle with issues of identity.[79]

Shoki Coe did much to shape Christianity in a Chinese context. According to John Bailey, his ideas of contextualisation, though not followed up well in the motifs of the Chinese church, do assist in removing certain unnecessary 'stumbling blocks' to genuine faith.[80] One example of this is arguably prayer and the manner in which it is carried out. Other hurdles may include the veneration of the dead and the use of the circular *ichthus* symbol or 'sign of the fish' and the cross. Courtney Handman's research on the Guhu-Samane Christians in rural Papua New Guinea explores this 'obstacle-removal-technique' much further by examining the manner in which the indigenous church produces an indexical and genealogical connection to biblical Judaism in order to discover certain prophetic revelations about their Christianity.[81] The impediment for some is historiographical. The notion that 'we black people' do not feature in the Bible is, therefore, by extension, an argument that 'the Guhu-Samane [people] are not accounted for in the histories of the Bible, [and as such they] are not Christian and maybe should not be'.[82] To counter this many believe that they are descendants of ancient biblical Jews and so are rightfully connected to an anticipated future Christianity. This is not unique to Papua New Guinea; some African Americans, since the nineteenth century, have

77 Ibid.

78 For a comprehensive study of scholars working on Taiwan democracy see Shelly Rigger, 'Political science and Taiwan's domestic politics: The state of the field', *Issues & Studies*, 38, 4 (2002), 49-92; also Murray Rubinstein, ed, *The other Taiwan: 1945 to the present* (Armonk, NY: M.E. Sharpe, 1994), especially chs.3-5.

79 For a well edited volume on Taiwanese identity see Gunter Schubert & Jens Damm, eds, *Taiwanese identity in the twenty-first century: Domestic, regional and global perspectives* (London: Routledge, 2011). On Coe's quest for identity, see 'Is Time Still on Our Side [*Huang Zhanghui rongyan jilupian* 黃彰輝容顏紀錄片]', Shoki Coe blog 黃彰輝, http://shokicoe.blogspot.co.uk/2012/09/is-time-still-on-our-side.html (accessed 25 June 2015).

80 John Bailey, 'What is contextualization and is it biblical?' *Asian Mission* (September, 2007), 5.

81 Courtney Handman, 'Figures of history: Interpreting Jewish pasts in Christian Papua New Guinea', *HAU: Journal of Ethnographic Theory*, 6, 1 (2016), 237-260.

82 Ibid., 238.

established communities of Black Israelites.[83] In the Chinese context the Jewish association is best represented among the Kaifeng Jews. However, this small community does not contextualise Judaism as being a precursor to Christianity but rather as one of the lost tribes. It is in Confucianism that this pathway to Christianity has been made. Confucius is perceived as a wandering sage, and his *Analects* have been compared to teachings of Jesus and the gospels.[84] Li Chungsheng (李春生, see Kuo in this volume), a Taiwan Christian at the turn of the century, took this further by arguing that Confucianism itself is an uncorrupted form of Christianity.[85] It was not just Coe's theology that has shaped Christianity in the Chinese speaking work. His own political activism and that of the PCT in general has in many ways – either directly or indirectly – fashioned certain forms of Christian activism in mainland China. The most recent case was the imprisonment of Hu Shigen (胡石根), a leader of the underground Church movement, for subversion.[86]

It is perhaps his transnational identity that marks Coe out as having truly shaped Chinese Christianity. The different identities that Coe espoused and the manner in which he contextualised them translates for many as an idea that being Christian and Chinese can be synonymous and are for them two sides of the same reality. For Shoki Coe, it is within the metamorphism of his name that the transnationality of his identity is most visible. He was an advocate of self-determination but argued that this came at a cost. At the very centre of both his ecumenical and political life was Winifred Coe, who in many ways held the family together. While he was still in Taiwan and she alone with the children in England, she often wrote to people on his behalf.[87]

As the PCT celebrated its 150th anniversary the political situation is gladly 'contextually' different, unlike its 100th when "a parade would be permitted, but there shall be no sound; During the parade no hand-out of documents will be permitted; there are quite a few ruffians in Tainan, there must be no contacts or fights with them; all activities must end by 11 p.m."[88]. The campaigning for selfhood continues in earnest. The 'between two worlds' of domesticity and activism transcends the shaping of Christianity in Taiwan and by extension the whole Sinophone world. Shoki Coe's message of civic activism can be found in

---

83 See Jacob S. Dorman, *Chosen people: The rise of American black Israelite religions* (Oxford: Oxford University Press, 2013).

84 Ralph R. Covell, *Confucius, the Buddha, and Christ: A history of the gospel in Chinese* (Eugene, OR: Wipf & Stock, 2004), 117.

85 Li Chunsheng 李春生, *Li Chunsheng zhuzuoji 李春生著作集 vol.2* [Collected Works of Li Chunsheng] (Taipei: SMC Publishing Inc., 2004), 90-94.

86 Stuart Leavenworth, 'Christian church leader jailed in Chinese human rights crackdown', *The Guardian* (Wednesday, 3 August 2016), https://www.theguardian.com/world/2016/aug/03/christian-church-leader-hu-shigen-jailed-chinese-human-rights-crackdown (accessed 4 August 2016).

87 For example, see PCE/FMC/6/01/87, Winifred to Mr Fenn (23 May 1961).

88 Chou Lien-hwa, *Memoir* (Taipei: United Literature, 1983), 271-72; also Chang, *Shoki Coe*, 117.

the leaders of all social movements on both sides of the Taiwan Strait.[89] From the Kaohsiung Eight in 1979 to Tiananmen Square ten years later. From the democratic movements of the Wild Lily Movement in 1990, the Wild Strawberries Movement in 2008, to the Sunflower and Umbrella movements of 2014 in Taiwan and Hong Kong, to the continued struggles of Chinese Christians in the People's Republic of China (PRC) today. Yet what is perhaps most important is that behind every great figure there are those who remain hidden, private, domestic, that play an equally, if not more, influential role.

89 See, e.g., Fan Yun 范雲, 'Jingmozhong gengyun xijie de fuyun geming 靜默中耕耘細節的婦運革命 [The silent development of the Women's Movement]', in Wu Jiemin 吳介民, Gu Erde 顧爾德, & Fan Yun 范雲, eds, *Zhixu binfen de niandai: yijiujiuling – erlingyiling*, 秩序繽紛的年代：1990-2010 [*The Era of Colourful Order: 1990-2010*] (Taipei: Rive Gauche Publishing House, 2010); Fan Yun 范雲, 'Shuogushi yu minzhu taolun: Yige gongmin shehui neibu zuqun duihua luntan de fenxi 說故事與民主討論:一個公民社會內部族群對話論壇的分析 [Story-telling and democratic discussion: An analysis of ethnic dialogue workshop in civil society]', *Taiwan Democracy Quarterly*, 7, 1 (2010), 65-105; Ho Ming-sho, 'Taiwan's state and social movements under the DPP government, 2000-2004', *Journal of Asian Studies*, 5 (2005), 401-425; Ho Ming-sho, 'Weakened state and social movement: The paradox of Taiwanese environmental politics after the power transfer', *Journal of Contemporary China*, 14, 43 (2005), 339-52; and Stephen Phillon, 'The impact of social movements on Taiwan's democracy', *Journal of Current Chinese Affairs*, 39, 3 (2010), 149-63.

The Hybridization and Localization of the Colony and the Making of Hong Kong Christian Leaders: Three Oral History Accounts

Kwok Wai Luen

The Hong Kong Church before 1970

The Hong Kong Church's relation with Western missionaries and the Mainland Church is important for understanding Christianity in China after 1949. On the one hand, most of the denominational churches (i.e., Baptist, Methodist, Church of Christ in China, Tsung Tsin Mission/Evangelical Missionary Society in Basel, Rhenish, and Anglican) in Hong Kong founded before 1949 were self-financed and self-governed. On the other, the influence of Western missionaries and Mainland Chinese Christian leaders was overwhelming after 1949. For political and social instability, and to gain the trust of the colonial government, Western missionaries in Hong Kong shouldered heavy responsibilities in relief work, education, and medical services from the 1950s to early 1970s. Besides social services, some missionaries that retreated from the Mainland after 1949 started new churches and ministries in Hong Kong. Prominent Mainland leaders, such as Calvin Chao (趙君影) and Timothy S. K. Dzao (趙世光) stayed in Hong Kong and started new churches. Therefore, Hong Kong became a centre of ministries, resources, and manpower.

This new input brought changes to the churches, the early 1950s seeing revivals among young Chinese Christians influenced by conservative theology. They were urged to hate sin, be uncompromising in matters of faith and zealous in evangelism. Their spiritual leaders were Woo Yan Tak (胡恩德), the leader of Hephzibah Evangelistic Centre,[1] and David Adeney, the Associate General Secretary for the Far East of the International Fellowship of Evangelical Students from 1956 to 1968.

In 1961, Chan Hay Him (陳喜謙) led a group of young Baptists to protest against the unspiritual and unbiblical practices of some pastors, eventually causing a break with the Baptist churches and the founding of several "evangelical" centres and churches.[2] In the meanwhile, Adeney's campus

1 The Hephzibah Evangelistic Centre was founded in 1918 by Julia Meadows, an evangelist of the Southern Baptist Foreign Mission, who later became an independent missionary. See *Our Church—Hephzibah* (Hong Kong: Hephzibah Evangelistic Centre, 2002), 65.

2 They are Kowloon City Evangelical Church from Kowloon City Baptist Church; Bonham Road Evangelical Church from Hong Kong Baptist Church; Shum Shui Po Peace Evangelical Centre from Shum Shui Po Baptist Church.

ministry helped the Christian Association of Hong Kong University regain momentum in evangelism. Chan was finally recruited by Adeney as a staff member for the Fellowship of Evangelical Students. According to Chan, Adeney used disciple training and Bible study groups to form committed young Christians.[3]

The period 1949 to 1970 was a time of rapid change and development for Hong Kong protestant churches. More importantly, Hong Kong was a territory in social, economic, and political flux, which in turn affected the Church. The establishment of the Communist regime in China, the Korean War, and political movements on the Mainland caused Hong Kong's population to grow rapidly. In 1946, it was 1.6 million,[4] growing to 2.67 million by 1956, and reaching 3.78 million in 1966.[5] The protestant churches also grew significantly during this period. In 1955, there were 188 churches with 53,917 members,[6] with 294 churches and 74,470 members just three years later.[7] The year 1962 saw 344 churches with 112,200 members.[8]

Political instability on the Mainland caused more and more Hong Kong people to consider the city their permanent home, and a sense of belonging developed from the 1960s. The rise of manufacturing industry generated many career opportunities for the younger generation. Carroll suggests that these changes resulted in the growth of a Hong Kong identity.[9] This paper explores a similar identity building process among Hong Kong Protestants by looking at the life and work of three significant Christian leaders.

Three leaders that have participated in and led ministries with social impact since the 1970s are Dr. Philemon Choi (蔡元雲) of the Breakthrough Movement, Rev. Dr. Lo Lung Kwong (盧龍光) of the Methodist Church and Chung Chi Divinity College, and Yu Miu Wan (余妙雲) of the Hong Kong Industrial Evangelical Fellowship. This paper draws on oral history accounts supplemented with other historical materials to portray their personal journeys and self-interpretation of their ministries. I also examine this emerging identity in terms of theological influence.

From the 1970s onwards, Hong Kong church leadership underwent a process of localization. In existing ministries and church organizations, missionaries

---

3 Wai Luen Kwok, 'Keeping tradition and introducing innovation: David Adeney's student ministry as a case for studying the interaction and changes of Hong Kong Church and Society', *Jian Dao*, 32 (July 2009), 123-152.

4 *Hong Kong Annual Report 1947* (Hong Kong: Government Printer, 1948), 9.

5 Census and Statistics Department, *Hong Kong Statistics, 1947-1967* (Hong Kong: Government Printer, 1969), 14.

6 Earl H. Cressy, *City churches in Hong Kong: With a supplementary survey of all churches in the colony* (Hong Kong: By the author, 1956), 1, 9.

7 Earl H. Cressy & Loren E. Noren, *Urban church growth in Hong Kong, 1955-1958: Second Hong Kong Study* (Hong Kong: By the author, 1960), 3.

8 Loren E. Noren, *Urban church growth in Hong Kong 1958-1962: Third Hong Kong Study* (Hong Kong: By the author, 1964), 1.

9 John M. Carroll, *A concise history of Hong Kong* (Hong Kong: Hong Kong University Press, 2007), 167-168.

were replaced, but more importantly, a new generation of leaders launched new ones, significantly impacting society as well as the church.

Although these successful ministries or movements were led by locals, we can trace how western missionaries and evangelical theology nurtured and shaped the theology, worldview, and working strategies of these leaders. For this reason I will analyze their thought and work through the lenses of hybridization and localization.

Philemon Choi

Philemon Choi (蔡元雲) founded *Breakthrough* magazine with Josephine Yan Pui So (蘇恩佩)[10] in 1973 and later became its president. When *Breakthrough* grew into a multi-ministry Christian youth organization, Choi was its General Secretary until 2003 and remains its Honorary General Secretary. Today, Breakthrough is a large organization with 200 workers and an annual expenditure of HKD 75.2 million in the 2013-14 financial year.[11] Choi is a Lausanne Committee member and a member of the Cape Town 2010 Advisory Council.[12] He is very active in community affairs and has held various public offices such as Chairman of the Commission on Youth, Chairman of the Action Committee Against Narcotics, a member of the Fight Crime Committee, the Committee of Services for Youth at Risk, a member of the Commission on Poverty and a member of the Vocational Training Council.

He was born in 1945 in Mainland China and his family moved to Hong Kong because of the civil war.[13] He became acquainted with Christianity while attending a Christian primary school. Next, during his time at King's College, a very good government secondary school, he began to have contact with David Adeney's student ministry and the student evangelistic "Rally".[14] Also, a good friend of Choi, George Hsu (徐理強),[15] had strong ties with the "evangelistic church" movement of the young Baptists, which was indirectly connected with Adeney. Hsu was Head Prefect when Choi was studying in the Lower Sixth. Choi mentioned that Hsu's enthusiasm for evangelism and Christian apologetics with a rational and scientific mind impressed him. As Hsu's junior, Choi was motivated by him to attend the Rally and have consistent Bible study,

---

10 Josephine Yan Pui So joined Campus Evangelical Fellowship in Taiwan as a staff member under the influence of David Adeney in 1966. When she founded *Breakthrough* magazine in 1973, it was under the management of the Fellowship of Evangelical Students.

11 *Breakthrough Annual Report, 2013-2014* (Hong Kong: Breakthrough, 2014), 8, 38.

12 'Records of the Lausanne Committee for World Evangelization - Collection 46', *Billy Graham Centre Archive*, http://www2.wheaton.edu/bgc/archives/GUIDES/046.htm (accessed 1 May, 2015); 'Cape Town 2010 Leadership', *Lausanne Movement*, http://www.lausanne.org/gatherings/related/cape-town-2010-leadership (accessed 1 May, 2015).

13 Philemon Choi, *My life path: 10 lessons with my mentors* (Hong Kong: Breakthrough, 2010), 14.

14 'Philemon Choi's Oral History Record', interview by Wai Luen Kwok on 16 February 2007, Hong Kong: Breakthrough Counseling Centre.

15 Choi, *My life path*, 51.

book reading, devotion, and prayers. In this period, he joined North Point Alliance Church and received baptism.[16]

However, Choi considered that his "awakening of the soul" actually happened at university.[17] In 1964, he was admitted to medical school at the University of Manitoba, staying in Winnipeg for 7 years. On arrival, he was invited to join the Winnipeg Chinese Christian Fellowship (WCCF), whose influence on him Choi recognizes. In the West Canada Youth Winter Conferences, he heard sermons by David Adeney, Stephen Knights, Philip Teng (滕近輝), Calvin Chao, and Thomas Wang (王永信). Adeney and Knights' passion and love for China impressed him very much. Choi questioned why a Westerner could love the Chinese so much, while he could not identify himself as a Chinese.[18] At the same time, Choi read Josephine So's novel *Narrow is the Way*, through which he felt the need to reflect on his "sense of belonging".[19] Choi also mentioned the great political and social events around him that let him witness "the ignition of dreams": the dream of rebuilding identity among Canadian immigrants, the examples of Martin Luther King and J. F. Kennedy as encouragements that young people should dream of transforming tomorrow, the nightmare of the Cultural Revolution in China and the dream of transforming the nation, and the "Six Day War" as a reminder of the imminence of the end times and the duty to evangelize the earth. Choi believes that this period of his life was marked by the search for identity and a passion for dreams and mission.[20]

For Choi, the WCCF of the 1960s was a very active and mission minded student fellowship. He was very moved when members of the fellowship met him at Winnipeg train station; the WCCF acted not only as a Christian fellowship, but also a student association connecting Chinese students in Winnipeg. The Fellowship not only preached to non-Christian students but also served and helped them. Choi was very impressed by this outward looking mindset. Also, he appreciated the choice of English as medium of communication, which helped Chinese students from Singapore, Taiwan, South East Asia, Hong Kong, and North America feel equal and respected. He was amazed that English helped them to cross potential barriers between different dialect groups.[21]

---

16 'Philemon Choi's Oral History Record', 16 February 2007; 'Philemon Choi's Oral History Record', interview by Wai Luen Kwok on 30 April 2015, Hong Kong: Breakthrough Youth Village.

17 Philemon Choi, 'Those years: He awakened my soul', in Robert Chan & Ruth Chan, eds, *The Red River years: The Winnipeggers in the potter's hand* (Hong Kong: MI Design, 2014), 224.

18 Philemon Choi, 'Preface: Those years: Times for Ignition of dreams', in *The Red River years*, 18. 'Philemon Choi's Oral History Record', 16 February 2007; 'Philemon Choi's Oral History Record', 30 April 2015.

19 Philemon Choi, 'Preface', 18; 'Philemon Choi's Oral History Record', 30 April 2015;

20 Philemon Choi, 'Preface', 16-18; 'Philemon Choi's Oral History Record', 30 April 2015.

21 Ibid.

Since 1965, WCCF has organized a summer gospel trip, Christian students visiting churches and doing street evangelism across cities and villages in Canada and the United States. In 1966, WCCF began to publish *Fountain*, a student magazine aimed at Chinese students (Christian and non-Christian) in North America. Choi marvelled at how a small university student fellowship could carry out such large-scale ministries and believes that the experience in Winnipeg planted the seed of his biblical faith and vocation in youth and China ministries.[22]

Choi returned to Hong Kong to share a common ethos with the young people of his generation: "Serve Hong Kong, contribute to the motherland".[23] He initially intended to be medical doctor, but his meeting with Jackie Pullinger[24] and Josephine So at Kowloon Walled City, home of disadvantaged people and den of gangs and drug addicts, motivated him to consider the urgency of youth work and Christian engagement in society. When Choi was agonizing about whether he should leave the medical profession and become a Christian youth magazine journalist, So told him, "I have worked with you for a period of time. I feel that you are passionate for young people. When you spend your spare time to share with the youth in schools, you are very dedicated and enjoy it. I truly believe that you have a sincere love for this city and the young people in it."[25] Choi emphasized that So did not push him to make a decision, but asked him to take time to think about it. After a retreat, Choi decided to join Breakthrough.[26]

At this point, it should be noted that spirituality rather than strategy played the vital role in directing the course of Choi's ministry. After deciding to work for Breakthrough full-time, he felt the need to be more equipped in theology and wanted to study counselling to meet the growing need in this area. In 1976, he went to Trinity International University, USA, to study psychological counselling, receiving a Master's in the subject in 1977. After he returned to Hong Kong, he worked for Breakthrough full-time.

In the area of spirituality, two points are noteworthy. Choi recalled that Jackie Pullinger influenced him to be aware of the difficulties of lower class people. Through her, he also learned to appreciate Charismatic Christians and their ministry.[27] John White's involvement in the Vineyard Church also compelled Choi to think again about the Charismatic movement. Choi considers him one of his life mentors,[28] through whom he deepened his understanding of the movement. He has openly supported White and shown

22 Choi, '*Those Years*', 230-231.
23 Choi, *My Life Path*, 62.
24 Jackie Pullinger is a British Charismatic missionary who has been in Hong Kong since 1966. Some of her missionary experience can be found in Jackie Pullinger, *Chasing the Dragon* (London: Hodder & Stoughton, 1980).
25 Choi, *My life path*, 64.
26 Ibid., 65.
27 'Philemon Choi's Oral History Record', 30 April 2015.
28 Choi, *My life path*, 15.

sympathy towards John Wimber.[29] Choi has been criticized by Arnold Yeung (楊牧谷) for becoming a Charismatic Christian leader in Hong Kong,[30] but Choi insists that he is not Charismatic but Evangelical. He wonders if a failure to recognize God as Triune is the reason for Chinese Christians' rejection of the work of Holy Spirit.[31]

Another of Choi's life mentors is Hans Burki, the person who "saved his life"[32] through his "Life Revision Seminar". Choi says that the seminars helped him to slow down and reorder his inner life; he learned to face the dark side of his life and put it under God's light. He also learned to leave his comfort zone and overcome fear of the unknown through the spiritual exercise of "letting go". Strikingly, he considered his decision to become the Chairman of the Commission on Youth an example of this.[33] In this sense, his public and political life can be viewed as an extension of his spiritual one.

When we discussed life mentors, Josephine So was the top of Choi's list. He states that she influenced him to love Hong Kong and young people devotedly. She opened his theological eyes, leading her colleagues to read the works of Dietrich Bonhoeffer, Jacques Ellul, and other theologians less known to conservative Christians. Choi mentioned that So did not limit Christian salvation to the merely personal, viewing it rather from the perspective of the city. Thus, *Breakthrough* magazine discussed many issues which the Church did not consider directly related to Christian faith. Choi appreciated the broader understanding of salvation So brought. Choi pointed out that the Church tends to limit itself within a narrow vision for the gospel and laments that it cannot see things socially and globally, which hinders the development of parachurch ministries.[34]

In the oral history interview, I asked Choi to identify milestones in his life. Apart from university studies and joining Breakthrough, Josephine So's death in 1982 and the start of the Breakthrough Youth Village building project in 1993 are important milestones. When So passed away Choi was lost and stressed. At the same time, as the British and Chinese governments started to negotiate the future of Hong Kong after 1997, society became pessimistic and panic-stricken. Choi needed to set the future direction of Breakthrough in order to meet the political challenges and the loss of Josephine So, and launched the "Rooted in Hong Kong" movement in 1983, believing that Christians should help Hong Kong people to be rooted in their city and respond to China and the world.[35]

29 'Philemon Choi's Oral History Record', 30 April 2015.
30 Arnold Yeung, *Charisma and diakonia* (Hong Kong: Christian Excellence, 1991).
31 'Philemon Choi's Oral History Record', 30 April 2015.
32 Philemon Choi, *Interaction of lives* (Hong Kong: Breakthrough, 2001), 200.
33 Choi, *My life path*, 130.
34 'Philemon Choi's Oral History Record', 30 April 2015.
35 Ibid.

Concerning the Breakthrough Youth Village milestone, Choi mentioned that he was invited to join the Central Policy Unit in the early 1990s. He met Leo F. Goodstadt, its Chief Adviser, and learned that political conflict between the British and Chinese governments meant that the Hong Kong colonial government would not have any policy plan for post-1997. Choi was alarmed by this and worried that Hong Kong would stagnate, political deadlock reducing opportunities for the youth to grow. He approached David R. Ford, the colonial government Chief Secretary, to explain that though the government could not plan beyond 1997 the citizens could. He proposed that Breakthrough could shape Hong Kong's young people to become leaders in the twenty-first century, who could break through their limitations and achieve an abundant life. Ford was moved by his plan and quickly gave a piece of land to Breakthrough for the Youth Village.[36]

For Choi, the building of the Youth Village put Breakthrough onto the public stage, as increasing numbers of the public and political leaders in Hong Kong and Mainland China visited it. Choi mentioned that after 1997, Chief Executive Tung Chee Hwa paid several visits to the Village and was very impressed, appreciating that Breakthrough could help young people face their motherland and the world. Tung then invited Choi to join the Commission on Youth. Notably, Choi believes that his horizons on youth problems widened after he joined the Commission and reflected on his mission and perspective on youth work. He stated, "initially, I focused on the individual problems of the youth. Then, I was concerned for family, education, and culture. Then, I was aware of the need of the city…Finally, I found that problems are not only systemic but also structural. The public policy affected the young people much. It is a structural sin."[37] He recalled his friend Lee Kam Hon,[38] Chairman of the Board of Directors of Breakthrough, reminding him that Breakthrough was founded to "counteract the culture". While the government was giving Choi and Breakthrough public support to change the culture, Lee suggested that he should take responsibility. Choi believes that this ministry landmark influenced the broader Hong Kong protestant churches, as they began to recognize that the Church should engage with society's structural problems; he sees the Hong Kong Church Network for the Poor as an example.[39]

Lo Lung Kwong

Lo Lung Kwong (盧龍光) was born in 1951 in Hong Kong, baptized as an infant at the Wo Mei Church of the Tsun Chun Mission (Basel Mission), and

36 'Philemon Choi's Oral History Record', 30 April 2015.

37 Ibid.

38 Lee taught at the Business School of the Chinese University of Hong Kong for many years. He was an active supporter of the Fellowship of Evangelical Students. He is now Emeritus Professor of Marketing, School of Hotel and Management, Chinese University of Hong Kong.

39 'Philemon Choi's Oral History Record', 30 April 2015.

confirmed in Kwun Tong Methodist Church in 1967. He studied Forestry at Taiwan's National Chung Hsing University, graduating in 1973. He obtained his Bachelor of Divinity from the Divinity Division of Chung Chi College, Chinese University of Hong Kong, in 1976. From 1978 to 1985, he was Pastor-in-charge of Epworth Village Methodist Church in Chai Wan and Officer-in-charge of the Methodist Epworth Village Community Centre. In 1985 he went to Durham University, obtaining his PhD. in 1992. From 1988 to 1995 he was Pastor-in-charge of the Hong Kong Methodist Church, the territory's largest Methodist congregation. From 1995 to 2014, he was the Director of the Divinity Division of Chung Chi College. He was President of the Methodist Church, Hong Kong from 2006 to 2012. He is a Life Member of Clare Hall, Cambridge University, and Visiting Professor at several universities in China. He was chairperson of the Association for Theological Education in Southeast Asia (2001-2005), and the Hong Kong Theological Education Association (1996-1998; 2003-2005).[40]

In an interview, I asked Lo to share milestones from his life and ministry, noteworthy people who influenced him or people he influenced, and changes in his theology and idea of ministry. At the beginning Lo talked about his time at university, stating that tight political control meant that there was little choice of student activities. He joined various activities organized by evangelical Christian organizations, such as Campus Crusade for Christ, Campus Evangelical Fellowship, and the Navigators.[41] I believe that Lo participated actively in these organizations because he was already very keen on evangelism. Lo said he chose to study Forestry in order to be a missionary in forest regions.[42] However, he believes that the visions of mission and national salvation can come together. On another occasion, Lo commented, "the political atmosphere of Taiwan influenced me much. They wanted to fight Communism in order to save their compatriots. But, is military action the only way to save the country? [I] studied Forestry because I wanted to use agriculture to save the country."[43] Lo recalled that his family gave him deep patriotism, and in his contact with evangelical student fellowships he had been forced to think whether God or Country is the greatest. He finally admitted that God is the greatest master and can save China through various means. China is still where his heart belongs, a point that we should note.

40 Fuk Tsang Ying, Sui Man Kwan, & Qing Wu, eds, *Festschrift in honor of Professor Lo Lung-Kwong* (Hong Kong: Chinese Christian Literature Council, 2014), 773-775.

41 'Lo Lung Kwong's Oral History Record', interview by Wai Luen Kwok on 8 May 2015, Hong Kong: Vietnam Woods.

42 Ying et al., *Festschrift*, 767.

43 Li Ying Ran, 'Sheyun yuanlao Lu Long Guang (The Veteran of Social Movement: Lo Lung Kwong', *Eastweek* (20 November, 2013), A034-A038. Retrieved from Wisers electronic service, 10 April, 2015.

Lo met Morley S. Lee (李秀全) at the Campus Evangelical Fellowship,[44] finding him a "very interesting" person. He admired him as a brilliant graduate of the Foreign Languages Department of Taiwan University, the elite of the time. Lo named several of Lee's coursemates – Pai Hsien Yung (白先勇), Wan Wen Hsing (王文興), and Leo Lee (李歐梵)[45] in support of this assessment. Lo notes that though Lee is an evangelical in theological and faith position, he is very open-minded theologically and culturally. He remembered Lee attending fellowship and summer camp wearing jeans, considered un-Christian and a sign of corruption by Chinese Christians in the late 1960s and early 1970s. Lee introduced Lo to Paul Tillich's theology. He also invited Wang Hsien-Chih (王憲治) to speak at summer camp. Wang is proponent of the Theology of Land (鄉土神學) in Taiwan and considered a liberal and anti-government theologian. Lo is very thankful to God that he met Lee in his early days, believing that he would have become a different person otherwise. Lee also discipled Lo, visiting him weekly for devotions and book reading. Lo recalls that they read Stott's *Christ the controversialist.* In the midst of his studies, the China Graduate School of Theology (CGST) was in the process of founding and organizing, and Lo attended classes by Tan Che Bin (陳濟民) and Wilson Wing Kin Chow (周永健), who became his friends. He also stated that some "uncles" he met in the fellowship belonged to Watchman Nee's Church Assembly Hall. Thus, his university life exposed him to a broad range of Chinese Christianity.[46]

Lo mentioned that though the evangelical student movement in Taiwan influenced him heavily, he finally decided to study theology at Chung Chi. Lee advised him against this because of Chung Chi's liberal theological position but did not insist on this. However, Lo chose Chung Chi for the quality of the faculty and because the Methodist Church is a supporting member. He felt that if the Church sent him for theological training, he was obliged to attend the seminary it preferred. This exposed him to liberal theology, but he also joined the Chinese University Fellowship of Evangelical Students, where he connected with Hong Kong's evangelical student movement.[47]

After graduation, Lo had to decide which Methodist church he wanted to serve in. He was not willing to serve under the authoritarian leadership of Wong Tsok (黃作),[48] and thus applied for a position at Epworth Village Methodist Church, Chai Wan. The denomination sent him to Chai Wan, and he found a community in poor condition, most residents still living in squatter areas or government temporary housing.

---

44 Morley S. Lee was born in 1938. He graduated from the Foreign Languages Department of Taiwan University in 1961. He studied theology at the Disciple Training Centre, Singapore under David Adeney, graduating in 1970. He served at Campus Evangelical Fellowship from 1963 to 1976. See http://www.chineseoverseas.org/index.php/celebrity/show/id/272.

45 Pai and Wan are prominent novelists and writers. Lee is a writer and professor of literature.

46 'Lo Lung Kwong's Oral History Record', 8 May 2015.

47 Ibid.

48 Wong Tsok (1922-1995) was the first President of the Methodist Church, Hong Kong from 1975 to 1982.

In November 1980, the Hong Kong Christian Council organized a consultation conference for the mission of the territory's Church in the 1980s. The agenda contained five main areas: evangelism to low-income citizens, student evangelism, concern for Mainland Christians, participation in public policy making, and influencing the attitude of the general public. At the end, Lo raised his hand and spoke to the audience, saying that though the conference wanted to show concern for the lower class, it had not presented any concrete action. He then voiced his concern about the proposed bus fare rises, which would significantly increase the financial burden of the lower class. Because of this speech, the conference leaders rapidly proposed Lo as the one to focus on this issue. Then, Raymond Fung (馮煒文) and Lau Chin Shek (劉千石) of the Christian Industrial Committee (CIC) immediately organized a press conference at which Fung, Lau, and Lo announced the founding of a joint committee to protest against the bus companies' proposal. Apart from this campaign, Lo also organized the owners of Shan Tsui Court, who had paid the full purchase price for their property in advance, to protest against the delay in completion of construction work in 1981. He also initiated a petition campaign for the building of the Eastern Hospital in 1982.[49]

Lo stated that during the 1980s many community issues emerged in which he was heavily engaged. There were at least six in which he helped the community in their response and coping strategies.[50]

Lo reflected that his participation in social action draws on his family background, character, and theology. He emphasized that the student fellowship at university had already taught him the importance of integrating life and faith; Christian faith should have its praxis and Christians should be disciples of Christ. When he studied at Chung Chi, he learned that he should read and understand the biblical message and carry out his pastoral work in the context of people's lives. Lo also sees his social participation as somehow related to the decolonization process. He remembers that the colonial government did not suppress his social actions; rather, whenever British officials visited Hong Kong, he was invited to meet them as a representative of public opinion. He guessed that the colonial government wanted to use public opinion to negotiate with China.[51] Not only did the colonial government want to contact him, but also the Chinese government; he was the youngest delegate of the first Hong Kong Christian Delegation to Beijing in September 1984.

At the grassroots level, Lo started discipleship training for evangelists among factory workers in Chai Wan. Four members of his church responded his call and he trained them to care for the worker class. He asked Raymond Fung and Lau Chin Shek to teach them the labour ordinance and taught them experiential biblical studies to give the workers a better understanding of the

49 'Lo Lung Kwong's Oral History Record', 8 May 2015.
50 Ibid.
51 Ibid.

Bible.[52] Also, he organized summer gospel camps for these workers. Because of these efforts, his church gathered more and more newcomers. He proudly said, "I do not only organize social movements, but also evangelize people. My Church has a strong basis. I cannot only be survived by social movements."[53] Among the workers he trained was May Yuk Kuen Poon (潘玉娟), a factory worker without secondary school examination certificate. Poon wanted to study theology and become a pastor, but most Hong Kong seminaries would not admit her. Lo concluded that although the Church wanted to evangelize the lower class, they did not have any apparatus or ministry to meet the need. Lo brought this issue to Wilson Chow and Tan Che Bin, and urged CGST to consider offering a theological programme to Christians without secondary education. As Chow and Tan were young teachers and could not make the decision, Lo went to Philip Teng for support and was amazed that Teng responded: "this is the era of grass-roots evangelism. Your plan should be supported."[54]

Yu Miu Wan

Yu Miu Wan (余妙雲) was born in 1951 in Hong Kong.[55] She obtained her Bachelor's in Economics from Tunghai University, Taiwan and her Master's in Economics from the University of Ottawa. In 1977, she became a voluntary worker with the Industrial Evangelistic Fellowship (IEF). In 1978, she was admitted to the Master of Christian Studies programme of CGST. After she graduated from CGST in 1980, she became a full-time worker with IEF,[56] leaving for several years to take care of her children. From 1989 to 2014, she was the fellowship's General Secretary.[57] In 2005, she was awarded the Secretary for Home Affairs' Commendation and in 2007 the Chief Executive's Commendation for Community Service.[58]

Yu describes herself as from a grass-roots family with deep experience of the hardships of the lower class.[59] She studied at True Light's Girls College and became a Christian at secondary school, joining North Point Alliance Church. At that time, the Church already offered a wide range of training and Yu

---

52 Lo gives the example of Zacchaeus as a story of exclusion and alienation. He used grouping and matching exercises to explain the problem of alienation in an interesting way.

53 'Lo Lung Kwong's Oral History Record', 8 May 2015.

54 Ibid.

55 Miu Wan Yu & Ching Hang Poon, *Xing yun liu shui [Floating cloud and running water]* (Hong Kong: Logos, 2014), back cover.

56 Yu, *Industrial Mission Movement of Hong Kong*, viii-x.

57 'Jiao bang [Passing the torch]', *Christian Weekly* 2612 (14 September 2014), http://www.christianweekly.net/2014/ta2022979.htm.

58 Miu Wan Yu, *Good news to the poor: From disconnected to connected* (Hong Kong: Industrial Evangelical Fellowship, 2014), front cover.

59 Miu Wan Yu, *Industrial mission movement of Hong Kong: The profile of ten leaders* (Hong Kong: The Industrial Evangelistic Fellowship, 2000), vii.

remembered that she learned bible study methods, regular devotion practice, individual evangelism methods, and prayer.[60]

Yu remembered that when she studied at Tunghai University, the Chaplain, Felix Liu (劉富理), brought the Christian students together and gave them discipleship training very similar to that of the Navigators, which was his background. This training made Yu keen to do evangelism and equip herself to deal with the challenges of non-Christians. She also joined some activities of the Campus Evangelical Fellowship, and by that time knew Lo Lung Kwong and Morley Lee. She also read Josephine So's works in *Campus* magazine and books published by the Campus Evangelical Fellowship. So's "They also have souls" (他們也有靈魂) impressed her much and she began to attend to the needs of grass-roots people. In Canada she joined the newly founded Ottawa Chinese Alliance Church, actively participating in their evangelistic and publication ministry. She recollected her need to decide where to go after graduation, and how Josephine So influenced her to serve the grass roots people and brought her to know Jackie Pullinger and her ministry. The ethos of intellectuals of her generation compelled her to reflect on her national identity and to love her Motherland. She also remembered that her family had yet to receive the Christian faith and felt the obligation to share the gospel with them.

When she came back to Hong Kong, she joined the prison ministry of North Point Alliance Church. On one occasion she invited some female former inmates to dinner and their behaviour greatly embarrassed her; however, her partner urged her to think how Jesus would respond instead of feeling embarrassed. This experience reinforced her desire to serve the grass roots.

In 1977, Yu joined IEF as a volunteer and met Chan Tin Cheung (陳天祥), founder of IEF. Chan was a graduate of Hong Kong Technical College (now Hong Kong Polytechnic University) and also of the conservative and fundamentalist Overseas Theological Seminary (OTS), founded by John L. Tsang (曾霖芳) in 1966. Chan was an actionist rather than a theorist, but had a clear theological position. He had been part of the Christian Industrial Committee before he founded IEF. The CIC claimed that the Church "should stand by the side of the workers", promoting their rights through resistance and movements, and claiming that if workers had justice in their workplace they were receiving God's salvation. However, Chan did not like a confrontational approach in seeking workers' welfare and asserted that workers are also sinners in need personal salvation. Thus, he left the CIC and founded the IEF. Interestingly, Chan borrowed the FES reading room as temporary office for IEF.[61]

Chan identified the worker class as a significant population group in Hong Kong with little chance to know the gospel and established the IEF to meet this

---

60 'Yu Miu Wan's Oral History Record', interview by Wai Luen Kwok on 23 April 2015, Hong Kong: Hong Kong Baptist University.
61 'Yu Miu Wan's Oral History Record', 23 April 2015.

need.[62] Yu recalled that Chan was mainly concerned about the conversion of working people, and explored various methods, such as drama class, picnics, media, entertainment, and night schools to attract the workers to the Christian faith. Though these activities did bring some people to Christ, they found it very difficult to survive in the churches. Thus, Yu organized disciple training – "Christian Soldiers Fellowship" for them, and through close interaction gained a deep and real understanding of the lower class. Yu remembered that learning by experience was the most significant at this stage of her ministry.

According to Yu, when Agnes Lau (劉達芳) joined IEF in 1976, she changed its direction to "Demolish the wall of the Church culture, Build the regenerating power of the workers". Lau asked Church leaders to stand by the labourers, provide disciple training, and establish workers' fellowships in the factories. Yu appreciated that this was the right step for IEF, because it could be more relevant to the workers. Yu saw Lau's move as similar to CIC's position. After Yu graduated from CGST in 1980, she worked in IEF as full-time staff. CGST made her rigorous in studying the Bible and eager to apply biblical insights to real life.[63] In the same year, Yu participated in the consultation conference for the mission of the Hong Kong Church. She stated that the conference, especially its campaign against bus fare increases, helped her reflect on how she could help grass-roots people concretely.[64] After this, Yu served as part time tutor of the Grassroots Evangelistic Training Ministry of China Graduate School of Theology. In 1988, she resumed work for IEF on a part-time basis and the next year became General Secretary. She mentioned the June-Fourth Incident as one of the reasons she took on the leadership of IEF. After she became the General Secretary, she found that Hong Kong society had changed a lot, as had the circumstances of workers and the lower class. At the same time, the population of factory workers was steadily decreasing and she needed to find a way forward for IEF. She insisted that the mission of IEF should be: working together with the churches, bringing the gospel to the lower class, and equipping lower class Christians with regenerative power. She found that IEF could help the workers and lower class through retraining and thus the fellowship has undertaken various social services for the poor in society.[65]

Hybridization and the Making of Hong Kong Christian Leaders

Since Edward Said's *Orientalism* in 1978, the dichotomy between East and West has been questioned in colonial studies of Asia.[66] However, when

62 Wai Luen Kwok, *Self-defence or social concern? The social and political participation of Hong Kong Church* (Hong Kong: Alliance, 2014), 43-45.
63 'Yu Miu Wan's Oral History Record', interview by Wai Luen Kwok on 30 April 2015, Hong Kong: Hong Kong Baptist University.
64 'Yu Miu Wan's Oral History Record', 23 April 2015.
65 Ibid.
66 Edward Said, *Orientalism* (New York: Vintage, 1979).

studying the rise of local leaders in the colonies, it is easy to fall into the "European and Asiatic" divide again. Homi Bhabha suggested that this Self-Other encounter is not simply dualistic; rather, it is a process of innovation, collaboration, and contestation.[67] Bhabha suggests that the colonial subjects used hybridization to escape the control of the authorities:

> I have developed the concept of hybridity to describe the construction of cultural authority within conditions of political antagonism or inequity. Strategies of hybridization reveal an estranging movement in the 'authoritative,' even authoritarian inscription of the cultural sign. At the point at which the precept attempts to objectify itself as a generalized knowledge or a normalizing, hegemonic practice, the hybrid strategy or discourse opens up a space of negotiation where power is unequal but its articulation may be equivocal. Such negotiation is neither assimilation nor collaboration. It makes possible the emergence of an "interstitial" agency that refuses the binary representation of social antagonism. Hybrid agencies find their voice in a dialectic that does not seek cultural supremacy or sovereignty. They deploy the partial culture from which they emerge to construct visions of community, and versions of historic memory, that give narrative form to the minority positions they occupy: the outside of the inside; the part in the whole.[68]

In this study, I find a similar hybridization experience among the leaders. They are influenced by Western theology through their education or life mentors, but (in the cases of Choi and Lo especially) do not feel that their hybridity pushed them into a peripheral position. Their experience helped them to tap resources from different theological traditions and maintain a strong national identity in their Christian faith. Also, the interviews showed that transitions of contexts and needs required the three leaders to integrate faith, life and political circumstances. A sense of solidarity with their people helped them change their methods or ministry strategies in something "hybridized", compounds of Western experience and their own invention. Their accounts showed self-confidence and self-reliance in implementing their vision.

These leaders are very different from "typical" postcolonial Asian Christian leaders such as Choan-Seng Song and Byung-Mu Ahn in terms of theological affinity. Song emphasized that Asian Christians should take "a leap from Israel to Asia" to develop a non-Western, truly Asian theology for themselves,[69] while Ahn "wished to free myself once and for all from Western theology and ask from a different perspective" as "a Korean or an Asian".[70] However, in my oral history accounts I cannot identify an obvious calling to break away from Western theology; the interviewees do not reject their evangelical affiliation and affinity and consider themselves aligned with Western theological

67 Homi K. Bhabha, *The Location of culture* (London: Routledge, 2004), 2.

68 Homi K. Bhabha, 'Culture's in between', *Artforum*, 32, 1 (1993), 212.

69 Choan-Seng Song, 'From Israel to Asia: A theological leap', *Ecumenical Review*, 28, 3 (July 1976), 252–65.

70 Volker Küster's interview with Ahn May 14, 1988. Cf., Volker Küster, *A Protestant theology of passion: Korean Minjung theology revisited, Studies in systematic theology, vol.4* (Leiden; Boston: Brill, 2010), 61.

traditions. More interestingly, these young leaders of the 1970s very actively participated in social movements and services, constructing a Christian identity radically different from the conservative Chinese Christian leaders of the previous generation and similar to the Western Neo-Evangelicals of the 1970s.

However, this evangelical identity does not mean that they are under Western dominance. Although we can identify significant missionary influence on them, it is already indirect, mediated via institutions like FES. Also, Western denominational confessions play very little part in their ministry and these leaders can cross the so-called evangelical, liberal, and charismatic boundaries if they wish. More importantly, if we define localization and decolonization as a process of shifting leadership to the locals, then this generation has assumed full leadership of the Hong Kong Church. The "Western" influence and hybridity in the interviewees' Christian experience is a result of discipleship, education, spiritual literature, and interpersonal networking. In this area, we may claim that Christian social participation shaped by life experience and cultures has the nature of a localized *didache*.

Finally, the most interesting finding is that the interviewees' hybridity has helped them gain access to Hong Kong's political sphere; the intersection of national, religious, educational and professional identities seems to have secured them political and social recognition from both colonial and post-colonial Hong Kong administrations.

In this sense, Hong Kong Christian leaders of the late colonial period give us unique examples of the interaction between Western "colonial" powers and their subjects in the process of localization and decolonization. They also shed light on the factors contributing to the development of Chinese Christian thought and practice after 1970.

This project is funded by the General Research Fund of the Research Grant Council, Hong Kong (project reference: 12638516).

Faith-Based Engagement in China's Harmonious Society: A Study of an Indigenous, Faith-Based NGO's Organizational Culture and Response to the 2008 Sichuan Earthquake

Easten Law

Introduction

The rise of modern China has been both celebrated and viewed with concern around the world. While recent policies have brought material riches and global prestige, these have been accompanied by a worrying rural-urban income gap, corrupt business and political practices, environmental disasters, and a moral-spiritual void within its latest generation. The Chinese government has not been unaware of these developments, and at the outset of a new millennium the Chinese Communist Party under President Hu Jintao began promoting a new national ethos entitled, "the Harmonious Society". The goals of the new push were to correct and balance the inequalities that have come with China's economic and political rise. In the midst of this, the Chinese church found itself with a new opportunity to build a stronger and more public foundation. Today, Chinese Christians are in a position of great potential and risk, and many, especially young urban professionals, are realizing that their Christian values and identity can have a public impact. Throughout the nation, Christians are beginning to see participation in social service as an important component of a robust faith life. All these signs point to the writing of a new and exciting chapter in the story of China's church.

This article summarizes a study completed at the close of the last decade (2009), a time when there was little published literature on the growing phenomenon of Christian social action in China via registered NGO structures. Literature searches revealed only a handful of editorial articles. Among them, Samuel Ling's 2001 piece entitled, "Charting Two Critical Maps for PRC Service Work", assessed the status of Christian mission in China, identifying eight developing ministry trends he believed important for the coming decade.[1] Other than the phenomenon of "Cultural Christians", which has already been

1 Samuel Ling, 'Charting two critical maps for PRC service work', *China Horizon*, http://www.chinahorizon.org/Articles/Microsoft%20Word%20-%20C-PRC%20MINISTRY.pdf (accessed 18 November, 2008).

researched,[2] none displayed any leaning toward social action by the church in the larger context of Chinese society. Much of Ling's assessment focuses on issues of indigenous theologies and their role in traditional conceptions of evangelism and discipleship, emphasizing the importance of indigenous Chinese leadership in the areas of education and congregational life.

What Ling may have missed in his 2001 survey was the increasing presence of social ministry by Chinese churches, intentional work focused on the needs of society. When thinking about social ministry in the Chinese Christian context, Ling's three key questions are still important today: "(a) Do we understand who our coworkers are in the PRC field? (b) Can we identify their unique emphases and approaches? (c) Can we discern the pertinent issues in ministry methods and in philosophy/theology, which will shape PRC minds and PRC ministries in the twenty-first century?"[3] This article is an attempt to answer these questions in the context of the Chinese church's most recent involvement in the field of social action.

With this in mind, the broader question guiding this research is: How can indigenous Chinese Christians create a socially impactful, culturally appropriate, and politically acceptable presence consistent with the push for a "Harmonious Society?" The question reflects a convergence between the church's conception of mission and the nation's larger sociocultural formation. As China begins to take its social ills seriously, the Christian community must find a niche that is not only acceptable to government authorities, but also supported by society at large. A greater social witness is not without challenges; relations with the government, perception by the public, and many other organizational issues related to funding, administration, and service delivery accompany churches in their attempt to serve in a name other than that of the Communist Party.

One illustrative example of the Chinese church's pioneering work in social engagement is the story of one legally registered NGO working in Sichuan Province, which, for security reasons, will be referred to simply as XNGO. In addition, names of persons have also been changed throughout the essay. XNGO is unique in its connection to the registered church organizations the Three-Self Patriotic Movement and the China Christian Council and is effectively one of China's first formally accepted faith-based NGOs, one that can declare its faith-based motivations for service in implicit ways short of verbal declaration. Starting as an education center for underserved youth in urban and rural Sichuan, XNGO's work has steadily expanded to include small rural development projects and the delivery of medical supplies to church clinics. XNGO's connections to church networks became especially important

2 For a short introduction, see Leung Ka Lun, 'Cultural Christians and Christianity in China', *China Rights Forum* 4 (2003), 28-31. For an extended reflection on the phenomenon see Fredrik Fallman, 'Faith, hope, love and modernity reflections on "Cultural Christians" in Contemporary China', *Monumenta Serica*, 54 (2006), 405-415.

3 Samuel Ling, 'Charting', 4.

in its grassroots response to the disastrous 2008 Sichuan Earthquake, an event now widely recognized as a major catalyst for the advancement of China's civil society.[4]

The unique standing and success of XNGO make it an appropriate case study from which to glean themes and patterns which show how Chinese Christians can develop a socially impactful, culturally appropriate, and politically acceptable presence. The research presented in this paper examines the influence of XNGO in Sichuan Province leading up to their response to the 2008 earthquake. In particular, the paper investigates how the internal culture of XNGO contributes to its external influence, exploring how the organization balances Christian conviction with political realities, and how it manages its connections to support from outside the country.

Methods

Ethnographic field research was conducted with XNGO staff and members of its network from September of 2008 to June of 2009 in order to gain holistic answers to these questions. A thorough understanding of its social-cultural influence was attempted by looking specifically at XNGO's (a) missional goals, (b) organizational culture, and (c) activities. This information was collected via three approaches: (1) individual interviews with important members of XNGO's leadership, (2) focus groups with XNGO office staff and ministers of the churches who receive XNGO's support, and (3) participant observations conducted over the course of approximately six months (September 2008 – February 2009). Three interviews were held with the leaders: Mr. Chen, XNGO's founder and director; Ms. Xi, the program manager; and Mr. Ben, a foreign national working in partnership with the organization. Three focus groups were also held, one with XNGO's permanent office staff and two others with local ministers leading churches in two prefectures in Sichuan. The purpose of these focus groups was to understand the current state of some of Sichuan's registered churches (before and after the 2008 quake) and how their relationship with XNGO has influenced their work and impact on society. In addition, participant observation was undertaken during XNGO's daily operations, according to four general categories (1) everyday office matters such as staff meetings, (2) current projects in development work, (3) English training programs, and (4) XNGO's minister leadership training conference.

Summary of Key Findings

From this research a number of themes emerged, findings grouped under the six headings below. The first three concern XNGO's missional goals and current

4 Shawn Shieh & Guosheng Deng, 'An emerging civil society: The impact of the 2008 Sichuan earthquake on grassroots civic associations in China', *The China Journal*, 65 (2011), 181-194.

activities while the latter three revolve around XNGO's organizational culture. Each carries lessons for how other faith-based NGOs might operate in the Chinese context.

1. XNGO's role as an international/domestic resource bridge.
2. XNGO's role as a change agent within traditional church culture.
3. XNGO's reconnection of social action with Christian witness.
4. XNGO's balance of politics and mission within Chinese civil society.
5. XNGO's balance of international influences and support with indigenous leadership and resources.
6. XNGO's operations reflecting culturally normative, hierarchical, relational Chinese networking.

International/Domestic Resource Bridge

When asked what services XNGO provides as a faith-based NGO in China, Ms. Xi stated, "communication and bridging (for) outside resources with the internal needs of Sichuan." Ms. Xi fulfills this by speaking monthly at Chengdu's International Fellowship, updating them on ministry among registered Chinese churches. These presentations help various groups to see needs and respond with appropriate resources. For example, following Xi's reports on Chinese church responses to the 2008 earthquake, members of the international church worked with her to organize short term quake recovery teams which helped with church building reconstruction and the coordination of toy donations for an orphanage.

One of the staff members commented that XNGO's dual purpose revolved around "reception and training." "Reception" essentially refers to how XNGO receives resources and volunteer support from various outside groups and coordinates their respective actions. Focus groups with ministers from around Sichuan confirmed this as they spoke in detail about XNGO's ability to connect volunteers and material resources for both quake relief and other ministries. One example is XNGO's management of a $124,000 donation from abroad to purchase and distribute winter clothing and blankets. In focus group discussions, ministers from one prefecture expressed gratitude to XNGO for connecting them with an international development group exploring a possible investment in their local orphanage.

XNGO's response to the 2008 Sichuan earthquake is an amplified example of this phenomenon at work. In the immediate aftermath, a key issue was clear communication and assessment of needs. Due to XNGO's extensive relational network with churches throughout quake stricken areas, there was above-average relaying of information on the situations in these locations by local ministers. XNGO staff posted regular updates from quake areas that helped the outside world understand the needs and respond accordingly with the immediate aid if necessary. In the early days following the quake, larger international NGOs had yet to mobilize effective relief projects as they had to work through political and bureaucratic systems, and XNGO therefore acted as a buffer for immediate relief care, channeling over half a million dollars into various sectors through both local government bodies and churches. The response of XNGO to the quake has earned them a great deal of respect and honor throughout Sichuan Province and raised the reputation of the church in the region.

Cultural Change Agent within Traditional Church Culture

Since XNGO's founding, local churches and the provincial branch of the China Christian Council and Three Self Patriotic Movement have increasingly contacted XNGO for assistance with social services whether for rural development, medical training, or educational projects. Through such relationships, church leadership throughout Sichuan is developing new ideas for ministry and conceptions of the role that faith can play in society, modes of thinking that accelerated in the months following the quake. Testimony from the two focus groups with ministers from two Sichuan prefectures provides contrasting evidence for this effect. These are two very different contexts; Prefecture A is a well-developed urban center whose level of development benefits surrounding rural areas, while Prefecture B is a rather isolated mountainous region lacking dependable transportation networks. Though both churches desire social outreach within their ministry models, they have very different circumstances and views of what is possible.

For ministers of Prefecture A, the quake has opened up a plethora of new and unimagined opportunities for witness through social action. What began as distribution of drinking water to quake stricken areas kept growing through local and international partnerships to include provision of material aid to quake-affected citizens, medical aid at a large hospital, building of new homes, construction of a cafeteria for temporary schools, and counselor training. Prefecture A church's extended involvement in relief work has earned them great praise from local government authorities. Their vision is to establish a new church in one of the prefecture's hardest quake-impacted areas, hoping the new building will be not only a place of worship, but also a community center, with facilities for counseling and vocational training. If Prefecture A is a success story, than Prefecture B is an example of struggle. There, the ministers have slowly established a social presence thanks to XNGO's injection of resources for rural development and education, but the church community itself struggles to maintain their own building. They feel their ability to witness through social action is weakened by their limited resources.

Overall, the success of Prefecture A is the exception rather than the norm. Prefecture B's struggles seem more representative of the larger body of registered churches, under pressure in terms of personnel and material resources while juggling a sensitive relationship with local authorities. These communities have been more dependent on XNGO itself for social action. Resources aside, XNGO's influence has shifted the mentalities of church leaders. According to Ms. Xi, concerning the rebuilding of churches post-quake two key questions have become common for pastors: 1) What is currently the most pressing social need in our community, and 2) How can we design our church building to meet that need? One rural church has identified the difficulties elderly grandparents have raising children whose parents have left for work in the city and have designed their new church building's third floor to have a library and student activity center.

Reconnecting Christian Witness with Social Action

While XNGO has exerted great effort connecting resources with social needs and has had a strong positive influence on the development of social engagement by churches via partnerships with them, the organization aims at a larger cultural shift. Mr. Chen was very open in his identification of XNGO as a faith-based organization with a duty to provide Christian witness. However, explicit witness in confessional terms is not necessarily the means to this end. Instead, XNGO seeks to form a stronger connection between charity and social action and the church, such that when people think of Christians, what comes to mind is the tangible contribution to the public good instead of superstitious beliefs or foreign influence. Mr. Chen was saddened that churches are not known for social development today when many of China's Christian forefathers were active in the building of hospitals and schools. It seems that XNGO is seeking to revive this spirit, to reinstate social change as part of Christian proclamation. Despite this grand goal, Mr. Chen admitted that the organization's name and public programming were not growing; their training programs include a modest English language tutoring effort, individual piano lessons, and some computer training classes.

On the topic of Christian witness, statements made by the organization's staff were mixed; some reinforced the director's comments while others made things more complicated. One staff member stated that she chose to work at XNGO after graduating from the local seminary to learn a new way of Christian service and witness. However, another staff member felt XNGO's community development work and training were not faith-based at all. When asked for clarification, this person stated that those benefiting from many of XNGO's services might never understand that Christians provide them. In fact, some of the staff are not professing Christians and one identified as a Communist Party member. Many of XNGO's music teachers are not Christian either. Another staff member stated that while XNGO is filled with Christians, it is not exclusively Christian and it is not necessary to be a Christian to work there. Nonetheless, Christian faith permeates the work and one must support Christian values. Another Christian staff member added that while there are real differences in beliefs, the values are a driving force for teamwork, unity, and good relations, a viewpoint affirmed by all the staff present at the focus group.

XNGO's office decor serves as an appropriate metaphor for this low-key ethos. The office walls feature many Bible verses written in Chinese calligraphy side by side with photographs of XNGO's founding ceremony and pictures of its training and community development projects. While there are many pictures of summer youth camps, the opening of a medical clinic, and relief work for poor villages in drought, there are no images of pastoral training, XNGO's support for churches, or the resources it provides. Is there any association between the Scripture and the pictures? In both what is displayed and what is not, nothing is stated outright, but anyone walking through the office could not help but think about the connection between the two.

Balancing Politics and Mission within Chinese Civil Society

Balancing security with Christian witness is a constant struggle for all believers in China. How does one explain all of XNGO's focused work with the churches of the province? Staff members commented that church based work occurs as a by-product of their "reception work" (i.e. XNGO's connection of local churches with outside resources). If outside groups such as international churches or companies come to XNGO desiring to work with the local churches, XNGO facilitates the partnerships as requested. The staff avows that such arrangements are not their primary work; XNGO's main task is training and community development for all, not only the churches. In this way, any focus on the church is more a matter of circumstance than intention. Perhaps such statements reflect a certain security protocol for talking about XNGO's work with outsiders, especially researchers.

According to Mr. Chen, XNGO's very conception and officially registered status is a testament to God's guidance; a series of auspicious events and political relations made it possible. Of particular significance is that XNGO is registered under the Education Bureau (EB) and has no relation with the Religious Affairs Bureau (RAB). The EB affiliation provides the organization a greater degree of freedom than would be available under the RAB as its primary focus is educational rather than religious. Church partnerships are less of an issue as long as the organization does not proselytize and advances the EB's objectives. Mr. Chen also reports a positive relationship with the local branch of the RAB, pointing to pictures of various officials welcoming him and other Christian workers to celebrate XNGO's beginning. At the ribbon cutting for XNGO's new office there was a speech from an RAB official and a blessing from a high-ranking TSPM minister. It seems that XNGO's initial success has given people in government enough face and credibility to allay any fears about supporting a potentially politically sensitive faith-oriented endeavor.

XNGO's very existence is a sort of testimony, a witness not only to the recipients of its services but also the leaders who allow them. While not witnessing to the masses of the city or province, it does to many within government leadership. XNGO's work and publicity demonstrate to government agencies how positive a faith-based group can be for society. At the same time, they must be especially careful how they declare their beliefs and purpose for their work. A staff discussion about where to hold a summer event revealed some of the sensitivities. Although small English training camps have been held in church buildings, a proposal to take a flagship, two-week Summer Youth Camp into an explicitly Christian space was problematic. Although Mr. Chen argued against it because of the complex relationships between XNGO, the RAB, and the EB, at the same time he emphasized the importance of the Christian teachers and counselors at the camp providing Christian witness through their actions. In any project or circumstance, XNGO must walk a careful path to maintain social integrity in relation to Christian mission.

Balancing International Influences and Support with Indigenous Leadership and Resources

Faith-based or not, non-profit groups are a very new category in China and many struggle to obtain adequate financial support. XNGO's international partnerships are especially sensitive. The organization has had a number of non-Chinese staff working under its umbrella, often with the official status of visiting expert advising on training or community development. The contrast between the "international" staff meetings and the "all staff" meetings is very interesting. In both meetings, a foreign co-worker led the agenda, yet while the international staff meeting involved much greater detail in planning and event organizing, the one including the Chinese national staff seemed more like a reporting and updating session. No concrete conclusions should be drawn from these observations alone, since not all staff meetings are the same; however the impression was that foreign staff have a much greater influence in the decision-making process than national staff, apart from Mr. Chen, the director.

When staff members were asked what element of XNGO's work was most successful, most referred to the Summer Youth Camp, which, interestingly enough, relies greatly on foreign support. Mr. Ben commented that he acts more or less as the unofficial "camp coordinator", finding volunteers, producing the curriculum, and so on. XNGO staff takes care of the logistics of where and when the event happens, but the *how* rests with Mr. Chen and the foreigners. Suffice to say, XNGO's operations appear to rely on significant foreign support in areas of program design, consultancy, and finances. Perhaps this is inevitable given China's current social-cultural context, although this is sure to change.

Culturally Normative, Hierarchical, Relational Chinese Network

This final theme explores XNGO's organizational culture as a normative example of Chinese cultural relations, including the very dynamics that brought the organization into existence. XNGO's functioning and success are almost completely dependent on its relationships, at the center of which is Mr. Chen himself. This is a common characteristic of many Chinese organizations; indeed Mr. Ben joked that if Mr. Chen were to be hit by a bus, XNGO would have to close its doors. All of XNGO's relationships with churches and government agencies stem from Mr. Chen in one way or another. The relational nature of Chinese culture means that all organizational decisions require his guidance in order to proceed. Mr. Chen's final approval is needed at the end of staff meetings, regardless of who leads them. Similarly, throughout any given day, people will be walking in and out of Mr. Chen's office for advice and approval about on one matter or another. His wisdom and authority rest at the top of the organizational pyramid, above any foreigner's influence. No matter how well anyone else may know the house, Mr. Chen has all the keys and only he can open or close the doors.

When asked what XNGO's greatest challenges were, several mentioned capacity building for staff and leadership and the need for clearer long-term goals and objectives. Mr. Chen also spoke about this difficulty, noting that it was hard to find good people to train for leadership roles and mentioning the important skills of international relationship building, managing relationships with the government, and stressing strong Christian conviction. All of these are very hard to find and Mr. Chen's limited free time leaves him ill-equipped to train a new leader as well versed and connected as he is. The question of leadership is a serious one for the organization's future.

Concluding Impressions

The main question at the heart of this study was, "how can Chinese Christians create a socially impactful, culturally appropriate, and politically acceptable presence within China's overall push for a *Harmonious Society*?" Answers were sought via a case study exploring the influence of XNGO in Sichuan Province leading up to their response to the 2008 earthquake, both in its public service to society at large and its private work to support Chinese churches. The research shows that XNGO's social influence is most effectively felt in two areas, its influence on church leadership and its witness to governing bodies that oversee it. It is within these two contexts that XNGO can serve as a model for other Christian leaders seeking engagement with Chinese society.

XNGO's influence on existing, registered, churches throughout the province can be summed up by examples of local ministers gaining a social consciousness and desire for community service. Through XNGO's role as a bridge to bring resources from the outside to churches and other communities at large, the holistic gospel is being re-planted in the hearts and minds of ministers. The destruction caused by the 2008 earthquake has served to speed up this awakening as churches seek ways to contribute in ways big and small.

The other area in which XNGO's strength is felt is with local government and leadership in the locations they serve. Because XNGO is a legally registered organization with nothing to hide concerning its Christian motivation, its works of service function as public relations for God with political leadership. Traditionally skeptical and wary of any faith-based work, the government of Sichuan's various cities and counties can see how Christianity can contribute to the goal of a "Harmonious Society" through the powerful testimony of XNGO, and may support more faith-based NGOs in the future. Though the organization cannot yet undertake explicit witness, such support will allow Christianity to expand its influence indirectly and legally.

Yet despite these strengths, this study also reveals limitations within XNGO's current operations, internal and external. Externally, the faith based motivations of XNGO and their hope to spread the gospel make their service a very sensitive matter. Up to this point XNGO has been blessed with supportive relationships with government, churches, and international groups, but these must be continuously managed and leveraged upon so that XNGO can continue to support church ministries alongside their officially sanctioned role as an education center. At any moment changes in political climate could result in major obstacles to the organization's work with churches. Internally, much of XNGO's power seems centralized on Mr. Chen and the organization's growth appears to depend exclusively on his ability to lead and guide. Thus, Mr. Chen's struggle to train new indigenous leaders within the organization limits its growth.

Overall, XNGO's work of encouraging churches to engage actively in social service and its ability to leverage political support for such work are impressive. While its impact is clear, it will take greater political openness, expanded leadership, and new financial resources for it to become sustainable. XNGO is a good model for the Chinese church to follow as they begin to take on a socially active role, but whether it is the best or only option is a question for future research.

Extended Analysis: Putting the Snapshot from 2009 into the Context of 2015

This study was completed in late 2009, the concluding impressions stated above providing a snapshot of church-state and NGO-state relations in China at that time. This extended analysis looks again at the picture described above in the light of new literature and developments in Chinese civil society as they relate to Chinese Christianity and social engagement. Chinese NGOs and civil society were, and still are, difficult to track given their ambiguous legal status within Chinese law; like unregistered church communities, China's NGOs have operated for years in a grey space under various government entities. Some were registered as businesses while others worked without any formal government recognition. Growing literature on civil society in China seek to clarify NGO-state relations beyond Western neo-Tocquivillian approaches that give priority to volunteer associations and their role in democratization. Rather, attention is paid to the ways in which NGOs balance dependency on and autonomy from the government. Many shape their work to complement state priorities to ensure political support while implementing elements of their own visions of social good within their operational contexts.[5] Such realities put Chinese NGOs in precarious situations similar to that of registered religious communities. Given the government's sensitivities to both NGOs and religious groups, XNGO was one of the most compelling organizations I met in my years of work in China. The organization's founding and recognition within local provincial government structures coupled with its relational link to TSPM church ministries presented a hybrid organization that dwelled within the grey spaces of religious organization and civil association.

An amazing story unfolded against the backdrop of the 2008 Sichuan Earthquake. Bin Xu conceives the impact of the quake as a "consensus crisis," "characterized by challenges to the state's managerial capacity, a critical need for civil society's services, a general agreement on priorities and goals, and the state's efforts to construct a morally respectable image. These features amplify the structural conditions favorable for relatively amicable state–society interactions."[6] Today, it is even clearer that the 2008 Sichuan Earthquake served as a watershed moment for Chinese civil society. According to an extensive review of NGO action and development in response to the quake conducted by the China Development Brief, some 263 NGO groups, domestic and international, gathered to engage in relief work.[7] Shieh and Deng identify the many ways NGOs networked and collaborated to access and connect with devastated communities throughout the province, often via personal relationships with local community contacts both within and outside the government.[8] The work of XNGO following the Sichuan earthquake is a portrait of Chinese Christian social engagement at a historic moment when, given the immensity of the crisis, the state appeared to support a greater diversity of organizations than it would normally allow. Shieh and Deng's

5 For detailed analysis of NGOs in China, see Yiyi Lu, *Non-governmental organizations in China: The rise of dependent autonomy* (London and New York: Routledge, 2009); and Qiusha Ma, *Non-governmental organizations in contemporary China: Paving the way to civil society?* (London: Routledge, 2006).

6 Bin Xu, 'Consensus crisis and civil society: The Sichuan earthquake response and state-society relations', *The China Journal*, 71 (2014), 91-108.

7 Shawn Shieh & Guosheng Deng, 'An emerging civil society'.

8 For another study of how NGOs navigate their work in the context of the 2008 Earthquake, see Trey Menefee & Bjorn Harald Nordtveit, 'Disaster, civil society and education in China: A case study of an independent nongovernment organization working in the aftermath of the Wenchuan earthquake', *International Journal of Educational Development*, 32 (2012), 600-607.

observations of NGO actions built on relational networking explain XNGO's relief work during the 2008 earthquake via church networks through government and non-government channels.

Shawn Shieh presents a framework for how Chinese NGOs operate within a complicated political and legal environment, identifying three distinct processes: (1) regulation, where the state formally controls and manages NGO action, (2) negotiation, where consensual and informal state-society interactions allow NGO action, and (3) socialization, where NGOs create space for action outside formal state relations.[9] This framework is easily applied to the work of XNGO, whose educational/training activities reflect regulated actions while its various church capacity building projects are arguably consistent with processes of socialization. The extensive work XNGO took on in response to the 2008 Sichuan Earthquake is likely an example of negotiation on multiple levels, not only between the organization and the state, but also between churches. XNGO was able to participate and expand within this consensus, because first, their legal status as a registered NGO gave them credibility in the eyes of the government, and second, their relational links with church communities throughout the province gave them a vast informal network of resources to mobilize.

This mix of formal and informal assets produced a win-win situation for both the government and the church. On the one hand, the government received expanded support for disaster relief that projected the image of a strong, capable, and responsive government to the world. On the other, the church's contributions brought greater government trust and opportunities for gospel witness through new social ministries. This dynamic is reinforced in Gerda Weilander's assessment of the influence of Christian values on China's larger social, cultural, and intellectual fabric, arguing that Christian understandings of "agape" love have not only consciously shaped Hu Jintao's vision of a harmonious society, but directed some of its policy in regards to Christian-state relations:

> Through reference to core values in Chinese Christian theology, the government gives a covert signal to the growing Christian population that their contributions are valuable and valued. Thus, the national project of building a Harmonious Society offers the Chinese Christian population a chance to prove its mettle. This is a very clever way of tacitly recognizing and enlisting the support of a potentially critical and growing social group, and has a number of advantages for the government. Not only does it mean that the energies and resources of this sector of society are channeled into (from the government's perspective) a constructive project, but, more crucially, it also enables the government to pass on

9 Shawn Shieh, 'Beyond corporatism and civil society: Three modes of state-NGO interaction in China', in Jonathan Schwartz & Shawn Shieh, eds, *State and society responses to social welfare needs in China: Serving the people* (New York: Routledge, 2011), 22-41.

certain duties to the community while at the same time re-establishing its own legitimacy.[10]

Paralleling studies of the Chinese NGO sector, there has also been an increase in literature examining Christianity's specific role in civil society, including cultural shifts in congregations and the contexts of their ministry. Of particular interest is Carsten T. Vala's analysis of the relationship between protestant churches and civil society in regard to the church's role in democratization from a political science perspective.[11] Drawing from 40 interviews with protestant church leaders, many of whom serve within registered TSPM church structures, Vala highlights the ways church leaders manage government oversight and gospel inspired social service along lines similar to Shieh and Deng's conceptions of negotiation and socialization between state and civil society. One dynamic Vala notes is the generally positive attitude church leaders have concerning state support for their social ministries.

> As an officially sanctioned part of society, Protestants are called upon by the regime to play important roles in meeting societal needs, as President Hu Jintao's 2007 announcement shows. Protestant leaders are eager to do so, yet they complain that they often lack the resources they need. In this context, some official church pastors and leaders go so far as to see the regime as benefitting churches that 'need the government's help' by offering the party-state's resources and recognition in society, help without which churches would have a 'hard time participating in society.' Such Protestants view the regime not as suppressing Protestant churches, as many overseas observers assume, but rather as empowering them.[12]

In this way, church leaders broker agreements with government leaders that provide churches means for addressing social concerns shared by both groups. Seen in this light, XNGO's work can be understood as a vehicle of such negotiation, an institutional link not formally part of the church yet capable of providing support for church ministries that serve the interests of society. In this way, churches sidestep certain limitations set by formal religious regulation. Vala also notes, "leaders in the Protestant associations, official seminaries, and registered churches may express cooperative attitudes toward the regime, reflecting their status as state appointees in regime-recognized institutions, but at the same time reserve their capacity to outflank the authorities to defend church interests."[13] In the case of XNGO, it is clear that those involved in its work are committed first to the work of the gospel. Its support for church ministries is motivated by spiritual as well as social well

---

10 Gerder Weilander, 'Beyond repression and resistance: Christian love and China's harmonious society', *The China Journal*, 65 (2011), 139.
11 Carsten T. Vala, 'Protestant Christianity and civil society in authoritarian China: The impact of official churches and unregistered "Urban Churches" on civil society development in the 2000s', *China Perspectives,* 4 October, 2012 [Online], http://chinaperspectives.revues.org/5949.
12 Ibid., 48.
13 Ibid.

being. In this way XNGO and the churches it serves exhibit elements of socialization where social service opens up new environments where the gospel can be better received despite government limitations on evangelism.

Another dynamic revealed in the aftermath of the Sichuan Earthquake was the potency of social capital amongst Chinese NGO groups. Shieh and Deng offer the following observation concerning the unprecedented response of Chinese NGOs in the aftermath of the 2008 Sichuan Earthquake:

> The rapid emergence of NGO networks is also an indication of the social capital that has accumulated over the past decade or so in China's associational community. This reserve of social capital is impressive given long-standing problems in the NGO community, such as weak organizational capacity, lack of legitimacy, and fragmentation, in addition to the constraints imposed by an authoritarian state that remains suspicious of NGOs. As scholars of civil society point out, this social capital should not be seen as leading to democratization. But the display of social capital in the societal response to the earthquake shows that NGOs are able to come together to address broader issues that transcend their own parochial interests.[14]

This statement can easily be applied to the Chinese church as well. The social capital inherent in the Chinese church has yet to be organized in a way that explicitly engages society at large, given many of the limitations mentioned and others associated with the extra element of religion. The work of XNGO highlights just how powerful and expansive social capital within church networks can be, especially in time of crisis. A recent piece by Evan Osnos states, "The Party is under increasing pressure to change the way it regards the desire for faith; China today has sixty to eighty million Christians, a community as large as the Communist Party. Li Fan, a secular liberal writer, told me, 'Christianity has probably become China's largest nongovernmental organization.'"[15]

It is perhaps because of this potency within NGO and church networks that the social-political climate of 2015 has changed from that of 2009. Despite the government's willingness to work with churches in some areas of public life, many registered churches are coming under increased control, particularly in coastal cities where many of their church buildings are being demolished. In addition, the growth and success of civil society in China have necessitated government responses to clarify and strengthen policies to regulate NGO functioning better. Most recently, the Chinese government has begun a move to legislate a comprehensive new "Charity Law," that will bring a greater standardization to NGO operations and relations that critics believe would

---

14 Shawn Shieh & Guosheng Deng, 'An emerging civil society', 194.

15 Evan Osnos, 'Five things you need to know about faith in China', *On Faith*, 13 May, 2014 [Online], http://www.faithstreet.com/onfaith/2014/05/13/five-things-you-need-to-know-about-faith-in-china/32061.

severely limit autonomy.[16] Despite the difficult new realities in both realms of church-state and NGO-state relations, XNGO's work has not only survived but thrived. As of 2015, XNGO continues to focus on education and training initiatives. What's more, the relief and development work birthed from their 2008 quake response has been formalized as a new foundation focused explicitly on relief and poverty alleviation. This officially registered foundation has given further legitimacy to much of XNGO's initial community development work, providing new links and resources to advance its faith-based missions. In an affirmation of the 2009 study's initial conclusions, XNGO's engaged social service and effective management of relationships with government, church, and international groups continues to yield fruit. The crisis consensus rendered by the 2008 earthquake and the contributions made by XNGO appear to have provided the organization further means to grow and expand despite the a negative turn in church-state relations in other parts of the country. Encouragingly, there has also been greater intentionality in building up new leadership to sustain such endeavors. Pastors from other provinces have also since connected with XNGO with a desire to replicate its model in their own settings.

For scholars and missionary agencies seeking to understand how indigenous Christians are advancing the work of the church, the realms of NGOs and civil society are important components. Brent Fulton notes, "The question of NGO reform is particularly salient for China's Christians. Many belong to unregistered groups whose lack of legal status denies them a valid platform for social engagement. Creating a level playing field for NGOs in China would require acknowledging the legitimate role these Christians play in society."[17] The double complexity of religious and civil society dynamics at work in faith-based NGOs within the context of China make this a difficult phenomenon to track, but a vital one to study. Its implications extend beyond structural relations and social dynamics to questions of public theology and the role of Christian faith in society at large.

How are organizations like XNGO contributing to the shaping of Christianity in China? In addition to its role in reshaping the theology/mentality of pastors and its witness to secular authorities, XNGO's continued growth signals a renewal of the vibrant social witness that once accompanied Christian mission before 1949, normalizing social good with gospel witness. This expansion of Christian social ministry by the Chinese church itself brings the gospel presence into new parts of society, providing means of injecting Christian values into social services typically conducted by non-Christian government organizations. For example, Cathy Neimitz' 2014 study of a

16 'New draft of charity law submitted to China's National Legislature', *China Briefing*, 16 January, 2015 [Online], http://www.china-briefing.com/news/2015/01/16/ china-drafts-new-charity-law.html#sthash.rEfRrp8c.dpuf.

17 Brent Fulton, 'China's schizophrenic NGO policy', *China Source*, 30 June, 2014 [Online], http://www.chinasource.org/resource-library/chinasource-blog/chinas-schizophrenic-ngo-policy

Christian operated Chinese orphanage highlights the missiological impact Christian values bring to orphan care.[18] Just how Chinese Christian social ministry differs from other forms of social service in China is an area of interest for future research.

This normalizing of social ministry in China is evident in Manhong Lin's 2011 publication, "What is Needed for Church-Run Social Service in China." Lin suggests that in their theological teachings churches instill a spirit of gratitude and charity that encourages social service. Also, there should be an expansion of Christian social service via NGO work into new areas that reflect the growing presence of the church in all of society:

> Currently, charitable activities that are centered on disaster relief, assistance for education, the disabled, the ill, and orphans and widows have become the main work of religious social service bodies, including the church. However, religious circles have a fine tradition and great potential in the areas of environmental protection, culture, education, and health. Religious circles are filled with enthusiasm, but this potential has not yet been tapped. As a result, some scholars argue that the role of religious groups is not simply to solve problems for the government or to remedy defects, nor is it simply to share the work and cooperate with the first and second sectors, but rather to become one means by which social values become reality.[19]

Third, Lin lists a number of recommendations for expanding church capacity for social ministry including formal training on public service and the building of public trust. As dean of Nanjing Union Theological Seminary, Lin's suggestions highlight a changing mindset amongst pastors across China. The instinct to hide for the sake of Christian survival is being replaced with a desire step out into new spheres of society. Whereas Samuel Ling's 2001 survey of Chinese Christian ministry neglected social ministry, a decade later Manhong Lin's work explicitly highlights and supports it. Seen in this greater context, XNGO's 2008 work can be viewed as an important part of reclaiming this spirit of social ministry grounded in gospel witness that echo that of their Christian forebears but in a new time and place.

18 See Cathy Neimetz, 'Christian distinctives in orphan care in China: Reflections on an agency visit', *Social Work and Christianity*, 41, 1 (2014), 66-67.

19 Mahong Lin, 'What is needed for church run social service in China', *Chinese Theological Review*, 23 (2011), 25–37.

Contributors

David Killingray is Emeritus Professor of Modern History, Goldsmiths, and Senior Research Fellow in the School of Advanced Study, both University of London. He has written books and articles on aspects of the history of Africa, the Caribbean, Empire, Christianity, the black diaspora, and English localities.

Lian Xi is Professor of World Christianity at the Divinity School of Duke University. He is the author of *The conversion of missionaries: Liberalism in American Protestant missions in China, 1907-1932* and *Redeemed by fire: The rise of popular Christianity in modern China*. He currently serves as associate editor of *Church History*.

Kuo Ya-pei is University Lecturer at the University of Groningen, the Netherlands. She is a historian of modern China, and has published articles on the concept of religion and its formation in the late nineteenth century, and on intellectual debate on culture in the 1910s-20s.

Liu Yanyan is currently pursuing a PhD degree at the Department of Sinology, University of Bonn. Her research concerns intercultural exchanges between Jesuits and China in the late Ming dynasty.

Stephen Donoho is a PhD student in Religious Studies at the University of Edinburgh. His main research interest is the history of English-language writing about East Asia, 'Formosa' in particular. His PhD thesis contrasts the ways in which the anti-Japanese insurgency in early colonial Taiwan was portrayed in two Presbyterian missionary periodicals.

Zhou Yun is writing her PhD dissertation on the transformation of homes by Christian women in Republican China at the Australian Centre on China in the World. Her research interests include the history of Protestantism in East Asia and contemporary overseas Chinese Protestants. Her article 'The making of Bible women in the Fujian Zenana Mission from the 1880s to the 1950s', will be published in *Christian women in Chinese society: The Anglican story* this year.

Monica Romano is a lecturer in Chinese philosophies, religions and Christianity at the Pontifical Gregorian University. She is a sinologist, social scientist, and development professional who has been researching Bible translation into Chinese for nearly 20 years. She also founder of *TherAsia*, a charity organization supporting the Church in Asia.

Peter Cunich has been teaching European history at the University of Hong Kong for nearly twenty-five years. He has written extensively on the history of Benedictine missionaries in Australia, and on the missionary activities of the Church Missionary Society and the London Missionary Society in Hong Kong and South China.

Lauren F. Pfister is a Professor in the Religion and Philosophy Department, and Director of the Centre for Sino-Christian Studies, Hong Kong Baptist University. He is associate editor of the *Journal of Chinese Philosophy*. His specialities include Qing Dynasty and twentieth century Chinese philosophy, China's missionary-scholars, Ruist-Christian dialogue, and hermeneutics.

Liu Jihua is Associate Professor in the School of History and Culture, Lanzhou University. His speciality is the history of Christianity in China.

Christina WONG Wai Yin is a lecturer at the Divinity School of Chung Chi College, the Chinese University of Hong Kong, teaching feminist theology, women in World missions, and gender in ministry. She is committed to the historical reconstruction of Chinese Christian women.

Bai Limin is senior lecturer in Chinese Studies at Victoria University of Wellington. She has published extensively on Chinese history, society and education in both English and Chinese. Among her publications is *Shaping the ideal child: Children and their primers in late Imperial China.*

Charles Weber is Professor of History Emeritus at Wheaton College. His teaching and research are focused on how African and Asian cultures have developed historically and how they influence the modern world. He is interested in how Christians have impacted these societies and the role they have played in developing national identity.

Niki J.P. Alsford is a Lecturer in Asia Pacific Studies at the University of Central Lancashire and Research Associate at the Centre of Taiwan Studies at SOAS. His research focuses on Taiwan's transnational social history and recent publications include: *Chronicling Formosa: Setting the foundation for the Presbyterian Mission, 1865-1876* (2015) and *A barbarian's house by the River Tamsui: One house and the history of its many occupants* (2015).

Kwok Wai Luen is an Assistant Professor in the Department of Religion and Philosophy and Associate Director Centre for Sino-Christian Studies at Hong Kong Baptist University. His research interests include Chinese Christianity, narrative theology, theological hermeneutics, and Christian doctrine.

Easten Law is a doctoral student in theological and religious studies at Georgetown University in Washington, DC. His research focuses on Christian identity, religious pluralism, and public life in contemporary China.

Paul Woods is a Research Tutor at the Oxford Centre for Mission Studies, specialising in East Asia. He is the author of *Theologising migration: Otherness and liminality in East Asia.* His areas of interest are identity and otherness and post-socialism. In previous incarnations he obtained doctoral degrees in Chinese Linguistics and in Biblical Theology.

Stephen Williams is Professor in the Systematic Theology and Church History Department at Union Bible College, Belfast. He has published in different areas in theology, ethics, and intellectual history, and his books include *Revelation and reconciliation: A window on modernity, The Shadow of the Antichrist: Nietzsche's critique of Christianity,* and the Kantzer lectures, *The election of grace: A riddle without a resolution?*